The Mexican Revolution's Wake

Throughout the 1920s Mexico was rocked by attempted coups, assassinations, and popular revolts. Yet by the mid-1930s, the country boasted one of the most stable and durable political systems in Latin America. In the first book on party formation conducted at the regional level after the Mexican Revolution, Sarah Osten examines processes of political and social change that eventually gave rise to the Institutional Revolutionary Party (PRI), which dominated Mexico's politics for the rest of the twentieth century. In analyzing the history of Socialist parties in the southeastern states of Campeche, Chiapas, Tabasco, and Yucatán, Osten demonstrates that these "laboratories of revolution" constituted a highly influential testing ground for new political traditions and institutional structures. *The Mexican Revolution's Wake* shows how the southeastern Socialists provided a blueprint for a new kind of party that struck calculated balances between the objectives of elite and popular forces, and between centralized authority and local autonomy.

Sarah Osten is an assistant professor of history at the University of Vermont. She has published research on Mexican politics, the history of the Mexican Southeast, and women's suffrage.

T0382586

CAMBRIDGE LATIN AMERICAN STUDIES

General Editors
KRIS LANE, Tulane University
MATTHEW RESTALL, Pennsylvania State University

Editor Emeritus
HERBERT S. KLEIN
Gouverneur Morris Emeritus Professor of History,
Columbia University and Hoover Research Fellow,
Stanford University

Other Books in the Series

(Continued after Index)

The Mexican Revolution's Wake

The Making of a Political System, 1920–1929

SARAH OSTEN

University of Vermont

CAMBRIDGE
UNIVERSITY PRESS

CAMBRIDGE
UNIVERSITY PRESS

University Printing House, Cambridge CB2 8BS, United Kingdom

One Liberty Plaza, 20th Floor, New York, NY 10006, USA

477 Williamstown Road, Port Melbourne, VIC 3207, Australia

314-321, 3rd Floor, Plot 3, Splendor Forum, Jasola District Centre, New Delhi - 110025, India

79 Anson Road, #06-04/06, Singapore 079906

Cambridge University Press is part of the University of Cambridge.

It furthers the University's mission by disseminating knowledge in the pursuit of
education, learning and research at the highest international levels of excellence.

www.cambridge.org
Information on this title: www.cambridge.org/9781108401289
DOI: 10.1017/9781108235570

First published 2018
First paperback edition 2020

A catalogue record for this publication is available from the British Library

ISBN 978-1-108-41598-9 Hardback
ISBN 978-1-108-40128-9 Paperback

For John and Micah

Contents

Photographs

Maps

ix

Acknowledgments

I went to graduate school with the intention of researching women's and indigenous rights movements in Mexico in the late twentieth century. I hope that readers will still find vestiges of my original, unrealized research plans in the pages that follow, even though my abiding interest in those topics eventually led me to quite a different one, in a very different historical period. I came to the subject of this book and conducted the research it required thanks to some strokes of good research luck, a few instances of serendipity, and above all, the training, guidance, and encouragement I have received from teachers, mentors, colleagues, friends, and family over the past fourteen years.

I owe significant debts of gratitude to many people who have helped me with this project in myriad ways. The largest of these is to my former graduate advisor Emilio Kourí. No one has done more to help me to write this book, or to become a professional historian. I am profoundly grateful to him for his mentorship and for all of his support over the years. I am also very grateful to Dain Borges, who guided me throughout my graduate studies from the very beginning. I benefited tremendously from Dain's extraordinary breadth of knowledge but also from his excellent practical advice about life in academia. I am also extraordinarily grateful to John Womack, who provided me with critical insights and advice about the research and writing of my dissertation, and who has always been so generous with both his time and his wisdom.

At the University of Chicago, Claudio Lomnitz was the one who initially encouraged me to research women's suffrage in socialist Chiapas, a project that eventually became this book. I was also extremely fortunate to have the remarkable opportunity to take classes with the late Friedrich Katz, and to discuss my research with him. I also studied with Tom Holt, Amy Dru Stanley, and Mae Ngai, as well as Fernando Escalante Gonzalbo of the Colegio de México, who taught at the University of Chicago in 2005. I am grateful to all of them for all that I learned in their courses, much of which still informs my research and teaching. I also benefited enormously from the wisdom of my fellow graduate students, particularly the members of the Latin American History Workshop, where I presented the early research for this book on several occasions. Many thanks to Pablo Ben, Carlos Bravo, Ananya Chakravarti, Lauren Duquette-Rury, Stuart Easterling, José Angel Hernández, Mac James, Ben Johnson, Greg Malandrucco, Jaime Pensado, Romina Robles Ruvalcaba, Diana Schwartz, Ann Schneider, Antonio Sotomayor, Jackie Sumner, and Mikael Wolfe for their insight, as well as their camaraderie.

As a Mellon postdoc and then visiting assistant professor of history at Northwestern University, I benefited from the wisdom of colleagues in the history department, and in Latin American and Caribbean Studies. I am particularly grateful to Brodie Fischer and Regina Grafe for their support and mentorship. Since 2013, I have been fortunate to be a member of the history department of the University of Vermont. It is an extraordinary community of scholars where I have not only found wonderful colleagues but also many friends. I am grateful to all of them for their support and guidance as I found my way during my first years on the tenure track, with special thanks to Abby McGowan and Harvey Amani Whitfield for their mentorship, kindness, and friendship since before I even arrived in Burlington.

I have also been fortunate to have a wonderful group of colleagues with expertise in various topics of this book, many of whom have also become mentors and friends. Justus Fenner gave me invaluable guidance on archival research in Chiapas, as well as tireless support for both me and my work from the time we met. I thank him for all his generosity and kindness. I could not have done the research I did for this book without him. Jan Rus has also been exceedingly generous with his advice and wisdom about the history of Chiapas since the very early stages of this project. I am very grateful to him for his kind assistance and support of me and my research over the years. Juan Pedro Viqueira was another valuable source of insight and advice on Chiapas history, particularly in the early stages of my research. I am also very grateful to Ben Fallaw for his invaluable advice and guidance on the history of Yucatán, and for his input on my research on the Southeast in general. I would also like to thank Martha Loyo for her help at various stages of my research, and for alerting me to the existence of the Vidal papers, which at the time were in storage at the Archivo General de la Nación (AGN) and uncatalogued, forgotten by nearly everyone but her.

Particular thanks are due to Julia Young, Casey Lurtz, and Matt Vitz for their careful reading and thoughtful comments on various drafts of sections of this book over the years, as well as for their encouragement and friendship. Other friends have been crucial sources of support, input, and companionship during my research and writing, particularly Anna J. Baranczak, Harlan North, Luisa Ortiz Pérez, Ulysses de la Torre, Dora Sánchez Hidalgo, Erika Robb Larkins,

Richard Conway, Nicole Mottier, Amanda Hartzmark, Patrick Iber, Scott Richmond, Rob Karl, Mike Lettieri, Angel Ortiz, Tania Munz, Christine Percheski, Elizabeth Smith, Mike Amezcua, Kate McGurn Centellas, Miguel Centellas, Matt Pillsbury, and the late Christina Jenkins, who I will miss always.

I also owe a large debt of gratitude to the many archivists, archive directors, and staff members in Mexico who have been such a great help to me throughout my research for this book. At the Calles Archive (FAPECFT), Patricia Cordero González was always patient as I requested document after document, and I am immensely grateful to her for all of her help, kindness, and laughter. I am also very grateful to Amalia Torreblanca Sánchez and Norma Mereles de Ogario for their support of my research and for making their archive feel like a second home to me in Mexico City, along with the rest of the wonderful FAPECFT staff. At the Mexican National Archive (AGN), I am very grateful to César Montoya Cervantes, Enrique Melgarejo Amezcua, Raymundo Álvarez García, Albertano Guerrero, Joel Zúñiga Torres, and Arturo Librado Galicia for their assistance, humor, and kindness, as well as to the many other staff members of the AGN who helped me with this project. In Chiapas, I would like to thank Noé Gutiérrez, Armando Martín Sánchez García, and the staff at the UNICACH archive for all of their help with my research. In Mérida, I would like to thank Dr. Piedad Peniche Rivera and the staff at the Archivo General del Estado de Yucatán for their assistance with my research there. My research assistant, Daniela Pineda, was also a critical asset to me in completing my research at the Calles Archive.

I could not have spent the time I did in those archives without generous funding from numerous sources. This includes the institutions with which I have been affiliated in various capacities: The University of Chicago, Northwestern University, and the University of Vermont. It also includes the Tinker Foundation, the Mellon Foundation, and the Doris G. Quinn Foundation. I was also very fortunate to receive a Fulbright-Hays grant that enabled me to conduct the bulk of my dissertation research in 2006–7, work on which this book is also heavily based.

At Cambridge University Press, I would like to thank my editor, Deborah Gershenowitz, who has been so supportive of this book project and who has helped to guide me through its completion. I am also grateful to my series editors, Matthew Restall and Kris Lane, for their support of this book and for their advice and feedback, and to Kristina Deusch for her assistance in turning the manuscript into a book. I would also like to thank the two anonymous readers of my manuscript who provided me with such useful feedback and advice.

I am very fortunate to have had the support and encouragement of my family. I am especially grateful to my parents, Fran and Bob Osten, who have always encouraged and supported my intellectual curiosity and exploration. I don't know that they foresaw that I would become a historian, but I can't imagine that I would have if not for them. I am also grateful to my husband's family, the Davys and the Keanes, who have always been so supportive of my career and my work. Special thanks are also due to my cousin Frank Siteman, who advised and helped me with some of the photographs in this book.

Above all, I could not have written this book without the support and encouragement of my husband, John Davy. I have been working on this project in one capacity or another since well before John and I met. In ways both big and small, he has not only enabled me to finish it, but also has been its most enthusiastic champion, even as he pursued his own career, and we moved from Chicago to Vermont. I am so grateful to him for all of it. Small children are often regarded as impediments to scholarly work and production, but I have found the opposite to be true since our son Micah was born in June of 2015, as I was completing the first draft of this book. He is an unmatched bright spot in every day. I am a better historian, a better teacher, and a better person in general because of John and Micah. This book is for them.

Introduction
Mexico's Search for Peace and Postrevolutionary Political Institutions

A good government depends on the wellbeing of the people, and for the government to do right, it unquestionably needs the support of the governed.

> Letter from a constituent to Governor Felipe Carrillo Puerto
> of Yucatán, 1922

In the first weeks of 1924, in a region that many said had been left out of the Mexican Revolution of 1910–20, a small army was formed by Socialists in the state of Chiapas, in far southeastern Mexico. Most of its members were likely coffee workers and poor farmers. These men did not take up arms against an oppressive, elite-led federal government as so many Mexicans had done during the Revolution. Instead, they organized and armed themselves to defend the federal government and local political institutions that they had helped to build. When Mexico's first postrevolutionary government came under attack during the de la Huerta rebellion of 1923–24, southeastern Socialists rose up in the government's defense and in defense of their rights that they believed it could best guarantee.

One of their brigades was named for Felipe Carrillo Puerto, the Socialist governor of the nearby state of Yucatán who had been executed by rebel forces a few weeks earlier (see Photograph 1.1). As workers and *campesinos* across the Southeast took up arms to combat the rebels and to avenge Carrillo Puerto's murder, former Secretary of the Interior and presidential candidate Plutarco Elías Calles recognized their organized resistance as emblematic of a sea change in Mexico.[1] In a private letter to his brother, he described the popular outcry in Yucatán, and marveled, "All of the worker and agrarian organizations have raised the alert to now like never before punish the reactionaries, and to demonstrate that the working people of Mexico are not the herd of

---

[1] For a discussion of the particular Mexican postrevolutionary meanings of "campesino," see Christopher R. Boyer, *Becoming Campesinos: Politics, Identity, and Agrarian Struggle in Postrevolutionary Michoacán, 1920–1935* (Stanford, CA: Stanford University Press, 2003), 1–12.

Photograph 1.1 The Felipe Carrillo Puerto Brigade, Chiapas, 1924
Source: Archivo General de la Nación, Colección Carlos A. Vidal. Sección: Actividades militares, políticas y administrativas, serie: fotografías sobre eventos públicos y sociales y obras públicas en Chiapas, caja 3, sobre: 14, foto: 2.

sheep that they were twelve years ago."[2] It was a lesson that Calles would not forget. Five years later he laid the foundations for Mexico's single party-dominated political system when he founded the party that would eventually become the Institutional Revolutionary Party (PRI). Its design was conspicuously influenced by precedents of party-driven politics that he observed in the Southeast, where Socialists took power in the states of Campeche, Chiapas, Tabasco, and Yucatán between 1920 and 1925. In the years that followed, Calles' party was adapted to usher in the era of mass politics in Mexico, again following southeastern examples.

This book is a new genealogy of the modern Mexican political system that looks to the Socialist Southeast to explain its origins. Its chief purpose is to examine how and why short-lived political experiments conducted in a far-flung region that the Mexican Revolution nearly bypassed became so important to the development of Mexico's postrevolutionary political institutions and traditions. This is the story of Mexico's remarkable, decade-long transition from civil war to a lasting postrevolutionary peace, and of some of the people, ideas, and movements that made it possible. It is also the story of the very high political and human costs that process entailed.[3]

---

2   Fideicomiso Archivos Plutarco Elías Calles, Fondo Plutarco Elías Calles (hereafter FAPECFT-PEC), expediente: 53: ELIAS, Arturo M. (1919–1926), legajo: 9/22, foja: 362, inventario: 1717. Calles to Arturo M. Calles, January 5, 1924.
3   By "peace" I refer to postrevolutionary pacification, rather than to an end to all political violence; this was certainly not achieved, and in many cases in the decades that followed it was state-

Revolutionary Promises and Postrevolutionary Dilemmas

The Mexican Revolution was a prolonged struggle fought by numerous heterogeneous factions, each with its own vision of the kind of country Mexico could and should become. As revolutionary armies clashed throughout the 1910s, their leaders also fought a war of words, ideas, and egos. In the process, they mobilized workers and campesinos across Mexico, often recruiting them as soldiers and partisans with ambitious promises of labor reform, land redistribution, political freedom, and a more just social order once the war was over. But when the Revolution ended in 1920, few if any revolutionaries had clearly articulated plans for how they would fulfill all of those revolutionary promises or, just as critically, how they would maintain long-term alliances with the popular constituencies they had exhorted to action.

Most politicians of the 1920s recognized that workers and campesinos could no longer be ignored or excluded wholesale from the political sphere, but translating the Revolution's ambitious ideals into a workable system of governance was a daunting challenge by any measure. From the beginning, there was a broad range of opinions on how and to what degree commitments to reform and redistribution of resources should be implemented by government, or for how long. Well into the twentieth century, federal reform efforts were also endlessly complicated by the resiliency of entrenched local elites and power brokers, and the durability of existing political traditions and power structures, both formal and informal. With no established traditions of electoral democracy or mass politics, but with its popular legitimacy rooted in strong rhetorical and constitutional commitments to both, the 1920s was a time of both trial and transition for the infant postrevolutionary political system. Mexico was wracked by violence and political upheaval in those years, which included the executions and exiles of numerous revolutionary heroes and political innovators. On several occasions the country nearly descended into civil war again.

The National Revolutionary Party (PNR) was meant to solve all of these ongoing dilemmas. Its creation was announced by its founder, president Plutarco Elías Calles, when he declared in 1928 that "we must see to it, once and for all, that Mexico passes from the historical condition of being a 'country ruled by one man' to that of 'a nation of institutions and laws.'"[4] After a decade of violence and political turmoil, this was a frank acknowledgment that Mexico had to abandon some of its old political habits and to embrace new ones in order to move forward and to secure a lasting peace. Calles' proposed solution was the building of a singular,

---

sponsored. However, large-scale armed rebellions against the federal government were principally confined to the 1920s.

4   Plutarco Elías Calles, *Pensamiento político y social: antología (1913–1936)*, ed. Carlos Macias (México, D.F.: Fideicomiso Archivos Plutarco Elías Calles y Fernando Torreblanca, 1994; repr., 1), 240–51.

uniquely powerful political party that united the majority of the political class under one institutional roof. It was to be based in Mexico City, but, crucially, it would also have a strong presence at the local level across Mexico, via a network of affiliated organizations. Through a hierarchy of alliances, citizens at the grassroots level could become connected to the political agendas of leaders at the highest echelons of power, even if their only direct contact with the political class was via the local branch office or an individual representative of the national organization.

For all of its amply documented flaws and failures, the party that eventually became the PRI has proven to be one of the most successful and powerful political parties that emerged during the twentieth century. The era of the PRI put an end to what one Mexican journalist in the mid-1920s despairingly described as a century of "imprisoning, exiling and murdering presidents," and ushered in an era of unprecedented institutional stability and continuity.[5] From 1929 to 2000, three successive versions of the "revolutionary" party dominated politics at all levels, only relinquishing the presidential palace after seven decades. Although it was restructured, its name changed three times, and its political direction changed many more times than that, several essential features of the party remained constant.[6] It continued to participate in elections and to run elaborate campaigns, even when the competition was negligible. It continued to actively court popular support, although its ability to win it waned over time. For decades, it largely succeeded in quarantining intra-elite political conflict within the party, preventing the kind of schisms and power struggles that had consistently provoked violence and upheaval in previous periods. To this day it continues to insist, in its very name as well as in its rhetoric, that its political legitimacy is derived from its self-ascribed status as the sole institutional heir of the Mexican Revolution.

Lastly, the government controlled by the parties of the Revolution generally preferred collaboration or cooptation of popular movements to rule by overt force. The breaking of this unwritten compact with the Mexican electorate was politically calamitous, as the PRI's popular legitimacy was gravely compromised and its landmark 2000 electoral defeat was hastened by the accumulated instances in which it violently repressed opposition groups and dissidents. The massacre of hundreds of peaceful protesters at the Plaza de Tres Culturas in Tlatelolco in 1968 is the most

---

5   Alonso Capetillo, *La rebelión sin cabeza: génesis y desarrollo del movimiento delahuertista* (México, D.F.: Imprenta Botas, 1925), 12. "Un siglo hemos pasado encarcelando, desterrando y matando Presidentes!"
6   The National Revolutionary Party (PNR) was founded in 1929. It was reorganized and its name was changed to the Party of the Mexican Revolution (PRM) in 1938. It became the Institutional Revolutionary Party (PRI) in 1946. In referring to these parties collectively, I do not mean to minimize the differences between them, but to emphasize that each served as the institutional foundation for its successor, and to express the continuities of the political system that they dominated.

notorious example of many. It was not a violently repressive system by design; indeed, quelling recurrent, destabilizing political violence was one of the party's foundational objectives. Practice was another matter from the outset, for reasons explored in this book. State-sponsored violence over the course of its long incumbency is inescapably one of the PRI's defining legacies.

This was not a democratic system, but nor was it straightforwardly authoritarian.[7] It was a system that depended on popular support, in spite of never making a serious commitment to electoral democracy. Under PRI governance, Mexican citizens could not count on ballots they cast being freely or fairly counted, but nor did they endure a brutal military dictatorship like those that took hold in much of Latin America during the mid-late twentieth century, nor the scale of state-led violence that resulted in so many countries. Although at times it was very dangerous to be an outspoken dissident, it was a system that did not include the extreme, ongoing purges of the political class perpetrated in other contemporaneous postrevolutionary contexts (comparisons with China, Russia, and Cuba are particularly revealing). As Friedrich Katz underscored, the importance of this difference cannot be overstated.[8] Mexico under the PRI did not have a strong record when it came to the protection of human rights or basic political and civil liberties, but real opportunities for political participation and even contestation did exist, albeit circumscribed.

I do not mean to overstate the strength and efficacy of the party, nor to suggest the perfection of the Mexican political system as it stood by 1929, or as it functioned in practice in the years that followed. On the contrary, one of my goals in writing this book is to provide a better historical understanding of the party's inarguable successes in spite of its notable

---

7   Mario Vargas Llosa famously described the PRI as "the perfect dictatorship." Recent scholarship across disciplines has reevaluated this assessment from a variety of angles, particularly in terms of how much political control the PRI ever really had. See, in particular, Paul Gillingham and Benjamin T. Smith, eds., *Dictablanda: Politics, Work, and Culture in Mexico, 1938–1968* (Durham, NC: Duke University Press, 2014). See also Kenneth F. Greene, *Why Dominant Parties Lose: Mexico's Democratization in Comparative Perspective* (Cambridge, England: Cambridge University Press, 2007), Beatriz Magaloni, *Voting for Autocracy: Hegemonic Party Survival and Its Demise in Mexico* (New York, NY: Cambridge University Press, 2006).

8   Friedrich Katz, "Violence and Terror in the Mexican and Russian Revolutions," in *A Century of Revolution: Insurgent and Counterinsurgent Violence during Latin America's Long Cold War*, ed. Greg Grandin and Gilbert M. Joseph (Durham, NC: Duke University Press, 2010). Luis Medina Peña stresses that another essential difference between these cases was that Mexican revolutionaries did not have a preexisting political party to manage postrevolutionary political reconstruction, which Russian and Chinese revolutionaries did. Luis Medina Peña, *Hacia el nuevo estado: México, 1920–1994*, 2nd edn. (México, D.F.: Fondo de Cultura Económica, 1995; repr., 6), 50. See also Garrido's comparison of the PRI and the communist parties of Russia and China: Luis Javier Garrido, *El Partido de la Revolución Institucionalizada: la formación del nuevo estado en México, 1928–1945* (México, D.F.: Siglo Veintiuno Editores, 1982), 13.

defects and weaknesses.[9] Scholars in many disciplines have examined how and why the Mexican single party-dominated system was so durable once it was already in place, even in the face of substantial and nearly constant contestation, but relatively little attention has been paid by historians to how or why this system took root in the first place.

However specious the notion of an "institutional revolution," and despite the fact that over time the PRI lost all popular legitimacy as the representative of Mexico's revolutionary heroes and the champion of their ideals, the party's core traits may all be traced directly back to the search for peace and stability by politicians in the years immediately following the Mexican Revolution. While groundbreaking in its implementation, the idea of a single party-dominated system was not a new one. As they designed the PNR, Calles and his collaborators looked to recent precedents of party formation, political organizing, and multi-class alliance building in Mexico. The Southeast provided a number of especially useful and relevant examples.[10] During the 1920s, the states of the region collectively constituted a testing ground for new political traditions and institutional structures, for the practical limits of radicalism and reformism, and for a total redefinition of the working relationship between Mexican citizens and their government, one that was critically mediated by a new style of political party. In recognition of the importance of these experiments, President Lázaro Cárdenas (1934–40) once famously described Socialist Tabasco as Mexico's "laboratory of revolution."[11]

9 As Benjamin T. Smith has underscored, state hegemony and federal control on the one hand and decentralization and regional independence on the other should not be understood to be mutually exclusive in Mexico in the late 1920s and early 1930s. Benjamin T. Smith, *Pistoleros and Popular Movements: The Politics of State Formation in Postrevolutionary Oaxaca* (Lincoln, NE: University of Nebraska Press, 2009), 43.

10 The geographical delimitation of this book to the states of Campeche, Chiapas, Tabasco, and Yucatán conforms to the contemporary conception of the Southeast as a region. When politicians of the era referred to the Southeast, these were the four states they almost invariably included in that designation. The exclusion of neighboring Veracruz, particularly considering its history of radical politics in the same period, might seem arbitrary to readers today, but the line that was consistently drawn around what was considered to be the Southeast is an interesting historical fact in and of itself. I have chosen to respect that line in my analysis in order to illuminate what it was that people at the time understood to be special and unique about the political experiments undertaken there, and to address the particular political significance of the Southeast in those years. On radicalism in Veracruz in this period, see Heather Fowler-Salamini, *Agrarian Radicalism in Veracruz, 1920–38* (Lincoln, NE: University of Nebraska Press, 1978).

11 Carlos R. Martínez Assad, *El laboratorio de la revolución: el Tabasco garridista*, 5th edn. (México, D.F.: Siglo Veintiuno Editores, 2004), 14. Thomas Benjamin ascribes the first use of the term "laboratory" to describe Mexico's regional political experiments to Carleton Beals, in 1923. Thomas Benjamin, "Laboratories of the New State, 1920–1929: Regional Social Reform and Experiments in Mass Politics," in *Provinces of the Revolution: Essays on Regional Mexican History, 1910–1929* (Albuquerque, NM: University of New Mexico Press, 1990), 73.

The Southeastern Revolution

At the turn of the century, the Southeast was not a region that seemed likely to produce a highly influential school of revolutionary reform. In those years it was a region legendary for the wealth it produced, and notorious for the de-facto enslavement, systematic oppression, and political marginalization of its large indigenous population. The Southeast was far removed from Mexico City as the crow flew, but also crippled in many parts by a lack of transportation infrastructure across an often difficult terrain that was divided by rivers, canyons, and mountain ranges in some places, and by wetlands and bodies of water in others; in the early twentieth century, travel both to and within the region was often difficult and sometimes outright impossible. It was also a part of Mexico with

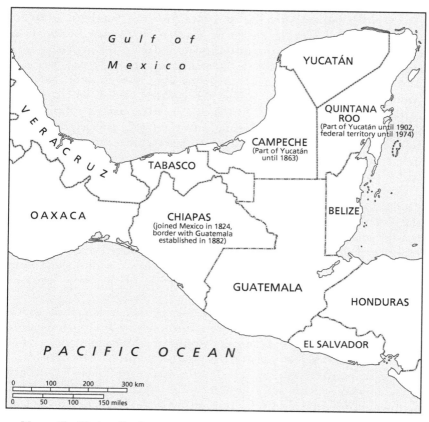

Map 1 The Mexican Southeast

a deeply entrenched tradition of local sovereignty, which many elites and some non-elites were prepared to defend vigorously. All of these factors together meant that for several years, while revolutionary armies clashed across the North and center of Mexico, the Southeast remained relatively peaceful. It was not until the mid-1910s that the region became a theater of the Revolution. Drawn by the economic potential of its primary exports and desperately in need of political territory to which he could credibly stake a claim, Venustiano Carranza, the so-called First Chief of the Constitutionalist revolutionary faction, dispatched troops and a series of military governors to the region beginning in 1914.

The following year, General Salvador Alvarado was recruited to lead the effort as Carranza's proconsul for the state of Yucatán. Alvarado embarked on an ambitious program of social, political, and economic reform, and founded the region's first Socialist political party. He started a regional political movement in the process, as local politicians and organizers picked up where he left off after his departure from the Southeast in 1918. Governors Felipe Carrillo Puerto in Yucatán (1922–24), Ramón Félix Flores in Campeche (1921–23), Carlos A. Vidal in Chiapas (1925–27), and Tomás Garrido Canabal in Tabasco (1921–24 and 1931–34) each substantially adapted Alvarado's programs and strategies to fit their own political objectives and to address the political, social, and economic particularities of their states. Although they were markedly different in some respects, their Socialist governments commonly pursued substantial land and labor reform and the increased enfranchisement of women and indigenous peoples. While they all called for state-led economic reform and redistribution of resources, none argued for the overthrow of capitalism. They collaborated with one another to varying degrees, and all cultivated similar alliances with national politicians, parties, and organizations. Most importantly, the southeastern Socialist leaders all used similar organizational frameworks to put together cohesive and powerful political organizations and popular coalitions in their respective states. These parties used their combined elite power and grassroots support to conduct some of the most progressive and far-reaching programs of reform in postrevolutionary Mexico.

Political parties already existed in Mexico by the 1920s, but the southeastern political laboratories produced something new. Built in response to the social, political, and economic realities of the region, they crafted innovative solutions to many of the greatest political challenges of the immediate postrevolutionary period in the nation as a whole. For the first time, Mexico had relatively depersonalized organizations that endured across multiple electoral cycles and ran multiple candidates, and established constituent bases well beyond elite political circles. Above all, the southeastern Socialist parties constituted vital, institutionalized, two-way conduits of influence, support, and communication between politicians and their constituents, all the way down to the grassroots.[12]

This was a highly idiosyncratic brand of Socialism, an extremely diverse and ill-defined political label to begin with, even just within Mexico.[13] Southeastern Socialism was adamantly nationalist, but its leaders nevertheless selectively borrowed from and referenced political movements in other countries, from US progressivism to anarchosyndicalism to Marxism, among other influences.[14] The southeastern Socialists repeatedly stated their desire to belong to a political wave of the future that they perceived to be sweeping the world, but insisted that radical change and reform must only be implemented by Mexicans, and on Mexican terms.[15]

It was a school of politics that was adamantly participatory, but never fully democratic. When the southeastern Socialists frequently spoke of democracy, they referred to their core principle of enfranchisement of a broad spectrum of citizens through their active participation in a corporatist, hierarchical political system that was for all intents and purposes dominated by a single political party led by elite and middle class politicians. While elections remained a key feature of the practice of politics in the Socialist Southeast, it was not a system that lent itself to multi-party competition or electoral democracy.[16] Even as the Socialists actively sought to depersonalize the Mexican political system and to politically mobilize groups that had long

12 Machine politics were nothing new in Mexico (or the Southeast), but parties with genuine popular constituencies were. On the politics of Porfirian and early revolutionary Yucatán, see Allen Wells and Gilbert M. Joseph, *Summer of Discontent, Seasons of Upheaval: Elite Politics and Rural Insurgency in Yucatán, 1876–1915* (Stanford, CA: Stanford University Press, 1996).

13 On the origins of Mexican Socialism, see Barry Carr, *Marxism and Communism in Twentieth-Century Mexico* (Lincoln, NE: University of Nebraska Press, 1992), 14–46. See also Heather Fowler-Salamini, "De-Centering the 1920s: Socialismo a la Tamaulipeca," *Mexican Studies / Estudios Mexicanos* 14, no. 2 (1998): 292–95. On southeastern Socialism in the 1920s, see Gilbert M. Joseph, *Revolution from Without: Yucatán, Mexico, and the United States, 1880–1924* (Durham, NC: Duke University Press, 1988); Daniela Spenser, *El partido socialista chiapaneco: rescate y reconstrucción de su historia* (México, D.F.: Centro de Investigaciones y Estudios Superiores en Antropología Social, 1988); Martínez Assad, *El laboratorio de la revolución*; Paul K. Eiss, *In the Name of el Pueblo: Place, Community, and the Politics of History in Yucatán* (Durham, NC: Duke University Press, 2010).

14 On Mexican communism, see Carr, *Marxism and Communism*; Daniela Spenser, *Stumbling Its Way Through Mexico: The Early Years of the Communist International* (Tuscaloosa, AL: University of Alabama Press, 2011). Fowler-Salamini has documented the influence of the Mexican Communist Party on agrarian radicalism in the state of Veracruz in the 1920s. Its influence was far less decisive in the Southeast. See Fowler-Salamini, *Agrarian Radicalism*, 29–33.

15 Spenser argues that Mexican radicals in the 1920s admired and sought to learn from the Bolsheviks, rather than to emulate the Russian example. Daniela Spenser, *The Impossible Triangle: Mexico, Soviet Russia, and the United States in the 1920s* (Durham, NC: Duke University Press, 1999), 63.

16 On the lack of a democratic tradition in postrevolutionary Mexico, see Katz, "Violence and Terror," 51.

been excluded from the political process, in practice their model perpetuated the concentration of power in the hands of a relatively small number of people. The important difference was that those people were now at least theoretically held accountable to represent the needs and wishes of a much broader spectrum of much more politically engaged constituents.

The reformers of the Southeast had peers in many other parts of Mexico that pursued similar political projects and reformist goals, sometimes via similar institutional apparatuses. By the late 1920s there were Socialist parties across all of Mexico. Some were more similar to the southeastern Socialist parties than others. The nearby state of Veracruz was home to one of the more radical and well-known agrarian reform movements in the 1920s that had many similarities to its Socialist peers to the east. Elsewhere, the northern state of Tamaulipas had a Socialist party that became influential in its own right and was modeled in part on southeastern precedents, led by future president and PNR leader Emilio Portes Gil.[17] So did the southwestern state of Michoacán, led by noted radical General Francisco Múgica in the early 1920s, after he briefly served as the revolutionary proconsul of Tabasco in the mid-1910s. As governor of Michoacán (1928–32), future president Lázaro Cárdenas also established reformist institutional structures that resembled those of the southeastern Socialist parties, such as a statewide workers' confederation.[18] By the end of the 1920s, "Socialism" was adopted as a designation by politicians throughout Mexico to describe a diverse collection of political projects. For the most part, these were reformers who intended to distinguish themselves for their relative radicalism in a political milieu that was comprised almost entirely of "revolutionaries;" thus, some Mexican Socialists of the era often used the designation interchangeably with "radical."[19]

Although it is impossible to ascribe Mexican Socialism as a political style as it was at the end of the 1920s to any one regional party or movement, southeastern Socialism was particularly influential on national politics.[20] By the mid-1920s some Mexican politicians were arguing that the southeastern Socialist model might be usefully applied at the national level, and several attempts to do this were made previous to the founding of

17 Heather Fowler-Salamini has written about both of these political experiments and projects. See Fowler-Salamini, *Agrarian Radicalism*; Fowler-Salamini, "De-Centering the 1920s." Another point of comparison is the Socialist Confederation of Parties of Oaxaca, founded in 1926. See Smith, *Pistoleros and Popular Movements*.

18 On both Múgica and Cárdenas in Michoacán, see Boyer, *Becoming Campesinos*.

19 Barry Carr has argued that "Socialism" frequently served as a distinguisher between revolutionaries and reactionaries in this period. Carr, *Marxism and Communism*, 15.

20 On the influence of regional politics during the 1920s, and the Socialist governments of the Southeast in comparative perspective with reformist state governments elsewhere in Mexico, see Benjamin, "Laboratories of the New State."

the PNR.[21] In the longer-term, it was a blueprint that helped to make possible the rise of the populist, progressive corporatism led by Cárdenas in the 1930s. The inclusion of previously disenfranchised sectors of society in the political process, even within the pronounced limits of a political system controlled by one political party, gave the notion of Mexico's postrevolutionary government being fundamentally grounded in revolutionary principles a degree of credibility that helped to legitimize the long tenure of the PRI for generations.

Reexamining the Origins of the System

Mexican history has offered surprisingly few explanations for how a singular "revolutionary" party emerged out of the 1920s, a period in which political factions were anything but united in their goals or rhetoric, and the meanings of the Mexican Revolution were actively and hotly contested. The frequent portrayal of the PNR as emerging suddenly and fully formed out of an institutional vacuum at the end of the 1920s is immensely unsatisfying, but also analytically troublesome. The absence of alternative narratives of the development of the single party-dominated system has gifted the PRI's mythology of itself as the sole institutional heir of the Mexican Revolution with an undue pride of place within historical interpretations of the postrevolutionary period. Worse, it has enabled a treacherous drift toward teleological explanations of how a very well-organized political hierarchy suddenly emerged from alleged total political disarray with the founding of the PNR. Oversimplification of the origins of the party that became the PRI, and of the social and political contexts from which it emerged have been to the detriment of both scholarly and popular interpretations of its legacies.

Historical scholarship on Mexico of the past several decades has emphasized that a constant process of dialogue and negotiation with communities, constituents, and power brokers at the local level was one of the most important keys to the success and near-total dominance of the PRI and its predecessors for so many years. This body of historical work has also stressed the relative weakness of the postrevolutionary state, and has shown that the federal government was only ever able to impose its political will unevenly, often through resort to violence and coercion, and through informal channels and intermediaries. In particular, historians have emphasized the significance of *camarillas* (cross-class local alliances of politicians and power brokers) to the functioning of politics, outside the bounds of formal political institutions. For quite some time now, historians have also

21 Two examples are discussed in detail in Chapter 6.

demonstrated that processes of cultural transformation were just as critical to postrevolutionary state formation as political ones.[22]

I focus on the creation of Mexico's political institutions and traditions in this book as a different but complementary approach to these same questions and preoccupations. The high degree of congruence between party and state in postrevolutionary Mexico poses a host of methodological challenges for scholars, but the distinction between the two is important.[23] The power wielded by postrevolutionary Mexican politicians via the parties they created was not ever unilateral, even when their parties were successful (and readers will find that this is a history that includes at least as many political failures as it does triumphs). Even so, the institutions themselves, both in design and in practice, are important artifacts and testaments to the time and places in which they were created. From the outset, the southeastern Socialist parties were intended to be formalized, institutional expressions of the Mexican Revolution; by scrutinizing the organizational systems, justifications, and bylaws their founders created to achieve this, and the ways their intentions did and did not conform to political practice, this book offers new insight into the ancestral relationship between the Revolution and the political parties that staked claims to its legacy for the rest of the twentieth century, and beyond.

I have chosen to treat the 1920s as a distinct period within Mexico's history. The decade of the 1920s is typically described by historians as either an epilogue to the Mexican Revolution or as a preamble to the era of the PRI, but it is rarely treated as a crucial period of political development, institutionalization, and social transformation in its own right.[24] In spite of ongoing debates among historians about the true character and long-term legacies of *Cardenismo*, the much-studied decade of the 1930s is unanimously regarded as the zenith of postrevolutionary reform and state building.[25]

22   In their examinations of processes of state formation in postrevolutionary Mexico, historians have increasingly called into question what constitutes the state. As Ben Fallaw succinctly puts it, "the state is less a thing than a process." Ben Fallaw, *Religion and State Formation in Postrevolutionary Mexico* (Durham, NC: Duke University Press, 2013), 3.

23   As Garrido argued, "The word 'PRI' has been used in some instances with great facility to indicate much more than the organization is in reality, and in others with great restriction to define much less than what it is." Garrido, *El Partido de la Revolución Institucionalizada*, 16.

24   On characterizations of the 1920s as either a period of political failures or the lead-up to Cardenismo, see Fowler-Salamini, "De-Centering the 1920s," 288–89.

25   Some of this comes down to a disagreement on periodization of the Mexican Revolution. I argue for a clear distinction between the armed phase of the Revolution (1910–20), and the period that followed it. On the other end of the spectrum, some historians argue that the Revolution ended at the finish of Cárdenas' presidency in 1940. These disagreements notwithstanding, compared to the 1920s, the literature on *Cardenismo* and the debates it has inspired are vast. In 1994, Alan Knight published what is still regarded as one of the definitive analyses of the Cardenista period: Alan Knight, "Cardenismo: Juggernaut or Jalopy?," *Journal of Latin American Studies* 26, no. 1

The decade of the 1920s was both violent and politically fraught, but the nearly constant crises that Mexico faced in those years did not preclude decisive steps toward state consolidation. It was precisely the process of political trial and error in these years that gave shape to Mexico's political system. When Calles founded the PNR in 1929, it was not the dawn of a new political era, but the definitive formalization of a trend that had been rapidly developing for most of the decade.

Geography and regionalism play critical roles in this book, as they have in histories of Mexico over the past several decades. The regionalized history of Mexico of the past several decades has typically been focused on states as the largest geographical unit of analysis, rather than on regions in the traditional sense of the word, and has generally precluded or eschewed comparative examinations between states within particular regions.[26] Particular Mexican states have commonly been used by historians either as illustrations of broader national trends or case studies that complicate previous assumptions about national trends. State-specific histories have contributed a wealth of valuable data about local particularities, but have frequently underplayed the significance of regional and national political trends. Over the years, historians have pointed to individual Socialist parties of the Southeast as likely influences on the design of the party that Calles founded in 1929.[27] Examining state, regional, and national politics in tandem reveals the extensive but previously little-understood

(1994). Since then, the character of Cardenismo and its long-term legacies have been taken up by historians in a number of monographs focusing on different topics and regions (and this is not even to mention the large number of articles on related topics). See, for instance, Jocelyn Olcott, *Revolutionary Women in Postrevolutionary Mexico* (Durham, NC: Duke University Press, 2005); Ben Fallaw, *Cárdenas Compromised: The Failure of Reform in Postrevolutionary Yucatán* (Durham, NC: Duke University Press, 2001); Boyer, *Becoming Campesinos*; Marjorie Becker, *Setting the Virgin on Fire: Lázaro Cárdenas, Michoacán Peasants, and the Redemption of the Mexican Revolution* (Berkeley, CA: University of California Press, 1995); Amelia M. Kiddle, *Mexico's Relations with Latin America during the Cárdenas Era* (Albuquerque, NM: University of New Mexico Press, 2016).

26 On the regionalized historiography of the Mexican Revolution, see, in particular, Thomas Benjamin and Mark Wasserman, *Provinces of the Revolution: Essays on Regional Mexican History, 1910–1929* (Albuquerque, NM: University of New Mexico Press, 1990). Recent scholarship has begun to look beyond state and regional lines. See, in particular, Ben Fallaw's examination of the role of Catholics in resisting (and thereby shaping) postrevolutionary reform initiatives in Campeche, Hidalgo, Guerrero, and Guanajuato. Fallaw, *Religion and State Formation*.

27 Thomas Benjamin argued that the Socialist governments of the southeastern states of Chiapas, Tabasco, and Yucatán were among the most politically influential regional administrations during the 1920s (he also cites Jalisco, Michoacán, San Luis Potosí, Tamaulipas, and Veracruz). Benjamin, "Laboratories of the New State." Over the years, various scholars have suggested that the Yucatecan Socialist party model was particularly influential on the design of the PRI and its predecessor parties. See, in particular, Joseph, *Revolution from Without*, 112. Fowler-Salamini also argues for the example of the radical agrarian movement in Veracruz as important to the course of national politics. Fowler-Salamini, *Agrarian Radicalism*.

relationships between all of the Socialist parties of the Southeast and political elites of Mexico City in the 1920s. These alliances and mutual influences across state lines are crucial for explaining the decisive impact of the Socialist experiments in party formation on national politics by the end of the decade.

As much as the Socialists' political programs were driven by an abiding desire for peace, political violence is an inescapable element of this history of the consolidation of the Mexican political system. Although the revolutionary armies largely disbanded by 1920, the impulse to protect political gains by force of arms remained endemic in postrevolutionary politics. While the Southeast largely escaped the violence that engulfed other regions during the revolutionary years and then again during the Cristero War of 1926–29, this was a profoundly violent period in the region, as everyday people sometimes lost their lives during political campaigns or while attempting to cast ballots for particular candidates. It was also a period in which politicians knowingly took their lives in their hands in order to oppose the initiatives of the ruling national political clique as it closed ranks and consolidated its power. Southeastern Socialists defended the government during the de la Huerta rebellion of 1923–24, but some helped to lead the Gómez-Serrano rebellion of 1927, both with decisive consequences. Over the course of the 1920s it became increasingly dangerous to be a radical or even a moderate dissident in Mexico. The history of the Socialist Southeast lays bare this legacy: Most of the individuals that appear most prominently in this book were either executed or assassinated, and a lucky few were exiled.[28] The credible fear of violence, whether generalized or targeted against individuals, informed the decisions that both elites and non-elites alike made about their participation in political processes.[29]

Recurring violence was formative to the postrevolutionary Mexican political system, both positively and negatively. As Mexicans grew ever wearier of war, politicians actively sought a means to permanently pacify the country, and to quell the fratricidal propensities of the political class that chronically threatened to derail the process of postrevolutionary state consolidation. After experiencing so much violence and witnessing so

---

28 Claudio Lomnitz argues that political assassination was a defining characteristic of Mexican politics particular to the period of 1910 to 1929. Claudio Lomnitz-Adler, *Death and the Idea of Mexico* (Brooklyn, NY: Zone Books, 2005), 386–91.

29 Jocelyn Olcott argues that struggles over the meanings of postrevolutionary violence in Mexico were both driven and complicated by the government's efforts to declare the Mexican Revolution definitively over. Jocelyn Olcott, "*Mueras y matanza*: Spectacles of Terror and Violence in Postrevolutionary Mexico," in *A Century of Revolution: Insurgent and Counterinsurgent Violence During Latin America's Long Cold War*, ed. Greg Grandin and Gilbert M. Joseph (Durham, NC: Duke University Press, 2010), 63.

many deaths, many Mexican citizens also became more willing to sacrifice some of their political freedoms and independence in exchange for peace and security, or were convinced that it was in their best interest to do so.[30] It was a system that was explicitly designed to prevent both elite coups and popular uprisings, but also to ensure that it would be strong enough to withstand either should they arise.

Methodology and Structure

This book relies heavily on the correspondence of its protagonists as its source base. The personal papers of most of the politicians in question are held in archives in Mexico City. At the Calles Trust Archive (FAPECFT), I worked with the papers of Presidents Plutarco Elías Calles and Álvaro Obregón, Secretary of War Joaquín Amaro, and Fernando Torreblanca, who served as the personal secretary to both Calles and Obregón at different times. At the Mexican National Archive (AGN), I worked with the papers of Socialist governors Tomás Garrido Canabal and Carlos A. Vidal, and Secretary of War Francisco R. Serrano. This is the first historical monograph to make use of the Vidal papers, which were only catalogued for the first time in 2011. I conducted the first inventory of the collection over the course of several months between 2006 and 2008.[31]

I additionally conducted research in various other collections at the AGN, as well as in the state archives of Chiapas and Yucatán.[32] I also worked in the archives of the Mexican Ministry of Defense (SEDENA), where I was able to access the personnel files of many of the generals and politicians that appear in this book, as well as track the administration of military governance and campaigns in the Southeast. I found an additional wealth of documents posted online by the SEDENA historical archive in 2010 in commemoration of the centennial of the Mexican Revolution. I also make use of documents from the United States Embassy collection held at the FAPECFT, which includes United States confidential diplomatic and military intelligence correspondence on Mexican politics.[33]

I counterbalance personal papers with official government documents, legislative debates, newspapers, and other archival collections to give the

---

30 On the relationship between violence and "state making" in postrevolutionary Mexico, see, in particular, Wil G. Pansters, ed. *Violence, Coercion, and State-Making in Twentieth-Century Mexico: The Other Half of the Centaur* (Stanford, CA: Stanford University Press, 2012).

31 My citation of documents from the Vidal papers is based on a rudimentary system I developed during this inventory. The cited documents are readily findable with the new catalog system. My preliminary guide to the collection is available at the AGN.

32 The bulk of the archival material for Tabasco is held at the AGN in Mexico City.

33 On the provenance of this document collection, see Jürgen Buchenau, *Plutarco Elías Calles and the Mexican Revolution* (Lanham, MD: Rowman & Littlefield, 2007), 134.

most balanced account of events that extant sources allow. By cross-referencing these various sources, I reconstruct a relatively complete accounting of the larger conversations taking place between the politicians in question. I also trace the genesis, development, and unraveling of their long-term political relationships over the course of the 1920s; alliances and enmities alike frequently had profound effects on Mexican national politics in the postrevolutionary period.

These sources illuminate the connections that were forged between politicians and their constituents in these years. An extensive body of correspondence received by Socialist and national leaders from people in communities across the Southeast reveals the tangible, quotidian impact of political changes and upheavals in the states in question. Through these governors' and party leaders' own accountings of their grassroots organizing efforts in both official and personal records, along with local and national newspaper coverage, I show the ways in which both state-level policymaking and national political events unfolded on the ground in local communities in the Southeast. My sources also enable me to show the direct connections that existed in the 1920s between national political campaigns and local politics in the Southeast. They demonstrate that what was taking place in the remote corners of states like Campeche, Chiapas, Tabasco, and Yucatán was sometimes taken very seriously in elite political circles in Mexico City, especially during the fraught presidential election cycles of 1923–24 and 1927–28. Lastly, I use the archived records of the early Mexican intelligence service (Dirección General de Investigaciones Sociales [DGIPS]) at the AGN to show how closely the federal government was tracking particular actors and events at the local level in the Southeast during the 1920s.[34]

This book is roughly chronological. First it traces the development and the spread of Socialism across the Southeast and then examines its influence on national politics. The first chapter is devoted to the early years of Socialism in Yucatán as it was first developed by Salvador Alvarado and then adapted by Felipe Carrillo Puerto in the mid-late 1910s. The second chapter examines how and why Yucatecan-style Socialism spread rapidly across state lines to Campeche, Chiapas, and Tabasco in the early 1920s. The third chapter is a study of the de la Huerta rebellion of 1923–24 that focuses on its particular impact and significance in the Southeast, and the repercussions for the Socialist parties there. The fourth and fifth chapters are studies of Socialism in Tabasco and Chiapas, respectively; together these introduce the growing divergence of Socialism as a school of politics within

34   For background on this document collection, see Aaron W. Navarro, *Political Intelligence and the Creation of Modern Mexico, 1938–1954* (University Park, PA: Pennsylvania State University Press, 2010), 4–5.

the region by the mid-1920s, fueled in part by the mutual antagonism between governors Tomás Garrido Canabal and Carlos Vidal. The sixth chapter is a history of the Gómez-Serrano rebellion, which was led in part by Socialists from Chiapas, and the failure of which meant the defeat and suppression of Socialism there, among its many long-term consequences. The final chapter traces the influence of southeastern Socialism on the design and consolidation of the National Revolutionary Party in the late 1920s and early 1930s.

Taken together, these chapters provide an account of a political experiment that was radical in its reformist ambitions and groundbreaking in its implementation, even when the practice of southeastern Socialism didn't always achieve all of its many lofty principles. It began in one state in a distant corner of Mexico, then expanded outward to three more, and then to the national stage in the space of less than a decade. Despite its geographic and temporal limits, it was a set of political ideas and ideals that was decisively influential to the course of Mexican politics from that point forward.

I

The Socialist Crucible

Yucatán, 1915–1922

I dream of a nation that is free, powerful, abundantly civilized and happy, and I cherish the conviction that if Mexico has the help of all of its children, as it should, the dream will not be long in becoming a dazzling reality, which I want to have its beginning in Yucatán.

Salvador Alvarado, 1916

On the eve of the Mexican Revolution in 1910, the state of Yucatán was home to many people who longed for economic, social, and political change, and a powerful, deep-pocketed few that were fiercely determined to resist it. Ricardo Flores Magón and his collaborators lambasted the regime of Porfirio Díaz from exile in the United States, and Francisco I. Madero toured Mexico as an opposition presidential candidate, while Pancho Villa soon raised an army in northern Durango and Emiliano Zapata did likewise in central Morelos. Some Yucatecan politicians had already successfully mobilized workers and campesinos at various moments for their own purposes during the *Porfiriato* (1876–1911), but well-oiled mechanisms of political repression had prevented a popular uprising there. As the Revolution engulfed other regions, reform remained out of reach in Yucatán until the Constitutionalist army of Venustiano Carranza arrived there in 1915 under the command of General Salvador Alvarado.

Occupying the apex of the peninsula that divides the Gulf of Mexico from the Caribbean, Yucatán lies roughly halfway between Mexico City and Miami. Within Mexico, the state has historically been regarded as singular, peripheral, and isolated. United States journalist John Kenneth Turner famously described Yucatán as one of the parts of Mexico most desperately in need of reform. "The portion of the people of Yucatán who are born free possess no 'inalienable right' to their freedom," Turner wrote in 1910, in his explosive serial exposé of the practice of slavery in Porfirian Mexico.[1] Yucatán was notoriously unequal, and Yucatecan elites were

---

1   John Kenneth Turner, *Barbarous Mexico* (Austin, TX: University of Texas Press, 1969), 13. On Turner's political activism, his exposé of slavery in Mexico and his research trip to Yucatán, see

experienced and adept at putting down popular challenges to their power and authority. They were also deeply fearful of an uprising by the oppressed and marginalized indigenous population of the state, with good reason. Nevertheless, by the mid-1920s the state was home to the most important model for postrevolutionary reform and institution building in Mexico, and was the crucible from which southeastern Socialism emerged. Yucatecan Socialism was a school of postrevolutionary politics that was acclaimed by its allies, and grudgingly lauded even by its enemies for its efficacy and integrity. It was the product of both homegrown organizing and the influence and interventions of outsiders. Its history is the indispensable entry point into this book's examination of the history and significance of southeastern Socialism.

This chapter explores how and why Yucatán came to pave the way for the creation of Mexico's postrevolutionary political system. It examines the particular features of the state in the 1910s that gave rise to Socialism, the political, intellectual and philosophical roots of the movement, and the histories of two Socialist governments in the state between 1915 and 1922. In many respects, the same features that made Yucatán unusual and exceptional within Mexico also made it a uniquely fertile ground for the kind of political experimentation that led to the formation of the groundbreaking Socialist Party of the Southeast (PSS) in 1921.

First, Yucatán's geographic distance from the revolutionary battlefields in 1910–15 meant that when the state did become involved in the Mexican Revolution, all factions had relatively more elaborated political programs, and their national strategies – both political and military – were likewise more clearly articulated. Second, from the perspective of de facto head of state Venustiano Carranza, Yucatán's physical distance from Mexico City made it a relatively low-risk site for political experimentation in the mid-1910s, with potential for high political and economic rewards. Third, as Yucatán became increasingly strategically important on the political map, national political leaders were willing to tolerate such experimentation on an ongoing basis – provided that it facilitated their control of the peninsula. Two generations of Yucatecan Socialists thrived under these circumstances and with these caveats from their respective national patrons.

Salvador Alvarado's Revolution in Yucatán, 1915–17

In the late nineteenth century, Yucatán experienced an unprecedented economic boom thanks to the development of the henequen industry in the state. The fibrous, spiky leaves of the henequen plant, a relative of the agave cactus, were shredded to make durable rope and twine. The plant flourished in Yucatán's climate, where little else did.[2] Yucatán's henequen became the principal source for the cords used to bind the crops and hay bales of farms all over the United States, almost all of which was purchased by the US-owned company International Harvester.[3] With increased mechanization, the new profitability of the fiber led to the dramatic intensification of its cultivation in the late nineteenth century and the rise of an extremely wealthy planter class. By the time of the Mexican Revolution, Yucatán was one of the wealthiest states in Mexico, even as the planters suffered through the inevitable booms and busts of a monocrop economy.[4]

Yucatán's plantation economy, initially dedicated to sugar production, depended heavily on a system of debt peonage and the de facto enslavement of indigenous campesinos. The haciendas also inevitably and inexorably expanded into lands formerly used by Maya communities for subsistence agriculture. The increasing pressures on indigenous communities in the peninsula in the nineteenth century boiled over into what is known to history as the Caste War, a revolt by the Maya that began in 1847 and lasted in some places into the early twentieth century.[5] As the henequen industry grew even more dramatically in the latter half of the century once the peninsula was pacified, so did land hunger among the Maya.[6] In short, Yucatán was transformed by the turn of the century as henequen became the state's undisputed monocrop and the planters' pockets were lavishly lined at the expense of an increasingly impoverished and disenfranchised indigenous workforce. Further, as indigenous communities lost progressively more lands to the haciendas, more people were forced into debt peonage on the henequen estates.[7]

2   On the ecological and climatological challenges posed for agriculture in Yucatán, see Joseph, *Revolution from Without*, 16–18.
3   On the particularities of the henequen plant and competing fiber sources elsewhere in the world at the turn of the century, see ibid., 13–14. On the history of mechanization of its processing, see ibid., 24, 26, 41.
4   On the politics and economics of Yucatán's Porfirian-era henequen economy, see Wells and Joseph, *Summer of Discontent*, chapters 3 and 4.
5   On the Caste War, see Terry Rugeley, *Rebellion Now and Forever: Mayas, Hispanics, and Caste War Violence in Yucatán, 1800–1880* (Stanford, CA: Stanford University Press, 2009); Terry Rugeley, *Yucatán's Maya Peasantry and the Origins of the Caste War* (Austin, TX: University of Texas Press, 1996); Paul Sullivan, *Xuxub Must Die: The Lost Histories of a Murder on the Yucatán* (Pittsburgh, PA: University of Pittsburgh Press, 2004).
6   Joseph, *Revolution from Without*, 26–27. They were joined in the henequen fields by Yaqui slaves imported from northern Mexico, as famously documented by Turner, along with other entrapped and recruited workers from elsewhere. Ibid., 29, 72.
7   For a case study of this process and its consequences, see Eiss, *In the Name of el Pueblo*, chapter 2.

When the Revolution began in 1910, the Yucatecan plantocracy initially succeeded in maintaining its grip on political and economic power. Gilbert M. Joseph has underscored that the memory of the Caste War lingered on the peninsula at the turn of the century; elites constructed a system that was explicitly designed to strip workers of their indigenous identity and to forestall any further uprisings by campesinos.[8] The planters and their political allies were also notably successful at keeping political ferment among organized workers and their advocates to a minimum until the later years of the Porfiriato via various forms of political repression.

It wasn't that no backlash against the political and economic elite occurred in Porfirian Yucatán. On the contrary, there was significant unrest in the state in the years leading up to the Revolution, including among campesinos, who increasingly allied with elite political factions by the end of the Porfiriato. As henequen boomed and then crashed in 1907–8, resident peons on haciendas found themselves with less to gain from quiescently participating in the henequen economy, and increasingly resisted their subjugation in numerous ways. Meanwhile, their "free" counterparts in surviving Maya pueblos experienced growing political repression and economic deprivation. They were correspondingly more receptive to outreach efforts by dissident political factions seeking to bolster their standing in ever-more direct confrontations with the ruling, Díaz-supported state government and the camarilla that controlled it. Although this was a potentially formidable coalition, Allen Wells and Gilbert M. Joseph argue that attempts at revolts were unsuccessful for several reasons, principally perpetual dissent and suspicion between rival dissident elite factions, and lingering elite reluctance to arm Maya campesinos with the collective memory of the Caste War still relatively fresh.[9] Nevertheless, by the end of the Porfiriato, most Yucatecan political elites recognized that workers and peasants had to be part of the political conversation, but generally regarded them as objects of reform, rather than agents. Even when they sought Maya campesinos as allies, they actively feared and guarded against the autonomous mobilization of the workers that kept the henequen economy running with their indebted labor.[10]

Finally, when Díaz was overthrown in 1911 and all elite factions decided they did indeed need popular support, they were unsuccessful at controlling the factions of workers and campesinos they had mobilized and spurred to action. Madero allies took power and largely perpetuated the status quo,

8　Joseph, *Revolution from Without*, 71, 82–85. Ben Fallaw, "Cárdenas and the Caste War That Wasn't: State Power and Indigenismo in Post-Revolutionary Yucatán," *The Americas* 53, no. 4 (1997): 552–53.

9　Wells and Joseph, *Summer of Discontent*, chapters 6 and 7.　10　Ibid., chapter 8.

leaving restless rival elite factions, mobilized workers and campesinos alike all dissatisfied, at best.[11] Workers and campesinos soon realized that none of the three competing elite factions had any intention of implementing significant political or economic reform, even now that the dictatorship was over. This resulted in a period of significant unrest in the state, as haciendas were destroyed and hacendados and overseers were killed by bands of enraged villagers and hacienda workers. Thus, when Madero was overthrown and assassinated by General Victoriano Huerta in 1913, most elites welcomed the military governor imposed by Huerta. Under the dictatorship, the clock was turned back in Yucatán, as any popular unrest or destruction of property met with harsh reprisals by the state. Above all, any political opening that might have fostered further uprisings among workers and campesinos was now shut. Yucatecan elites, in spite of their other differences, found common ground in their now reaffirmed preference for law and order over even the possibility of indigenous people rising against them.[12]

Even so, Yucatán's elites could not keep the Revolution at bay, nor forestall significant reform once Huerta was defeated by a coalition of revolutionary forces in 1914. The lucrative henequen economy, the obvious military advantages of controlling the narrow Isthmus of Tehuantepec, and Chiapas' international border with Guatemala, among other factors, eventually made the Southeast a key part of national political and military strategies. Venustiano Carranza, so-called First Chief of the Constitutionalist faction, was not the only one to recognize the region's importance on the revolutionary map, but he was the first to make a concerted attempt to take control of it.[13]

The Constitutionalists' political and economic interests in Yucatán were effectively one and the same. It was by far the most economically important state of the Southeast, and one of the most important in all of Mexico. This was all the more true in the last years of the Revolution, as the First World War fueled a spike in global demand for henequen. This windfall drew the attention of Carranza and the Constitutionalists, as they sought funds to prosecute their ongoing war against their revolutionary rivals. By 1914 Carranza was reportedly prepared to spend as much as a million pesos to build up his forces in Yucatán in the hopes that this investment would pay for itself many times over.[14] Even as Carranza's armies battled against Villa

11 Ibid., 239.   12   Ibid., 232–38; Eiss, *In the Name of el Pueblo*, 79–96.
13 Pancho Villa was also aware of the potential advantages of controlling the Southeast, but made no concerted effort to do so. Alan Knight, *The Mexican Revolution, Volume 2* (Lincoln, Nebraska: University of Nebraska Press, 1986; repr., 1), 236.
14 Historical Archive of the Ministry of National Defense, 2010 online archive commemorating the centennial of the Mexican Revolution and the bicentennial of Mexican Independence (www.archivohistorico2010.sedena.gob.mx) (hereafter AHSDN-W), Operaciones Militares, Yucatán, 1914. XI/481.5/325. Eleuterio Avila to Carranza, October 16, 1914.

and Zapata in the center and north of the country, Constitutionalist money, troops, and arms flowed into Yucatán to lay the groundwork for a new military government there.[15]

Yucatán's henequen riches were what made it so strategically important, but they also made the state a uniquely difficult territorial conquest for the Constitutionalists. The planter elite was unwelcoming at best, and was also equipped with nearly limitless funds and had close relationships to powerful international business interests, particularly in the United States. For their part, foreign firms, above all International Harvester, were deeply invested in maintaining an undisturbed, cheap supply of Yucatecan henequen. Carranza was a passionate nationalist, but the value of henequen was in its salability abroad. As Carranza's proconsul in the state in 1915–17, General Alvarado's tasks were therefore to bring Constitutionalism to Yucatán, to pacify the ongoing uprisings in the state, to reform its economy, and to bring the state's elite planter class to political heel, all without disrupting the henequen economy and its valuable flow of exports to the United States.

If there was anyone up to the task, it was Alvarado. His first predecessor, Colonel Euleterio Avila, had the advantage of being a Yucatecan, but had local political baggage that proved to be more of a detriment than an advantage in his ability to govern and pacify the state. Nor did he have the political skill required to walk the fine line between reforming Yucatán and enflaming it.[16] He was soon replaced with General Toribio de los Santos, a northerner who took the opposite tack and was uncompromising in his application of Constitutionalist reform in the state. In his short time in office he succeeded in alienating a diverse spectrum of Yucatecans in their shared distaste for Constitutionalist interference to such a degree that he succeeded in uniting former political enemies in a push for greater local sovereignty and autonomy.[17]

Carranza's savvy choice of Alvarado as the state's next proconsul constituted both a course correction and a doubling down: Alvarado had a stiffer spine and a greater talent for politics than his predecessors, and as another northerner, he had no sense of local political obligation to constrain him. Unlike most of his revolutionary colleagues, Alvarado was a politician who became a soldier, rather than the other way around. Born in the state of Sinaloa in 1880, he grew up and was educated in neighboring Sonora. Like many other northern revolutionaries, Alvarado came from a solidly middle

---

15 Much of the weaponry destined for Yucatán was purchased in Cuba. AHSDN-W, Operaciones Militares, Yucatán, 1914. XI/481.5/325. Manuel Amaya to Carranza, November 5, 1914. On the significance of Yucatán in Carranza's national strategy, see Joseph, *Revolution from Without*, 6-8, 94–95.

16 Wells and Joseph, *Summer of Discontent*, 267–74.   17 Ibid., 275–79.

class background. He first entered politics in 1906, as a local elector, and took inspiration from the Flores Magón brothers and the Mexican Liberal Party (PLM).[18] However, unlike Ricardo Flores Magón, Alvarado was an early supporter of Madero, and following Madero's death he joined Carranza and rose quickly in the ranks of the Constitutionalist army.[19] As one of the rising stars of the revolutionary generation, Alvarado's appointment in Yucatán was testimony to Carranza's commitment and seriousness when it came to taking control of southeastern Mexico.

The "Constitutionalist" revolution was based on notions of modernizing and rationalizing politics, society, and the economy in order to install a new regime of law and order in Mexico. In 1915, Carranza and the Constitutionalists issued decrees intended to reorganize everything from labor laws to family relations, and in Yucatán (as elsewhere) moved quickly to abolish debt peonage once and for all. Alvarado brought this decidedly moderate but still highly ambitious reformist impulse with him to Yucatán. This put him immediately at odds with the henequen planters, whose exploitative labor system was one of Alvarado's principal targets for reform on his arrival to the state. His predecessor, Avila, had abolished debt peonage in the hopes of pacifying the countryside, but the planters had fought back fiercely, and the governor quickly acquiesced and rendered his own reform nearly meaningless in practice.[20]

By contrast, Alvarado's reorganizations of the politics and economy of Yucatán between 1915 and 1917 were ambitious and far-reaching. It was a process that required striking delicate political and administrative balances and forging strategic compromises, and Alvarado proved to be adept at both. He tempered the imposition of his sweeping reform program with the purposeful inclusion of Yucatecans from diverse social classes into the new political administration that he constructed and controlled in the state.[21] In later years, Alvarado would repeatedly tout all that he achieved in Yucatán in 1915–17 as a successful example of the implementation of the brand of revolutionary politics that he espoused for Mexico as a whole.

18 Salvador Alvarado, *La reconstrucción de México: un mensaje a los pueblos de America, Volume 1* (México, D.F.: Partido Revolucionario Institucional (PRI), 1919; repr., 1982), 21. Alvarado subscribed to *Regeneración*. See James D. Cockcroft, *Intellectual Precursors of the Mexican Revolution, 1900–1913* (Austin, TX: University of Texas Press, 1968), 124.

19 Roderic Ai Camp, *Mexican Political Biographies, 1884–1935* (Austin, TX: University of Texas Press, 1991), 10.

20 Wells and Joseph, *Summer of Discontent*, 270–1; Eiss, *In the Name of el Pueblo*, 100–2.

21 As both Joseph and Alan Knight have argued, Alvarado's success as a proconsul lay in his ability to forge a multi-class coalition in Yucatán, organized to work toward what was ultimately a relatively moderate program of reform. Joseph, *Revolution from Without*, 98. Knight, *The Mexican Revolution, Volume 2*, 238.

Alvarado called his brand of politics "Socialist," a decision that would mark the politics of the Southeast for many years to come. Alvarado's version of Socialism was always more about political practice than a clearly articulated ideology or a consistent philosophy. He worried that lofty ideals inscribed into law, and into the 1917 Constitution, were meaningless if they were not applied effectively and regularly in practice, and invoked "Socialism" as such quite rarely in his extensive political writings.[22] These treatises were largely based on his work in Yucatán, but he used them to offer political prescriptions for Mexico as a whole. In one instance, he described Socialism as "a new light in the midst of the confusion born of the failure of all of the systems that humanity has tested in search of happiness."[23] Subsequent generations of Socialists in the Southeast and beyond would employ similarly vague and romantic descriptions of the global uplift that the advent of Socialism promised as justifications for their otherwise heterogeneous political programs. The ambiguity, and therefore the flexibility, of the term "Socialist" paradoxically became one of the defining characteristics of Mexican Socialism.

While not entirely unrelated, it is essential that Mexican Socialism of this era is not conflated with other variants of Socialism that were developed elsewhere in the world in the early twentieth century. The closest political relative of Alvarado's mid-1910s brand of "Socialism" was mainstream United States progressivism; later variations of Mexican Socialism incorporated other, more radical political and intellectual influences.[24] In the United States, the Progressive Era brought about the advent of programs providing child welfare, mother's pensions, veteran's benefits, among others, intended to ameliorate the rapid changes and upheavals of the modern era while preserving certain idealized elements of eras past. Progressivism, as Richard Hofstadter underscored, posed an ideological paradox in its insistence on reform but its simultaneous nostalgia for something its protagonists sensed had been lost (or imminently would be) and therefore its conservatism in the most literal sense.[25] An analogous contradiction lay similarly close to the heart of Alvarado's Socialist project.

22 FAPECFT-FAO, serie: 20700, expediente A-2 30: ALVARADO, Salvador (Gral.), legajo 1, fojas 4–22, inventario: 778. Open letter from Alvarado to Carranza, Obregón, and Pablo González, 13 Aug 1919. On Alvarado's ideology, as such, see also Joseph, *Revolution from Without*, 101.

23 Salvador Alvarado, *Actuación revolucionaria del General Salvador Alvarado en Yucatán* (México, D.F.: B. Costa-Amic, 1918; repr., 1965), 55.

24 I use the term "progressivism" in a very general sense, acknowledging that its meanings are many and are actively debated by historians of the United States. Joseph has suggested that Alvarado may have purposefully adopted progressivist language at times, particularly in his dealings with North American business interests and politicians. Joseph, *Revolution from Without*, 158.

25 Richard Hofstadter, *The Age of Reform: From Bryan to F.D.R* (New York, NY: Knopf, 1955), 12–16.

Like US progressivism, Alvarado's version of Socialism in Yucatán combined new and innovative social programs with nostalgia for an idealized
social past, strong notes of paternalism, and protections for business interests, which were nevertheless concurrent with plans for targeted social
equalization between classes.[26]

These similarities were not accidents. Alvarado cited a broad spectrum of
US reformers of the era as his political role models. He admiringly quoted
Woodrow Wilson, and applauded numerous examples of reform movements
and measures undertaken in the United States and Britain throughout his
published prescriptions for postrevolutionary Mexican policymaking.[27]
Alvarado's Socialism was a creative amalgam of political strategies he cobbled
together to address the particular political challenges of both governing and
reforming the Southeast. He was given license for the experiment for several
years. At least for a while, as long as Alvarado continued to restock the
Constitutionalist treasury, he could pursue his reform projects in Yucatán.

Alvarado began with labor reform. In 1915 he issued a new labor law
that was regarded at the time to be one of the most radical and progressive
in Mexico, and which he proudly described as having freed indigenous
Yucatecans from bondage.[28] Historian Paul Eiss has emphasized that while
the Constitutionalists inarguably did away with some of the most abusive
and outmoded practices on Yucatán's henequen plantations and ensured
basic labor rights and protections, their efforts on behalf of workers were
not otherwise especially radical or extensive.[29] Yet the changes that were
made were transformative. Alvarado estimated that the labor law reduced
henequen production in the state by 15 percent by 1917, but argued that
this was the entirely justifiable cost of guaranteeing workers an eight-hour
workday, indemnification for unjustified dismissal, fair wages, and the
right to strike, all for the first time. To offset the lost work hours the new
labor rights regime entailed, Alvarado spent state resources to recruit
immigrants to work on the henequen plantations.[30] Alvarado succeeded
in part by offering Yucatecan hacendados and foreign investors favorable

---

26 Alvarado, *Actuación revolucionaria*, 42. Ben Fallaw argues that "Yucatecan socialism owed as much
    to classical liberalism and anarchosyndicalism as to historical materialism." Fallaw, *Cárdenas
    Compromised*, 11.

27 Perhaps more surprisingly for a Latin American nationalist in the era of the Roosevelt Corollary,
    Governor Carlos Vidal of Chiapas later quoted Theodore Roosevelt in his own propaganda
    materials.

28 AHSDN-W: Operaciones Militares, Yucatán, 1917. XI/481.5/327. Alvarado to Carranza,
    April 24, 1917.

29 Paul K. Eiss, "A Measure of Liberty: The Politics of Labor in Revolutionary Yucatán, 1915–1918,"
    ed. Edward Davis Terry, et al., *Peripheral Visions: Politics, Society, and the Challenges of Modernity in
    Yucatan* (Tuscaloosa, AL: University of Alabama Press, 2010). 60.

30 AHSDN-W: Operaciones Militares, Yucatán, 1917. XI/481.5/327. Alvarado to Carranza,
    May 13, 1917.

terms for their business dealings in the state while pushing them hard to adopt more equitable labor practices, so that, in his words, "they might fill the social function that the community has the right to demand of them."[31] Alvarado's labor law would subsequently be a model for Article 123 of the 1917 Constitution that guaranteed a nearly identical set of workers' rights.[32]

Alvarado had little patience for planters who sought to undermine his political and economic projects, and he wasn't above retaliation to exert his political dominance and keep the southeastern elite in line.[33] Yet his most successful ploy to this end was to make the planters rich. To further reform the Yucatecan economy, in 1916 Alvarado reorganized the state Regulatory Commission of the Henequen Market ("la Reguladora") that had been founded several years before. Nearly all planters but the most elite initially participated in the commission, which purchased their henequen and then brokered its sale when the best price could be secured. Alvarado substantially expanded the purview and the power of the *Reguladora*, all-but compelling nearly the entire planter class to participate, and concocting a variety of creative sanctions for those that defied him.[34] This was an explicitly nationalist effort to take control of a resource that had for many years principally enriched the wealthiest planters and the foreign companies that bought their crop, at the expense of nearly everyone else in the state. Like many of Alvarado's reforms, it required a firm but delicate hand. Alvarado literally could not afford to alienate the cordage buyers and manufacturers in the United States, even as he actively sought to undermine the privileges to which they were accustomed. Even so, he made it clear to them that the henequen trade would henceforth be conducted on Mexican terms – including a mandate that the fiber could only be transported on Mexican-owned ships.[35] In relatively short order Alvarado succeeded in making the state-run Reguladora the sole supplier of henequen to International Harvester and the other cordage firms. The results spoke for themselves. As world demand for the crop spiked as competing fiber supplies were disrupted by the First World War, the new arrangement made money hand over fist for Alvarado's state government, the planters, and Carranza's government.[36]

31   Alvarado, *Actuación revolucionaria*, 45.   32   Joseph, *Revolution from Without*, 110.

33   FAPECFT-FEC, expediente: 19: ALVARADO, Salvador (Gral)., legajo: 1, fojas 7–8, inventario: 874. Alvarado to Calles, October 23, 1917. "Precisely because [the reactionaries] want to puff up their chests these days, I am going to tighten the screws on them a bit, just to rid them of their good mood."

34   On the creation and subsequent reform of the Reguladora, see Joseph, *Revolution from Without*, 136–39.

35   AHSDN-W: Operaciones Militares, Yucatán, 1917. XI/481.5/327. Alvarado to Carranza, January 17, 1917. On the possible origins of this idea, see Lomnitz-Adler, *The Return of Comrade Ricardo Flores Magón*, 80–81.

36   Joseph found that under Alvarado's leadership, the price fetched in the United States by Yucatecan henequen increased four-fold between 1916 and 1918. Joseph, *Revolution from Without*, 141–42.

When it came to land policy, Alvarado was markedly more conservative than most of the southeastern Socialist politicians that he inspired. While he saw land reform as a crucial step toward modernizing Yucatán and the redemption of its indigenous campesinos, Alvarado was not enthusiastic about the redistribution of lands into communally held ejidos, and instead espoused a system that would ideally lead to the predominance of small, privately held lands ("pequeñas propiedades"). In large part, this was because henequen was so crucial both to the economy of the state and to his political projects.[37] However, he stipulated that the return of enormous estates was unacceptable, and was unsparing in his written attacks on Mexico's wealthiest classes, particularly in Yucatán.[38] "The Creels and the Terrazas were nothing more than poor apprentices who should have gone to Yucatán for lessons," he wrote, referencing the infamously wealthy landowning clans of northern Mexico before the Revolution.[39] However, Alvarado was quick to distinguish between "capitalists" and "aristocrats," arguing that the former were hard working and productive, while the latter were reactionary parasites devoted purely to consumption.[40]

Alvarado's land reform law of 1915 reflected these conflicted agendas, and left expropriation of the haciendas as a measure of last resort when the supply of unused lands was exhausted.[41] Alvarado also made clear that he did not intend to bring about the supremacy of henequen workers over their employers, and he intervened to keep the haciendas up and running when he deemed it necessary.[42] Still, Alvarado believed that the indigenous recipients of land should be equipped to protect their holdings from the onslaught of landowners by force of arms if necessary.[43] In spite of its clauses designed to protect the henequen sector, Alvarado faced a major setback when Carranza's government deemed his land law too radical and in conflict with federal law, but local agrarian officials pressed on with

37   Ibid., 126. On Alvarado's intersecting ideas about land and race, see Eiss, *In the Name of el Pueblo*, 99–100.

38   Joseph discusses Alvarado's agrarian policies in depth in his chapter "The Theory and Practice of Bourgeois Reform: Land and the Export Economy," including an exploration of the idealization by Alvarado and other revolutionary leaders and thinkers of the time of the pequeña propiedad as the basic unit of postrevolutionary landholding. Joseph, *Revolution from Without*. See pages 122–25, in particular.

39   Alvarado, *Actuación revolucionaria*, 69. This was a reference to their wealth rather than the extent of their landholdings. Joseph has underscored that in terms of acreage, by national standards, never mind in comparison to the (in)famously vast landholdings of these particular families, Yucatecan henequen plantations were relatively small. Joseph, *Revolution from Without*, 36.

40   Salvador Alvarado, *La reconstrucción de México: un mensaje a los pueblos de America, Volume 2* (México, D.F.: Partido Revolucionario Institucional (PRI), 1919; repr., 1982), 6–7.

41   Joseph, *Revolution from Without*, 127.

42   Eiss, "A Measure of Liberty: The Politics of Labor in Revolutionary Yucatán, 1915–1918," 54.

43   Alvarado, *La reconstrucción de México, Vol. 2*, 56–57.

provisional land distributions to petitioners with Alvarado's guidance.[44] By his own estimate, Alvarado's land reform law cost the planters of Yucatán 240 million pesos by 1917.[45]

For Alvarado, a new program of federal public education was another indispensable cornerstone to the functioning of all of the social programs he envisioned for Yucatán and for Mexico as a whole.[46] Echoing the progressives to the north once more, Alvarado wrote that the redemption of Mexico's lower classes was contingent on the civilization and betterment of its indigenous peoples, through effective public education.[47] When it came to federal programs for indigenous people, Alvarado issued one of his only sharp critiques of United States policy, decrying the reservation system and declaring that Mexico's indigenous communities must not be similarly sequestered; he shared this view with the politician and intellectual Emilio Rabasa, who had served as the Porfirian governor of Chiapas.[48] Yet in many other respects, particularly when it came to education programs, Alvarado openly admired precedents set in the United States.[49] As governor of Yucatán, he built a teachers college for indigenous students that was modeled on Booker T. Washington's Tuskegee Institute, designed to produce indigenous teachers that could go on to lead new schools in their own communities.[50] Alvarado argued that because the 1917 Constitution guaranteed universal suffrage (for men), it was of the utmost necessity for the government to educate the masses. Otherwise, he warned, the true political force of the nation would rest with illiterates; if Indians were to vote as they had the right to do, they had to be educated so they would "not be fooled." "We have two problems in the countryside," Alvarado surmised, "the agrarian, and the educational. If we manage to resolve both, we will have resolved the problem of Democracy."[51]

Alvarado also argued that equal education for women was an essential step for Mexico to become a modern nation.[52] In 1915 and 1916, he helped to organize two feminist congresses in Yucatán, the first of their kind in Mexico. At these congresses, "feminism" was represented as a natural

44 Eiss, *In the Name of el Pueblo*, 123–24.
45 AHSDN-W: Operaciones Militares, Yucatán, 1917. XI/481.5/327. Alvarado to Carranza, April 24, 1917.
46 AHSDN-W: Operaciones Militares, Yucatán, 1917. XI/481.5/327. Alvarado to Carranza, July 28, 1917. See also Alvarado, *La reconstrucción de México, Vol. 2*, 182–86.
47 Ibid., 13–15.
48 Ibid., 20. Emilio Rabasa, *La evolución histórica de México* (Paris, France: La Vda. de C. Bouret, 1920), 80, fn1.
49 See, for instance, Alvarado, *La reconstrucción de México, Vol. 2*, 22–43. Alvarado wrote that he was strongly influenced by an indigenous education program in Alaska.
50 AHSDN, Operaciones Militares, Estado de Yucatán, 1917. XI/481.5/327. Alvarado to Carranza, July 28, 1917.
51 Alvarado, *La reconstrucción de México, Vol. 2*, 53–55. 52 Ibid., 302–3.

subsidiary and ally of Socialism.[53] "Love and virtue, when they are true, are not born of conventionality, and are not sustained by oppression and hypocrisy," Alvarado wrote in defense of women's rights within their marriages, and argued that women should be educated and allowed to work outside of the home.[54] Although much of Alvarado's rhetoric regarding women's rights was driven by his acknowledgment of international trends toward women's emancipation and political enfranchisement, particularly in the United States, he stopped short of making the case for women's right to vote.[55]

Alvarado was a nationalist with an ambitious, long-term vision for a peaceful and modern Mexico that could pursue its own interests and defend its own borders. At the heart of his vision for Mexico was a political system grounded in popular elections and led by strong political parties. In an era in which Mexican political parties were typically little more than a loose alliance of elites brought together by their support of a particular candidate for a particular office, Alvarado was an innovator who presciently argued that political parties would be the key to Mexico achieving a peaceful postrevolutionary order.[56] Alvarado called for a new kind of political party: one that was depersonalized in its activities and that would unite "working men, thinking men, and men of action" within its ranks, to truly represent the needs of the nation.[57]

He founded the Socialist Workers' Party of Yucatán in 1916 with these goals in mind.[58] The leaders of the party, chosen with Alvarado's support, were drawn principally from the urban middle and working classes.[59] These were the most obvious constituencies for the brand of reformism

53 Salvador Alvarado, *El primer Congreso Feminista de Yucatán: anales de esa memorable asamblea* (Mérida, Yucatán, México: Ateneo Peninsular, 1916), 5.

54 Alvarado, *La reconstrucción de México*, Vol. 2, 306.

55 Ibid., 113. On Alvarado's policies regarding women's rights and legal status in Yucatán, particularly in regards to divorce, see Stephanie Smith, "'If Love Enslaves . . . Love be Damned!': Divorce and Revolutionary State Formation in Yucatán," in *Sex in Revolution: Gender, Politics, and Power in Modern Mexico*, ed. Jocelyn Olcott, Vaughan, Mary K., Cano, Gabriela (Durham, NC: Duke University Press, 2006), 99–104.

56 This was much commented on within the political class in 1919, as Alvarado began writing open letters to prominent politicians and publishing manifestos in newspapers. See the conversation between Obregón and Benjamin Hill on the subject: Fideicomiso Archivos Plutarco Elías Calles y Fernando Torreblanca, Fondo Álvaro Obregón (hereafter denoted as FAPECFT-FAO), fondo: 9, serie: 030100, expediente: H-1 355, HILL, Benjamin G. (Gral.), legajo: 5/6, fojas 223–30, inventario: 1425. Hill to Obregón, September 24, 1919.

57 FAPECFT-FAO, fondo: 6, serie: 020700, expediente: A-230, ALVARADO, Salvador (Gral.), legajo 1/1, fojas 1–19, inventario 778. Alvarado to Obregón, January 21, 1919. On the tradition of personalismo and arguments against it in Mexican politics in the early twentieth century, see Lomnitz-Adler, *The Return of Comrade Ricardo Flores Magón*, xxvii–xxxiii.

58 Fallaw, "Cárdenas and the Caste War That Wasn't," 554.

59 Joseph, *Revolution from Without*, 110.

that Alvarado brought with him to Yucatán. In forging alliances with workers whose fight for economic justice and political representation predated his arrival, Alvarado echoed the model of reform preferred by the northern revolutionary factions, especially the Sonorans Álvaro Obregón and Plutarco Elías Calles, who themselves came from relatively modest blue collar backgrounds.[60] Like Alvarado, they could much more easily relate to urban workers than they could to Maya campesinos.

Making the Southeast intelligible to northern revolutionary leaders was an important step toward integrating the region into a national reform movement, which was always part of Alvarado's project. It was no accident that his collaborators in founding this first Socialist party were organizers from the Casa del Obrero Mundial (COM, "House of the World Worker"), who arrived in Yucatán to organize workers as they had already done in Mexico City and elsewhere.[61] Although Alvarado renamed the party the Socialist Party of Yucatán in 1917 after parting ways with the COM and closing their local office, southeastern Socialism was integrated with national political trends toward the enfranchisement of workers from the outset.[62] By design, southeastern Socialism was a regional political project that never lost sight of the national political picture.

Winning the support and the trust of the working people of Yucatán through reform programs and popular political organizing was essential to the success of Alvarado's Socialist project, but it was not immediate nor organic. Local communities in Yucatán had good reason to be skeptical after they had been opportunistically mobilized by elite factions at the end of the Porfiriato, and then denied meaningful reform by the Maderistas after Díaz's overthrow.[63] Eventually, Alvarado's effort was successful, at least in some quarters. "We were pleasantly surprised to find that the men of the Revolution were not the vulgar assassins that [the reactionaries] had led us to believe they were," local Socialist leaders recounted in a letter to Carranza in 1917. "The man that we believed came here to exterminate us and to commit outrages against our homes has turned out to be the strongest bond of love between our beloved homeland and the great

60 On urban labor unrest in Yucatán before the Revolution, see Allen Wells and Gilbert M. Joseph, "Clientelism and the Political Baptism of Yucatán's Urban Working Classes, 1876–1929," in *Citizens of the Pyramid: Essays on Mexican Political Culture*, ed. W. G. Pansters (Amsterdam: Thela Publishers, 1997).

61 Joseph, *Revolution from Without*, 109–10. On the Casa's activities across Mexico and relationship to the Constitutionalists, see John Lear, *Workers, Neighbors, and Citizens: The Revolution in Mexico City* (Lincoln, NE: University of Nebraska Press, 2001), 288–91.

62 On the downfall of the COM and the rise of the Mexican Regional Labor Confederation (CROM) between the mid-1910s and early 1920s, see Kevin J. Middlebrook, *The Paradox of Revolution: Labor, the State, and Authoritarianism in Mexico* (Baltimore, MD: Johns Hopkins University Press, 1995), 72–83.

63 Wells and Joseph, *Summer of Discontent*, 224–29.

Mexican nation."[64] In other, less auspicious cases, henequen workers clashed with state officials when they found that Alvarado's vision for reforming their workplaces was more limited than their own and they were sometimes harshly reminded that their "liberation" was not to be at the expense of the henequen economy.[65]

A large part of the community outreach on behalf of Alvarado's Socialist Party was undertaken by a political organizer named Felipe Carrillo Puerto who had worked in a variety of trades before becoming an agronomist. In 1907, Carrillo Puerto joined a dissident elite faction supporting the gubernatorial candidacy of Delio Moreno Cantón, in an unsuccessful attempt to unseat the dominant Díaz-supported camarilla in Yucatán.[66] His work as a Morenista agent landed Carrillo Puerto in prison twice, in 1909 and 1911, the second time for killing a would-be assassin. He became progressively more radical in his politics, influenced by the writing of Ricardo Flores Magón, and eventually also of Marx. He joined the Zapatistas in Morelos in 1914, and returned to Yucatán a year later, allegedly once he heard of Alvarado's land reform efforts there.[67] Carrillo Puerto quickly made a reputation for himself in the state as a highly capable grassroots organizer and agrarian advocate.[68] He spoke fluent Yucatec Maya, and acquired extensive experience organizing in rural indigenous communities that Alvarado's political machine had scarcely acknowledged. As Alvarado's collaborator, Carrillo Puerto became the most important coordinator of the Socialist Party's constituent organizations and the creation syndicates at the local level, known as ligas de resistencia ("resistance leagues"), as well as forging ties between Alvarado's government and preexisting, sympathetic organizations in the state.[69] The liga system was Alvarado's creation, but building it was Carrillo Puerto's mission. Under his watch, the party base was expanded dramatically into rural areas to politically mobilize indigenous campesinos.[70]

---

64 AHSDN-W: Operaciones Militares, Yucatán, 1917. XI/481.5/327. Carlos Castro et al. to Carranza, January 29, 1917.

65 Eiss, *In the Name of el Pueblo*, 136–37.

66 On the Morenistas, and Carrillo Puerto as their agent, see Wells and Joseph, *Summer of Discontent*, 187–92, 226.

67 Francisco Jose Paoli Bolio and Enrique Montalvo Ortega, *El socialismo olvidado de Yucatán: elementes para una reinterpretación de la revolución mexicana* (México, D.F.: Siglo Veintiuno Editores, 1977), 75–85.

68 Joseph, *Revolution from Without*, 191–92. See also Gilbert M. Joseph, "Caciquismo and the Revolution: Carrillo Puerto in Yucatán," in *Caudillo and Peasant in the Mexican Revolution*, ed. D. A. Brading (New York, NY: Cambridge University Press, 1980), 207–9.

69 Some of these were already organized into their own syndicates prior to Alvarado's arrival. Joseph, *Revolution from Without*, 86, 113–14.

70 For a case study of the activities of ligas de resistencia in the late 1910s, see Eiss' examination of the town and region of Hunucmá: Eiss, *In the Name of el Pueblo*, 136–42.

Alvarado was ambivalent on Carrillo Puerto's organizing achievements. He intended for the ligas to be constituent pieces of a corporatist political system dominated by his political party, and a means of organizing and mobilizing a popular constituent base in common cause with elite politicians. But he did not expect the ligas to be the system in and of themselves. Nor did he intend for liga members to feel empowered to organize strikes or confrontations with the henequen planters that employed them, as some did in 1918.[71] Further, in spite of Carrillo Puerto's impressive successes in organizing within rural communities, Alvarado had doubts about the strength and allegiances of rural ligas and their largely indigenous membership. "I have always supported those below, the Indian, the poor, in the face of the abuses and unjust intentions of the privileged caste with the hope of forming a party of the people that owes its rights and its wellbeing to our beloved Mexico, and to thereby have a nationalist party," he wrote to Carranza in 1917. "But these poor people have lived in a state of the most absolute slavery, and I fear that they won't stand firm should a conflict arrive."[72] As doggedly as Alvarado advocated the political enfranchisement of Yucatecan workers, the Maya, and the poor, this was intended to be a government for the people, but not necessarily of or by the people, and he remained apprehensive about campesinos' dependability as full and engaged citizens.[73]

With the ratification of the 1917 Constitution, Alvarado's days as the military governor of Yucatán were numbered. Under new federal law, states could only elect governors born in those states, or who had resided there for five years or more. Alvarado nevertheless held out hope that an exception might be made. "I wish that you could come and see, just once, how the multitudes of Indians receive me in their communities, where the women and children come to embrace me," he pleaded with Carranza.[74] Alvarado minced no words in attempting to persuade Carranza of what was at stake, pointedly remarking to the President that the planter elite intended to take back the entirety of the peninsula (including the neighboring state of Campeche) from Constitutionalist rule, given the chance to do so.[75]

---

71 Ibid., 138.

72 AHSDN-W: Operaciones Militares, Yucatán, 1917. XI/481.5/327. Alvarado to Carranza, April 24, 1917.

73 Eiss argues that control of indigenous workers was one of the main objectives of Alvarado's reform of labor in the state. Eiss, "A Measure of Liberty: The Politics of Labor in Revolutionary Yucatán, 1915–1918," 55–56.

74 AHSDN-W: Operaciones Militares, Yucatán, 1917. XI/481.5/327. Alvarado to Carranza, April 25, 1917.

75 AHSDN-W: Operaciones Militares, Yucatán, 1917. XI/481.5/327. Alvarado to Carranza, April 24, 1917.

Yucatecan Socialists promised Carranza that Alvarado enjoyed extensive popular support, but their pleas for him to stay were to no avail.[76]

In 1917, members of the planter class organized and financed the Yucatecan Liberal Party to run a gubernatorial campaign in the upcoming state election. Its candidate was Bernardino Mena Brito, a young colonel, and its platform was principally defined in opposition to everything that the Yucatecan Socialists stood for.[77] This was a marked change in strategy by the Yucatecan Liberals, who, consonant with Porfirio Díaz's antipathy toward political parties, had eschewed forming one before the Mexican Revolution, but now found it necessary in order to confront the well-organized Socialists.[78] New party notwithstanding, the Yucatecan Liberals had long feared the potential consequences of real popular mobilization in the state, and now they plainly resented the suggestion that elite politicians might ever have to placate a popular base, never mind collaborate with one on substantive matters of governance. This was not just a conflict about ideology or power, but also a fundamental difference of opinion about the long-term practical implications of the Mexican Revolution in Yucatán. For the Liberals and their planter allies, Alvarado's brand of revolutionary politics was an unwelcome imposition. Yucatecan elites clung fiercely to their accustomed privilege, isolation, and autonomy and argued that they had no reason to change, while Alvarado marveled at their stubborn insensibility and warned that any reversal of reform would provoke a second Caste War.[79] Alvarado's enemies countered that it was Alvarado that would provoke another Caste War by weakening Yucatán's political institutions and stirring up racial hatred among the Maya.[80]

In spite of the pointed attacks that the Liberals led against Alvarado's administration and against Constitutionalism more generally, Alvarado gave explicit orders that Socialist workers were not to interfere with Mena Brito's campaign and propaganda efforts.[81] Nevertheless, the campaign was marked by violent clashes between Socialists and Liberals in which as many as twenty people lost their lives.[82] On Alvarado's orders, all gubernatorial candidates were assigned armed escorts of federal soldiers for their protection. This was typical of a pattern of recurring violence surrounding local elections in the early postrevolutionary era, as new

76 AHSDN-W: Operaciones Militares, Yucatán, 1917. XI/481.5/327. Carlos Castro et al. to Carranza, January 29, 1917.
77 Joseph, *Revolution from Without*, 116.   78 Wells and Joseph, *Summer of Discontent*, 34.
79 AHSDN-W: Operaciones Militares, Yucatán, 1917. XI/481.5/327. Alvarado to Carranza, April 25, 1917.
80 AHSDN-W: Operaciones Militares, Yucatán, 1917. XI/481.5/327. Pedro Manzanilla to Carranza, May 22, 1917.
81 AHSDN-W: Operaciones Militares, Yucatán, 1917. XI/481.5/327. Alvarado to Carranza, January 29, 1917.
82 Joseph, *Revolution from Without*, 117.

political traditions clashed with old habits, particularly as political parties were introduced as mechanisms of popular mobilization and organizing. "Everything is political in Yucatán these days, from a brawl between two drunks to the arrest of a thief," Alvarado reported back to Mexico City in October.[83]

Liberals grew desperate and preemptively spoke of having the results of the state election nullified on the basis of anticipated fraud by the Socialists. Felipe Carrillo Puerto vividly described their complaints as "the contortions of a crushed viper" and responded by organizing a rally of thousands of Socialists and their allies as a demonstration of their shared unwillingness to tolerate any loss of hard-won political rights. "The people who love and bless and sustain revolutionary principles and the government that embodies them have made themselves into an electoral army," he declared to Carranza. He estimated that 50,000 Yucatecans were willing to lose their lives in defense of Socialism and their newly guaranteed rights and freedoms.[84] "Suspending the election is the reactionaries' last hope," Alvarado reported to Carranza as Carrillo Puerto rallied the Socialist base in a convincing show of popular support for reform and the gubernatorial candidacy of Socialist leader Carlos Castro Morales.[85]

The Socialists may have been gaining ground in Yucatán, but they were losing it in Mexico City as Carranza's patience for Alvarado's political experiment wore thin. Carranza's support of Alvarado was never a blank political check, and he now sought to curb the extent of his proconsul's reforms, starting with his nullification of Alvarado's celebrated labor law in 1916.[86] Now that Yucatán was pacified and set solidly on a path toward reform, Carranza no longer believed that it was in his best interest to allow one of his most ambitious and talented subordinates to continue to amass power and popular support. Alvarado was one of a handful of credible competitors for the presidency and therefore a potential problem for Carranza's plans to impose his own presidential successor. The threat Alvarado posed was significant enough that well in advance of the 1920 presidential election, Carranza chose to sever his powerful lieutenant from the political party he founded in Yucatán and the independent constituent base he had established. Alvarado was effectively punished for his success in Yucatán. For the first but not the last time, the effectiveness of the southeastern Socialist model of party formation was regarded in Mexico

83 AHSDN-W: Operaciones Militares, Yucatán, 1917. XI/481.5/327. Alvarado to Carranza, October 30, 1917.

84 AHSDN-W: Operaciones Militares, Yucatán, 1917. XI/481.5/327. Carrillo Puerto et al. to Carranza, October 24, 1917.

85 AHSDN-W: Operaciones Militares, Yucatán, 1917. XI/481.5/327. Alvarado to Carranza, October 24, 1917.

86 Eiss, "A Measure of Liberty: The Politics of Labor in Revolutionary Yucatán, 1915–1918," 61.

City as a potential spoiler in a national election. Carranza removed Alvarado from the state for several months, first reassigning him as the military commander of the whole Southeast in the summer of 1917, briefly allowing him to return to Yucatán, and then permanently removing him from the region in 1918.[87]

Felipe Carrillo Puerto now became the leader of Yucatecan Socialism. He spent the rest of 1917 expanding the Socialist party's organizing efforts further into rural areas and indigenous communities, and preparing for the first test of the Socialist Party at the ballot box with the upcoming gubernatorial election. He did so with limited support from Alvarado, who gave Carrillo Puerto the reigns of the Socialist Party but threw his support behind the gubernatorial candidacy of Socialist leader Carlos Castro Morales.[88] Carrillo Puerto nevertheless spent the next several years building a political machine and establishing a popular base of support that made him indisputably the most important political figure in the entire Southeast within the space of just a few years.

The Socialist Party carried the 1917 election, and Castro Morales became Yucatán's first postrevolutionary governor, but the planter elite and their Liberal allies were not going anywhere. As Carrillo Puerto moved to radicalize the Socialist party and broaden its popular base, the multi-class alliance Alvarado had carefully constructed quickly began to unravel. The Liberals were both resentful and startled by their electoral defeat, and insisted that the Socialists had won only by force of arms and subterfuge. One Liberal leader described the Socialists as inferior to Liberals in "both number and quality." Racist and classist overtones permeated Liberal rhetoric, as they described themselves as the "true people of Yucatán," drawing sharp contrasts between themselves as peaceful pillars of respectability and the illiterate, rabble rousing Socialist workers and campesinos.[89]

Yet even as they steadfastly resisted progressive reform, Yucatecan Liberals adapted their strategies to the decidedly more populist political climate. They conspicuously adopted the language of revolutionary political change, if not embracing its spirit or content, in their insistence that most of their own party's members were humble working people. In practice, their peremptory efforts to recruit popular support were frequently met with resistance. New postrevolutionary ideas about how politics were done in Mexico were embraced by Socialist state officials, workers, and campesinos, and these clashed with the Yucatecan Liberals'

87   Joseph, *Revolution from Without*, 114.

88   Joseph argues that this was a ploy by Alvarado to stymie Carrillo Puerto's consolidation of power. Ibid., 116–17.

89   AHSDN-W: Operaciones Militares, Yucatán, 1918. XI/481.5/328. Lorenzo Gómez et al. to Bernardino Mena Brito. Undated; Undated memo by Dr. Barriga, "El Estado de Yucatán es un Caos."

throwback strategies for getting their political way.[90] What communities had always resented, they now refused to accept, and they often used revolutionary rhetoric and law to justify their intransigence in the face of Liberal attempts to politically impose themselves on them. Campesinos of Hocabá wrote to the state government to complain that they were being persecuted for refusing to join the Liberal Party, when they only wanted to work in peace and to stay out of politics entirely.[91] Some Socialists in Cenotillo chose to take their families and flee their community under pressure from local Liberals after one of their fellow partisans was beaten and locked in a dungeon.[92] For workers and campesinos that did wish to participate in politics, for the first time they had other, better political options than shallow, opportunistic, and sometimes semi-consensual alliances with local elites. In another case of abuses against campesinos who refused to support the Liberal Party, state officials sternly reminded the municipal president that "citizens are absolutely free to adopt the political credo that is most in accordance with their way of thinking."[93]

Dealt what increasingly looked like a losing political hand, Liberals resorted to violence and fear mongering. Governor Castro Morales bluntly described Liberal attacks against campesinos as a "politics of terror."[94] He complained to Carranza that Liberals not only provoked violence but also sought to annul all acts by his state government.[95] Liberals countered by accusing Carrillo Puerto of personally inciting crimes against both their persons and their property. Stories of arrests, physical assaults, and arson by Socialists abounded. In one particularly inflammatory case, Liberals sent Carranza a list of their supporters that Felipe Carrillo Puerto allegedly intended to have assassinated.[96] Liga members were also accused of following orders from the Socialist Party to attack and even to kill non-members within their communities.[97] Liberal leaders were well aware that what

90　AHSDN-W: Operaciones Militares, Yucatán, 1918. XI/481.5/328. José G. Corrales to Bernardino Mena Brito, April 19, 1918.
91　Archivo General del Estado de Yucatán (hereafter AGEY), Fondo: Ejecutivo, Serie: Gobernación, Caja 712, 1920. Juan Vela et al. to Secretaría de Gobernación, April 9, 1920.
92　AGEY, Fondo: Ejecutivo, Serie: Gobernación, Caja 712, 1920. Secretaría de Gobernación to Feliciano Lara, March 15, 1920.
93　AGEY, Fondo: Ejecutivo, Serie: Gobernación, Caja 712, 1920. Secretaría de Gobernación to Municipal President, March 15, 1920.
94　AHSDN-W: Operaciones Militares, Yucatán, 1920. XI/481.5/330. Castro Morales to Carranza, March 22, 1920.
95　See, for example, AHSDN-W: Operaciones Militares, Yucatán, 1918. XI/481.5/328. Castro Morales to Carranza, June 26, 1918.
96　AHSDN-W: Operaciones Militares, Yucatán, 1918. XI/481.5/328. Lorenzo Gómez et al. to Bernardino Mena Brito. Undated.
97　AHSDN-W: Operaciones Militares, Yucatán, 1918. XI/481.5/328. José María Marín N. to Bernardino Mena Brito, April 16, 1918.

Carranza most wanted in Yucatán was law, order, and steady henequen revenues. They tailored their missives to him accordingly, fuming that the Socialist state government was dedicated to disrupting public order rather than guaranteeing it, and urging Carranza to intervene to protect their constituents from Socialist threats and attacks.[98]

Carrillo Puerto tried to reassure the president that the Socialists remained his truest allies in Yucatán, promising him that the great majority of the population was Socialist and, as such, unconditionally allied with Carranza's government.[99] But Carrillo Puerto and Carranza were gravely ill-matched as allies. Yucatecan elites had worked tirelessly to have Alvarado removed as the state's proconsul and schemed to undermine his position there, believing that ridding themselves of the man would likewise rid them of revolutionary reform.[100] Now that they were faced with a more radical, civilian successor to Alvarado who lacked his national political connections, they smelled blood.

Carranza was unmoved by Carrillo Puerto's attempts to convince him that the Socialists' ongoing organization of workers and campesinos into ligas was in his best interest. Carranza never had much interest in radical experiments, nor was he invested in a fight for social justice. He had tolerated Alvarado's populist reformism because it had kept the peace and henequen profits flowing. With the state's economy in crisis by 1919 as henequen's market value dropped precipitously, Yucatán's political value to Carranza also plummeted. Further, from Carranza's point of view, aside from the unrest provoked at the local level by clashes between Socialists and Liberals, the political chaos in Yucatán was a win-win situation, as the two competing political factions sought to curry favor with him and demonstrate their loyalty to his federal government.

As Carranza turned his back on the Yucatecan Socialists when they faced an onslaught of attacks and schemes against them by the planter class, Carrillo Puerto and the Socialists rededicated themselves to the formation of new ligas de resistencia across the state, all allied with a *Liga Central* that the party established in Mérida. As Carrillo Puerto remade the institutional structures he inherited from Alvarado, the liga system came into its own, setting a precedent that would reverberate throughout the region, and then beyond. Carrillo Puerto's independence from Carranza gave him the freedom to push Yucatecan Socialism in a much more radical direction.

98 AHSDN-W: Operaciones Militares, Yucatán, 1918. XI/481.5/328. Bernardino Mena Brito to Secretaría de Gobernación. Undated (April 1918). AHSDN-W: Operaciones Militares, Yucatán, 1917. XI/481.5/327. Victor J. Manzanilla to Carranza, September 29, 1917.

99 AHSDN-W: Operaciones Militares, Yucatán, 1917. XI/481.5/327. Carrillo Puerto to Carranza, September 24, 1917.

100 AHSDN-W: Operaciones Militares, Yucatán, 1917. XI/481.5/327. Alvarado to Carranza, April 24, 1917.

The primary function of the ligas de resistencia was to serve as the point of contact between local communities and the Socialist Party, and by extension, the Socialist state government. In practice they served as syndicates, mutual aid societies, and community-level branch offices of the party. Sometimes they were organized by particular interest groups across communities, such as feminist ligas de resistencia, but most often they were organized to represent the workers of a particular locale. Each liga was led by a president, secretary, treasurer, an agent dedicated to petitions by members, and an agent dedicated to labor matters, each of which were directly elected by members each year. Members paid monthly dues of one peso and fifty cents and met at weekly assemblies. Some ligas chose to form consumer cooperatives. Others formed cooperatives that shared resources such as electricity, grain mills, and even cinemas. Others formed agrarian cooperatives that were dedicated to henequen production and members collectively worked shared ejido fields. At least in theory, all ligas were required to have a night school for workers where they could learn to read and write, and for many, to learn Spanish.[101] The liga system was also used as a mechanism for promoting and sometimes implementing state-sponsored social programs at the local level, such as an anti-alcohol campaign in the early 1920s.[102] By Carrillo Puerto's (likely inflated) estimates, in some communities as much as 95 percent of the working population had joined a liga by 1918, by which time the right of workers to form ligas was guaranteed by the state labor code.[103] Four years later, Juan Rico of the Mexican Regional Workers' Confederation (CROM) reported that every public servant in Yucatán was a liga member.[104]

Crucially, all of the fifty-eight distinct, local ligas belonged to the Socialist Party, and their members comprised the party's constituent base.[105] Through the ligas, Yucatecan workers and campesinos had an unprecedented degree of contact with their leaders and with the political process. They were also offered extensive protections under state law, which explicitly prohibited the dismissal of employees for joining organizations or unions, or for participating in strikes. Workers who lost their jobs for any of these reasons could claim an indemnity of three months' wages. The

101 AHSDN-W: Operaciones Militares, Yucatán, 1918. XI/481.5/328. Carrillo Puerto to Carranza, December 22, 1918.
102 FAPECFT-PEC, expediente: 25, CARRILLO PUERTO, Felipe, legajo 3/7, fojas 151–5, inventario 830. Carrillo Puerto to Calles, April 3, 1922.
103 AHSDN-W: Operaciones Militares, Yucatán, 1918. XI/481.5/328. Carrillo Puerto to Carranza, December 22, 1918. Labor Code of Yucatán, 1918. Reproduced in: *Leyes y decretos del gobierno socialista de Yucatán* (Mérida, Yucatán, México: Talls. Pluma y Lápiz, 1924).
104 Juan Rico, *Yucatán: la huelga de junio*, 2 vols. (Mérida, México 1922), 1:7, 19.
105 Ibid., 1:19, 104–5.

Socialist labor code of 1918 emphasized the rights and responsibilities of both workers and employers, but also included measures to improve quality of life for workers. No one was allowed to be required to work more than seven hours at night. Child labor was prohibited. Women workers were given further protections, including protection from firing during pregnancy and for two months following childbirth, and mandated breaks for breastfeeding with dedicated spaces for nursing at their workplaces. The labor code was also designed to incentivize workers to join ligas: It specified that workers that did not join ligas or other associations would not be granted the same salary benefits as their organized counterparts.[106]

The institutionalization of the alliance between affiliate organizations at the local level within a centralized party structure was perhaps Carrillo Puerto's most important political innovation; certainly it was the most influential, moving forward. The relationship between the ligas and the party was mutually beneficial by design. Carrillo Puerto routinely used his position as the leader of the Socialist Party to directly advocate for communities across Yucatán, intervening on their behalf with the Socialist state government. These petitions most often concerned land and labor rights, from communities waiting for access to particular pieces of land, to campesinos demanding justice following illegal eviction or unjust firing from haciendas.[107] Often these petitions were made in collaboration with the presidents of the ligas in question, who represented their members' interests to party leaders, who then took the petition further up the political hierarchy. The liga system therefore empowered its allies at the local level as representatives of their communities.[108] The ligas also became an institutionalized means of implementing revolutionary reform at the local level. Often liga representatives were explicit in their communications with the party that there were "pre-constitutional" problems that had to be addressed in their communities, underscoring that old abuses and irregularities at the expense of the working poor would no longer be tolerated.[109] In making demands of their employers with the assistance of liga representatives, campesinos scrupulously cited relevant laws and

106 AGEY, Fondo: Ejecutivo, Serie: Gobernación, Caja 620, Legajo II, 1918. Gregorio Vargaz and Gerardo Baeza to the Department of Labor, June 3, 1918; Labor Code of Yucatán, 1918. Reproduced in: *Leyes y decretos del gobierno socialista de Yucatán*.
107 AGEY, Fondo: Ejecutivo, Serie: Gobernación, Caja 685, Legajo II, 1919. Carrillo Puerto to Vicente Ocampo Alonso, August 20, 1919; Carrillo Puerto to Vicente Ocampo Alonso, April 24, 1919.
108 AGEY, Fondo: Ejecutivo, Serie: Gobernación, Caja 685, Legajo II, 1919. Manuel Berzunza to Vicente Ocampo Alonso, September 3, 1919.
109 See, for example, AGEY, Fondo: Ejecutivo, Serie: Gobernación, Caja 685, Legajo II, 1919. H. Valencia López to Vicente Ocampo, April 30, 1919.

established a paper trail through their local ligas and, by extension, through the Socialist Party.[110]

The ligas also served as a mechanism for the diffusion of crucial information about new laws and the new political systems under both the 1917 federal Constitution and the Socialist state government. There was an evident popular awareness at the local level of the sea changes taking place in Yucatán, and in Mexico more broadly, particularly in terms of land administration. Eiss found that ligas' petitions for land reform often failed in this period, either because hacendados mounted successful legal defenses of their lands, or because the Socialist state government failed to intervene on behalf of claimants.[111] Even so, their communications with the party make clear that Yucatecan campesinos who joined ligas de resistencia in this period came to have an entirely new conception of their own relationships to the state government, and that they sought to take advantage of what was being offered to them by an unprecedentedly sympathetic administration. Most of the problems that the ligas helped their members to solve were not new, but the solutions they were able to offer were.

Perhaps most urgently, the Socialist Party and the Socialist state government frequently intervened in henequen labor disputes using the state's new labor laws. Department of Labor inspectors were tasked with sorting out the postrevolutionary legality of arrangements made between landowners and campesinos, such as contracts that defined how the campesinos' time would be divided between their work in the henequen fields and working their own fields on hacienda lands, and when and how often they were to be paid. The inspectors met with both workers and overseers and then made their judgments and recommendations.[112] In some cases this was a matter of simply advising petitioners and respondents of relevant laws. In other cases, the inspectors proposed solutions, such as the regularization of payroll cycles and the establishment of cooperatives on haciendas to manage the purchase of goods and foodstuffs and to keep prices down for resident workers.[113] In one such case in July of 1918, an investigation was opened after workers on the Cholul hacienda wrote to the Department of

---

110 See, for example, AGEY: Fondo Ejecutivo, Serie: Gobernación, Caja 620, Legajo II, 1918. Carlos Pacheco A. to Plácido Lope, June 13, 1918.

111 Eiss, *In the Name of el Pueblo*, 140–41.

112 AGEY, Fondo: Ejecutivo, Serie: Gobernación, Caja 620, Legajo II, 1918. Inspector report to Department of Labor, June 19, 1918.

113 AGEY, Fondo: Ejecutivo, Serie: Gobernación, Caja 620, Legajo II, 1918. Inspector report to Department of Labor, June 12, 1918. This was particularly important in Yucatán where many basic food items were imported, since the state's arable land was so overwhelmingly dedicated to henequen cultivation. On food hoarding and price gouging, see Joseph, *Revolution from Without*, 144–5.

Labor complaining of the poor treatment they received from the foreman and the slave-like conditions in which they were forced to work.[114] An inspector was dispatched to the hacienda in a matter of days, and the Department of Labor ordered that the owner remove the foreman from his post in order to ensure "both the tranquility of the workers and the well-being of the finca."[115] A replacement foreman was then chosen by the state.[116] Landowner Adolfo Bolio allowed this intervention by the state government, and subsequently reported that he saw no reason for campesinos not to use the lands they requested on his hacienda, provided that they pay him the tax mandated by law, and that he be allowed to demarcate the borders of said lands.[117]

New state laws were issued to regularize arrangements between hacendados and campesinos who resided on their property, to obviate such interventions. In January of 1919, the Socialist government passed a law that resident campesinos owed no more than 5 percent of their harvest to the landowners whose fields they used to farm their own subsistence crops.[118] This was not so much an effort to change existing land tenure patterns, but to renegotiate and regulate the terms of existing arrangements, and prevent abuses. The new law was frequently cited in complaints by landowners and campesinos alike in the years that followed, as a means of combatting nonpayment and overcharging, respectively.[119]

Campesinos in Yucatán increasingly turned to the state government in these years as a means of bypassing corrupt and abusive local officials whom they had no hope would uphold their postrevolutionary rights. "We are poor people," campesinos of Tekantó wrote to Governor Castro Morales. "We don't have anyone to defend our rights that are being attacked, and in this town there is no authority to administer justice for us, because they

---

114   AGEY, Fondo: Ejecutivo, Serie: Gobernación, Caja 620, Legajo II, 1918. Workers of the Cholul Finca to the Department of Labor, July 1, 1918. Joseph has underscored that workers on henequen plantations rarely had personal contact with landowners by the 1910s and instead dealt with administrators. Ibid., 75. On the creation and operation of the Department of Labor, see Eiss, "A Measure of Liberty: The Politics of Labor in Revolutionary Yucatán, 1915–1918," 61.

115   AGEY, Fondo: Ejecutivo, Serie: Gobernación, Caja 620, Legajo II, 1918. Head of the Department of Labor to Owner of the Cholul Hacienda, July 5, 1918.

116   AGEY, Fondo: Ejecutivo, Serie: Gobernación, Caja 620, Legajo II, 1918. Head of the Department of Labor to Superintendent of the Cholul Hacienda, July 5, 1918. Eiss argues that the firing of overseers as a means of addressing worker complaints was typical of Yucatán in this period. Eiss, "A Measure of Liberty: The Politics of Labor in Revolutionary Yucatán, 1915–1918," 58.

117   AGEY, Fondo: Ejecutivo, Serie: Gobernación, Caja 685, Legajo II, 1919. Consulting Lawyer of the Local Agrarian Commission to Liga Central de Resistencia, October 1, 1919.

118   AGEY, Fondo: Ejecutivo, Serie: Gobernación, Caja 712, 1920. Secretaría de Gobernación to Jefe de las Operaciones en el Estado, March 11, 1920.

119   For one example of such a landowner complaint, see AGEY, Fondo: Ejecutivo, Serie: Gobernación, Caja 712, 1920. L. Matos Pérez to Francisco Vega y Loyo, February 13, 1920.

have conspired to torment us."[120] The ligas were a means of combatting such abuses, but also of dealing with this political reality. The liga system and the Socialist Party could not immediately, systematically replace entrenched local power brokers, and indeed sometimes relied on them as allies.[121] Still, liga membership was understood to proffer protections that local officials either could not or would not. In registering a complaint to the Socialist governor about the abuses he suffered at the hands of local authorities in Chapab, one liga member tellingly concluded, "If all of the outrages that I have reported to you can be committed against a Socialist liga member, imagine what might be committed against people who aren't."[122]

In the late 1910s, Liberal elites and Socialist workers and campesinos in Yucatán all adopted a shared language of postrevolutionary politics as they sought to win disputes at the local level, but also to curry favor in Mexico City by emphasizing their dedication to democracy, freedom, and the Revolution. Liberals frequently stressed their status as hardworking, productive members of society, a notion they clearly felt was under attack by Socialists.[123] It was a strategic adjustment to a new political reality, even as they refused to embrace it. The working people of Yucatán also adjusted to the rapidly changing political culture. Complaints by workers and campesinos to the Socialist government about abuses by corrupt local officials and hacendados were frequently made, employing a language of political rights and citizenship, and almost invariably invoked the new federal constitution.[124] In 1920, campesinos from Tekantó complained that they were suffering the same abuses by local authorities as they had in Porfirian times, in spite of the protections afforded them by the 1917 Constitution. They emphasized that it was local elites and officials that seemed unable to accept that political times had irrevocably changed in Mexico.[125] "Perhaps the mayor is not aware of it, but the Constitution of the Republic gives me

---

120 AGEY, Fondo: Ejecutivo, Serie: Gobernación, Caja 712, 1920. Esteban Kú et al. to Governor Carlos Castro Morales, March 13, 1920.

121 Joseph has emphasized that caciques frequently continued to operate in Yucatán in this period, often in collaboration with Carrillo Puerto and the Socialist party and state government, which recruited them as a stop-gap means of establishing a grassroots base in relatively short order. See Joseph, "Caciquismo and the Revolution: Carrillo Puerto in Yucatán," 220–21.

122 AGEY, Fondo Ejecutivo, Gobernación, c. 645, 1918. Pedro Ortíz to Castro Morales, November 4, 1918.

123 AHSDN-W: Operaciones Militares, Yucatán, 1918. XI/481.5/328. Lorenzo Gómez et al. to Bernardino Mena Brito. Undated. On Liberal use of reformist rhetoric in Yucatán, see also Eiss, *In the Name of el Pueblo*, 133–34.

124 See, for example, AGEY, Fondo: Ejecutivo, Serie: Gobernación, Caja 712, 1920. Antonia Ricalde de Chí to Castro Morales, January 27, 1920.

125 AGEY, Fondo: Ejecutivo, Serie: Gobernación, Caja 712, 1920. Esteban Kú et al. to Castro Morales, March 13, 1920.

the right to be involved in the politics of my country without being harassed," a political organizer wrote to Governor Castro Morales in 1920 in his complaint of politically motivated abuses in the town of Acanceh.[126] In 1920, campesinos of Tunkás requested not just logistical or legal assistance from the state government, but also "moral support" in their struggles with local landowners. These were people that for the first time believed that the state government was on their side, particularly, as they specified, in its capacity to enforce postrevolutionary federal reforms.[127]

It would be impossible to overstate the enormity of the task of putting an entirely new set of laws and political traditions into practice as mandated by the 1917 Constitution, particularly considering that Mexico still had several more years of civil war ahead of it. In Yucatán these challenges were even more acute with the advent of Socialist governance and its relatively radical remaking of local law, and all the more so in the face of ongoing elite resistance to reform and redistribution of land and resources. Making both state and federal reform initiatives work in practice at the local level was sometimes a rocky process. In one case, an Inspector of Public Offices reported in 1918 that the town of Cacalchén's new town council was yet to meet. When questioned, local officials admitted that they weren't yet familiar enough with new municipal laws to carry out their newly required responsibilities. One of the inspectors' tasks was therefore to provide local politicians with the training they needed to implement the state's new legal regime. Such visits by state officials also provided communities with a valuable opportunity to report back to the government about things they needed and reforms that were difficult to implement for various reasons, whether it was the lack of appropriate land or facilities, matters of public health, or insufficient resources for the upkeep of public buildings.[128] Sometimes the Socialist Party also intervened in the management of liga affairs at the local level, dispatching mediators to assist in resolving disputes that inevitably arose.[129]

The liga system was also an integral part of the Yucatecan Socialist Party's national political agenda. Felipe Carrillo Puerto commonly sent petitions and made demands of the federal government in the name of the

126   AGEY, Fondo: Ejecutivo, Serie: Gobernación, Caja 712, 1920. Filomeno Monteforte to
        Secretaría de Gobernación, April 15, 1920. The mayor in question defended himself, and clarified
        that he was very much aware of the rights guaranteed by the constitution. L. Escobedo to Castro
        Morales, April 24, 1920.

127   AGEY, Fondo: Ejecutivo, Serie: Gobernación, Caja 712, 1920. Ildefonso Medina et al. to
        Secretaría de Gobernación, March 11, 1920.

128   See, for instance, AGEY, Fondo Ejecutivo, Gobernación, c. 645, 1918. Antonio Rosel H. to Jefe
        de Visitadores de Oficinas Públicas, February 25, 1918.

129   See, for instance, AGEY, Fondo Ejecutivo, Gobernación, c. 645, 1918. Unsigned letter to Castro
        Morales, December 2, 1920.

thousands of liga members that he represented, emphasizing that this popular base was both powerful and politically legitimizing. At the heart of these missives was a radical new interpretation of the relationship between citizens and the federal government, as mediated by the Socialist Party. In April of 1918 Carrillo Puerto implored President Carranza to intervene on behalf of his base when it came to the redistribution of lands, and bemoaned federal injunctions that protected many of the henequen haciendas from expropriation. He emphasized to the president that these thousands of land-hungry campesinos were bound to Carranza as his own constituents as members of the Socialist Party with which he was theoretically still allied.[130]

This rationalization was not just for Carranza's benefit. Carrillo Puerto's systematic fusing of local, state, and national political interests was an integral element of his vision of what the Socialist Party was and what it could accomplish in the long-term. From the beginning, he understood his role as the leader of the party to be that of a liaison between the local communities of Yucatán and the highest echelons of power in Mexico City. Perhaps even more importantly, he intended for any resulting influence, political pressure, and power to be channeled through the institutional structures of the Socialist Party; his own empowerment was inarguable, but a corollary benefit. This was a visionary, unprecedented way of organizing political power in Mexico. It was initially designed to solve specific Yucatecan political dilemmas, but the influence of the idea could never be contained within state lines.

Practice was inevitably more difficult, as the closeness of the relationship between the ligas and the state government often became a source of local conflict. Liberals from Hunucmá and Tetiz complained that the Socialist government was extorting them in order to fund ligas de resistencia. They also protested that local Socialist officials were forcing the wealthy to pay a minimum of 20 pesos a week for an ineffectual new program of infrastructural improvement, funds that they claimed were largely pocketed by the directors of the program.[131] Liberals in Ekmul complained that their partisans were being forced to unionize and could not work without Socialist credentials that had to be purchased from the party.[132] Some campesinos alleged that they had been dismissed from jobs on haciendas

---

130 AHSDN-W: Operaciones Militares, Yucatán, 1918. XI/481.5/328. Carrillo Puerto et al. to Carranza, April 1, 1918.

131 AHSDN-W: Operaciones Militares, Yucatán, 1918. XI/481.5/328. José María Martín to Bernardino Mena Brito, April 30, 1918. On tensions between Liberals and Socialists in Hunucmá and Tetiz, see Eiss, *In the Name of el Pueblo*, 136–42. See also Wells and Joseph, *Summer of Discontent*, 229–33.

132 AHSDN-W: Operaciones Militares, Yucatán, 1918. XI/481.5/328. Undated and unsigned memo, "Atropello cometido por las autoridades del pueblo de Ekmul."

because they had formed ligas and joined the Socialist Party, something that was prohibited by the state employment code.[133] Conversely, campesinos in Kini complained in 1918 that although they had the legal right to ejidos, the local agrarian commissioner denied their petition for land because they didn't belong to a liga de resistencia.[134]

With the liga system, Carrillo Puerto sought to strike a calculated balance between local autonomy and centralized authority in order to meet the needs both of the party and the communities it hoped to serve. This was a substantial refinement and amplification of Alvarado's blueprint. Carrillo Puerto and his fellow party leaders relied on liga members as their committed constituent base, but the liga system was also designed to be responsive to the needs of the grassroots and to provide an institutional context for communities and individuals to participate in the political system. Electoral democracy and popular agency were integral elements of Carrillo Puerto's political rhetoric. He told his supporters: "It is dependent on you that men branded as thieves, assassins, and traitors never return to be rulers."[135] He was also insistent that the rule of the day in Yucatán was political freedom, whether citizens supported the Socialist government or not.[136]

The obvious drawback to a system that counted on the local administration of the branches of a central organization meant that the Socialist Party as an organization, and Carrillo Puerto himself, forfeited a significant amount of local control. Further, the diverse and sometimes redundant ways in which the groups that constituted the party were labeled, including both ligas and unions of various stripes, exaggerated the organizational and numerical strength of the party, to an unknown degree.[137] This was not just a Socialist problem: in 1922, Juan Rico of the CROM argued that many of Yucatán's trade unions outside of the Socialist system existed solely on paper.[138]

Carrillo Puerto's remaking of Alvarado's Socialist Party was formalized and its policies and programs were extensively codified at two party congresses in 1918 and 1921. Under Carrillo Puerto, the party was redesigned

133 See, for example, AGEY, Fondo: Ejecutivo, Serie: Gobernación, Caja 620, Legajo II, 1918. Gregorio Vargaz and Gerardo Baeza to the Department of Labor, June 3, 1918.
134 AGEY, Fondo Ejecutivo, Gobernación, c. 645, 1918. Cirilo Matos et al. to Castro Morales, November 12, 1918.
135 Rico, *La huelga de junio* (vol. 1), 57.
136 FAPECFT-PEC, expediente: 25, CARRILLO PUERTO, Felipe, legajo 3/7, fojas 136–37, inventario 830. Carrillo Puerto to Calles, February 20, 1922.
137 On the inflation of Socialist membership numbers and its long-term consequences, see Gilbert M. Joseph "The Fragile Revolution: Cacique Politics and Revolutionary Process in Yucatan." *Latin American Research Review* 15, no. 1 (1980): 55–56.
138 Rico, *La huelga de junio* (vol. 1), 19–20.

to be more responsive to the demands of its members, was substantially expanded to more actively address the needs of the agrarian poor, and was more tailored to Yucatecan political realities. Part of this transformation included a much closer integration of the rank and file of the party with the leadership than had ever existed under Alvarado, including at the congresses themselves, which were active dialogues between the leaders of the party and representatives of communities across the state. The statutes the delegates produced demonstrate an ambitious political vision and a long-term plan for reforming Yucatán that strongly emphasized political practice over dogma.

The first congress, held in Carrillo Puerto's hometown of Motul in 1918, was the first time that representatives of the ligas and the leaders of the Socialist Party met collectively to forge a plan for the organization moving forward. After nearly a year of planning, 144 delegates gathered to discuss their goals. The attendees were divided into thematic committees that produced recommendations to be shared with the whole of the congress. These accords were ambitious and far-reaching. Delegates drafted plans for handling liga finances, defining the roles and rights of female liga members, the codification of dues, and the establishment of liga cooperatives and schools, among other topics.[139] Committees of delegates also committed to paper extensive codification of the expected behaviors of liga members, down to the forms of identification they were expected to present to one another. The final accords made explicit the favoritism that was to be shown to liga members over non-members when it came to employment, mandated a minimum of one year of membership before an individual could be nominated for leadership positions within a liga or for political office, required that members vote only for Socialist political candidates, and formally established the organizational structure of the Liga Central. Liga members were directed to categorically reject accusations against the ligas by their political enemies, to celebrate Labor Day as well as the birthday of Karl Marx each year, and to voice any dissent or complaint within liga assemblies. This was a visible effort by the Socialists to forge partisan discipline, and to formalize the basic framework via which individual members were to interact with the party to which they belonged, and by extension, with the Socialist-led state government.[140]

Another goal articulated by the delegates was to build stronger ties to sympathetic national political organizations and international political movements. One of the central figures at the 1918 congress was Robert Haberman, a Romanian-born lawyer and Socialist labor organizer Alvarado

139   Ibid. (vol. 1), 79–97.   140   Ibid. (vol. 1), 97–100.

first invited to Yucatán in 1917.[141] Haberman became one of Carrillo
Puerto's advisors, helping him to organize workers and to remake the
Socialist Party.[142] Haberman attempted to imbue Yucatecan Socialism
with more ideology and political philosophy, introducing party leaders to
the writings of Marx, Lenin, and Engels.[143] At the first congress, he also
contributed to drafting an accord on how foreign Socialists visiting
Yucatán were to be received by the party.[144]

Although Carrillo Puerto and Haberman continued to work together
throughout the early 1920s, the radicalization of the Socialist Party would
always be on Yucatecan terms.[145] One of the principal questions posed to
the delegates at the second Socialist congress at Izamal in 1921 was whether
or not their party should be formally affiliated with Comintern.[146] Despite
his own membership in the Third International, by 1921 Carrillo Puerto
was adamantly opposed to the "communizing" of Yucatán.[147] The final
disposition by the delegates was a qualified negative, with the stipulation
that they were "emphatically in agreement with all movements on a path
to social transformation of the universe." The delegates' refusal to join
Comintern demonstrated a decided reluctance to relinquish their political
autonomy.[148] Under Carrillo Puerto's guidance, Socialism in southern
Mexico was to remain a unique and independent brand of revolutionary
politics.

141   Fideicomiso Archivos Plutarco Elías Calles y Fernando Torreblanca, Colección Documental de la
      Embajada de Estados Unidos en México (hereafter denoted as FAPECFT-CDEEUM), expediente:
      070101: AGREGADO MILITAR DE ESTADOS UNIDOS: Informes, legajo: 2/11, fojas 47–51,
      inventario: 23. Summary of Mexican Intelligence, No. 221, March 8, 1922. On Haberman, see
      Gregg Andrews, "Robert Haberman, Socialist Ideology, and the Politics of National
      Reconstruction in Mexico, 1920–25," *Mexican Studies / Estudios Mexicanos* 6, no. 2 (1990);
      Gregg Andrews, *Shoulder to Shoulder?: The American Federation of Labor, the United States, and the
      Mexican Revolution, 1910–1924* (Berkeley, CA: University of California Press, 1991), chapter 6.
142   Alma M. Reed and Michael Karl Schuessler, *Peregrina: Love and Death in Mexico* (Austin, TX:
      University of Texas Press, 2007), 243.
143   Haberman was an anti-communist Socialist. See Andrews, *Shoulder to Shoulder?* Joseph argues
      that the leaders of the PSS, including Carrillo Puerto, were never truly able to absorb or fully
      assimilate Marxist or Leninist political theory, even though they read it avidly. Joseph, *Revolution
      from Without*, 201.
144   Rico, *La huelga de junio* (vol. 1), 100.
145   Archivo General de la Nación de México, Fondo Obregón-Calles (hereafter AGN-OC), 428-c-6.
      Dr. José G. Parres to Secretario de Gobernación, May 12, 1921.
146   Originally scheduled for 1919, this second meeting was delayed by two years because of the
      difficulties caused by the Carrancista persecution of the Socialists during the 1920 presidential
      race. This included Carrillo Puerto's temporary exile from the state. Rico, *La huelga de junio*, 105.
      Reed and Schuessler, *Peregrina*, 252–53, 56.
147   Reed and Schuessler, *Peregrina*, 257.
148   Rico, *La huelga de junio* (vol. 1), 128. On Carrillo Puerto and Comintern, see Spenser, *Stumbling Its
      Way Through Mexico*, 53–54, 109–10. Spenser suggests that Rico attended the congress of Izamal
      to prevent the PSS from joining Comintern, on behalf of the CROM.

A 1920 party program outlining the objectives and responsibilities of Socialists at the local level (*ayuntamiento*) provides further insight into how the party was meant to work in practice. Socialist agents on the ground were required to be vetted for their sincerity and their civil valor. They were expected to carry out their own propaganda efforts, and to provide monthly written reports of what they had achieved. What they were asked to pursue on behalf of the party was far-reaching. These included efforts to reduce taxes on working people; to carry out a municipal takeover of basic services such as public transportation, telephones, electricity, water and garbage collection; to pursue more effective public education; to ensure that municipal workers had access to communal lands to work; to provide instruction in public defense in order to create an "army of workers" to substitute the federal army; to found a "House of the Indian" in each town that would "introduce Indians to modern life;" to found experimental farms; to create a special municipal police force dedicated to education, hygiene, and "public moralization;" and to prohibit alcohol at the municipal level.[149] These guidelines bear the marks of both Alvarado, in the paternalism and rationalization of politics they prescribed, and Carrillo Puerto, in the idealism, relative radicalism, and dedication to reform experiments they expressed.

Beginning in 1918, President Carranza moved to limit the activities of the Socialist party and to curtail Carrillo Puerto's power, and put two successive new military commanders in charge of a federal campaign against the Yucatecan Socialists.[150] "The ligas don't threaten anyone," Carrillo Puerto protested to Carranza. "They are well organized and disciplined and constitute a great strength for the government." By the end of 1918, he estimated the total liga membership in the state to be 62,000. "These are humble working people," he wrote of the liga members. "They are loyal to the revolutionary cause and have never considered the separatism that is constantly instigated by the majority of Yucatecan hacendados."[151] The President was unmoved, and did everything in his power to undermine or preferably to destroy the Socialist Party of Yucatán in his last months in office, including offering direct support to the Liberal Party.[152] In a private letter to Álvaro Obregón, Carrillo Puerto accused Carranza of not only colluding with the federal army and the henequen

149　FAPECFT-FAO, fondo: 11, serie: 30400, expediente: 135: CARRILLO PUERTO, Felipe, legajo 1, foja 6, inventario 2151. "Programa del Partido Socialista que Sustentarán los Componentes de los Ayuntamientos del Estado." Submitted to Obregón by Carrillo Puerto, July 9, 1920.
150　Joseph, *Revolution from Without*, 169.
151　AHSDN-W: Operaciones Militares, Yucatán, 1918. XI/481.5/328. Carrillo Puerto to Carranza, December 22, 1918.
152　Joseph, *Revolution from Without*, 170–71.

planters to destroy the Socialist Party, but of purposefully destabilizing the state as a pretext to impose another military government there.[153]

Although Carranza's campaign against the Socialists was devastating to their organization in the short-term, in the longer-term it was a politically tone-deaf stratagem that dramatically backfired. First, it was far too late to put the Socialist genie back in the bottle in Yucatán; Carrillo Puerto was just getting started. Second, Carranza's moves against the Socialists drove them into the arms of his emerging rival, General Álvaro Obregón. In 1919 Carrillo Puerto led the way, declaring his support for Obregón's opposition presidential candidacy against Carranza's handpicked successor, Ignacio Bonillas, in an early cry of all-but open rebellion against Carranza.[154] The Yucatecan Socialists' enthusiastic embrace of Obregón as their presidential candidate in defiance of Carranza underscores that for many young politicians and revolutionary soldiers of the era, Obregón's candidacy represented a much-desired changing of the political guard in Mexico City. It also established an important precedent with long-term consequences in the Southeast.

Obregón needed Carrillo Puerto, too. The late 1910s and early 1920s was a period in which regional caudillos continued to operate and thrive across Mexico, not always in a markedly different manner than they had before the Revolution. The national government's toleration and even cultivation of these alliances was emblematic of a period in which the infant postrevolutionary government sometimes relied on proxies to accomplish what it could not do itself, and outsourced local political control to individuals or groups with the proven ability to maintain peace and stability at the local or state level. But Carrillo Puerto was not simply a caudillo, and his alliances with Obregón and Plutarco Elías Calles came to be much more politically sophisticated than simple patronage relationships. They were forged out of a desire by all parties to build more substantive relationships between local, state, and national politics, and between national politicians and local constituencies. The Yucatan Socialists already had the institutional mechanisms in place to attempt it. For the very same reasons that Carranza feared Carrillo Puerto and his Socialist political machine with its mobilized and well-organized popular base, he was an indispensable ally for Obregón in 1919.

Carrillo Puerto and Obregón may have needed each other, but they had little natural affinity for one another. The former was a lifelong civilian activist who was influenced by Marxism and had fought with Zapata,

153 FAPECFT-FAO, fondo: 11, serie: 30100, expediente: C-7114: CARRILLO PUERTO, Felipe, legajo 1/1, fojas 6–7, inventario 1183. Carrillo Puerto to Obregón, July 22, 1919.
154 Joseph, *Revolution from Without*, 205. See also Linda B. Hall, *Álvaro Obregón: Power and Revolution in Mexico, 1911–1920* (College Station, TX: Texas A&M University Press, 1981), 221.

and who had both an ideological and a personal commitment to radical social and political reform. The latter was a brilliant military commander on a seemingly inexorable rise to the top of the power structure who saw radical reform projects like Carrillo's principally as a means to the end of consolidating political control and securing a postrevolutionary peace. Their differences notwithstanding, they were brought together in February of 1919 in an arranged political marriage by General Benjamin Hill as part of his early organizing work for Obregón's presidential campaign.[155] In early 1919, Hill asked Alvarado to help him to arrange a meeting with Carrillo Puerto in order to formalize an alliance between Obregón and the Yucatecan Socialist Party. The Southeast had historically been a region that had been notoriously difficult for Mexico City to control either politically or militarily, and Carranza's efforts to that end had conspicuously mixed results.[156] While Carranza sought to undermine the Yucatecan Socialists, Hill believed that the support that they could give to Obregón's presidential campaign was essential to winning support for his candidacy in the entire Southeast.[157] After meeting personally with Obregón in Mexico City, Carrillo Puerto returned to Mérida and immediately put the Socialist party to work on behalf of Obregón's presidential campaign. It was the beginning of a sea change in how national political campaigns were conducted at the regional level in Mexico.

Carrillo Puerto was quick to begin making demands of his new ally. Just as Obregón sought to consolidate his power at the national level, Carrillo Puerto was struggling to consolidate his own in Yucatán, to protect the workers and campesinos that he was working to organize, and to definitively establish the Socialist Party of Yucatán as a political force with which to be reckoned. One of his first requests of Obregón was that he intercede in Yucatán to limit the actions taken against the Socialists by General Luis Hernández, who Carranza had sent to Yucatán with orders to carry out a campaign of repression against the Socialist Party.[158] The pressure that Carranza's forces were putting on the Socialists in Yucatán following Alvarado's departure was enough to force Carrillo Puerto into exile in the

---

155 Hill was a longtime ally of Obregón's. See Hall, *Álvaro Obregón*, 182–83, 98–99, 238. He was also related to Obregón by marriage. See Knight, *The Mexican Revolution, Volume 2*, 267.

156 FAPECFT-FAO, fondo: 11, serie: 20700, expediente: H-5138: HILL, Benjamin G. (Gral.), legajo 1/1, fojas 5–14, inventario 886. Hill to Obregón, February 27, 1919.

157 FAPECFT-FAO, fondo: 11, serie: 20700, expediente: H-5138: HILL, Benjamin G. (Gral.), legajo 1/1, foja 29, inventario 886. Hill to Obregón, March 13, 1919.

158 FAPECFT-FAO, fondo: 11, serie: 30300, expediente: 33: YUCATAN, legajo 1/2, fojas 3–4, inventario 2015. Carrillo Puerto to Obregón, May 6, 1919. See also Joseph, *Revolution from without*, 169–70.

United States for several months.[159] "We know that everything will change when you become President," Carrillo Puerto told Obregón in 1919. He did not mince his words: "In the meantime, it is necessary for popular political parties – the ones that will help you – not be debilitated by the actions of revolutionaries that have not known how to understand the Revolution."[160] In return for Obregón's support, Carrillo Puerto promised to embark on a grassroots campaign in Yucatán for his presidential candidacy.[161] His ability to do so was his trump card. It worked.

Obregón's forging of an alliance with Carrillo Puerto was part of a larger push to build a base of popular support for himself leading up to the 1920 election. It was followed closely by a now-famous secret pact that Obregón signed with Luis Morones, the president of the Mexican Regional Labor Confederation (CROM), in August of 1919.[162] In exchange for the CROM's support during his presidential campaign, Obregón would establish a new Ministry of Labor should he become president, and would recognize the central committee of the CROM as a legal entity that would be empowered to negotiate with this new ministry. The Mexican Labor Party (PLM), the political branch of the CROM, also threw its support behind Obregón's candidacy.[163]

Obregón's alliance-building during his presidential campaign was intended to consolidate his network of support among political leaders like Morones and Carrillo Puerto, but just as importantly, to connect himself with local parties and unions that they were equipped to organize and mobilize their members on his behalf. Not only had this never been done before in Mexico, but it would not have been possible before on a similar scale. The Revolution had made it necessary, as workers and campesinos mobilized by revolutionary armies and ideals now expected to be rewarded with a place at the political table. In the absence of national

159   Carrillo Puerto would later tell his lover, Alma Reed, that he had been planning to visit the United States for some time preceding his exile, and that he used the opportunity to make contact with Socialists there. Reed recalled that Carrillo Puerto told her of his strong desire to participate in an international Socialist movement, and to make his peers in the United States aware of his political projects in Yucatán. Reed's memoir, which is largely concerned with her time in Mexico and her interactions with Carrillo Puerto, was published posthumously in 2007, after the manuscript was discovered in an abandoned apartment in Mexico City. While her discussions of Carrillo Puerto are obviously colored by her tremendous love for him, her accounts of conversations that she had with him about Yucatecan politics in this period nevertheless provide valuable insights into the nature of the man, as well as his politics. Reed and Schuessler, *Peregrina*, 245.

160   Rico, *La huelga de junio* (vol. 1), 39.

161   FAPECFT-FAO, fondo: 11, serie: 30300, expediente: 33: YUCATAN, legajo 1/2, fojas 3–4, inventario 2015. Carrillo Puerto to Obregón, May 6, 1919.

162   Alan Knight and others have suggested that it was Calles the brokered the deal between Obregón and the CROM. Knight, *The Mexican Revolution, Volume 2*, 488.

163   Hall, *Álvaro Obregón*, 217–18.

political parties that could command electoral discipline of both politicians and popular constituencies, this kind of networking and alliance building was critical for Obregón, particularly in a region like the Southeast where he had no independent base of support of his own. As Carrillo Puerto emphasized, he could put his political party and its well-organized constituent base to work for Obregón. Scarcely a month after their alliance was formalized, Carrillo Puerto boldly promised to deliver nearly the entire Southeast (Yucatán, Campeche, Chiapas, and Tabasco) for Obregón in the presidential election. If this offer seemed overly confident and ambitious, Obregón was intrigued enough to accept it. Carranza's ongoing struggle to control the Southeast was undoubtedly an important consideration. Carrillo Puerto was quick to make clear what was at stake for his new ally. He argued that Carranza's attacks against the Socialists were now aimed equally at Obregón, and were regional in scope. "The principal object is to cause your presidential campaign in the Southeast to fail," Carrillo Puerto warned Obregón.[164]

When the Sonorans issued their Plan de Agua Prieta in April of 1920 rebelling against Carranza, who was then assassinated, Carrillo Puerto's political gamble in attaching himself to Obregón paid tremendous political dividends. When Obregón became President, the political leaders and factions that had supported him were quickly empowered, and those that had supported Carranza fell out of favor, and were often also removed from elected offices. This included Governor Carlos Castro Morales, who had pinned his political hopes on Carranza's ability to cling to power and to successfully impose Bonillas as his presidential successor.[165]

In 1921, Carrillo renamed his party the Socialist Party of the Southeast (PSS).[166] The change was in more than just the name. Alvarado had designed his Socialist party as the institutional apparatus of a more moderate and circumscribed reformist project. Carrillo Puerto's redesign of the party included far greater popular mobilization, a more extensive geographic scope (in practice as well as in name), and the establishment of political institutions in Yucatán that were intended to endure beyond the horizon of Carrillo Puerto's political career. Although he himself was one of the driving forces behind the successes of the PSS in the 1920s, the party was far less personalist in character than nearly all other parties and political clubs in Mexico in this period.

Carrillo Puerto's new allies were largely supportive of his ambitious plans for the party. In particular, Plutarco Elías Calles, now Secretary of the Interior in Obregón's cabinet, was plainly intrigued by the political

164   FAPECFT-FAO, fondo: 11, serie: 30300, expediente: 33: YUCATAN, legajo 1/2, fojas 15–16, inventario 2015. Carrillo Puerto to Obregón, July 18, 1919.
165   Joseph, *Revolution from Without*, 205–6.   166   Ibid., 195.

experiment in Yucatán. In Calles Carrillo Puerto found the ally that neither he nor Alvarado ever had in Carranza, and that neither would have found in Obregón. Calles was not a radical in the same way Carrillo Puerto was, but he was very much interested in radical experimentation with new forms of political organization in a way that Obregón wasn't. For Carrillo Puerto, Socialism was the goal unto itself, and he referred to Calles as the "paladin of the working classes" for his support for radical projects like his.[167] But for Calles, the most interesting feature of southeastern Socialism was not the reforms it achieved, but the institutional structures the Yucatecans pioneered to reach their reformist goals.

Calles quickly became Carrillo Puerto's most important ally. No other politician of the Southeast had such evidently extensive access to Calles, or engaged in a similarly extensive correspondence with him, regarding matters big and small, and national as well as local. Through Calles' agents Robert Haberman and Juan Rico of the CROM, who reported back to him from the PSS congress in 1921, Calles was intimately involved with the development of the party nearly from the outset.[168] Calles also became Carrillo Puerto's most ardent defender in Mexico City, and one of the Socialist Party's most enthusiastic supporters. On a visit to Yucatán in 1921, Calles gave a speech praising the goals and the achievements of the PSS, ratifying his support of the party's programs, and expressing his strong support of Carrillo Puerto. What seemed to impress Calles most was the level of political institutionalization that the PSS had achieved by 1921:

In Yucatán, the people have already achieved their liberties and its rights; the authorities are the legitimate representation of the people, and the new ones that will come will also be the result of the conscious vote of all of the citizens of the state. This beautiful feat that the people of Yucatán have achieved is because of not one man, nor myself, nor the President of the Republic, nor of any other official; this feat belongs exclusively to the Socialist Party of the Southeast.[169]

What the PSS had managed to do in Yucatán, Calles inferred, was no less than to have made good on the promises of the Mexican Revolution. It is hard to imagine a more ringing endorsement of a regional political project by the second most powerful man in Mexico.

The closeness of the relationship between Carrillo Puerto and the new Secretary of the Interior was not lost on their political enemies in Yucatán. Anti-Socialist Yucatecans of many stripes complained to President

167 FAPECFT-PEC, expediente: 25: Carrillo Puerto, Felipe, legajo 1/7, fojas 27–28, inventario 830. Carrillo Puerto to Calles, May 4, 1921.
168 Haberman would subsequently become an advisor to Calles as Secretary of the Interior (1920–24), as well as the only foreign-born member of the policymaking committee of the CROM. Andrews, "Robert Haberman," 189–91.
169 This speech is reproduced in Calles, *Pensamiento político y social: antología (1913–1936)*, 57–59.

Obregón that Calles was protecting Carrillo and the PSS.[170] Calles was also accused of covering up the crimes of the PSS, and of scaring the Yucatecan opposition into silence.[171] Bernardino Mena Brito, the former Liberal gubernatorial candidate, accused Calles of being prejudiced against Liberals, and offered to personally enlighten Calles as to the true state of political affairs in Yucatán.[172] The rancor that Calles' support of Carrillo Puerto and the PSS inspired in Carrillo Puerto's political enemies in Yucatán demonstrates the extent to which Calles' strong support of the Socialists was understood as a serious social threat as well as a political liability for Yucatecan Liberals. In November of 1920, Yucatecan Liberals bitterly complained that Calles had shipped two thousand rifles to Carrillo Puerto to arm indigenous campesinos that supported the PSS. Once again, the specter of a race war unnerved elites of the peninsula, and they resented the soon-to-be Secretary of the Interior, yet another northern outsider, for inciting the Maya against them.[173] For all that most Yucatecan elites had come to dislike about Carranza, the Constitutionalists had at least worked to disarm the popular bands that had risen against them in the early 1910s, prior to Alvarado's arrival.[174] In Carrillo Puerto, "the people of Yucatán believed they saw the well-known and detestable figure of Alvarado, smiling with a diabolical squint," a Liberal legislator complained to Obregón, registering his horror at the "chilling" sight of armed Maya campesinos marching through the streets of Mérida, "threatening whites and mestizos with their rifles and their classic war cries."[175]

Much of the elite anger and resentment was aimed at Carrillo Puerto personally. The ongoing concentration of political power in his hands was undeniable. However, it was not unequivocal, nor is it fair to describe the PSS as straightforwardly personalist. On the contrary, by 1921 the PSS was pushing to depersonalize itself as a political organization. At the Socialist congress of Izamal that year, self-nomination of Socialist candidates for political office was prohibited with the penalty of expulsion from the party. This was not a party organized around the sole, central purpose of seeing Carrillo Puerto elected as governor or of solely empowering other

170 See, for example, AGN-OC, c. 165, exp. 424-h-2, leg. 1. María del Pilar Pech to Don Manuel Carpio, January 8, 1921.
171 AGN-OC, c. 165, exp. 424-h-2, leg. 1. F. Gamboa et al. to Obregón, December 2, 1922.
172 AGN-OC, c.165, exp. 424-h-2, leg. 1. Bernardino Mena Brito to Álvaro Obregón, January 19, 1921. For a discussion of Mena Brito's founding of the PLY, see Joseph, *Revolution from Without,* 116–17.
173 On pervasive racial anxiety among Yucatecan elites in the 1910s, see Wells and Joseph, *Summer of Discontent,* 208–9.
174 Ibid.
175 FAPECFT-FAO, serie: 030500, expediente: 913: MANZANILLA, D.A. (Dip)., legajo 1, fojas 1–2, inventario: 3787. D.A. Manzanilla to Obregón, November 12, 1920.

individuals, in the model of most political organizations in Mexico in the immediate postrevolutionary period. Indeed, Carrillo Puerto only became governor of Yucatán in 1922, and spent most of the previous five years methodically building the party as an institution with a much longer-term vision than a single election or gubernatorial term.

Even more revolutionary for the time, Carrillo Puerto worked to build the PSS into a regional party with national political clout. In 1920–22, he served as one of Yucatán's federal legislators.[176] This office gave Carrillo Puerto direct access to the national political stage, and unparalleled national exposure for the Socialists' political projects and ideas. He made the most of the opportunity to both publicize and defend the achievements of the PSS and his political ideas from the floor of the Chamber of Deputies, conspicuously using the legislature as a public forum in which to lay a foundation of support and sympathy in Mexico City for Yucatecan Socialism.[177] At the same time, Carrillo Puerto pushed the PSS to adopt a national political agenda. This was done in collaboration with a number of prominent outsiders who sympathized with their politics and had come to have vested interests in the success of the Socialist project in Yucatán, including Juan Rico and Samuel Yúdico of the CROM and General Francisco Múgica. All three attended the Izamal congress as Calles' personal representatives, along with Robert Haberman, who became one of Calles' agents and advisors.[178]

When Carrillo Puerto took his oath of office as governor of Yucatán in 1922, he added to the text mandated by law that he would uphold the accords of the congresses of Motul and Izamal.[179] This was a powerful recognition of the forces that had contributed to his assumption of the governorship. In vowing to enact the program that the workers' congresses had agreed on, Carrillo Puerto honored his relationships to grassroots delegates who had attended the congresses, as well as the outsiders, particularly Haberman and Rico, who had helped to shape the accords produced at both congresses. The PSS' relationships with communities at the

176   Camp, *Mexican Political Biographies, 1884–1935*, 40.
177   "Diario de los Debates de la Cámara de Diputados," H. Congreso de la Unión, http://cronica
      .diputados.gob.mx/DDebates/index.html. Legislatura XXIX – Año I – Período Ordinario –
      September 2, 1920 – Número de Diario 11.
178   Plutarco Elías Calles, *Correspondencia personal (1919–1945)*, ed. Carlos Macías, 2 vols., vol. 2
      (México, D.F.: Fideicomiso Archivos Plutarco Elías Calles y Fernando Torreblanca, 1991; repr.,
      1), 470–3. Carrillo Puerto to Calles, August 21, 1921. Yúdico was one of the original members of
      the Grupo 2, Acción of the CROM, along with Morones and Rico, was the regional PLM
      representative in Veracruz and Tlaxcala in 1920, and founded the CROM's National Railway
      Federation in 1925. See Marjorie Ruth Clark, *Organized Labor in Mexico* (New York, NY:
      Reissued by Russell & Russell, 1934; repr., 1973), 63, 73, 74, 113, 77.
179   Rico, *La huelga de junio* (vol. 1), 53–54.

grassroots and with power brokers in Mexico City became equally important elements of Carrillo Puerto's Socialist regime once he came to power.

As governor, Carrillo Puerto dramatically stepped up both the scale and the pace of agrarian reform and distribution of ejidos.[180] While this land reform had both practical and ideological objectives, Carrillo Puerto also intended for it to build further popular support for both his state government and for the federal government with which he was now closely allied. "The humble workers have become convinced that we will not betray them with promises and praise, but rather that the revolution concerns itself with them and does everything it can to favor them," he wrote to Calles.[181] This was characteristic of Carrillo Puerto's perennial efforts to make his allies in Mexico City aware of the relevance and the significance of his political project in Yucatán to their own. His reports about the successes of the PSS were not just boasts. They were also theses on methods of postrevolutionary popular organizing. As Carrillo Puerto envisioned it, the institutionalization of parties and respect for the rule of law was the best hope for peace for Yucatán, and for Mexico as a whole.[182] He explained to Obregón that through regularization of political processes, democratic elections, and the institutionalization of laws and civil rights, he was hopeful that Yucatán could finally find peace. He argued that with the Socialists' takeover of the government, peace and justice had triumphed in the state, that political violence was no longer justified, and that the political adversaries of the Socialists must be recognized as their fellow citizens.[183]

By the close of 1922, it seemed that Carrillo Puerto was successfully managing the broad spectrum of challenges of governing Yucatán. However, many threats to his Socialist government remained, and the combined strength of the PSS and the ligas de resistencia was yet to be truly tested. Even as he emphasized the political peace that Socialism had achieved in Yucatán, Carrillo Puerto always made it clear to his allies in Mexico City that he was willing to protect Socialist political gains and institutions by force of arms, and that it might become necessary.[184] He continued to work assiduously to prepare his party and his government for

180   Joseph, *Revolution from Without*, 237–41. Eiss, *In the Name of el Pueblo*, 150–51.

181   FAPECFT-PEC, expediente: 25, CARRILLO PUERTO, Felipe, legajo 3/7, fojas 151–55, inventario 830. Carrillo Puerto to Calles, April 3, 1922.

182   See Ben Fallaw, "Felipe Carrillo Puerto of Revolutionary-Era Yucatán: Popular Leader, Caesar, or Martyr?," in *Heroes and Hero Cults in Latin America*, ed. Samuel Brunk and Ben Fallaw (Austin: University of Texas Press, 2006), 132. "Unlike other political parties of the day, which served as electoral vehicles, under Carrillo Puerto the PSS was to be an instrument of permanent mobilization aimed at connecting popular demands with state power."

183   FAPECFT-FAO, fondo: 11, serie: 30400, expediente: 135: CARRILLO PUERTO, Felipe, fojas 31–35, Carrillo Puerto to Obregón, November 20, 1920.

184   FAPECFT-PEC, expediente: 25, CARRILLO PUERTO, Felipe, legajo 3/7, fojas 136–37, inventario 830. Carrillo Puerto to Calles, February 20, 1922.

armed attacks against them. In January of 1923 the governor pleaded with Calles for assistance in adequately arming the local police force in Yucatán, requesting over a thousand new rifles for the authorities of various communities across the state, and more for a new state police cavalry detachment that he was forming.[185] Carrillo Puerto knew better than anyone that the Socialists faced many threats from within the state. However, it would ultimately be a national political conflict that would bring his Socialist experiment to breaking point.

Conclusions

If Salvador Alvarado's idiosyncratic brand of Socialism changed one thing in the Southeast, it was that it forced politicians and power brokers of the region to confront the reality that workers and campesinos could no longer be ignored or politically quarantined. What this meant in practice varied a great deal from state to state in the region in the years that followed, but this basic recognition of how the Mexican Revolution had transformed the country was at the heart of every so-called Socialist project undertaken in Mexico from that point forward.

Alvarado's government in Yucatán constituted a middle stage between Mexico's revolutionary and postrevolutionary politics. The same could be said for the brand of "Socialism" that he invented. Alvarado borrowed from older ideas, such as the idealization of the pequeña propiedad, willfully copied contemporary US progressivist policies, and at the same time pushed relatively audacious new programs such as the emancipation and politicization of women and indigenous people. Similarly, he did not seek to destroy capitalism, but rather, to promote its development along with the advent of a just relationship between capital and labor, for the enhancement of the greater social good.[186] It was a creative political amalgam, unique to the time and place in which it unfolded, which nevertheless proved to be tremendously influential beyond that time and place. From the beginning, one of the central functions of the Socialist political machine of Yucatán was to be a mechanism of local propagation and enforcement of the precepts of the Mexican Revolution as they were enshrined in the 1917 Constitution. The Yucatecan Socialists provided an important model for accomplishing this at a time when very few politicians were attempting anything nearly as ambitious when it came to building new political

---

185 FAPECFT-PEC, expediente: 25, CARRILLO PUERTO, Felipe, legajo 5/7, fojas 245–46, inventario 830. Carrillo Puerto to Calles, January 26, 1923.

186 Joseph summarizes Alvarado's stance on labor relations thusly: "In Alvarado's roseate vision, the responsible forces of capital and labor would come to regard their interests as complementary, rather than conflictive." Joseph, *Revolution from Without*, 102.

institutions, and often struggled just to stay in power and maintain law and order. For Carrillo Puerto and his allies, Socialism truly was the Mexican Revolution transformed into a system of government.

From a very early point, Plutarco Elías Calles saw great promise in this bold political experiment. Calles' interest in the politics of the Southeast was always greater than that of Obregón's, and his knowledge of the particulars of southeastern regional politics were accordingly always more profound. As president, Obregón commonly delegated the handling of southeastern political matters to his Secretary of the Interior. Carrillo Puerto's shift away from Obregón and toward Calles as his chief ally and Calles' investment in the development of southeastern Socialism were precedents that would be repeated across the larger region, with important national consequences in the years to come.

Revolutionary Laboratories

The Spread of Socialism across the Southeast, 1915–1923

> Workers' associations without organized political parties are bodies without heads.
>
> Letterhead of the Socialist Agrarian Party of Campeche, 1921

Venustiano Carranza became president of Mexico in 1917 by making a large number of compromises with other revolutionary leaders and factions, and because he was lucky enough to have General Álvaro Obregón prosecuting his wars against the forces of Pancho Villa and Emiliano Zapata. Even so, Carranza came to power with a minimal mandate and was still struggling to control the whole of national territory. One part of Mexico where he had made decisive progress was in the state of Yucatán, thanks to the efforts of his proconsul General Salvador Alvarado to govern the state and keep its henequen export economy running and profitable. Now Carranza sought to replicate those results across the larger Southeast, and he turned to Alvarado once again to make it happen. Carranza was not interested in giving further encouragement to radicals like Felipe Carrillo Puerto. This time Alvarado's task was to achieve political control of the region, without engaging in any of the extensive political and social reforms that he had undertaken in Yucatán.

The results were mixed, at best, as Alvarado himself was quick to acknowledge. In 1918, he described the politics of the Southeast to Carranza as "a vicious circle." "To improve the economic situation there must be peace, and for there to be peace the economic situation must improve and there must be a well-organized Army, and for there to be a well-organized Army there must be peace and economic wellbeing," he wrote, and concluded: "these problems will only be resolved slowly, with the efforts of well-intentioned men."[1] Alvarado's assessment was accurate, and prescient. For the rest of the 1910s, the imposition of Constitutionalism sewed both discontent and strife in the Southeast. Yet the Socialist experiment

---

1 AHSDN-W: Operaciones Militares, Tabasco, 1917. XI/481.5/285. Alvarado to Carranza. Undated report from 1918 (misfiled).

survived under Carrillo Puerto's leadership. By 1920, it had also spread across state lines, as radicals, reformers, and other groups and factions alienated by the civil wars that Carranza unleashed in the region saw in Carrillo Puerto's experiment a new and better means of achieving peace and political stability. Many also benefited from his guidance and direct support.

In some places, the spread of Socialism outward from Yucatán seemed all but inevitable, especially to neighboring Campeche. In terms of climate, geography, and economy, the Southeast can be divided between the states of the Yucatecan peninsula – Yucatán, Campeche, and Quintana Roo (then a federal territory), and their southern neighbors, Chiapas and Tabasco (see Map 1).[2] On the peninsula in the 1910s and 1920s, henequen was one of the only crops to flourish on the hot and humid plains. In mountainous Chiapas and tropical, low-lying Tabasco, different climates, topographies, and political histories meant a different set of social, political, and economic circumstances. Socialism took root later in both places, and assumed markedly distinct forms in the years that followed, as is explored in later chapters.

Carrillo Puerto's renaming of his party as the Socialist Party of the Southeast (PSS) in 1921 was not grandstanding, but a statement of intent. He believed that his model of political organizing could be expanded and applied across the larger region, and he worked to cultivate and champion Socialist movements in Campeche, Chiapas, and Tabasco. Carrillo Puerto's political plans were not limited to the Southeast. One of the accords at the Yucatecan Socialists' Congress of Izamal in 1921 declared that it was incumbent upon the ligas de resistencia in the Southeast to send propagandists to all Mexican states in which there were not already ligas.[3] Like Alvarado, Carrillo Puerto believed that Yucatecan-style Socialism was a model of politics that could someday be applied at the national level.

When Carranza was assassinated and the Sonoran revolutionary faction came to power, Carrillo Puerto was already the Sonorans' most important ally in the region. With Obregón as president and Calles as Secretary of the Interior, Carrillo Puerto could now count on federal support for his political projects, both in Yucatán and in the larger Southeast, particularly from Calles; so could many of the Socialist leaders and parties Carrillo Puerto had inspired and supported in neighboring states. The Sonorans proved to be much more open to political experimentation and radicalism than Carranza had been, and sometimes actively encouraged it. Carrillo Puerto and his counterparts in other states of the region made the most of this window of political opportunity. In the space of six years, the Southeast was

---

2 On the politics and economics of the partition of Quintana Roo from Yucatán in 1902, see Wells and Joseph, *Summer of Discontent*, 43–54.

3 Rico, *La huelga de junio* (vol. 1), 123–24.

transformed from a counterrevolutionary stronghold to a bastion of home-grown radicalism on the cutting edge of postrevolutionary reform and political institutionalization.

This chapter explores how and why this was possible, as politicians across the region began to experiment with Yucatecan-style Socialism. A closer look at the popular reception and social impact of these experiments in Tabasco and Chiapas as they developed follows in subsequent chapters. Although the Socialist movements in Chiapas, Tabasco, and Yucatán are the principle case studies compared in this book, an examination of the spread of Socialism to Campeche is included here as an important element of the history of southeastern Socialism as it became a regional phenomenon in the late 1910s and early 1920s.

Constitutionalism in the Southeast, 1915–1918

The arrival of Constitutionalist forces to the Southeast in 1914 sparked the political experimentation that became southeastern Socialism. Just a few years later, the Constitutionalists sought to put a brake on this growing wave of radicalism, which Carranza feared would undermine his chief objective of securing political control of the region. By 1918, the south-easterners that were most enthusiastic about land and labor reform were subjected to a sustained campaign of political persecution by federal forces and their proxies. Activists and organizers were routinely harassed and attacked, and sometimes killed. Nevertheless, the 1917 Constitution promulgated by Carranza became the sacred charter of reformers, workers, and campesinos alike, who were frequently galvanized and further radicalized by the repression they faced at the hands of Constitutionalist forces, local elites, or both. As in other parts of Mexico, elites across the Southeast strongly resisted even modest social and economic reform, irrespective of whether it was proposed by Constitutionalists or homegrown radicals. The outcomes of these shared circumstances varied a great deal state by state, according to a number of factors.

Campeche bordered Yucatán and also most resembled it in its climate, landscape, demographics, and economy, and elites there watched the Socialist experiment unfold in Yucatán with particular, understandable trepidation. Campeche was part of Yucatán until 1857, when a group of Liberals spearheaded a separatist movement that eventually led to the creation of the new state in 1863.[4] The two states still had much in common by the time of the Revolution. Perhaps most decisively, both had economies that were critically dependent on planters' control over the

---

4   José A. Abud, *Campeche: Revolución y movimiento social (1911–1923)* (México, D.F.: Universidad Autónoma de Campeche, 1992), 28.

labor of Maya campesinos. Like Yucatán, Campeche was still recovering at the turn of the century from the unrest and uncertainty provoked by the so-called Caste War on the peninsula, when a Maya faction rebelled against the Mexican government and declared their territory (in the present-day Mexican state of Quintana Roo) independent, with pockets of fighting that continued into the 1930s.[5] Campeche also went through a henequen boom at the same time as Yucatán, and it became the state's principle cash crop by the 1880s. As in Yucatán, inequality increased in Campeche as henequen came to reign supreme and the wealthiest residents of the state grew exponentially more so.[6] In spite of these commonalities, Constitutionalism took a markedly different form in Campeche, in large part due to the character and ambitions of the proxy Carranza dispatched there.

When proconsul Joaquín Mucel Acereto arrived in Campeche in 1914 his task was identical to that of his counterparts across the Southeast: to undertake a circumscribed and controllable process of much-needed reform in a state that was dramatically unequal, while at the same time stifling the proliferation of more radical reform movements. Mucel abolished debt peonage and canceled outstanding worker debts, mandated reduced work-weeks, required that planters pay their workers in cash, and recognized the rights of workers to organize. These reforms initially won him popular support, and Mucel briefly succeeded in forging a multi-class coalition.[7] But he was substantially more authoritarian than his fellow proconsuls. Mucel dissolved Campeche's legislature and replaced all of the state's courts with his own military tribunals, which he used to suppress dissent and opposition.[8] More than any of the Constitutionalist proconsuls, Mucel also abused his power. He imposed new regulations on the sale of alcohol in Campeche until he personally controlled a statewide monopoly on it, and he battled bootleggers to keep it that way.[9]

To the southwest of Campeche, Tabasco was quite different from the states of the peninsula in many respects. Its population was relatively small, and relatively less indigenous; in the late nineteenth century approximately a quarter of residents of the state were Chontal, and these were mostly concentrated in the northwest.[10] Tabasco's economy and its politics were decisively shaped by its distinct physical characteristics and climate. Debt peonage was common on large estates dedicated to typically tropical crops

5   Carlos Justo Sierra, Fausta Gantús Inurreta, and Laura Villanueva, *Breve historia de Campeche*, 2 ed. (México, D.F.: Fondo de Cultura Económica, 2011), 146–47.

6   Abud, *Campeche: Revolución y movimiento social (1911–1923)*, 30–31.   7   Ibid., 48–49, 51.

8   Ibid., 50–51.

9   FAPECFT-PEC, expediente: 98, HERNANDEZ, Santiago M., legajo 1/1, foja 32–3, inventario 2734. Santiago Hernández to Calles, August 26, 1922.

10 Carlos R. Martínez Assad, *Breve historia de Tabasco*, 2nd edn. (México, D.F.: Colegio de Mexico Fondo de Cultura Económica, 2006), 114, 25.

such as bananas, coconut, cacao, sugar, and coffee.[11] One of the lowest lying and most tropical states in Mexico, floods, insect plagues, and outbreaks of tropical diseases were constant threats, and natural disasters sometimes provoked political ones.[12] In the early twentieth century, travel to and within the state was limited by lack of infrastructure and further complicated by a high density of rivers, lakes, and swamps. Transportation and commerce alike often required a boat.[13]

In the nineteenth century, Tabasco's most important exports were tropical hardwoods, particularly mahogany, a business dominated by US and European lumber companies. These valuable trees were harvested under notoriously harsh working conditions in Tabasco's hot and humid climate, often by indigenous workers from both Tabasco and Chiapas. The work was so undesirable and recruitment of workers so difficult that lumber companies sometimes resorted to involuntary prison labor.[14] By the 1920s, bananas overtook lumber and became a wildly successful near-monocrop.[15] The decline of logging and the rise of the banana sector did little to change the day-to-day lives of Tabasco's working poor. It was another export commodity that meant immense profits for foreign corporations and required grueling labor by the men who tended the plants and harvested the fruit.[16]

In spite of the logistical challenges that Tabasco's inundated landscape posed, Carranza might have reasonably assumed that a Constitutionalist political takeover would be more easily accomplished there than in other parts of the Southeast. The state initially looked well-primed to receive northern revolutionaries, perhaps more so on paper than any other state of the region. In the early 1900s, a local anti-Díaz movement gained momentum and clashed with federal forces over the reelection of the Porfirian governor. A few years later, rebels in the western Chontalpa region of the state stockpiled weapons and recruited rural workers in support of Madero's call to overthrow Díaz, and triumphed in early skirmishes with federal troops. Once he became president, Madero installed Dr. Manuel Mestre Ghigliazza, a prominent but moderate Tabasco dissident, as governor.[17] However, after Madero was overthrown and assassinated in 1913, Mestre recognized the Victoriano Huerta dictatorship, provoking a new wave of revolution in Tabasco. Now led by Carlos Greene, the western rebels were

11 Martínez Assad, *El laboratorio de la revolución*, 95.
12 Kristin A. Harper, "Revolutionary Tabasco in the Time of Tomas Garrido Canabal, 1922–1935: A Mexican House Divided" (Ph.D. diss., University of Massachusetts Amherst, 2004), 30–31, 41.
13 Martínez Assad, *El laboratorio de la revolución*, 94.
14 Harper, "Revolutionary Tabasco," 19–24.
15 Martínez Assad, *El laboratorio de la revolución*, 98–110.
16 Harper, "Revolutionary Tabasco," 19.
17 Ibid., 35–41. See also Alfonso Taracena, *Historia de la Revolución en Tabasco*, 3 ed., vol. 1 (Villahermosa: Consejo Editorial del Estado de Tabasco, México, 1981).

soon joined in their fight by the Usamacinta Brigade in the east. This new faction was led by Luis Felipe Domínguez, who formed an early alliance with Carranza. Both rebel bands extensively recruited the urban and rural working poor into their ranks.[18]

Tabasco's incipient revolution was quickly derailed by regional jealousies and bitter infighting. When Carranza alienated Greene by making Domínguez governor, the local revolutionary factions turned on one another. Making Greene governor after Domínguez resigned did nothing to ease factional strife, and Carranza soon reassigned Greene elsewhere.[19] Exasperated by the inability of his local allies to resolve their differences and to pacify and govern Tabasco, Carranza finally dispatched General Francisco Múgica of Michoacán to the state as its proconsul in 1915.[20] Although he was welcomed by none of the warring local factions, within a year Múgica defeated most pockets of rebellion and consolidated his control over Tabasco.

Of all of the southeastern proconsuls, Múgica was the most like Alvarado in terms of the ambition of his reforms, but he was more radical in his politics. Múgica quickly set out to distribute land, reform labor relations, and implement sweeping anticlerical measures, something that became a defining feature of radical reformism in Tabasco.[21] He understood part of his task to be a campaign of "moralization and regeneration" of society in Tabasco, which included vigorous efforts to abolish the production and sale of alcohol.[22] Above all, Múgica was dedicated to land reform. This brought him into conflict with the more conservative Carranza, as well as North American investors whose holdings in Tabasco were imperiled.[23] Under pressure from US interests, the president overruled one of Múgica's land redistributions, and ordered that the property be returned to its former owners. Although Múgica eventually convinced Carranza to change his mind, Carranza removed him from Tabasco shortly thereafter, after only a year as governor.[24]

18 Harper, "Revolutionary Tabasco," 41–48.
19 Enrique Canudas describes the Constitutionalist revolution in Tabasco as little more than the beginning of a struggle between local factions. Enrique Canudas, *Tropico rojo: historia politica y social de Tabasco los años garridistas 1919/1934*, vol. 1 (Villahermosa, Tabasco: Gobierno del Estado de Tabasco, Instituto de Cultura de Tabasco, 1989), 12. See also Ramona Isabel Pérez Bertruy, *Tomás Garrido Canabal y la conformación del poder revolucionario tabasqueño, 1914–1921* (Villahermosa, Tabasco: Gobierno del Estado de Tabasco, Secretaría de Educación, Cultura y Recreación, Dirección de Educación Superior e Investigación Científica, 1993), 6.
20 Canudas, *Tropico rojo, Vol. 1*, 1, 13–14; Martínez Assad, *Breve historia de Tabasco*, 152–54; Taracena, *Historia de la Revolución en Tabasco*, 1, 345–47. Múgica would later become a noted leftist radical in Mexico, and very nearly a presidential contender in the late 1930s.
21 Martínez Assad, *El laboratorio de la revolución*, 156–57.
22 AGN-TGC, c. 1, exp. 8. Undated copy of Múgica's anti-alcohol statute.
23 Harper, "Revolutionary Tabasco," 52–53.   24 Ibid., 52.

The state sank into a period of violent upheaval following Múgica's departure as regional factionalism resurged. "Red" revolutionaries led by Carlos Greene and the Radical Party of Tabasco (PRT) were pitted against the more moderate "Blues," led by Greene's old adversary Luis Felipe Domínguez. As the Reds and the Blues clashed violently throughout the late 1910s, Carranza resorted to re-empowering Domínguez as governor in 1916.[25] Desperate to secure some semblance of political order, Domínguez attempted to soften the resistance of local elites to Constitutionalist government, and resorted to re-empowering local politicians of the Porfirian era that had only recently been driven out of office. This had the opposite of the intended effect, as these officials embarked on a retaliatory campaign of repression and terror against any person or community that identified as a revolutionary, and contrary local forces responded by forming militias to defend themselves.[26] The ceaseless infighting between multiple revolutionary factions that had once looked like promising local constituencies for the Constitutionalists now delayed any significant reform of Tabasco.

Even so, it was neighboring Chiapas that posed what was arguably the greatest political challenge for the Constitutionalists in the Southeast. Like their counterparts on the Yucatecan peninsula, the elite of Chiapas depended heavily on the coerced labor of indigenous workers, and they fought bitterly to maintain their control of it. But in many other respects, Chiapas was distinct from the rest of the states of the region, including in ways that decisively affected the course of its politics. Formerly part of Guatemala, Chiapas joined Mexico in 1824, but its borders were not finalized until the turn of the century.[27] The state was deeply divided, both literally and figuratively: It was profoundly segregated between indigenous people and non-indigenous *Ladinos*. The indigenous population was itself quite diverse: Whereas the Maya of the Yucatán peninsula all spoke one language, Chiapas was home to at least ten distinct Mayan language groups, which significantly complicated efforts at political organizing in the state.

Chiapas was also much more varied in its terrain than neighboring states, and these differences translated into both economic differentiation

25 Martínez Assad argues that the differences between the two parties were largely locally specific. Martínez Assad, *El laboratorio de la revolución*, 157. Canudas echoes this, describing the fleeting and constantly changing alliances between local factions and national political factions. Canudas, *Tropico rojo, Vol. 1*, 1, 15–6. Camp, *Mexican Political Biographies, 1884–1935*, 71–72.

26 AHSDN-W. Operaciones Militares, Tabasco, 1917. XI/481.5/285. Alvarado to Carranza. Undated report from 1918 (misfiled).

27 On Chiapas joining Mexico, see Thomas Benjamin, *A Rich Land, a Poor People: Politics and Society in Modern Chiapas*, Revised edn. (Albuquerque, NM: University of New Mexico Press, 1996), 6–11. See also Catherine A. Nolan-Ferrell, *Constructing Citizenship: Transnational Workers and Revolution on the Mexico-Guatemala Border, 1880–1950* (Tucson, AZ: University of Arizona Press, 2012) p 18–51.

and political polarization. Chiapas is sharply divided by mountains, rivers, waterfalls, and canyons; today, the state produces much of Mexico's hydro-electric power. Its lowlands are hot and humid while its highlands are cool and foggy. The colonial-era capital of San Cristóbal de Las Casas in the highlands is less than forty miles as the crow flies from the modern state capital of Tuxtla Gutiérrez in the lowlands, but the two cities are also separated by over five thousand feet in altitude; to arrive in Tuxtla from the highlands is literally to descend from the clouds. Travel between Chiapas' regions was not easy, another significant complication to political organizing in the state for generations. Historian Manuel B. Trens wrote in 1927: "As of today, except on the coast, the huff of a locomotive hasn't been heard in Chiapas."[28] In the early twentieth century many roads in the state were only passable seasonally and sometimes only on horseback, where there were roads at all.[29]

The state's main export crop at the turn of the century was coffee, grown on plantations along its Pacific coastline.[30] The rest of the lowland economy was dominated by cattle ranching, and the cultivation of rubber, cacao, and fruit. All of it depended on indigenous labor, which was perhaps Chiapas' most sought-after resource of all. While lowland planters and ranchers made their money on export commodities, highland elites made much of theirs as labor brokers and debt contractors, providing workers from highland indigenous communities to the lowlands.[31] Beginning in the 1890s, a series of mechanisms, including debts, fines, and a head tax, were put into place by the state government to coerce highland indigenous men to work on plantations throughout the state, where there were chronic labor shortages.[32]

The move of Chiapas' state capital from San Cristóbal to Tuxtla in 1892 reflected longstanding regional political divides that endured well into the twentieth century. In the nineteenth century this was a difference between highland Conservatives and lowland Liberals, but in practice their main bone of contention was over who controlled indigenous labor. Since the move of the capital to Tuxtla was part of a Porfirian effort to curtail the

---

28 Manuel B. Trens, *Vidal y Chiapas: su campaña política y su administración* (México, D.F., 1927), 25.
29 Calles was informed that part of his visit to Chiapas in 1923 would only be possible on horseback. FAPECFT-PEC, expediente 92: MENDOZA, Manuel (Tte Corl.), legajo 1/1, foja 22, inventario 3666. Calles to Manuel Mendoza, February 13, 1923.
30 On Chiapas' coffee economy, see Casey Marina Lurtz, "Exporting from Eden: Coffee, migration, and the development of the Soconusco, Mexico, 1867–1920" (Ph.D. dissertation, The University of Chicago, 2014); Nolan-Ferrell, *Constructing Citizenship*.
31 Jan Rus, "Revoluciones contenidas: los indígenas y la lucha por Los Altos de Chiapas, 1910–1925", *Mesoamérica*, no. 46 (2004): 60–62.
32 Jan Rus, "The End of the Plantations and the Transformation of Indigenous Society in Highland Chiapas, Mexico, 1974–2009" (Ph.D., University of California, Riverside, 2010), 4.

political power of the highland elite, they loudly declared themselves to be partisans of Madero when the Mexican Revolution began. They also took the Revolution as an opportunity to settle old scores closer to home. During the so-called Pajarito Rebellion in 1911, highland elites recruited and organized Tzotzil men from San Juan Chamula to attack their lowland rivals, officially in Madero's name.[33]

As elites used the revolution as an opportunity to score points in long-standing quarrels, very little changed in terms of how politics were done or who held power in Chiapas until 1914, when Carranza dispatched General Jesús Agustín Castro as his first proconsul to the state.[34] Their mutual distaste for the incursion of outsiders was enough to unite the elites of Chiapas, who found unprecedented common cause in their shared resistance to Carranza's clumsy attempts to control the state from the outside. Castro's arrival provoked a rebellion by the so-called Mapaches ("raccoons"), who were principally lowland planters and ranchers who took up arms to defend their political autonomy, and, in their words, "property and freedom of conscience."[35] They employed guerrilla tactics and nominally fought in support of Pancho Villa, but they became best known for their longstanding refusal to capitulate to the Constitutionalists.[36]

Other than their bitter resistance to the occupation of their state by northern revolutionaries, the Mapaches were not men who had much in common with the ultra-wealthy henequen planters of Campeche and Yucatán. Chiapas had no export crop that ever produced wealth on the scale that henequen did, and the men who fought as Mapaches were not the most elite of the state. Still, there were important similarities. Like the henequen barons, the Mapaches were resistant to change. Writing in 1927, Manuel B. Trens assessed that the Mapaches were inspired to fight against "the application of redemptive principles" – more specifically, the canceling of workers' debts and the liberation of the campesinos of Chiapas – and that they did so with the support and financing of wealthy landowners who saw their own interests imperiled by Constitutionalism.[37] Alluding to both their nickname and their reputation, a bemused federal agent in the

33   Rus, "Revoluciones contenidas," 68–71, 80.
34   On the limited revolutionary uprisings in Chiapas pre-1914, see Robert Wasserstrom, *Class and Society in Central Chiapas* (Berkeley, CA: University of California Press, 1983), 157–59.
35   April 1917 manifesto by Tiburcio Fernández Ruiz, quoted in Trens, *Vidal y Chiapas*, 21–23. Benjamin describes the Mapaches as "*finqueros* who valued their autonomy more than any assistance they might gain from regional or national government." Benjamin, *A Rich Land, a Poor People*, 125.
36   On the early days of the Mapache rebellion, see Benjamín Lorenzana Cruz, *Del maderismo al mapachismo en Chiapas: La Revolución Mexicana en la región de Tonalá*, Biblioteca Chiapas: Investigación del patrimonio cultural (Tuxtla Gutiérrez, Chiapas, México: CONACULTA / CONECULTA, 2013), 80–91.
37   Trens, *Vidal y Chiapas*, 19.

1920s described the Mapaches as "wild animals."[38] Led by General Tiburcio Fernández Ruiz, the Mapache counterrevolution delayed any significant reform in Chiapas for nearly a decade.

When General Pablo Villanueva was posted as Chiapas' new proconsul in 1916, he tried to appease the Mapaches by appointing several of their allies to positions within his government, much as Alvarado had done in forging a multi-class state bureaucracy in Yucatán. Violent confrontations between Villanueva's forces and rebel contingents in 1917 made clear that the effort at conciliation had failed, and so the Constitutionalists resorted to stopgap measures to build their power base in Chiapas.[39] Instead of carefully constructing a diverse coalition as Alvarado had in Yucatán, they fell back on the time-tested method of outsourcing political control to local strongmen, people whose power and prestige relied on maintaining the status quo. One concerned citizen in Comitán complained to Carranza in 1917 that federal agents in Chiapas had neither the "time, judgment nor tact" to replace corrupt local officials of the old regime with principled, sincere revolutionaries.[40]

In sum, by 1918, as Socialism in Yucatán was gaining strength and popularity with Felipe Carrillo Puerto's leadership, it was not clear that a similarly ambitious strain of reform politics would ever take hold in the rest of the Southeast, or who would spearhead it. For various reasons, none of Carranza's proxies were nearly as successful at constituency building, political stabilization, or pacification as Alvarado had been in Yucatán in 1915–17. This is likely why Carranza finally made Alvarado his military commander for the whole of the Southeast in 1918. In spite of their differences and disagreements, he had become Carranza's proconsul of last resort.

Alvarado was unimpressed with what his colleagues had achieved when he arrived in Tabasco. "[Múgica] seems to have had good intentions, but he didn't know how to maintain the equanimity that is necessary in the turbulent sea of passions that constantly agitate this state," he reported to Carranza. As for Múgica's successor, Domínguez, Alvarado bluntly described him as "the idol of all of our enemies."[41] Alvarado argued that what Tabasco most needed was a capable governor who could both resist the "seductions" of the old political order, and was willing and able to collaborate with the military authorities in the state. He further

---

38 Archivo General de la Nación de México, Dirección General de Investigaciones Políticas y Sociales (hereafter denoted as AGN-DGIPS), c. 192, exp. 17.

39 Trens, *Vidal y Chiapas*, 20–21. Benjamin, *A Rich Land, a Poor People*, 133–34.

40 AHSDN-W, Operaciones Militares, Chiapas, 1917. XI/481.5/54. Francisco Domínguez to Carranza, June 28, 1917.

41 AHSDN-W, Operaciones Militares, Tabasco, 1917. XI/481.5/285. Alvarado to Carranza. Undated report from 1918 (misfiled).

recommended a program of strategic ejido distribution across the Southeast, a campaign to publicize the ideals of the Revolution, the deportation of five hundred rebels from both Chiapas and Tabasco, and to postpone all elections until peace was secured.[42]

Alvarado was equally dismayed when he arrived in Chiapas, complaining that proconsul Pablo Villanueva had not been firm and aggressive enough in his dealings with the Mapaches.[43] Alvarado then embarked on an aggressive military campaign against the rebels and a draconian program of population reconcentration.[44] The war that ensued was disastrous for Chiapas.[45] Ranching families fleeing the state sold their equipment and livestock at bargain basement prices, decimating both agriculture and industry in the state and exacerbating the already dramatic concentration of wealth in the hands of a few. Prospectors flourished, reselling cattle in Yucatán for four times what they paid frightened ranchers seeking to liquidate their possessions in Chiapas.[46] As farms were abandoned or sacked by the Mapaches, parts of the state faced food shortages. There was famine in Chamula, where the war contributed to disrupting the labor migrations to the lowlands that Tzotziles there had come to depend on.[47]

The results of the campaign were mixed at best, even by Alvarado's estimation. Gone was all of his bravado and confidence of earlier days, as the general expressed frustration at his inability to reproduce in Chiapas the kind of reformist ferment he had generated in Yucatán. "All of my efforts to inculcate my collaborators with my patriotic fervor and my anguishes as a thinking man have failed," he admitted to Carranza.[48] In another letter, he concluded miserably that he hadn't even succeeded in convincing his own soldiers in Chiapas to regularly clean their weapons.[49] Chiapas was so politically fractured along so many social, economic, and territorial lines

42 AHSDN-W, Operaciones Militares, Tabasco, 1917. XI/481.5/285. Alvarado to Carranza. Undated report from 1918 (misfiled). AHSDN-W, Operaciones Militares, Tabasco, 1918. XI/481.5/286. Alvarado to Carranza, September 16, 1918.

43 AHSDN-W, Operaciones Militares, Tabasco, 1917. XI/481.5/285. Alvarado to Carranza. Undated report from 1918 (misfiled).

44 Benjamin, *A Rich Land, a Poor People*, 137. Lorenzana Cruz, *Del maderismo al mapachismo en Chiapas*, 130–31.

45 On the economic impact of the Mapache rebellion, see Lorenzana Cruz, *Del maderismo al mapachismo en Chiapas*.

46 AHSDN-W, Operaciones Militares, Chiapas, 1918. XI/481.5/55. Memo sent to Carranza, December 12, 1918. Signature indecipherable.

47 Lorenzana Cruz, *Del maderismo al mapachismo en Chiapas*, 131–33. Rus, "Revoluciones contenidas," 74–75.

48 AHSDN-W, Operaciones Militares, Tabasco, 1918. XI/481.5/286. Alvarado to Carranza, October 1, 1918. I have taken some liberty with the translation of "consciente" here.

49 AHSDN-W, Operaciones Militares, Tabasco, 1917. XI/481.5/285. Alvarado to Carranza. Undated report from 1918 (misfiled).

that coalition building there was an especially formidable challenge, even for a talented political strategist like Alvarado. With no urban working class predisposed to unionization on the scale of Yucatán, Tabasco, or Campeche, and no partner like Carrillo Puerto to handle rural grassroots organizing, popular support was not as forthcoming as it had been in Yucatán. Without this organizational effort at the local level and without the kind of cross-class alliances he had built in Yucatán through the Socialist Party, Alvarado frequently found himself pitted against recalcitrant municipal authorities who often favored the Mapache rebels.[50]

Without the institutional framework and bureaucratic apparatuses of a well-organized political party, managed in its day-to-day operations by cooperative local politicians and grassroots organizers, Constitutionalist efforts to govern and reform the Southeast were both ad hoc and ineffective compared to what Alvarado had achieved in Yucatán. The region's lack of progress toward any substantive postrevolutionary political institutionalization was further underscored as the 1918 gubernatorial elections approached. A new wave of political violence overtook the region as Carranza's appointed military proconsuls each attempted to stay in power by campaigning for full, elected terms, as Alvarado had in Yucatán. In Campeche, Chiapas, and Tabasco alike, the political aspirations of the proconsuls came up against stiff local resistance, both by factions that sought to protect local sovereignty against further Constitutionalist interference, and by radicals who were increasingly alienated by the proconsuls' limited efforts to address their demands for land and labor reform, and by Constitutionalist retaliation against those who tried to organize workers and campesinos. Socialist Yucatán served as a potent object lesson for all.

In Tabasco, Luis Felipe Domínguez's supporters argued that once he was elected as governor he would be able to solve all of the problems that had eluded him as proconsul.[51] This was less than convincing for disillusioned citizens across the political spectrum, particularly as the gubernatorial race exacerbated the ongoing political polarization that plagued the state. Old rivalries resurged when the Reds and reform-minded elites who had been alienated by the Constitutionalist campaigns in the state settled on Domínguez's old rival, Carlos Greene of the Tabasco Radical Party, as their gubernatorial candidate.[52] Domínguez preemptively complained that Greene and the Radicals were planning a significant electoral fraud, and warned that Tabasco would not find any peace should Greene

---

50 AHSDN-W, Operaciones Militares, Tabasco, 1918. XI/481.5/286. Alvarado to Carranza, September 16, 1918.

51 AHSDN-W, Operaciones Militares, Tabasco, 1918. XI/481.5/286. E. Sánchez Montero to Carranza, October 18, 1918.

52 AHSDN-W, Operaciones Militares, Tabasco, 1917. XI/481.5/285. Open letter to Carranza from A. Ocaña et al., May 3, 1917.

triumph.[53] It found no peace during the campaign, either. Domínguez stepped down as proconsul in order to campaign for the governorship, and was replaced by a young Constitutionalist from Chiapas, General Carlos Vidal. As Vidal struggled to maintain peace leading up to the election, his father was shot and killed in the street in Villahermosa, allegedly by Blues as retribution for the favoritism that Vidal had shown toward the Reds.[54] Tabasco continued to be rocked by political violence after Greene was elected in February of 1919, as Domínguez and his supporters refused to accept their defeat. In the end, Greene was only able to remain in the governorship for a year and a half.[55]

Proconsul Pablo Villanueva's efforts to stay on as governor of Chiapas in 1918 caused similar turmoil.[56] As the war between the Constitutionalists and the Mapache rebels dragged on into its fourth year, the perceived federal imposition of an outsider candidate on the state was an intolerable prospect for people across the political spectrum. Many in Chiapas sympathized with revolutionary ideals, but also bitterly resented the ongoing, particularly brutal Constitutionalist campaign there. If the Constitutionalists had prioritized substantive reform in Chiapas, they would have found ready allies. Instead, they unleashed a campaign of repression against radicals and aspiring reformers.

The repression experienced by a young political organizer in Chiapas named Ricardo Alfonso Paniagua is emblematic of the failure of Constitutionalism in the Southeast. Paniagua came from a family of activists in Mariscal, in the southernmost part of the state. His brother Hector and his father Juan Eduardo were both teachers who worked in local schools.[57] In the coffee growing region of Chiapas where the Paniaguas lived and worked, Constitutionalist labor reforms introduced in 1914 had initially helped to mobilize the organization of coffee workers, leading to a strike in 1918 and increasing labor radicalization. It was these organized coffee workers that served as the grassroots base for the Paniaguas' early organizing efforts.[58] However, the Paniaguas and their fellow activists in the coffee region quickly became alienated and then further radicalized as

53 AHSDN-W, Operaciones Militares, Tabasco, 1918. XI/481.5/286. Domínguez to Carranza, November 17, 1918. Operaciones Militares, Tabasco, 1917. XI/481.5/285. Domínguez to Venustiano Carranza, March 30, 1917.

54 Canudas, *Tropico rojo, Vol. 1*, 1, 17.   55 Harper, "Revolutionary Tabasco," 53–54.

56 AHSDN-W, Operaciones Militares, Chiapas, 1919. XI/481.5/56. Villanueva to Carranza, December 3, 1919.

57 Spenser, *El partido socialista chiapaneco*, 85–87. Both worked for the federal Public Education Ministry (SEP) after it was founded in 1922. Stephen Lewis, *The Ambivalent Revolution: Forging State and Nation in Chiapas, 1910–1945* (Albuquerque, NM: University of New Mexico Press, 2005), 28–29.

58 Emilio Zebadúa, *Breve historia de Chiapas* (México, D.F.: Fondo de Cultura Económica, 1999), 152–53. Spenser, *El partido socialista chiapaneco*, 72–73, 82–83.

they were persecuted for their opposition to the Constitutionalist-aligned local government of Motozintla in the late 1910s.[59] Members of the family were threatened, and one brother fled. The horse that Juan Eduardo used as his primary mode of transportation in his political organizing was stolen. More gravely, Hector was kidnapped at gunpoint by a lieutenant from the local garrison and thrown in prison. His family was permitted no contact with him, and told only that his arrest was ordered by President Carranza and governor Villanueva themselves.[60]

In Campeche, Carranza accepted Joaquín Mucel's authoritarianism as a preferable alternative to the chaos and violence his proconsuls oversaw in Chiapas and Tabasco. Of all of the ambitious Southeastern proconsuls, only Mucel was able to stay on for an elected term as governor, with Carranza's support. This was in spite of only a mixed record of political success. Mucel's blend of reform and repression antagonized elites, exasperated would-be reformers, and disappointed workers and campesinos. By 1918, as Mucel dragged his feet implementing land reform, campesinos began to lose their patience. In July, the warehouse of the Punto Paraíso hacienda was set on fire, causing an estimated 25,000 pesos worth of damage. An anonymous message was posted in the public market, signed only as "the farmers." It explained that the owners of the hacienda would be the subjects of further attacks if they did not give back the land they had long ago stolen from the men who worked it and who now impatiently awaited its return. The letter concluded: "if it is necessary to murder you, don't doubt that we will do it."[61] Mucel confirmed to Carranza that the incident was caused by a recent resolution that denied land grants to the campesinos of Punto Paraíso, who believed that the Revolution had promised it to them.[62]

Yet meaningful reform was not on the immediate horizon in Campeche, particularly as Carranza reinforced Mucel's mandate. Carranza's message to the Southeast was clear: Mucel was allowed to stay in power in Campeche because he prioritized control over reform, while Múgica was removed from the region for championing reform and popular organizing. Encouraged by Carranza's favoritism, Mucel's governorship was even more authoritarian than his term as proconsul. Workers and campesinos in Campeche now faced more extreme repression when they attempted to organize themselves outside of official government channels. In 1915, workers in the northern town of Nunkiní came together to found the Union of Workers and

59 Spenser, *El partido socialista chiapaneco*, 84–85.
60 Archivo General de la Nación, Fondo Carlos A. Vidal (hereafter AGN-CAV), c.4, t.2, f.10. Paniagua to Vidal, November 3, 1919.
61 AHSDN-W, XI/481.5/25, c. 4. Operaciones Militares, Campeche, 1918. Copy of letter from "los agriculturores" to los Señores Carpizo, July 15, 1918.
62 AHSDN-W, XI/481.5/25, c. 4. Operaciones Militares, Campeche, 1918. Mucel to Carranza, July 23, 1918.

Campesinos (UOC), to pursue land and labor reform. In terms of its scope and stated objectives, this was a less radical organization than its grassroots counterparts in Chiapas and Yucatán.[63] Even so, the organization now faced new threats and suppression by Mucel's government.[64]

Mucel was the most authoritarian of the proconsuls, but his crackdown on aspiring reformers in Campeche was emblematic of a larger pattern across the region. Perhaps even more revealing is master politician Salvador Alvarado's shift away from coalition-building and toward brute force in Chiapas. As the 1910s came to a close, the Constitutionalists grew increasingly ruthless in their treatment of southeastern dissidents of all stripes, but particularly of people and organizations that officials and local elites feared might be susceptible to radical ideologies, and above all to the ever-growing influence of Felipe Carrillo Puerto. In the meantime, outside of Yucatán, relatively little was accomplished when it came to implementing any sort of substantive reform in the Southeast, radical or otherwise.

The Rise of Southeastern Socialism, 1918–1920

As the Constitutionalists grew increasingly brutal in their treatment of southeastern dissidents, many working people and their elite sympathizers across the region were driven into the arms of relative radicals who sought to organize them to push for profound political, social, and economic reforms. Buoyed by this popular support, a new generation of reformers came to power in the region by the early 1920s. They also enjoyed the support of the ascendant Sonoran revolutionary faction in Mexico City. When Obregón became president in 1920, he and Calles found eager allies among long-stymied radicals and revolutionaries across the Southeast, just as they already had in Yucatán.

Felipe Carrillo Puerto served as a powerful inspiration for this new generation of Southeastern Socialists, and was their most important ally. He also embodied the greatest political fears of the elites of the region, with good reason. The privileged classes of Campeche in particular worried that Carrillo Puerto's radicalism might spill over state lines and succeed in politicizing Maya campesinos in their state. Nervous elites of Hecelchakán said so in as many words in 1920, writing to President Obregón after witnessing violent conflicts between Socialists and their antagonists, begging him to prevent "a situation analogous to Yucatán."[65]

---

63 Abud argues that the existence of an independent organization like the UOC in 1915 was much more radical than the UOC's actual demands. Abud, *Campeche: Revolución y movimiento social (1911–1923)*, 52–53.

64 Ibid., 61.

65 AGN-OC, 408-C-18. Gustavo Ortiz and Marcelino Pavón to Obregón, December 7, 1920.

A group of activists and reformers in Campeche founded the Pro-Campeche Political Party (PPPC) in 1919 after they lost hope that Joaquín Mucel's government would pursue meaningful reform.[66] Mucel did not take kindly to organized dissent, and the party's first gubernatorial candidate withdrew under the strain of the official repression he and his supporters faced.[67] The PPPC was also divided from the outset between its members who sought simply to reclaim power from the outsider Constitutionalists, and those who sought to pursue a more ambitious agenda of reform and grassroots organizing.[68] During the 1920 gubernatorial campaign, the PPPC therefore campaigned on promises of education reform and democracy, but purposefully avoided the question of land reform.[69] It was a compromise that proved impossible to sustain in the long-term. In May of 1920 the more radical branch of the party broke away as the Agrarian Socialist Party (PSA), with the intent to address the social and economic ills that the PPPC had declined to prioritize. Then, a few months later, with Felipe Carrillo Puerto and a contingent of Yucatecan Socialists present, a young reformer named Ramón Félix Flores announced the formation of the Pro-Campeche Socialist Agrarian Party as a Campeche-based branch of Carrillo Puerto's Socialist Party of the Southeast. Flores announced that the new party's most important priority was land reform.[70]

Even as Campeche's would-be reformers splintered into factions, elites and members of the state's old political order grew increasingly nervous about the potential arrival of Yucatecan-style radicalism to Campeche. Elites were losing accustomed ground at home, but they still had powerful friends in Mexico City. When a PPPC candidate was elected to the governorship in 1920, Campeche's senators successfully pressured interim President Adolfo de la Huerta to declare the state's powers disappeared in order to impose the more moderate Gonzalo Sales Guerrero as governor in July of 1920.[71] The new governor and his allies did their best to stymie the radicalization of the workers and campesinos of Campeche. By December of 1920, eighty-three Socialists were held in the prison of Hecelchakán, and a hundred more were held by federal forces in the state capital where they were reportedly not being fed. The Campeche Socialists recognized that they were the objects of a sustained campaign of violence

66 On the formation and early days of the PPPC, see Abud, *Campeche: Revolución y movimiento social (1911–1923)*, 64–72. On the proliferation of political parties in Campeche in this period, see Justo Sierra, Gantús Inurreta, and Villanueva, *Breve historia de Campeche*, 205.

67 Justo Sierra, Gantús Inurreta, and Villanueva, *Breve historia de Campeche*, 202–3.

68 Abud Flores, *Campeche: Revolución y movimiento social (1911–1923)*, 64–65. On the formation and character of the PPPC, see also Justo Sierra, Gantús Inurreta, and Villanueva, *Breve historia de Campeche*, 205–6.

69 Abud, *Campeche: Revolución y movimiento social (1911–1923)*, 69.   70 Ibid., 80–81.

71 Ibid., 77–79.

and intimidation that was designed specifically to limit their support among terrorized workers and campesinos, and to politically silence them. "The responsibility lies indisputably with the authorities who systematically trample the political rights of the people," a Campeche Socialist reported to Calles.[72]

More than their counterparts elsewhere in the Southeast, the Socialists of Campeche benefited from the direct support of Carrillo Puerto. This relationship included close supervision of local politics in Campeche by Yucatecan Socialists, as well as occasional direct intervention. Ramón Félix Flores and his collaborators followed the Yucatecan Socialists' model of popular organizing closely as they sought to counterbalance the power of the entrenched political elites with mass mobilization of people who had never before been included in the political process. As in Yucatán, this first and foremost meant courting the support of Maya campesinos, people who had much to gain in joining a fight for political and agrarian reform, and relatively little to lose. Party members all carried red cards, and paid monthly dues of fifty cents.[73] Campeche's ligas de resistencia were closely modeled on the ligas of Yucatán. They sponsored a wide variety of cultural and social events, which were often conducted in both Spanish and Maya. Flores himself also commonly spoke in Maya when visiting rural communities.[74] "The people of the state of Campeche all support the Pro-Campeche Agrarian Socialist Party, and are patiently tolerating the outrages with which the government of the state is victimizing them, but surely they will reach the point of exhaustion," one Socialist warned Calles.[75]

Their allies across the state line were quick to come to their aid. In December of 1920, Governor Sales Guerrero complained to Obregón, only two weeks into his presidency, that hundreds of Yucatecan Socialists armed with machetes had crossed into Campeche with the intent of "generalizing disorder," violating the state's sovereignty in the process.[76] The Sonorans were unmoved by such protestations. Carrillo Puerto had succeeded in convincing Obregón and Calles of the value of his political project, particularly as it became clear that the new generation of Socialist parties in the region were adept at organizing popular support for both

72 FAPECFT-PEC, expediente: 231, ROJAS MORANO, Manuel, legajo 1/1, fojas 1 and 4, inventario 5025. Manuel Rojas Morano to Calles, December 5, 1920.

73 FAPECFT-PEC, expediente: 24, FLORES, Ramón Félix, legajo 2/2, fojas 63–65, inventario 2115. Flores to Calles, November 29, 1923.

74 Abud, *Campeche: Revolución y movimiento social (1911–1923)*, 108–9; José A. Abud, *Después de la revolución: Los caciques y el nuevo estado, Campeche (1923–1943)* (México, D.F.: Universidad Autónoma Metropolitana, 2012), 36–37.

75 FAPECFT-PEC, expediente: 231, ROJAS MORANO, Manuel, legajo 1/1, foja 1, inventario 5025. Manuel Rojas Morano to Calles, December 5, 1920.

76 AGN-OC, 408-C-18. Obregón to Ministry of Interior, December 14, 1920.

local and national candidates.[77] The Sonorans now acted quickly and decisively to support the spread of Socialism across the larger Southeast, and into Campeche in particular. As the landed class fretted over what was to come and pleaded for federal intervention, Obregón's government delayed the state's elections to give the Socialists more time to organize and to prepare a credible gubernatorial campaign for a new election.[78]

When the Socialist candidate Enrique Gómez Briceño appeared to have won the election, Campeche descended into political chaos. From Yucatán, Socialist party president Miguel Cantón accused outgoing governor Gonzalo Sales Guerrero of attempting to impose defeated Liberal candidates for local office over the Socialists who had actually won the popular vote, lodging his protest in the name of 60,000 Yucatecan Socialists.[79] On the governor's orders, municipal presidents denied Socialist legislative candidates the credentials they needed to take office, or simply refused to cede power to Socialist successors to their offices. In Atasta, police imprisoned four Socialist operatives and tampered with ballots.[80] Arrests and violent attacks by local officials against Socialists were also reported in the towns of Pomuch, Tenabo, and Dziblanche.[81] Ramón Félix Flores fumed that with such attacks against his local operatives, the Liberals' goal was none other than to destroy the fundamental principles of the Mexican Revolution.[82]

Calles was losing his patience and issued statements to the national press describing Sales Guerrero's efforts to stifle the political will of the people of Campeche. Under pressure both from Mexico City and from popular forces at home, Sales Guerrero finally accepted the results and allowed the Socialist legislature to be installed, with federal agents in the state testifying as to its democratically elected legitimacy, along with thousands of Socialists who arrived to show their support for their candidates.[83] When Gómez Briceño was finally declared as governor, Socialist Manuel Rojas Morano reported to Calles that he was witnessing "indescribable joy among the previously oppressed people and the surprise of their infamous oppressors."[84] By that time Calles needed no convincing. If his sympathies

77 Of the nearly seven thousand votes cast for Obregón in Campeche, nearly three quarters were by registered members of the PPPC, and the rest by the PLC, which was, strictly speaking, Obregón's party. FAPECFT-FAO, serie: 30300, expediente: 4, CAMPECHE, legajo 1/1, foja 5, inventario 1986. Flores to Obregón, September 10, 1920.

78 Ernest Gruening, *Mexico and Its Heritage* (London: Stanley Paul & Co. Ltd., 1928), 404–5.

79 AGN-OC, 408-C-18. Miguel Cantón to Obregón, December 28, 1920.

80 AGN-OC, 408-C-18. Obregón to Ministry of the Interior, December 31, 1920.

81 AGN-OC, 408-C-18. Fernando Torreblanca to Ministry of the Interior, January 8, 1921.

82 AGN-OC, 408-C-18. Flores to Obregón, December 30, 1920.

83 AGN-OC, 408-C-18. Flores to Obregón, December 27, 1921.

84 FAPECFT-PEC, expediente: 231, ROJAS MORANO, Manuel, legajo 1/1, foja 5, inventario 5025. Manuel Rojas Morano to Calles, January 6, 1921.

in the state were not clear enough already, he made them even more so by personally attending Gómez Briceño's inauguration.[85] It was the beginning of a new era, in which Calles gave substantial, direct support to the Socialists of the Southeast.

In Chiapas, Socialism was led by Carlos Vidal, the Constitutionalist general who briefly served as interim proconsul in Tabasco in 1919. Vidal came from a relatively modest planter family in Pichucalco, on the northwestern frontier of Chiapas. While several of his siblings left Mexico to study abroad, Vidal stayed to manage family properties, and later, to join the Mexican Revolution. He led a local Constitutionalist faction in his hometown in 1913, and left Chiapas to join the Constitutionalist army later that year.[86] He rose rapidly in its ranks, leaving behind a wife and children that he only saw rarely thereafter. Highly articulate and passionate about reform, for the next fifteen years, Vidal became Chiapas' best hope for a reformist movement that came even close to approximating the one in Yucatán. Conspicuously influenced by both Alvarado and Carrillo Puerto as he circulated through various military and political postings across the Southeast, by 1920 Vidal had become a self-described Socialist. As the Mapache insurgency wore on, and with no opportunity or incentive to collaborate with the Constitutionalist state government, opposition leaders and organizers in Chiapas reached out to Vidal, who was both sympathetic and eager to build a base of popular support in his home state in preparation for a gubernatorial campaign. Still stationed in Tabasco, in 1919 Vidal authorized the political organizer Ricardo Alfonso Paniagua to found political clubs in his name, to coordinate among his allies in the state, and to run a propaganda campaign on his behalf.[87]

The merging of Paniagua's grassroots organizing with Vidal's national political connections was the genesis of Socialism in Chiapas. It was formalized with the founding of the Chiapas Socialist Party in January of 1920 by Paniagua, agronomist Raymundo Enríquez, and Ismael Mendoza of the Michoacán Socialist Party, with support and encouragement from Vidal, who immediately became the party's first gubernatorial candidate.[88] The party's constitution followed the example of Yucatecan Socialism in many respects. It called for land reform, labor reform, including a maximum workday and a minimum wage, social and political equality for women, and participation of the party in all electoral campaigns to elect

85   Abud, *Campeche: Revolución y movimiento social (1911–1923)*, 87–88.
86   Trens, *Vidal y Chiapas*, 55.
87   AGN-CAV c.4, t.2, f.10. Vidal to Paniagua. Undated, but most likely from November/December of 1919.
88   Benjamin, *A Rich Land, a Poor People*, 139–40. AGN-CAV c.6, f.13. Vidal to Raul Pola Muñoa, January 18, 1921.

Photograph 2.1 General Carlos A. Vidal, c. 1917
Source: Archivo General de la Nación, Colección Carlos A. Vidal. Sección: Asuntos
personales, serie: fotografías personales y familiares, caja 3, sobre: 2, foto: 13.

representatives of the working class.[89] Unlike in Yucatán, in Chiapas there
had been no groundwork laid by the Constitutionalists for undertaking
such an ambitious program of reform. Nor did the Chiapas Socialists
benefit from the extensive, direct intervention of the Yucatecan Socialists
that their counterparts in Campeche did. Nevertheless, in the years that
followed, Vidal and Paniagua transformed the Chiapas Socialist Party into
a statewide political organization, supported by Carrillo Puerto at the
regional level, and by Calles in Mexico City.[90]

In these same years, another ambitious young radical was rising through
the political ranks in Tabasco. From a wealthy, landowning family, Tomás
Garrido Canabal was raised on the Tabasco-Chiapas border, and educated

89   Spenser, *El partido socialista chiapaneco*, 183–84.
90   AGN-CAV, c.6, f.13. Vidal to Raul Pola Muñoa, January 18, 1921.

across the Southeast, finally earning a law degree in Campeche.[91] In 1916, he was appointed as the head of the legal department of Múgica's Constitutionalist government in Tabasco. He was rapidly promoted within the state's department of justice.[92] He was also appointed to the committee assigned to revise the state's legal codes, making him privy to the inner, workaday processes of Múgica's efforts to reform Tabasco's political system.[93] This included Múgica's efforts at "moralization": It seems likely that Garrido had a hand in drafting the governor's anti-alcohol statute.[94] Garrido also briefly worked for Alvarado's government in Yucatán. Felipe Carrillo Puerto regarded the ambitious young bureaucrat to be of "good faith," in his words, if not yet a close ally.[95] Garrido was strongly influenced by the Yucatecan Socialists' system of ligas de resistencia, but the balance that both Alvarado and Múgica struck between strong-arm politics and reform was also of critical importance to his political formation.[96]

Garrido took the political reins in Tabasco for the first time in 1919, briefly serving as interim governor when a state election devolved into a chaotic impasse. By then he had joined the Tabasco Radical Party, which was gaining popular support by that time. Like their counterparts elsewhere in the Southeast, the Tabasco Radicals were also working to forge alliances with the Sonorans, and were campaigning for Obregón's presidential candidacy.[97] Obregón's triumph in 1920 solidified the Radicals' growing importance in the state, but it was not enough to win them control of the state government. In 1920, as factional strife in Tabasco continued unabated, the state's powers were declared "disappeared" by the Senate along with those of numerous other states, as a means of purging Carranza's allies from state governments.[98] As in many other states in this period,

91 AGN-DGIPS, c. 171, exp. 12. Report on Garrido by Agent 18, October 15, 1924. See also Kristin A. Harper, "Tomás Garrido Canabal of Tabasco: Road Building and Revolutionary Reform," in *State Governors in the Mexican Revolution, 1910–1952: Portraits in Conflict, Courage, and Corruption*, ed. Jürgen Buchenau and William H. Beezley (Lanham, MD: Rowman & Littlefield Publishers, 2009), 110–11.

92 AGN-TGC, c. 1, exp. 8. Appointment letter to head of the legal department, January 10, 1916. Appointment letter as interim district attorney ("fiscal"), May 6, 1916.

93 AGN-TGC, c. 1, exp. 8. Appointment letter to the Junta of Code Revision, July 22, 1916.

94 AGN-TGC, c. 1, exp. 8. Two copies of Múgica's anti-alcohol decree are among Garrido's papers, one of which was corrected and revised by hand.

95 FAPECFT-FAO, fondo: 11, serie: 30400, expediente: 135: CARRILLO PUERTO, Felipe, legajo 1/1, foja 9, inventario 2151. Carrillo Puerto to Obregón, July 21, 1920.

96 As Martínez Assad has underscored, Múgica's government in Tabasco, despite its brevity, was the foundation upon which Garrido's political machine would later be built. Martínez Assad, *El laboratorio de la revolución*, 156.

97 FAPECFT-FAO, fondo: 11, serie: 30100, expediente: M-031 452, MARTINEZ DE ESCOBAR, Rafael (Lic.), legajo 1/1, foja 3, inventario 1522. Rafael Martínez de Escobar to Obregón, July 26, 1919.

98 The Plan de Agua Prieta withdrew recognition from the governments of Guanajuato, Nuevo León, Queréraro, San Luis Potosí, and Tamaulipas. On Mexico's constitutional clause empowering the

different factions in Tabasco recognized different governors and different state legislatures, ultimately leaving it to the federal government to sort out which was legal (and/or most favorable to its interests). Under pressure from Calles and Obregón, the Senate agreed to recognize Tomás Garrido Canabal as interim governor.[99] After so many years of turmoil, Tabasco was now in the hands of a dedicated reformer who had the strong support of the President and Secretary of the Interior, who was increasingly hailed by supporters as the person who might finally be able to put revolutionary principles into practice in Tabasco. One partisan presciently suggested to Garrido in 1919 that this might be accomplished not by violence, but by the elimination of any participation by counterrevolutionary elements in the political process.[100]

Southeastern Socialism in Practice, 1920–1923

As Socialism spread across the Southeast from 1920 onward, it became evident that Felipe Carrillo Puerto's model of grassroots organizing and party building was highly adaptable to local circumstances. The form that Socialism ultimately took in Campeche, Chiapas, and Tabasco depended on the priorities of the leadership of the Socialist parties in each place, which were driven by locally specific considerations, as well as the personalities of the individuals in question.

Of all of the states of the Southeast, Carrillo Puerto was most directly involved with helping to build the Socialist party of Campeche. Even so, the state's Socialist party was never as successful or powerful as its counterparts elsewhere in the region. Even with the strong support of Calles and Carrillo Puerto, Socialist governor Enrique Gómez Briceño faced formidable political challenges once he finally took office in 1921. He did so as a member of a Socialist party that had only recently been created, in a state in which any political consensus was painfully difficult to achieve. Liberals and landowners had only accepted his election under duress and with the direct intervention of the federal government. They now remained in active opposition to the Socialist takeover of the state government, and still had the ears of powerful friends and allies in Mexico City. Equally problematic, the new governor did not benefit from a unified cohort of allies, as

federal Senate to "disappear" the powers of states, see Manuel González Oropeza, *La intervención federal en la desaparición de poderes* (México, D.F.: Universidad Nacional Autónoma de México, Instituto de Investigaciones Jurídicas, 1983). On the pattern of state electoral crises and disappearances of powers in the 1920s, see Sarah Osten, "Trials by Fire: National Political Lessons from Failed State Elections in Post-Revolutionary Mexico, 1920–1925," *Mexican Studies/Estudios Mexicanos* 29, no. 1 (2013).

99   Canudas, *Tropico rojo, Vol. 1*, 1, 29–30.
100   AGN-TGC, c. 1, exp. 11. Felipe Bueno to Garrido, March 7, 1919.

reform-minded politicians in Campeche remained deeply divided over questions of ideology and political strategy. Lastly, while the Campeche Socialists had made great strides in organizing a popular base in the lead-up to the election, this was still very much a work in progress.

Gómez Briceño was understandably nervous about the political cards he had been dealt. He was plainly sympathetic to the demands of Campeche's workers, writing to Calles that he recognized that workers' demands were sincere and driven only by their desire to improve their situations, even when they were impossible to meet. But he worried in the same letter that local Socialists failed to understand the larger goals of Socialism, and instead took their new empowerment at the local level as an opportunity to take maximum advantage of their newfound authority. He also expressed his concern that agrarian reform would be extremely difficult without agricultural modernization.[101] Still, he forged ahead with his efforts to redistribute and restore lands to campesinos in the state.[102]

His shaky coalition was soon tested. In May of 1921, Campeche's railroad and port workers went on strike, protesting sixteen-hour workdays for extremely meager wages and seeking to make the most of the Socialists' electoral triumph.[103] The strikers described the Socialist Party's role as the local mechanism of enforcement of the 1917 Constitution and urged President Obregón to intercede on their behalf, so that "the promises of the Revolution will not be illusory."[104] The striking workers had the active support of their counterparts in Yucatán, who responded by boycotting the transport of cargo from Yucatán to the commercial houses in Campeche that were in conflict with the Socialists there.[105] This solidarity effectively paralyzed commerce on the Yucatecan peninsula during the summer of 1921 as the train service was repeatedly interrupted.[106]

Gómez Briceño's dilemma in the face of the strike provides a window into the difficult balance that Socialism embodied in its very nature as a principally elite-led movement that was dedicated to popular organizing, at least in the abstract, dependent on national political patronage, and under constant attack from wealthy, counterrevolutionary adversaries.

101 FAPECFT-PEC, expediente: 93, GOMEZ B., Enrique, legajo 1/1, fojas 1–2, inventario 2405. Enrique Gómez B. to Calles, April 28, 1921.
102 FAPECFT-PEC, expediente: 93, GOMEZ B., Enrique, legajo 1/1, foja 11, inventario 2405. Enrique Gómez B. to Soledad González, June 23, 1921.
103 AGN-OC, 407-C-6. Enrique Gómez B. to Obregón, June 6, 1921. AGN-G3, 407-C-6. Carrillo Puerto to Obregón, June 4, 1921. See also Silvia Teresa Marcial Gutiérrez, *Los tranvías: Un medio de transporte y su importancia social, económica, cultural, política y en la traza urbana de la ciudad de Campeche (1883–1938)* (Campeche, Campeche: Universidad Autónoma de Campeche, 2002), 106–7.
104 AGN-OC, 407-C-6. R. Castillo F. to Obregón, June 2, 1921.
105 AGN-OC, 407-C-6. Rafael Zubarán Capmany to Fernando Torreblanca, June 24, 1921.
106 AGN-OC, 407-C-6. Alejandro Mange to Obregón, June 4, 1921.

The Campeche port strike also illustrates the immense challenge Socialists faced in achieving a functional political consensus, even among workers that Socialist reforms were meant to benefit. The embattled governor established a labor tribunal in the state, which he proudly claimed had helped the workers of Campeche to unionize in order to claim their rights that had long been violated. He reiterated that he understood his mission to be to make revolutionary promises into tangible realities for the people of Campeche.[107] But not all workers in the state saw it that way. As the strike wore on, port workers who didn't belong to ligas de resistencia complained that they were no longer allowed to pick up or deliver cargo for the United Railroad of Yucatán if they didn't have Socialist party credentials.[108] Employers complained that the governor not only forced them to accept the unionization of their workers, but that he also insisted that only Socialist liga members be hired.[109] The railroad companies were incensed at the prospect of finding themselves at the mercy of the state's labor tribunals and the ligas de resistencia that were supported by the governor.[110] Former governor Sales Guerrero snidely remarked that the Yucatecan Socialist Party had been installed in the governor's mansion of Campeche.[111]

The Yucatecan Socialists did become involved. Carrillo Puerto urged Obregón to protect the Socialist workers of Campeche from any federal military interference in their strike, and reminded him that the workers' demands were perfectly in line with article 123 of the 1917 Constitution, which guaranteed them an eight-hour workday.[112] But Carrillo Puerto conspicuously treaded carefully, well aware that the Socialists' obstruction of trade was potentially contributing to the ongoing economic crisis on the peninsula. He was also careful not to allow the situation to imperil his relationship to Calles or Obregón. A booming henequen economy on the peninsula in the 1910s had been Salvador Alvarado's most important leverage with Carranza, and enabled him to carry out the reforms that he did in Yucatán. As the henequen economy collapsed in the 1920s, the Socialists' carefully crafted alliances with the Sonorans were their singularly most important political lifeline. Carrillo Puerto promised Obregón and Minister of Finance Adolfo de la Huerta that the Socialists would do anything necessary to resolve the peninsula's economic crisis.[113]

107 AGN-OC, 407-C-6. Enrique Gómez B. to Obregón, June 2, 1921; Enrique Gómez B. to Obregón, June 3, 1921.
108 AGN-OC, 407-C-6. Rosario Conde to Obregón, July 7, 1921.
109 AGN-OC, 407-C-6. Francisco A. Ortiz and J. MacGregor to Obregón, June 5, and June 9, 1921.
110 AGN-OC, 407-C-6. Francisco A. Ortiz to Obregón, June 1, 1921.
111 AGN-OC, 407-C-6. Gonzalo Sales Guerrero to Obregón, June 1, 1921.
112 AGN-OC, 407-C-6. Carrillo Puerto to Obregón, June 4, 1921.
113 AGN-OC, 407-C-6. Carrillo Puerto to Obregón, September 28, 1921.

The strike finally ended in disappointment for the workers, with few significant concessions made by the companies, other than respect for the federally mandated maximum workday.[114] In part, the strike failed because the Socialists were divided on strategy, with party president Ramón Félix Flores and the governor at odds over how to most effectively confront the intransigent companies on behalf of the workers.[115] One of the strike's lasting effects was therefore to corrode the fragile alliance that had brought Gómez Briceño to power. Won over by the more radical Flores, the Socialist base began to protest openly against the governor, including for not having been decisive enough in his confrontations with landowners over the question of agrarian reform.[116] Flores argued that the governor had failed to fulfill his responsibility to promote laws and policies favorable to the working classes. Finally, Gómez Briceño resigned in August of 1921. Flores was elected as his replacement and took office in November.[117]

As the Socialists repudiated their own governor, their enemies sensed an opportunity. From Mexico City, Campeche's Liberal senators pushed for another disappearance of the state's powers, as they had successfully done in 1920.[118] But the political times had changed. In spite of their differences with each other, the Campeche Socialists had still made impressive strides in assembling a coalition. Municipal presidents, ligas de resistencia, union leaders, and local Socialist parties across Campeche vociferously protested, arguing that such a move would critically undermine the sovereignty of the state, legitimately elected institutions and the hard-won political rights of Campeche's voters.[119] "The workers will not consent to the criminal attack on the rights of the people of Campeche," the president of the liga de resistencia of Calkini indignantly wrote to the president, in the name of 2,000 Socialists in his district.[120] Campeche labor leaders expressed their fear that if popular sovereignty were allowed to be so grievously violated, it would never be re-attained.[121] A Socialist party leader from the coastal town of Lerma put it bluntly: "the people of Campeche have forever broken the dictatorial and praetorian regimes and are not disposed to yield to a group of corrupt politicians taking shelter under the wings of the

114 Justo Sierra, Gantús Inurreta, and Villanueva, *Breve historia de Campeche*, 209. Abud, *Campeche: Revolución y movimiento social (1911–1923)*, 98–99.
115 Marcial Gutiérrez, *Los tranvías*, 107–10.
116 Abud, *Campeche: Revolución y movimiento social (1911–1923)*, 91–92.   117 Ibid., 102–3.
118 AGN-OC, 408-C-18. Alejo Aguilar to Obregón, December 21, 1921.
119 See, for instance, E. Ortegón, Municipal President of Hecelchakán, to Álvaro Obregón, December 21, 1921. This included Campeche's Liga Feminista. AGN-G3, 408-C-18. Lucia Cortti de Curmina to Obregón, December 23, 1921.
120 AGN-OC, 408-C-18. Luis G. Arcila to Obregón, December 22, 1921.
121 AGN-OC, 408-C-18. Liga de Carretilleros to Obregón, December 23, 1921.

Senate."[122] The Socialists' message was clear: They would not consent to a return to the politics as usual of pre-revolutionary days, in which the popular will could be summarily trumped by the whims of elites in Mexico City. And this time, the popular will could be channeled through the institutional structures of the Socialist Party to effectively challenge top-down meddling in state politics, even by the state's own federal legislators.

Campeche's sovereignty became something of a cause célèbre across Mexico. From Mérida the PSS leadership protested the disappearance of powers proposal in the name of all of the Socialists of Yucatán, Campeche, Tabasco, and the territory of Quintana Roo, as an illegal and unjustifiable contravention of Campeche's sovereignty.[123] Politicians elsewhere agreed, and the state legislatures of México, Michoacán, Nayarit, Querétaro, and Veracruz all lodged similar complaints with Obregón's government.[124] So did Adalberto Tejeda, the radical governor of Veracruz, and the Worker's Party of Veracruz, in the name of its 15,000 members.[125] The Mexican Labor Party (PLM) also submitted a protest in support of Campeche's Socialist state government.[126]

Faced with this onslaught of protest, Obregón reassured the Socialists and their allies that the Senate was sure to reconsider the disappearance of powers measure once he had provided its members with further information about the "true situation" in the state.[127] The Campeche Liberals were rebuffed and the Socialist state government retained federal recognition. But the standoff over the state's sovereignty had plainly hit a nerve across Mexico. At stake was whether or not the popular will at the state and local levels would be respected by the federal government in the postrevolutionary era. The southeastern Socialists ceaselessly sought to build political relationships that extended from their grassroots bases all the way to the President and back again, channeled and managed by their political parties. By 1923, the system appeared to be working. For the moment, Campeche's landed elites and their Liberal allies were defeated.

As governor, Flores was adamant that his Socialist government represented the interests of all of Campeche's citizens, and that he sought

122 AGN-OC, 408-C-18. Federico Aguilar to Obregón, December 23, 1921.
123 AGN-OC, 408-C-18. Miguel Cantón to Obregón, December 22, 1921.
124 AGN-OC, 408-C-18. Raymundo R. Cartena and Clemente Trueba to Obregón, 31 December 1921 (México). J. I. Lugo to Obregón, December 30, 1921 (Michoacán). [illegible] to Obregón, January 28, 1922 (Nayarit). J. T. Obregón et al. to Obregón, December 30, 1921 (Querétaro). Angel [illegible] to Obregón, December 29, 1921 (Veracruz). Carrillo Puerto and Miguel Cantón to Obregón, December 23, 1921 (Yucatán).
125 AGN-OC, 408-C-18. Adalberto Tejeda to Obregón, December 27, 1921. Leonardo Altamirano to Obregón, December 29, 1921.
126 AGN-OC, 408-C-18. Ricardo Treviño to Obregón, December 27, 1921.
127 AGN-OC, 408-C-18. Obregón to Ramón Martínez, December 26, 1921.

a sustainable and productive balance between the interests of business owners and the wealthy, and the working class and the poor. After just a few months in office, he proudly claimed to have achieved this. "We have harmonized the interests of Capital and Labor, and now they help and respect one another," he wrote to Obregón. He insisted that the only challenge that remained in Campeche was economic, rather than political.[128] In his first annual gubernatorial address, Flores reported that his government had redistributed 13,525 hectares of farmland to communities in need.[129] Flores also estimated that 80 percent of Campeche's workforce was unionized by that time.

Even with such a majority, Flores conceded that tensions still ran high between unionized and "free" workers.[130] Further, as in Yucatán, Liberal-aligned municipal presidents who had held onto their offices frequently clashed with Campeche's Socialist leadership and rank and file. Socialist candidates for local offices were still routinely threatened as local authorities attempted to impose Liberals in the offices in question.[131] On the other side, non-Socialist workers insisted that they were in the vast majority in Campeche, and that they were being brutally persecuted by the Socialist government.[132] Flores defended himself, writing to Obregón: "It is the responsibility of the government that I lead to provide guarantees to all of society, but its main function is to contribute to the improvement of the [situation of the] laboring classes, when they ask for all that our laws promise to them."[133]

Faced with ongoing infighting among his partisans and ongoing confrontations with Liberals and elites, Flores had an invaluable ally in Felipe Carrillo Puerto. At the Yucatecan Socialist congress at Izamal in 1921, the party's collaboration with Socialists across the Southeast was formalized, with the creation of a Federal Council that would consist of leaders from the Liga Central of each state that now belonged to the PSS, while stipulating that the Liga Central of Yucatán would serve as the parent organization of all of the local ligas across the region. The president of the PSS, who was also the president of the Liga Central, was also to be the president of the Federal Council, and was given veto power over the resolutions of the latter body. While the ligas of each state were to have sovereignty in the choosing of their candidates for local political offices, the Federal Council, led by

128   AGN-OC, 408-C-15. Flores to Obregón, May 5, 1922.
129   Abud, *Campeche: Revolución y movimiento social (1911–1923)*, 106.
130   FAPECFT-PEC, expediente: 24, FLORES, Ramón Félix, legajo 1/2, foja 4, inventario 2115. Flores to Calles, December 1, 1921.
131   AGN-OC, 408-C-18. Miguel Cantón to Obregón, December 27, 1921.
132   AGN-OC, 408-C-18. C. Góngora G. to Obregón, January 12, 1922.
133   AGN-OC, 407-C-6. Flores to Obregón, January 26, 1922.

Carrillo Puerto, was given control over the nomination of presidential candidates by the PSS as a whole.[134]

All told, this was a significantly large amount of political territory: The four states (Campeche, Chiapas, Tabasco, and Yucatán) and one federal territory (Quintana Roo) in question constituted over 12 percent of the area of Mexico (roughly 92,255 square miles). Carrillo Puerto was also in communication with and submitted petitions to Calles on behalf of organized workers in Veracruz, and in 1921 he claimed that his allies there would also soon be formally affiliated with the PSS.[135] It was Carrillo Puerto's relationships to the Sonorans that enabled the Yucatecan Socialists' sometimes blatant violations of the sovereignty of neighboring states. Calles and Obregón did not just tacitly accept Carrillo's political incursions into other states of the region.[136] Convinced that they stood only to gain from Carrillo Puerto's consolidation of a regional Socialist movement in the Southeast, the Sonorans facilitated his regional political project in ways large and small.[137]

Carrillo Puerto represented the interests of Socialists in both Campeche and Yucatán during his legislative term, often submitting petitions to the Chamber of Deputies in the name of the Socialist parties of both states.[138] Carrillo Puerto and Flores also jointly submitted petitions to federal ministries and described their respective political parties as collectively representing all of the communities of the entire peninsula.[139] This was an expression of solidarity, but also a question of survival, as both states faced a crippling economic crisis as henequen prices plummeted following World War I and their economies relied heavily on federal subsidies. The closeness of the relationships between the Socialists of both states and the Secretary of the Interior became even more important as the economic crisis wore on. Carrillo Puerto argued to Calles that together,

---

134 Rico, *La huelga de junio* (vol. 1), 109–11.

135 FAPECFT-PEC, expediente: 25, CARRILLO PUERTO, Felipe, legajo 1/7, foja 26, inventario 830. Carrillo Puerto to Calles, May 4, 1921. On Veracruz joining the PSS: AGN-TGC, c. 3, expediente 9. Carrillo Puerto to Garrido, April 14, 1921.

136 See, for instance, Calles' endorsement of Carrillo Puerto's electoral organizing efforts in Quintana Roo: FAPECFT-PEC, expediente: 25, CARRILLO PUERTO, Felipe, legajo 3/7, foja 150, inventario 830. Calles to Carrillo Puerto, March 31, 1921.

137 Sometimes their support was a matter of everyday logistics. In 1921 Obregón ordered that Carrillo Puerto be given a discounted rate for his telegrams to and from Yucatán, Campeche, and Chiapas as a political representative of all three states, subsequently adding Tabasco. AGN-OC, c. 367, expediente: 824-C-2. Obregón to Carrillo Puerto, January 12, 1921.

138 See, for example, "Diario de los Debates de la Cámara de Diputados." Legislatura XXIX – Año I – Período Ordinario – November 4, 1920 – Número de Diario 59.

139 FAPECFT-PEC, expediente: 25, CARRILLO PUERTO, Felipe, legajo 1/7, foja 6, inventario 830. Carrillo Puerto and Flores to Ing. Antonio I. Villareal, Srio. de Fomento, February 19, 1921.

Campeche and Yucatán constituted both the vanguard and the rearguard of Mexican Socialism.[140]

The Chiapas Socialists also had Carrillo Puerto's support, but never as directly as their counterparts in Campeche. The Chiapas Socialist Party also departed from the Yucatecan model in its organizational structure, as the only southeastern Socialist party that had no *ligas de resistencia*. Instead, it relied on preexisting political organizations as its local subsidiaries. In his capacity as Vidal's chief political organizer, Ricardo Alfonso Paniagua's first order of business was therefore to unite all of the scattered sympathetic political clubs, parties, and individuals that supported Vidal behind a singular political program, in lieu of building *ligas* from scratch. These groups were politically diverse, geographically dispersed, and frequently at odds among themselves over the slates of candidates that they supported at the local level.[141] Many reform-minded parties and political clubs had formed independently at the community level across Chiapas during the 1910s.[142] They were united in their distaste for the Mapaches, but heterogeneous in the political labels they chose for themselves (including "radical," "popular," "democratic," and "liberal"). They were also accustomed to their independence and had never been confederated within a larger organization. Channeling all of the various local interests that were frequently united only in their support of Vidal's gubernatorial candidacy was a monumental task, and Paniagua openly expressed his exasperation at the internecine conflict he confronted in his organizing work.[143]

The Chiapas Socialists' organizational efforts were both complicated and catalyzed by the fact that six years after the Mapache rebellion began, Chiapas was still at war. By that time, it was clear that compromises would have to be made on all sides to achieve peace. In the end, it was only their shared distaste for Carranza's efforts to govern the state from the outside that enabled the warring local factions to find some common ground. In February of 1920, Vidal agreed to recognize the Mapache leader Tiburcio Fernández Ruiz as head of a singular "revolutionary" movement in Chiapas, to incorporate his own forces into the Mapache-led División

140 FAPECFT-PEC, expediente 25: CARRILLO PUERTO, Felipe, legajo 2/7, fojas 136–37, inventario 830. Carrillo Puerto to Calles, February 20, 1922.

141 By early 1920, the Vidalista network included the Partido Popular de Chiapas, based in San Cristóbal, the Partido Radical Chiapaneco de Chiapa de Corzo, the Club Liberal "Union y Trabajo" in Tapachula, and the Club Benito Juárez in Pichucalco, to name a few, along with various otherwise nameless Vidalista clubs across the state. See AGN-CAV, c.6, f.5.

142 See, for example, the founding of the Constitutionalist club "Francisco I. Madero" in Comitán: AHSDN-W, Operaciones Militares, Chiapas, 1917. XI/481.5/54. Francisco Domínguez to Carranza, June 28, 1917.

143 AGN-CAV c.4, t.2, f.10. Paniagua to Vidal, December 24, 1919.

Libre de Chiapas, and to unite with the Mapaches in support of Obregón's anticipated effort to overthrow Carranza.[144] This was a secret, backroom deal; publicly, Vidal continued to assure Carranza of his loyal support, and to campaign for Carranza's chosen presidential successor, Ignacio Bonillas.[145] Finally, just days before Carranza's overthrow and assassination, Vidal signed a joint statement along with various Mapache generals, declaring that, like all other tyrants, Carranza must fall.[146]

As Vidal tried to play both sides of the political field, Fernández Ruiz acted decisively, brokering further deals for himself and the Mapaches. He was able to do so because pacifying Chiapas remained the Constitutionalists' priority there. In March, the Mapache leader and new interim Governor, Alejo González, declared a ceasefire and embarked on peace negotiations. Fernández Ruiz also reached out to the ascendant Sonorans. In exchange for abandoning his demand for the removal of all federal troops from Chiapas, Fernández Ruiz won the promise of formal incorporation of the Mapache forces into the federal army should Obregón triumph over Carranza.[147] When the Agua Prieta rebellion succeeded, Fernández Ruiz was further rewarded with Obregón's endorsement for the governorship. By coopting the Mapache counterrevolution, Obregón brought Chiapas into the national political fold in a way that Carranza never did by fighting against them. Carlos Vidal had been outplayed, and on June 1, he renounced his gubernatorial candidacy.[148]

Obregón's choice of Fernández Ruiz as Chiapas' new governor in 1920 pacified the state at long last, but it wasn't a solution that was built to last. The Mapaches had risen in rebellion against Carranza's violation of Chiapas' sovereignty and, by extension, their political autonomy, and once in power they treated the state as a Mapache fiefdom. Fernández Ruiz soon became notorious for his willingness to contravene local and federal laws to advance his own interests, provoking several armed rebellions against his government.[149] One federal agent reported that the governor was preoccupied chiefly with the crushing of any opposition political parties that arose

144 Fideicomiso Archivos Plutarco Elías Calles y Fernando Torreblanca, Archivo Fernando Torreblanca (hereafter denoted as FAPECFT-AFT), fondo 11, serie 30500, expediente 423, DIVISION LIBRE DE CHIAPAS, legajo 1/1, foja 16, inventario 3298. Text of agreement between Vidal and Fernández Ruiz. February 8, 1920.

145 AGN-CAV, c.4, t.2, f.4. Vidal to Carranza, April 16, 1920.

146 AGN-CAV, c. 6, f. 4. Open letter to the people of Chiapas from the "Revolutionary Forces of the State." May 8, 1920.

147 Benjamin, *A Rich Land, a Poor People*, 141. On Obregón's pattern of accommodation and collaboration with conservative governors and caudillos, including Fernández Ruiz, see Benjamin, "Laboratories of the New State," 72–73. See also Fowler-Salamini, "De-Centering the 1920s," 291–92.

148 AGN-CAV c.1. Vidal to Paniagua, June 1, 1920.

149 AGN-DGIPS, c. 192, Exp. 17, fojas 1–3. Report by Agent 6, October 22, 1924.

in the state.[150] By another account, he employed thugs and assassins that he sent after his opponents.[151] The Mapache leader was also accused of helping himself to a substantial share of a fifteen thousand peso monthly federal subsidy for the upkeep of the tracks of the Pan-American Railroad that crossed Chiapas.[152] By the time he left office in 1924, employees of the state government hadn't been paid in a year.[153] And while Fernández Ruiz was in power, reform was effectively out of the question. The Mapaches rebelled against the imposition of revolutionary reform and saw no reason to change course. Instead, the governor issued a land law in 1921 that was designed to protect landowners from expropriation.[154] The routine abuses of power, unapologetic corruption, and persecution of political enemies by Fernández Ruiz's government crystallized a diverse opposition movement across Chiapas, as the state's politics became polarized between Fernández Ruiz and the Mapaches on one side, and Carlos Vidal and the Socialists on the other.

Obregón may have readily abandoned the Chiapas Socialists in favor of peace and political expediency, but Calles wasn't ready to do so. Following his gubernatorial defeat Vidal received orders from Calles that he was to come to Mexico City along with the troops under his command.[155] Vidal spent the next few years there, and was promoted to a series of increasingly prominent positions within the Ministry of War, attaining the rank of General de Brigada in 1922.[156] But he did not give up his work back home. Days after the Mapache leader took power, an undeterred Vidal wrote to a supporter in Tonalá, "the salvation of our state will be the formation of a Great Socialist Party of Chiapas."[157] The Socialists there counted on Calles' support, and believed that his intervention on their behalf would be their only political hope.[158]

150 AGN-DGIPS, c. 175, Exp. 5, fojas 2–5. Report by Manuel Cervantes, May 26, 1924.
151 Trens, *Vidal y Chiapas*, 38.   152 Gruening, *Mexico and Its Heritage*, 406.
153 Congreso de la Unión, "Diario de los Debates de la Cámara de Senadores del Congreso de la República Méxicana, 1875–1984," www.senado.gob.mx/index.php?watch=13&mn=3. Año I, XXXI Legislatura. Tomo I, núm. 54. December 18, 1924.
154 María Eugenia Reyes Ramos, *El reparto de tierras y la política agraria en Chiapas, 1914–1988* (México: Universidad Nacional Autónoma de México, Centro de Investigaciones Humanísticas de Mesoamérica y del Estado de Chiapas, 1992), 48–49. Robert Wasserstrom found that Fernández Ruiz created nine ejidos, principally in order to quell labor unrest among coffee workers organized by the Socialists. Wasserstrom, *Class and Society in Central Chiapas*, 160.
155 AHSDN, XI/111/3–1838, Vidal, Carlos A., Tomo 1, foja 115. Calles to Vidal, June 15, 1920.
156 In 1921 he was appointed by Obregón the Jefe del Departamento del Estado Mayor de la Secretaría de Guerra y Marina. AHSDN, XI/111/3–1838, Vidal, Carlos A., Tomo 2, foja 282. Next, he served as the Jefe de Oficialía Mayor at the Ministry of War. AGN-CAV, c.6, f.2. "Datos Biográficos del General de Brigada Carlos A. Vidal," May 1944. A year later he was promoted to General de Brigada. AHSDN, XI/111/3–1838, Vidal, Carlos A., Tomo 1, foja 49.
157 AGN-CAV c.3. Vidal to Cesareo J. Antonio, November 20, 1920.
158 AGN-CAV, c. 6, f. 12. Lizandro Villafuerte to Vidal, November 29, 1921.

This was a period in which Vidal began to reflect on what he understood Socialism to mean. His rhetoric from this period reveals a more pronounced radicalism, suggestive of Carrillo Puerto's influence on him. He wrote to a supporter in Tuxtla Chico, "My wish is that very soon our working class be entirely unionized, so that we can seize power from Capital, for the day that the first workers' strike takes place in this state, the magnates will tremble."[159] Like Carrillo Puerto, Vidal was a nationalist who saw Mexican Socialism as part of an international movement, but insisted that it be implemented by Mexicans on their own terms. He wrote to a partisan that "Socialism is the future of the nations of the world, and before we are swept away by this global movement, we should go out to greet it. For it would be very sad if we should wait for this wave of evolution to come to us from elsewhere, when we have men who are capable of guiding our own destiny."[160]

The early 1920s was a period of development and consolidation for the Chiapas Socialist Party. The party dispatched agents to coffee plantations with the goal of organizing the workers and helping them in confrontations with their employers, initially with limited success, and provoking the consternation of the Mapache state government. In 1922, the Socialists, along with the CROM-affiliated Soconusco Union of Workers and Peasants, organized a strike by thousands of coffee workers, which succeeded in winning them some important concessions from planters.[161] Ricardo Alfonso Paniagua's grassroots political organizational efforts also began to pay off as he perfected his ground strategy. Paniagua personally traveled across the state and nominated delegates of the Socialist Party in each municipality who were then responsible for further recruiting and organizing within their own communities.[162] Letters poured in to Vidal from supporters across Chiapas, offering their support and detailing their involvement with the party, and often describing having been personally recruited by Paniagua.[163]

Felipe Carrillo Puerto counted on Vidal eventually coming into power in Chiapas to help him further Socialism as a regional movement in the Southeast.[164] For his part, Vidal understood cooperation with Carrillo Puerto and the PSS to be instrumental to furthering both his own political objectives in Chiapas and Socialism in the larger region, and the two

---

159 AGN-CAV, c.3. Vidal to Arturo M. Álvarez, December 15, 1920.

160 AGN-CAV, c.6, f.13. Vidal to Pablo Quiñones, December 16, 1920.

161 Benjamin, *A Rich Land, a Poor People*, 153–54.

162 AGN-CAV c.5, t.2, f.A. Pablo Quiñones to Vidal, April 6, 1921. See also CAV c.6, f.8. Pablo Quiñones to Vidal, March 24, 1922.

163 See, for example, AGN-CAV, c. 1, t. 2. Catarino Ramos to Vidal, December 19, 1922.

164 In October of 1920, Vidal's brother Amilcar wrote to him to report that Carrillo Puerto had assured him that Vidal would soon come to power in Chiapas. AGN-CAV c.1, f.2. Amilcar Vidal to Carlos Vidal, October 11, 1920.

Socialists were actively collaborating by the end of 1920.[165] Leaders of the PSS in Yucatán worked to support and protect their counterparts in Chiapas, including intervention with President Obregón in the summer of 1921 to protect Paniagua when he was arrested by the Mapache government for "intolerable behavior," which allegedly included firing his pistol in the air while shouting "long live the Bolsheviks."[166] In 1923 Carrillo Puerto lobbied Calles to replace Fernández Ruiz with Vidal, underscoring that "all of the Socialist elements of the region are calling for it."[167] By that time, even small, local political parties in rural Chiapas were declaring their direct affiliation with the PSS, suggesting both the breadth and the depth of Carrillo Puerto's ever-growing influence across the Southeast.[168]

In Tabasco, like his counterparts Flores in Campeche and Vidal in Chiapas, Tomás Garrido Canabal also followed Carrillo Puerto's example in allying himself as closely as he could to Obregón and Calles. Like Chiapas, Tabasco was not a place that the Constitutionalists had ever fully pacified or controlled. For Obregón and Calles, the prospect of having an ambitious young ally there, and what's more, one with proven political experience under difficult circumstances, had obvious advantages and appeal. For the ambitious Garrido, a close alliance with the Sonorans likewise held great promise. Calles visited Tabasco in February of 1921, accompanied by Carrillo Puerto, where he was feted by the Radical Party and its partisans. During the visit, Calles made his support of Garrido and the Radicals well known. With his ally Carrillo Puerto at his side, Calles bolstered his own network of like-minded allies throughout the Southeast by openly showing favor to radical reformers across the region.[169] Garrido also received advice and encouragement from Carrillo Puerto, who urged him to continue his efforts to organize workers in Tabasco.[170]

Calles took a marked interest in Garrido's prospects from an early point. He wrote to the young governor in July of 1921, advising him to think strategically, and to exercise great caution and restraint in the upcoming state legislative elections in Tabasco.[171] For his part, Garrido assured Calles

165   AGN-CAV, c.6, f.9. Vidal to Paniagua, December 14, 1920.

166   AGN-OC, c. 302, 811-P-21. Miguel Cantón to Obregón, June 14, 1921.

167   FAPECFT-PEC, expediente 25: CARRILLO PUERTO, Felipe, legajo 5/7, foja 254, inventario 830. Carrillo Puerto to Calles, February 20, 1923.

168   See, for instance, FAPECFT-FEC, fondo: 3, serie: 401, expediente: 5: ADHESIONES A LA CANDIDATURA PRESIDENCIAL DEL GRAL. PLUTARO ELIAS CALLES, CHIAPAS, legajo: 1/1, foja: 24, inventario: 1198. Memo by the Juntas del Partido Socialista Cintalapaneco, September 2, 1923.

169   Canudas, *Tropico rojo, Vol. 1*, 1, 34–35.

170   Archivo General de la Nación de México, Fondo Tomás Garrido Canabal (hereafter AGN-TGC), c. 3, expediente 9. Carrillo Puerto to Garrido, April 14, 1921.

171   FAPECFT-PEC, expediente: 54, GREENE, Carlos (Gral.), legajo 1/1, foja 35, inventario: 2506. Calles to Garrido, July 4, 1921.

that unlike his predecessors, he would be able to keep the political peace in the state once he took power. Garrido also urged Calles to remove or replace federal agents in Tabasco who were working against him, assuring the Secretary of the Interior that the working people of the state would be immensely grateful.[172] It likely didn't hurt his alliances with the Sonorans that Garrido was also an incorrigible political gossip; not all of his information was reliable, but his ear was always close to the ground. His reports to the Sonorans about alleged schemers and traitors remained a constant throughout all of their political correspondence over many years, as were his protestations of his loyalty. These efforts paid off. In 1921, the perennial rebel leader Carlos Greene was accused of plotting against the federal government and imprisoned. Garrido was initially implicated as one of his coconspirators, but Calles personally assured Garrido that he refused to believe that he would ever participate in a rebellion.[173]

Garrido started to sketch the shape of his long-term reformist program while still interim governor, beginning with a significant disbursal of federal funds to municipal governments for the construction of new public schools.[174] He also undertook ambitious infrastructural modernization projects in the state in this period, particularly the dredging of the port of Frontera.[175] And he declared himself amenable to the formation of workers' ligas in Tabasco, although he didn't begin to build his own for several more years.[176] Workers in Tabasco began to tentatively reach out to Garrido, in the hope of finding a champion for their rights, and for a more just political and economic regime in Tabasco in the not too distant future.[177]

In 1922, Garrido ran for his first elected term as Tabasco's governor. By this time, he had also assumed control and leadership of the Radical Party.[178] His gubernatorial candidacy was also supported by some Blues in the state and by the National Cooperatist Party (PCN) at the national level.[179] The election was marred by violence, like so many others that preceded it. After several complaints from Garrido about intrigues against him, Calles sent a sharply worded letter to the Chief of Military Operations in the state, reminding him that it was his duty to protect the lives of all of

---

172 FAPECFT-PEC, expediente: 140, GARRIDO CANABAL, Tomás (Lic.), legajo 1/7, foja 3, inventario: 2312. Garrido to Calles, March 23, 1921.
173 FAPECFT-PEC, expediente: 54, GREENE, Carlos (Gral.), legajo 1/1, foja 48, inventario: 2506. Calles to Garrido, February 14, 1922.
174 AGN-TGC, caja: 4, expediente: 4. Garrido to Presidentes Municipales, February 28, 1922.
175 AGN-TGC, caja: 4, expediente: 4. Garrido to Luis Pedrero, March 9, 1922.
176 AGN-TGC, caja: 3, expediente: 3. Garrido to Gonzalo Vargas Pino, July 6, 1921.
177 AGN-TGC, caja 4, expediente 4. José Pool to Garrido, August 27, 1922. On Garrido's support among workers and on José Pool more specifically, see Harper, "Revolutionary Tabasco," 72–73.
178 Canudas, *Tropico rojo, Vol. 1*, 1, 40.
179 AGN-TGC, caja: 4, expediente: 1. Undated memo from 1922.

the gubernatorial candidates, including Garrido's.[180] As the struggle for the governorship heated up over the course of 1922, Garrido and five of his associates received permission to carry pistols in order to defend themselves.[181]

In September, amid violent attacks on partisans of both sides, Miguel Torruco, the president of the Radical Party and a federal legislator, was assassinated in Mexico City, where he had been campaigning for Garrido.[182] Garrido was undeterred by the assassination, and was confident that he would still be able to triumph in the upcoming election with the help of his powerful national allies.[183] He was right. Torruco's murder crystallized President Obregón's resolve to support Garrido's gubernatorial bid, as he declared that the bloody political struggle that was taking place in Tabasco was an embarrassment for not just the state, but all of Mexico.[184] With the decided support of Obregón and Calles, Garrido's election as governor for the 1922–26 term was then effectively guaranteed when his opponent (and cousin) José Domingo Ramírez Garrido renounced his candidacy.

Garrido was elected and took office in January of 1923. He had promised his allies in Mexico City that if elected, he would save Tabasco from further political disorder, and within a few months, Calles was praising him for the state's political pacification.[185] But Garrido also had ambitious plans for reforming Tabasco. By this time, his reputation as a radical was growing. As red paranoia grew in the United States in the early 1920s, US military intelligence apprehensively reported that the new governor of Tabasco was a disciple of Felipe Carrillo Puerto and that he was already distinguishing himself by "practicing agrarianism in the most radical manner [sic]," and dividing up oil lands in Tabasco.[186] Although these particular fears were conjectural, the report correctly ascertained that Garrido had indeed joined forces with his Socialist counterparts across the region. By 1924, Garrido and the PRT began to establish their own ligas de resistencia in Tabasco.[187]

180 FAPECFT-PEC, expediente: 140, GARRIDO CANABAL, Tomás (Lic.), legajo 1/7, foja 58, inventario: 2312. Calles to Luis T. Mireles, June 25, 1922.
181 AGN-TGC, caja: 5, expediente: 6. Memo by Luis T. Mireles, September 13, 1922.
182 Martínez Assad, *El laboratorio de la revolución*, 158–59.
183 AGN-TGC, caja 4, expediente 3. Garrido, unaddressed memo, September 15, 1922.
184 AGN-OC, caja: 151, expediente: 408-T-25. Obregón to A. Casanova et al., September 21, 1922.
185 FAPECFT-PEC, expediente: 140, GARRIDO CANABAL, Tomás (Lic.), legajo 1/7, foja 74, inventario: 2312. Garrido to Calles, June 15, 1923.
186 FAPECFT-CDEEUM, expediente: 080201: DIVISION DE INTELIGENCIA MILITAR: Informes, legajo: 4/6, fojas 204–7, inventario: 19. Summary of Mexican Intelligence, No. 296, August 22, 1923.
187 Harper, "Revolutionary Tabasco," 73.

Conclusions

The Southeast was not the only place in Mexico where Socialist parties were founded in the 1920s, but it produced the earliest and most influential examples. The region also had the highest concentration of Socialist parties, in spite of the fact that the Constitutionalists had recently found the whole of the region to be uniquely difficult to control, never mind reform.

One of the things that made the Southeast unique was its large Maya population. The demographics of the states in question were both a challenge and an advantage for would be reformers. In Chiapas, where many Mayan languages are spoken, political organizers seeking to work with indigenous campesinos faced a significant logistical hurdle greater than that of their counterparts in Yucatán and Campeche, where Yucatec Maya predominated, and where many Ladinos spoke it at least a little, including Carrillo Puerto himself. Further, across the region, many indigenous people were understandably reluctant to welcome the overtures of any political faction or movement seeking their support, based on both recent and historical experience. Arguably, the greatest Socialist organizing success in the long-term was eventually in Tabasco, where the indigenous population is relatively small compared to the other states examined here (although other factors were also at play in that success).

It was also a region that was markedly hostile to interference from outsiders throughout the revolutionary period. In no small part, this was because local elites were accustomed to exerting, and felt entitled to exert, control over indigenous labor. For all of these reasons, for many political elites in Mexico City, the Southeast was deemed a relatively low-risk site for political experimentation compared to other regions of Mexico, because they had relatively little to lose and possibly something to gain in allowing radicals to attempt to reform places like Chiapas. This was a critical factor in the ability of several generations of southeastern Socialists to conduct the political experiments that they did, without extensive interference or hindrance from Mexico City. A top-down model of political control never worked in the Southeast for Carranza and the Constitutionalists, nor would it have worked for the Sonorans after them. In Chiapas it had the opposite of the intended effect, sparking a lengthy counterrevolution. In Tabasco, it dramatically exacerbated preexisting political divisions and enmities. In Campeche, the rapid rise and fall of the Pro-Campeche Party demonstrated that without genuine and broad popular support, reformist movements in the Southeast had no political teeth, nor the ability to credibly challenge either Constitutionalists or conservative elites. Nor was the opportunistic outsourcing of governance to provincial forces with power but no ideological or political commitment to reform a workable solution, as demonstrated by Obregón's empowerment of the Mapaches in Chiapas.

The Mapaches' disastrous time in power in the early 1920s demonstrated to Calles and Obregón that Mexico could not go back to how it was before the Revolution – not even in distant Chiapas.

The southeastern Socialists showed that federal initiatives at the state and local levels were much more effective and more widely embraced when implemented by local politicians who worked in dialogue with local communities and were responsive to local needs and objectives, and even more so with corporatist state- or regional-level organizations with strong ties to national political factions. In practice this took the form of political parties that balanced centralized authority with measured respect for local political autonomy, and articulated a relatively consistent populist and reformist program that addressed the preoccupations and expectations of workers and campesinos in both tangible and rhetorical ways. In spite of their differences, all of the southeastern Socialist governments adopted this same basic formula. There were adaptations of this formula from state to state, but the results spoke for themselves. Variations on the Yucatecan Socialist model of postrevolutionary political institutionalization largely pacified the whole of the long-recalcitrant Southeast by 1923.

This was also a pioneering model of single-party dominance at the state level in Mexico, in which political differences were debated and resolved within each Socialist party, in dialogue with grassroots constituencies organized into corporatist networks through ligas de resistencia at the local level (everywhere except Chiapas). Although the implementation of this model inspired conflict and sometimes violence, by 1923 the southeastern Socialists could credibly claim that their system was working, as the old, elite-dominated political class was effectively sidelined in three of the four states in question (the Socialist takeover of Chiapas would come a few years later). Politicians in Mexico City, and none more than Plutarco Elías Calles, took notice.

This became starkly clear when Felipe Carrillo Puerto's collaboration with Ramón Félix Flores broke down when it came time for Campeche to elect a new governor in 1923, and he and Flores disagreed over who should be Flores' successor. Both candidates were Socialist party insiders; Fernando Enrique Angli Lara, who was Carrillo Puerto's pick, was the party's secretary, while the more moderate Angel Castillo Lanz, who was supported by Flores, was its treasurer.[188] Carrillo Puerto remained reluctant to relinquish control over Campeche's politics, and likely also hoped to prevent Socialism there from taking a more moderate turn. He protested that Flores was trying to prevent the ligas de resistencia in the state from supporting Angli. In fact, Carrillo Puerto's open support of Angli was part

---

188   Justo Sierra, Gantús Inurreta, and Villanueva, *Breve historia de Campeche*, 211. On Angli Lara and
         Castillo Lanz in the 1930s, see Fallaw, *Religion and State Formation*, 36–37, 48–51.

of the problem; he himself acknowledged that some Campeche Socialists were campaigning against Angli because they perceived that Carrillo Puerto had violated the state's sovereignty by giving him such strong support.[189]

Observing the Socialists' infighting in 1923, Calles wrote to Flores, and copied Carrillo Puerto. In this extraordinary document, Calles did not take a side between the candidates, but instead laid out his vision for how the Socialist parties of the Southeast should behave and manage their elections:

As far as I am concerned, the electoral campaign should take place in a fully democratic setting, without any pressures of any kind by the authorities of that state, and with equal guarantees for all of the candidates that arise. Since the Socialist Party has an overwhelming majority, it doesn't need to resort to any torturous means of entering the campaign. Within the party, I am of the opinion that true democracy should be practiced. The Socialist Party should convene a convention at which all of the ligas are represented, and the representatives of those ligas should have absolute freedom to express their opinions, to discuss the candidates and to cast their votes. It seems to me that it would be a misstep if the leaders of the Liga Central tried to impose a candidate contrary to the will of the Ligas of the state. Any difficulty that arises within the party would be disastrous for the party itself and could cause its dissolution and its ruin as a consequence, something that I believe men of good will shouldn't allow. One should therefore work within the party in all honesty and with complete justice, allowing, I repeat, the representatives of the ligas ample freedom to designate their candidate, and that choice should obey the will of the people. The little differences that exist within the party should be stifled, harmony should be sought between all of the members, and all matters of a personal nature should be put aside for the good of the group.[190]

By 1923, six years before he founded the National Revolutionary Party, Calles was carefully considering how a party of this kind should be operated, how disagreements might be managed within a single-party-dominated political system, and what such a party might achieve if an appropriate balance could be struck between centralized control and popular representation. The Campeche Socialists followed Calles' prescriptions closely. The party held a convention of seventy-four delegates chosen by their respective ligas, committees, and towns across the state, who chose Castillo Lanz as their gubernatorial candidate, in defiance of Carrillo

189 FAPECFT-PEC, expediente: 25, CARRILLO PUERTO, Felipe, legajo 5/7, foja 249–51, inventario 830. Carrillo Puerto to Calles, February 14, 1923.
190 FAPECFT-PEC, expediente 25: CARRILLO PUERTO, Felipe, legajo 5/7, foja 267, inventario 830. Calles to Carrillo Puerto, March 8, 1923.

Puerto's wishes.[191] But it was Carrillo Puerto himself who had helped them build a political machine that enabled them to exert their independence from him. By 1923, southeastern Socialism was growing and changing, increasingly across state lines, and not always in the ways that its architects envisioned.

---

191   AGN-OC, 408-C-35. J. Acuña R. and Ignacio R. Yeso to Obregón, April 1, 1923.

3

Putting the System to the Test

The de la Huerta rebellion in the Southeast, 1923–1924

In love, suicide is romantic and beautiful. In politics, it is stupid.
The rebellion of December was eminently political. Only retrospect will
determine whether or not it was justified.

Alonso Capetillo, 1925

As the southeastern Socialists labored to build postrevolutionary political
institutions that would enable them to govern while implementing ambitious reformist promises, their efforts were imperiled by a political crisis as
the national government was nearly overthrown. Mexico had no precedents
for peaceful presidential succession following the Mexican Revolution, and
the political class was saturated with revolutionary veterans who now sought
political power. In 1923, their collective aspirations and anxieties inevitably
came to focus on the upcoming presidential succession. The result was the de
la Huerta rebellion of 1923–24.

In December of 1923, Minister of Finance Adolfo de la Huerta rebelled
against President Álvaro Obregón, taking at least half of the Mexican
military with him. The simplest explanation for the crisis is that de la
Huerta mutinied in protest of Obregón's choice of Secretary of the Interior,
Plutarco Elías Calles, to succeed him in the presidency in 1924. But this
moment of crisis for the infant postrevolutionary Mexican state was also
a symptom of several political diseases at once, as troubling gaps began to
emerge between the theory and practice of governance under the constitution of 1917. Above all, the rebellion was driven by prevailing uncertainty
surrounding processes of presidential succession and election. It was also
fueled by a cluster of overlapping power struggles: between the executive
branch and the federal legislature, between the executive and the military,
and between the federal government and regional power brokers (both
elected and otherwise).

This chapter examines the impact of the de la Huerta rebellion on the
Southeast. Socialists played important roles in the defense of the federal
government against rebel forces in the region. In the process, they mustered
popular support for the federal government, channeled through their

corporatist political parties. This set precedents that did not go unnoticed in Mexico City. The rebellion also forced both Calles and Obregón to reexamine the political, economic, and military significance of the Southeast as they worked to preserve their government. For all of these reasons, the Socialist Southeast gained unprecedented national attention during the de la Huerta crisis, with important consequences for the region once the rebellion was defeated in June of 1924.

The de la Huerta Rebellion of 1923–1924

In 1920, Álvaro Obregón plotted his succession to the presidency, in spite of President Venustiano Carranza's determined efforts to thwart his rise to power and impose his own handpicked successor. In April of 1920, Obregón and his fellow Sonorans Adolfo de la Huerta and Plutarco Elías Calles led a rebellion against Carranza with the declaration of the Plan de Agua Prieta, which repudiated the president. This was followed by Carranza's overthrow and assassination a few weeks later.[1] When Obregón became president that December, he brought Calles and de la Huerta with him to Mexico City as his Secretaries of the Interior and of Finance, respectively.[2]

By 1923, nearly everyone in Mexico expected Calles to be the next president, thanks to Obregón's strong support.[3] However, as the election drew closer, many ambitious politicians and generals grew increasingly uncomfortable with the continued political dominance of Obregón and Calles. For some, this was an unacceptable concentration of power in the hands of one revolutionary faction, and they saw a second consecutive Sonoran presidency in 1924 as imperiling their own presidential aspirations. Others worried that Obregón's choice of Calles as his successor signaled his intent to return to power for the subsequent term, in 1928, in blatant violation of Francisco I. Madero's by then nearly sacred precept of "no reelection."

In 1922, Obregón sent de la Huerta to New York to negotiate Mexico's foreign debt and revolutionary-era indemnities, in the hope of at last winning postrevolutionary diplomatic recognition from the United States and European powers.[4] This was a tall order. Countries with oil interests in Mexico, and the United States most of all, were chilly toward Obregón's

---

1   See Hall's explanation of the roots of the Agua Prieta rebellion, and de la Huerta's central role in it. Hall, *Álvaro Obregón*, 233–37.

2   See Buchenau's discussion of the power imbalance within the Sonoran Triangle at this time. He argues that politically Calles was the weakest of the three. Buchenau, *Plutarco Elías Calles*, 90.

3   Ibid., 102.

4   For a detailed discussion of the work of de la Huerta in New York, and the interactions between de la Huerta and Obregón during those months, see Pedro Castro Martínez, *Adolfo de la Huerta: la integridad como arma de la revolución* (México, D.F.: Universidad Autónoma Metropolitana Iztapalapa, Siglo Veintiuno Editores, 1998), chapter 4.

government. Article 27 of the 1917 Constitution declared that natural resources, including subsoil rights, belonged to the nation, and foreign-owned oil companies feared that Mexico would put it into practice. Under pressure from the powerful oil lobby, the administration of Warren G. Harding made it known that US recognition of Obregón's government was contingent on the nonretroactive application of Article 27, the upholding of property rights in Mexico of US citizens, and the payment of indemnities for property that US citizens had lost during the Mexican Revolution. As Minister of Finance, de la Huerta's unenviable task was to find a workable settlement that would expedite the renewal of diplomatic relations with the United States while still being politically acceptable at home. His negotiations with banks in New York produced the de la Huerta–Lamont Agreement. Signed in June of 1922, Mexico agreed to acknowledge and repay a billion dollars in foreign debt.[5] But the agreement did not win many of the concessions from the bankers that Obregón wanted, and the United States continued to withhold diplomatic recognition from Mexico. The standoff was not over.

As de la Huerta was negotiating the 1922 agreement, Calles was working through his own less official channels to win support for Obregón's government in the United States. In the fall of 1921, Calles sent Robert Haberman to the United States to work as a propaganda agent for the Mexican government, and as his emissary to Samuel Gompers and the American Federation of Labor (AFL).[6] Haberman had already worked for the Sonorans as a propaganda agent in the United States in 1920, encouraging North American investors to do business in Mexico following the Revolution.[7] In between, he had collaborated with Felipe Carrillo Puerto to strengthen the organization of the PSS at the Congress of Izamal, and served as an emissary between Calles and the Yucatecan Socialists. Haberman's work to help Calles to build his relationships with the Socialists of the Southeast and with the AFL were part of the same project, as Calles sought the support of organized labor on both sides of the border leading up to his anticipated presidential campaign in 1924. Minister of Education José Vasconcelos shrewdly accused Haberman of working to secure support in Yucatán for Calles' presidential candidacy.[8] In fact, Haberman was also working for Carrillo Puerto in New York, as an agent of Yucatán's state-run henequen export

5 Héctor Aguilar Camín and Lorenzo Meyer, *In the Shadow of the Mexican Revolution: Contemporary Mexican History, 1910–1989* (Austin, TX: University of Texas Press, 2001; repr., 5), 81–82.
6 See FAPECFT-PEC, expediente: 2: HABERMAN, Roberto, legajos 1 and 2. inventario: 2615. On Haberman's complex relationships with both the US and Mexican governments, as well as the AFL and Carrillo Puerto, as well as his time in New York, see Andrews, *Shoulder to Shoulder?*, chapter 6.
7 Andrews, "Robert Haberman," 200.   8 Ibid., 201, fn 37.

commission. When his work in the United States for Calles was complete, Haberman returned to Yucatán to continue his work with Carrillo
Puerto and the PSS.[9]

As he worked to fulfill Obregón's orders in New York, Adolfo de la
Huerta became suspicious of Haberman's activities there. He wrote to
Calles and Obregón to complain that Haberman was in New York, and
that he was meeting with US Socialist groups and journalists. He worried
that Haberman was "giving them the wrong impression," so they would
not accept the debt agreement he was working to secure. Further, de la
Huerta repeated rumors that Haberman was "inciting" the leaders of
Yucatán, Veracruz, and the state of México to declare general strikes at
the moment the agreement was achieved.[10] "I am absolutely certain that
the information you have been given about Haberman is completely
false," Calles responded, without revealing that Haberman was working
for him.[11] When Haberman's activities in New York were criticized in
the Mexican press in the fall of 1923, Calles warned Obregón not to take
any action until he was able to personally fill him in on the work
Haberman had been doing, and insisted on Haberman's unequivocal
loyalty to them.[12]

When de la Huerta returned to Mexico, it became more starkly clear that
he and Obregón had growing political disagreements. In particular, de la
Huerta strongly opposed the Bucareli Accords of 1923, in which Mexico
agreed to pay for lands expropriated from US citizens, and conceded that
Article 27 would not be applied retroactively to foreign-held properties
acquired before the ratification of the 1917 Constitution.[13] A claims commission was also established, to definitively settle what Mexico owed to
US citizens for damages incurred during the Revolution.[14] De la Huerta
protested that Obregón had granted foreigners special rights.[15] He also
evidently took Obregón's newfound willingness to cooperate with the
United States personally, particularly after Obregón had publicly criticized

---

9   See FAPECFT-PEC, expediente: 2: HABERMAN, Roberto, legajo 2/2, foja 64, inventario: 2615.
    Haberman to Calles, February 21, 1922.
10 FAPECFT-PEC, expediente: 2: HABERMAN, Roberto, legajo 2, foja 81, inventario: 2615. de la
    Huerta to Calles, June 24, 1922.
11 FAPECFT-PEC, expediente: 2: HABERMAN, Roberto, legajo 2, foja 82, inventario: 2615. Calles
    to de la Huerta, June 27, 1922.
12 FAPECFT-PEC, expediente 5: OBREGON, Álvaro (Gral.), legajo 4/13, foja 169, inventario
    4038. Calles to Obregón, September 23, 1923.
13 Buchenau, *Plutarco Elías Calles*, 105. David Allen Brush, "The de la Huerta rebellion in Mexico,
    1923–1924" (Ph.D. diss., Syracuse University, 1975), 99.
14 For a concise summary of these negotiations and accords see Aguilar Camín and Meyer, *In the
    Shadow of the Mexican Revolution*, 80–84.
15 Brush, "The de la Huerta rebellion in Mexico, 1923–1924," 99.

his earlier attempts to conciliate US business interests.[16] Nevertheless, thanks in part to de la Huerta's efforts, on August 31 the United States restored diplomatic relations with Mexico. The next day, many other countries followed suit and reopened their embassies.[17]

Obregón was politically strengthened by these diplomatic triumphs both at home and abroad, but many observers rightly began to worry that the growing strife between the Sonorans had the potential to disrupt the upcoming presidential election cycle. Although Obregon's choice of Calles as his successor was well known, Calles waited until US diplomatic recognition was restored to resign as Secretary of the Interior in order to begin his presidential campaign. On September 5, Calles publicly accepted his presidential nomination by numerous political parties across Mexico, including the Socialist parties of the Southeast.[18] However, in spite of his earlier enthusiastic declarations in favor of Calles' candidacy, it was no longer clear that de la Huerta would support his old friend's campaign.

There were other political tensions building that also had the potential to complicate the presidential succession. In the early 1920s, regional and national political parties began to emerge as important players for the first time in Mexico. These parties now competed against one another for power in Mexico City, especially within the Chamber of Deputies. This included a correlated struggle between the branches of the federal government, as legislators sought to stake out their power vis-à-vis the traditionally dominant executive branch.[19] A guardedly optimistic editorial in *El Universal* in September of 1923 declared that although Mexico might not have a perfectly democratic presidential election in 1924, the struggle that was taking place was nevertheless encouraging because it meant that Mexico was showing signs of moving toward a party system. The paper concluded that a sincere political struggle between parties would preclude further armed revolts over elections.[20]

The most powerful of these emerging parties was the National Cooperatist Party (PCN). Founded by lawyer Jorge Prieto Laurens in

---

16 Brush argues that the crisis within the Sonoran Triangle at this point was largely personal and that, in fact, the two Sonorans had far fewer substantive political differences than de la Huerta would subsequently claim. Brush, "The de la Huerta rebellion in Mexico, 1923–1924," 100–1.

17 *El Universal*, September 1, 1923, p. 1. "Inlgaterra, Francia, Cuba y Belgica Reconocerán al General Obregón."

18 *El Universal*, September 5, 1923, p. 1. "Aceptó su Postulación Formalmente el Gral. Calles."

19 This was a legislature that was much more powerful than has often been assumed. See the arguments made by both Valenzuela and Jean Meyer (in essays in the same edited volume) regarding the role of both houses of the legislature in driving policymaking alongside the executive branch in this period. Georgette Emilia José Valenzuela, "1920–1924: ¡ . . . Y Venían de una Revolución!," in *Gobernar sin mayoría, México 1867–1997*, ed. María Amparo Casar and Ignacio Marván (México: Taurus : CIDE, 2002). Jean Meyer, "La diarquía (1924–1928)," ibid.

20 *El Universal*, September 5, 1923, p. 3. Sección Editorial.

1917, it enjoyed a solid majority in both houses of the federal legislature by the early 1920s.[21] By 1923, the Cooperatists also controlled a large bloc within the Senate, had members on the Supreme Court, and counted six governors among their ranks. The party's principle weakness, in contrast to the Socialist parties of the Southeast, was that it never had much success in building a popular base of support.[22] It isn't clear that it made any serious attempts to do so. As the presidential election approached, the PCN's primary goal became mustering a credible challenge to Calles' campaign and to Sonoran hegemony in general.

Prieto Laurens was initially allied with the Sonorans, but he came into serious conflict with them when he ran for the governorship of San Luis Potosí in 1923, for several reasons. First, his opponent, Aurelio Manrique of the National Agrarian Party (PNA), was supported by Calles. Second, the election in San Luis Potosí proved to be a political disaster that had ramifications well beyond the borders of the state. Both candidates and their supporters claimed victory once the election was held in August, and when a straightforward resolution to the impasse wasn't forthcoming, the state descended into chaos and violence.[23] As in many other, similar cases in other states during this period, the federal government was forced to intervene in a deadlocked gubernatorial election. The first order of business was de-escalation, as Obregón ordered the federal troops in the state to attempt to disarm the feuding factions.[24] Then he withdrew federal recognition of the state government and referred the case to the Senate for resolution and the convocation of a new election.[25]

At a moment of already uncertain shifts in the balance of power in Mexico City, all of the national political parties saw the electoral crisis in San Luis Potosí as an opportunity to measure their relative strengths against one another.[26] The Cooperatists refused to accept what they perceived to be Obregón's moves against them in the state, even as the president refused to publicly support either party's candidate. The PCN appealed Obregón's

21 Georgette Emilia José Valenzuela, *El relevo del caudillo: de cómo y porqué Calles fue candidato presidencial* (México, D.F.: Ediciones El Caballito, 1982), 35–36.

22 On Prieto Laurens and the PCN, see Luis Monroy Durán, *El último caudillo: apuntes para la historia de México, acerca del movimiento armado de 1923, en contra del gobierno constituido* (México, D.F.: J.S. Rodríguez, 1924), 34–43; John W. F. Dulles, *Yesterday in Mexico: A Chronicle of the Revolution, 1919–1936* (Austin, TX: University of Texas Press, 1961), 133–4; Dudley Ankerson, *Agrarian Warlord: Saturnino Cedillo and the Mexican Revolution in San Luis Potosí* (DeKalb, IL: Northern Illinois University Press, 1984), 102–3.

23 On the San Luis Potosí election of 1923, see Romana Falcón, *Revolución y caciquismo: San Luis Potosí, 1910–1938* (México, D.F.: El Colegio de México, 1984).

24 Brush, "The de la Huerta rebellion in Mexico, 1923–1924," 80–81.

25 On the history of the disappearance of powers clause in Mexican constitutional law, see González Oropeza, *La intervención federal en la desaparición de poderes.*

26 On the details of this election and its ramifications, see Osten, "Trials by Fire."

handling of the election to the Supreme Court, but the result hardly mattered anymore when the court ruled in the Cooperatists' favor in November.[27]

By that time, various political maelstroms had begun to merge, as Prieto Laurens pressured Adolfo de la Huerta to be the Cooperatists' presidential candidate. Even in a period in which politics remained dominated by individuals, two of the most powerful men in Mexico could not run for President without the support of political parties. Calles had been working for various years to build an independent base of allies and constituents in anticipation of the 1924 election, but de la Huerta had no such support network of his own if he chose to defy Obregón and run against Calles. With the support of the PCN, de la Huerta was eventually convinced he might have a real opportunity to challenge his fellow Sonorans. He submitted his resignation from Obregón's cabinet in September.[28]

De la Huerta's break with Obregón was troubling to many, including Calles. He wrote to de la Huerta: "As your sincere and loyal friend, I urge you, after you reflect calmly on your conduct, to see that it gives the reactionaries who seek to divide us a powerful weapon, and to speak to our friend and chief [Obregón], withdrawing your resignation."[29] De la Huerta refused, convinced of the wisdom of his decision to join the Cooperatists. The weeks that followed seem to vindicate his incendiary choice. In October, the PCN succeeded in winning control of the Permanent Commission of the Chamber of Deputies, and outnumbered pro-Calles legislators 131 to 78.[30] A week later, the Cooperatists arranged an enormous public demonstration in favor of de la Huerta, with attendance reaching an estimated 25,000 people.[31] De la Huerta finally formally accepted the Cooperatists' nomination as their presidential candidate.[32] In de la Huerta, politicians and generals across the political spectrum that opposed Calles' presidential candidacy for a variety of reasons found the viable opposition candidate for whom they had already been searching for some time.[33]

Calles also transitioned into campaign mode. In a not-so-veiled dig at the Cooperatists, he publicly declared that he sought popular support for his candidacy rather than the support of political parties. Nevertheless, Calles

27 On the details of the Supreme Court's ruling, see González Oropeza, *La intervención federal en la desaparición de poderes*, 209–10.
28 Buchenau, *Plutarco Elías Calles*, 105.
29 Plutarco Elías Calles, *Correspondencia personal (1919–1945)*, ed. Carlos Macías, 2 vols., vol. 1 (México, D.F.: Fideicomiso Archivos Plutarco Elías Calles y Fernando Torreblanca, 1991), 107–8.
30 Brush, "The de la Huerta rebellion in Mexico, 1923–1924," 111.
31 Ibid. Brush mentions rumors that many of the demonstrators were likely paid to attend the rally.
32 Buchenau, *Plutarco Elías Calles*, 106. 33 Capetillo, *La rebelión sin cabeza*, 21.

worked diligently to build a coalition of parties to support his campaign.[34] The CROM and the PLM had already become crucial allies to both Obregón and Calles, mustering popular support for federal initiatives and now for Calles' presidential bid. Calles conspicuously put leaders of the CROM, the PNA and the PSS in many of the principal leadership positions within his campaign in October of 1923, as these parties became his most valuable and most reliable sources of support.[35]

The Socialists in the Southeast provided Calles with another important constituent base. Calles had carefully staked out the region as a bastion of support over the previous years, and now his relationships with the Socialists there provided him with firm political ground on which to stand, beyond what the CROM could provide, as he embarked on his presidential campaign. As allies, the southeastern Socialists posed the additional advantage for Calles of being relatively independent of Obregón, who had shown little interest in them once the region was pacified. Upon accepting his nomination, Calles announced that his first presidential campaign tour would be in the Southeast.[36]

The main opposition to Calles' candidacy before de la Huerta's defection lay within the military. A political system that affirmed the right of an incumbent to choose his successor meant that the Sonorans could potentially shut ambitious generals out of high-ranking political offices in perpetuity. At a time when political legitimacy was still very much derived from an individual's participation in the Mexican Revolution, many generals also felt that Calles' relatively lukewarm military credentials were not sufficient for him to become president.[37] His ties with the urban labor movement only further alienated many generals, while others were offended by his notorious anticlericalism.[38] The disaffected generals formed another nucleus of dissent that was drawn to de la Huerta's candidacy, even though he was the only civilian member of the Sonoran clique.[39] Obregón knew the Mexican

34   Ibid., 104. This may have been merely a rhetorical distancing of himself from the PCN by Calles, rather than an intended repudiation of all political parties, which he certainly did not carry out in practice.

35   FAPECFT-FEC, expediente: 4: INTREGRACION DEL CENTRO DIRECTIVO DE LA CAMPAÑA PRO-CALLES. COMISIONES DE HACIENDA JURIDICA Y DE PRENSA, legajo 1/1, inventario: 2615. Calles to various, October 22 and 23, 1923.

36   *El Universal*, September 6, 1923, p. 3. "Acepta su Candidatura el Gral. Elías Calles."

37   Enrique Plasencia de la Parra, *Personajes y escenarios de la rebelión delahuertista* (México, D.F.: Instituto de Investigaciones Históricas, UNAM, 1998), 18.

38   Martha Beatriz Loyo Camacho, *Joaquín Amaro y el proceso de institucionalización del Ejército Mexicano, 1917–1931*, 2 edn. (México, D.F.: Miguel Ángel Porrúa, 2003), 105. Buchenau, *Plutarco Elías Calles*, 104.

39   Medina Peña argues that the rebellious generals never considered de la Huerta one of their own, but opportunistically attempted to use his schism with his fellow Sonorans to their own advantage. Medina Peña, *Hacia el nuevo estado*, 43–44.

military better than anyone, and he understood that disaffected generals posed another serious liability for his government. That fall, he did what he could to try to ensure that active duty officers did not become involved in political campaigns.[40]

One of the most important of the disaffected generals was Salvador Alvarado. After the Agua Prieta rebellion, Alvarado very briefly worked for his longtime friend de la Huerta during his interim presidency in 1920 as his Minister of Finance, before departing to New York as a representative of the henequen regulatory commission of Yucatán that he had rebuilt, and to build confidence in Mexico's new government among the bankers and investors there.[41] But Alvarado always had his differences with Obregón, who doubted his loyalties, undoubtedly in part because it was widely understood that Alvarado had his own presidential ambitions. Obregón opposed Alvarado's appointment to the cabinet, but was overruled by Calles and de la Huerta.[42]

Their distaste was mutual, and increasingly bitter. In 1919, Alvarado called for the establishment of a competitive party system in Mexico, and stridently warned of the dangers of popular disaffection with the political system in places where candidates were imposed by the powerful and their camarillas. He further cautioned that the election of a caudillo would preclude meaningful political reform. He exhorted Obregón and General Pablo González to withdraw their presidential candidacies and to join him in forming a united, revolutionary political party that would then convene delegates to select a candidate.[43] Still, in 1920 he lauded Obregón for his patriotism and pledged his support of Obregón's government once he took power, protesting that he planned to retire from politics and would not accept a cabinet post if it were offered to him.[44]

By that time, he was also estranged from the Socialists of Yucatán. Upon hearing a (false) rumor in 1921 that Alvarado might be reassigned as a chief of military operations in the Southeast, Carrillo Puerto insisted to Calles that Alvarado's return would mean disaster for the Socialists there.[45] As a northern outsider, Alvarado had built the foundations of the political

40 FAPECFT-PEC, expediente 5: OBREGON, Álvaro (Gral.), legajo 4/13, foja 171, inventario 4038. Álvaro Obregón to Plutarco Elías Calles, October 1923 [date illegible].

41 Castro Martínez, *Adolfo de la Huerta*, 66, 81.

42 Ibid., 159–60. Dulles, *Yesterday in Mexico*, 80–81.

43 FAPECFT-FAO, serie: 20700, expediente A-2 30: ALVARADO, Salvador (Gral.), legajo 1, fojas 4–22, inventario: 778. Open letter from Alvarado to Carranza, Obregón, and Pablo González, August 13, 1919.

44 FAPECFT-FAO, serie: 30400, expediente 30: ALVARADO, Salvador (Gral.), legajo 1, fojas 6–8, inventario: 2046. Alvarado to Obregón, September 17, 1920.

45 FAPECFT-PEC, expediente 25, CARRILLO PUERTO, Felipe, legajo 2/7, fojas 83–4, inventario 830. Carrillo Puerto to Calles, August 12, 1921.

machine that Carrillo Puerto had made into something more uniquely southeastern. Carrillo Puerto was now powerful and well-connected enough that he saw no need to tolerate unwanted outsider interference in the politics of Yucatán. In August of 1922, Carrillo Puerto reported to Calles that Alvarado was organizing support for de la Huerta's presidential candidacy, long before it was declared.[46] By 1923, Alvarado was among a group of generals who formed the Union of Revolutionary Soldiers of 1910–1913 in support of de la Huerta, and became one of his presidential campaign managers.[47]

In early November, a group of governors from across Mexico collaborated in a futile effort to forge a reconciliation between Calles and de la Huerta. Their stated goal was to assure that the upcoming presidential succession was peaceful.[48] There were good reasons to fear that the rift between the Sonorans and the Cooperatists' political maneuvers could lead to violence. In November, a large group of Cooperatist legislators accused General Arnulfo Gómez of plotting to have them assassinated. Rumors of incipient armed rebellions by restless generals in Veracruz and Puebla circulated widely in the weeks that followed. Finally, on December 4, de la Huerta and Prieto Laurens fled Mexico City for Veracruz with a group of their supporters, as the ongoing political conflict now promised to boil over into an armed uprising.[49] The de la Huerta rebellion had begun.

The rebellion spread rapidly, centered on four loci: Veracruz, where de la Huerta himself was based and where General Guadalupe Sánchez presented a serious military threat to Obregón's regime, Jalisco, where General Enrique Estrada also presented a significant military challenge, and Oaxaca, where General Fortunato Maycotte was seconded in his rebellion by Governor Manuel García Vigil. Lastly, the rebellion spread into the Southeast, where army garrisons rebelled against the Socialist state governments of Campeche, Tabasco, and Yucatán. Despite the stated justifications that they shared, these rebellions were only tenuously related to one another, and only some of the generals who led these movements recognized Adolfo de la Huerta as their leader. De la Huerta scrambled to define the political tenets of the mutiny that took his name, but *delahuertismo* as such was coherent only in its adamant opposition to Álvaro Obregón's monopoly of power in Mexico, and in defiance of his choice of Calles to succeed him as president. De la Huerta himself never controlled any territory or troops, other than what rebel generals claimed in his name.

---

46   FAPECFT-PEC, expediente 25, CARRILLO PUERTO, Felipe, legajo 4/7, foja 219, inventario 830. Carrillo Puerto to Calles, August 15, 1922.

47   Plasencia de la Parra, *Personajes y escenarios*, 99.

48   *El Universal*, November 2, 1923, 1. "Labor de Acercamiento Entre los Candidatos de la Huerta y Gral. Calles."

49   Brush, "The de la Huerta rebellion in Mexico, 1923–1924," 120–3, 29.

President Obregón remained resolutely sanguine about the rebellion, even as it spread, or at least sought to minimize its seriousness. He gave orders to Secretary of War Francisco R. Serrano that federal forces should not engage the rebels militarily until it was possible to defeat them soundly, and to proceed judiciously with military recruitment, because he believed that the conflict would not last for long.[50] Both houses of the Mexican legislature continued to meet and to operate in Mexico City during the rebellion, in spite of the protests of rebel legislators that they could not legally operate without a quorum, which their collective absence made impossible.[51] Their objections were ignored. Undeterred, the Mexican Senate moved forward to ratify the claims commission previously agreed upon with the United States that had so incensed de la Huerta.[52] As a result of these efforts, Obregón was able to count upon the support of the US government throughout the rebellion. The lifting of an embargo on arms shipments from the United States to Mexico proved to be crucial, and Obregón quickly opened negotiations with US weapons manufacturers to arm loyal groups across Mexico.[53] One of the most important sources of arms for federal troops was the US government itself, which sold Mexico surplus weaponry and ammunition left over from World War I.[54] In January of 1924, the Coolidge administration also embargoed any shipments of arms to the Delahuertistas, a crippling blow to the chronically underequipped rebel armies.[55]

Obregón's government also enjoyed the support of the American Federation of Labor, undoubtedly thanks in part to the work that Robert Haberman had carried out on Calles' orders to convince Samuel Gompers of the Mexican government's pro-labor stance.[56] Gompers described de la Huerta as a reactionary bent on crushing the Mexican labor movement who was determined to "set Mexico back a decade or more."[57] Gompers' support proved to be instrumental in keeping armaments out of rebel hands. In late December, the AFL declared its full support for Obregón's

50 AHSDN, XI/111/1-243, Serrano, Francisco R., Tomo 4, foja 896. Álvaro Obregón to Francisco R. Serrano, December 11, 1923. AHSDN, XI/111/1-243, Serrano, Francisco R., Tomo 7, foja 1631. Obregón to Serrano, December 12, 1923.
51 *The New York Times*, December 13, 1923, p. 4. "Deputies Cross the Border."
52 *The New York Times*, December 12, 1923, p. 4. "Mexico Ratifies Treaties."
53 See, for instance, a discussion between Obregón and Serrano in January, in regards to purchasing arms in Texas. AHSDN, XI/111/1-243, Serrano, Francisco R., Tomo 4, foja 938. Serrano to Obregón, January 5, 1924.
54 For a more detailed discussion of these arms deals, see Brush, "The de la Huerta rebellion in Mexico, 1923–1924," 162–69.
55 Ibid., 179–80.
56 On the AFL's alliance with the Mexican government during the rebellion, see Andrews, *Shoulder to Shoulder?*, chapter 5.
57 *The New York Times*, December 22, 1923, p. 4. "Asks Watch on Smuggling."

government, and Gompers called upon AFL-affiliated union members in the United States who worked in shipping and at border posts to participate in blocking the shipment of arms to rebel forces in Mexico and to report suspicious activities to US authorities.

Mexican organized labor's support also became an essential element of the government's defensive strategies. At the beginning of the rebellion, Obregón wrote to Secretary of War Serrano: "If it is necessary, the Executive will convoke the rural classes and other working classes of the entire country, so that they will collaborate with their government to impose peace and to punish the treason of the rebels."[58] Facing huge numbers of defections within the military, with the assistance of the CROM and the PNA, Obregón launched an effort to arm and mobilize workers and campesinos, although he regarded the recruitment of these so-called irregular forces to be a measure of last resort.[59] Nevertheless, he was able to do so thanks in large part to Calles' persistent efforts to build strong alliances with popular groups and political parties, including the Socialists of the Southeast. Socialists elsewhere in Mexico also enthusiastically took up the cause of the federal government as the rebellion spread, requesting arms and ammunition to combat it.[60] The general that Calles enlisted to run popular recruitment efforts for the government was Carlos Vidal of Chiapas. Vidal and the Socialists of the Southeast had forged a model for mobilizing grassroots constituents and connecting them to political leaders that now proved very valuable.

By mid-January, several rebel factions had proposed a ceasefire. Obregón categorically rejected it and announced he was only willing to accept the rebels' unconditional surrender.[61] At the end of the month, after very few actual battles since the rebellion's start, federal troops finally inflicted a decisive military defeat on the rebel forces in Veracruz, with over 400 casualties and 1,300 rebel soldiers taken prisoner. The rebels' hopes for a military victory were dimmed from that point forward.[62] On February 5, de la Huerta and his supporters abandoned Veracruz, and departed for the port of Frontera in Tabasco. Federal forces retook the city within days, for the first time since the rebellion began.[63] A week later, federal forces also

58 AHSDN, XI/111/1-243, Serrano, Francisco R., Tomo 4, foja 888. Obregón to Serrano, December 6, 1923.
59 Plasencia de la Parra, *Personajes y escenarios*, 79–80.
60 See, for example, the Socialist Club of Puebla's request to this effect: FAPECFT-PEC, expediente 27: CLUB SOCIALISTA POBLANO, PUEBLA, PUE., legajo 1, foja 1, inventario 883. Aurelio B. Morales to Calles, December 12, 1923.
61 Brush, "The de la Huerta rebellion in Mexico, 1923–1924," 238–41.
62 Plasencia de la Parra, *Personajes y escenarios*, 70–73.
63 AHSDN, XI/111/1-243, Serrano, Francisco R., Tomo 6, foja 1464. Obregón to Serrano, February 11, 1924.

recaptured Guadalajara.[64] The tide of the conflict had turned definitively in the government's favor. At the end of March, de la Huerta and Prieto Laurens fled into exile in the United States.[65]

Even as the rebel commanders conferred on how to end the rebellion, the fighting waged on in the Southeast and continued long after the rebellion had been defeated everywhere else and its leaders were settling into their new lives in exile.[66] It resulted in some of the most grievous political wounds that Obregón and Calles sustained during the whole of the de la Huerta episode.

The de la Huerta Rebellion in Yucatán and Campeche, 1923–1924

There was no military rebellion in the Southeast that compared in size or seriousness to the uprisings in Veracruz or Jalisco. Even so, from a very early point in the brewing crisis, both Yucatán and Tabasco were rumored to be likely targets for rebel attacks.[67] As home to the still-valuable henequen industry, Yucatán in particular was a piece of extremely lucrative territory for both the government and the rebels, particularly the latter, who desperately needed money.[68] Further, as the rebellion in other regions was progressively defeated by federal forces, the Southeast gained new strategic significance for the rebels. Lastly, for both Calles and de la Huerta, as presidential hopefuls, the Southeast presented significant opportunities for political gain. Although the region was full of alienated elites and counterrevolutionary factions desperate for patronage in Mexico City, Calles unquestionably had the upper hand, having already invested significant time and energy in his alliances there. The results soon spoke for themselves, as it was Calles' network of Socialist allies that prevented the Southeast from falling wholesale to the rebels.

Calles also counted on the CROM and the PLM to bolster his political position in southern Mexico. Juan Rico of the CROM, who had worked closely with the PSS in its early years, was also one of the organizers of Calles' presidential campaign in the region. Rico reported directly to Calles about which parties in the South were supporting him, and which generals

---

64 AHSDN, XI/111/3-1838, Serrano, Francisco R., Tomo 5, foja 1021. Serrano to Obregón, February 11, 1924.

65 AHSDN, XI/111/1-243, Serrano, Francisco R., Tomo 7, fojas 1555–6. Serrano to Obregón, March 22, 1924.

66 *The New York Times*, December 21, 1923, p. 3. "Rebels Move to End Mexican Conflict."

67 *The New York Times*, December 11, 1923, p. 1. "Rebels Begin to March on Mexican Capital with New Artillery."

68 Brush, "The de la Huerta rebellion in Mexico, 1923–1924," 200.

and politicians could be counted upon to support his candidacy.[69] In the chaotic fall of 1923, such an inventory of supporters, along with evidence of their loyalty, was a critically important asset for Calles.

Rico was an assiduous point man for the campaign. In the Southeast and elsewhere, he strove to instill party discipline among the PLM's local affiliates, at least when it came to the presidential election, and to weed out opportunists and fair weather allies.[70] He was extremely suspicious of both politicians and parties who had only recently joined the PLM and/or professed support for Calles. Rico's efforts included monitoring Carrillo Puerto's political activities, as he reported to Calles that the Yucatecan Socialist had been "committing idiocies," which Rico believed might make Calles' campaign appear internally divided.[71] The stakes could not have been higher, at a time that Calles needed Carrillo Puerto as much as Carrillo Puerto needed him. The de la Huerta rebellion demonstrated that Calles' instincts were correct, and that control of the Southeast was essential to maintaining national political stability in Mexico. In practice, this meant supporting Carrillo Puerto and his government in Yucatán, first and foremost.

Nevertheless, Rico was right to be concerned. Although Carrillo Puerto's loyalty to Calles does not seem to have faltered, his grip on power was weaker than it seemed, and many of the henequen planters still feared the long-term implications of his reform program. Then, in November and December of 1923, Carrillo Puerto laid the legal groundwork for the collectivization of Yucatán's henequen plantations.[72] His girlfriend, the US journalist Alma Reed, recounted that Carrillo was in "high spirits" in these days:

Things were going well; there was no interference on the part of the Chief Executive with the ever-broadening measures that were being taken for the people's welfare. Hostility of the dispossessed *hacendados* could not be overlooked, but they were held in check and did not dare move against the new way of life, where the slave of former years was now a proud citizen, participating in government and enjoying the fruits of his labors.[73]

In these same days, under pressure from Obregón's forces, the de la Huerta rebellion swept toward the Southeast. The strength of the alliances between

69 FAPECFT-PEC, expediente: 48: RICO, Juan, legajo 1/1, fojas 1–2, inventario: 4870. Rico to Calles, September 18, 1923, and FAPECFT-PEC, expediente: 48: RICO, Juan, legajo 1/1, foja 11, inventario: 4870. Rico to Calles, October 25, 1923.
70 In one instance, Rico rejected the attempt of a local party in Mexico City to join the PLM, based on his assessment that it was an organization that lacked any moral qualities, and was an enemy of organized labor. FAPECFT-PEC, expediente: 48: RICO, Juan, legajo 1/1, foja 18, inventario: 4870. Rico to Eligio Hidalgo, March 14, 1924.
71 FAPECFT-PEC, expediente: 48: RICO, Juan, legajo 1/1, fojas 1–2, inventario: 4870. Rico to Calles, September 18, 1923.
72 Joseph, *Revolution from Without*, 260–62.   73 Reed and Schuessler, *Peregrina*, 291.

the region's Socialist governments and Obregón's federal government was about to be tested. Because of its economic importance, its internal political strife and the nature of Carrillo Puerto's Socialist political machine, Yucatán became ground zero of the rebellion in the region.

Carrillo Puerto's political triumphs in Yucatán had been underwritten by his integration of popular forces into the PSS via the ligas de resistencia. His usefulness as an ally to Calles and Obregón was therefore grounded in the ongoing success of the liga system once he became governor. Obregón eventually decided that the benefits of arming popular forces to fight the rebels outweighed the risks, but Carrillo Puerto had already decided to arm the ligas de resistencia and the municipal police across Yucatán in a preemptive defense of his government well before the rebellion began.[74] In January of 1923, Carrillo wrote to Calles pleading for weapons to protect his fragile political gains in Yucatán, particularly for communities on state lines.[75] He also insisted that General Fortunato Maycotte not be assigned as the Chief of Military Operations in Yucatán, as was rumored. He accused Maycotte of being a reactionary, and insisted that he would jeopardize the work of the PSS.[76] Carrillo Puerto's instincts were sound, as Maycotte soon helped to lead the rebellion in Oaxaca.

As he maneuvered to protect his Socialist government, Carrillo Puerto was also working for Calles' presidential campaign throughout the Southeast. In August of 1923, he met with Samuel Yúdico of the CROM and Emilio Portes Gil in Mexico City, and solidified plans for a PSS convention in Mérida and a PLM convention in Guadalajara to nominate Calles as their presidential candidate.[77] Carrillo Puerto intended for the PSS to collaborate with the CROM/PLM at both the regional and national levels. On the national political map in 1923, the PLM and the PSS were recognized to control the states of Yucatán, Chiapas, Tabasco, and Campeche.[78] Carrillo Puerto's willingness to link his grassroots constituency and his regional political machine to his allies' national political projects had the potential drawback of the loss of autonomy in the long run, but in the short term it made him an even more valuable ally to Calles. Carrillo Puerto's

---

74 A notable example is Governor Adalberto Tejeda of Veracruz, who was asked to recruit within his network of agrarista grassroots supporters to fight the de la Huerta rebels. See Plasencia de la Parra, *Personajes y escenarios*, 84. Some of these armed civilian groups also became targets of the rebels – in one case, Estrada's forces executed members of an Agrarian Committee in Jalisco that supported the government. AHSDN, XI/111/1-243, Serrano, Francisco R., Tomo 7, foja 1637. Obregón to Serrano, December 12, 1923.

75 FAPECFT-PEC, expediente 25, CARRILLO PUERTO, Felipe, legajo 5/7, fojas 245–6, inventario 830. Carrillo Puerto to Calles, January 26, 1923.

76 Carrillo Puerto to Calles, March 5, 1923. Calles, *Correspondencia personal (1919–1945)*, 2, 482–85.

77 FAPECFT, expediente 25, CARRILLO PUERTO, Felipe, legajo 5/7, fojas 290–91, inventario 830. Carrillo Puerto to Calles, August 8, 1923.

78 Capetillo, *La rebelión sin cabeza*, 15–16.

Photograph 3.1 The PSS nominates Calles as its presidential candidate in Mérida, August 1923. Carrillo Puerto is in the white suit.
Source: Fideicomiso Archivos Plutarco Elías Calles y Fernando Torreblanca (FAPECFT)

attempted expansion of the PSS into a truly regional political party also made him indispensable to his national allies, and to Calles most of all.[79]

The PSS hosted its convention of all of the southeastern Socialist parties in Mérida in August of 1923, and formally nominated Calles (see Photograph 3.1). This was the apogee of regional Socialist unity, as the Socialists of Campeche, Chiapas, the territory of Quintana Roo, Tabasco, and Yucatán came together to campaign for Calles. Carrillo Puerto personally reported to Calles that evening: "We have designated you as our presidential candidate, as we consider you to be an upright revolutionary, and a frank and loyal friend to the worker [...] In this peninsula we especially congratulate you, as you will surely be the true savior of the interests of the proletariat, and your conduct will bolster the prestige of the Mexican nation."[80] The Chiapas Socialist delegation to the convention described the mood in Mérida as "delirious" when Calles

79 FAPECFT, expediente 25, CARRILLO PUERTO, Felipe, legajo 6/7, foja 340, inventario 830. Calles to Carrillo Puerto, November 16, 1923.
80 FAPECFT-PEC, expediente 25: CARRILLO PUERTO, Felipe, legajo 5/7, foja 294, inventario 830. Carrillo Puerto to Calles, August 18, 1923.

was nominated.[81] As planned, the PLM convention followed suit and offered Calles its presidential nomination four days later.[82]

These alliances were not simple top-down patron–client arrangements, although they inarguably contained elements of that model. Nor were these simple marriages of political convenience, although they certainly proved to be beneficial to all parties, at least for a while. Carrillo Puerto was not willing to take unilateral orders from Mexico City. Nor was he content to merely carry out a state-level political experiment with the blessing of powerful friends and allies in the federal government. By consolidating his influence throughout the Southeast as well as building strong alliances in Mexico City, Carrillo Puerto made himself into a powerful national political figure in his own right. The kind of local-state-regional-national political linkages that Carrillo Puerto worked methodically to forge in the early 1920s were groundbreaking in Mexico.

Like other vigilant observers, Felipe Carrillo Puerto expected something akin to the de la Huerta rebellion, and he did what he could to mitigate the threats the brewing crisis posed to the Southeast. Several weeks before de la Huerta accepted the Cooperatist presidential nomination, Carrillo Puerto wrote to Calles to warn him that Guadalupe Sánchez was conspiring against him and was likely to attempt to overthrow Governor Adalberto Tejeda of Veracruz. A month later, he cautioned Calles that the Cooperatists were gaining a presence in Campeche, where Carrillo Puerto continued to lose influence as the Socialists there increasingly staked out their independence from the PSS. Nevertheless, two months later, Carrillo Puerto assured Calles that Yucatán and Campeche remained securely in federal hands. Across Yucatán, the PSS continued its recruitment efforts for the ligas de resistencia and its grassroots campaign for Calles.[83]

Carrillo Puerto began to panic in early December as the de la Huerta rebellion spread southward. He warned Calles that ships full of rebel troops under the command of Sánchez would imminently arrive in Yucatán. Carrillo Puerto cautiously trusted the colonel in command of the 400 federal soldiers that remained in Yucatán, but he feared that troops in Campeche would turn against both the federal government and his state government. After a year of fruitlessly pleading with Calles for shipments

---

81 FAPECFT, APEC anexo, Fondo 3, serie 401, expediente 5: ADHESIONES A LA CANDIDATURA PRESIDENCIAL DEL GRAL. PLUTARCO ELIAS CALLES. CHIAPAS. legajo 1/1, foja 5, inventario 1198. Pascual Córdoba to Calles, August 21, 1923.

82 FAPECFT-PEC, expediente 25, CARRILLO PUERTO, Felipe, legajo 6/7, foja 306, inventario 830. Carrillo Puerto to Calles, August 22, 1923.

83 FAPECFT-PEC, expediente 25, CARRILLO PUERTO, Felipe, legajo 6/7, foja 313, inventario 830. Carrillo Puerto to Calles, September 8, 1923; fojas 328–29, Carrillo Puerto to Calles, November 9, 1923; foja 325, Felipe Carrillo Puerto to Calles, November 5, 1923; fojas 335–37, Carrillo Puerto to Calles, November 12, 1923.

of arms, Carrillo Puerto was still not able to arm the ligas de resistencia to protect the Socialist state government. He reassured Calles that Yucatán was ready to defend the Mexican Revolution, but he again urged Calles to send soldiers and guns to allow the Socialists to protect the state from a rebel onslaught.[84]

Calles assured Carrillo Puerto that he had nothing to fear from Sánchez, but wrote him again a few days later to finally promise him a shipment of ten thousand arms.[85] Carrillo Puerto pointedly replied: "[The guns] will not only be potentially useful to us, but also to you {and Obregón} at any moment." He emphasized how ready and able the Yucatecan Socialists were to defend the federal government: "Once the ligas de resistencia are armed, they will easily be able to defeat the federal forces in Yucatán, without a doubt, because the compañeros are ready to defend {our} cause; great enthusiasm and determination reign here. If we bring forty thousand rifles, eighty thousand compañeros will arrive to take them up."[86] In the days that followed, efforts were made to purchase five thousand guns in Texas, almost certainly to be sent to Yucatán.[87]

According to Alma Reed, Carrillo Puerto also sent his own agent to the United States to buy weapons with 200,000 pesos from the Comisión Exportadora.[88] He also sought to liquidate and gather all available funds in the state to defend his government, but was prevented from accessing any funds of the federal monetary commission in the state by a federal agent

84 FAPECFT-PEC, expediente 25, CARRILLO PUERTO, Felipe, legajo 6/7, foja 344, inventario 830. Carrillo Puerto to Calles, December 5, 1923.

85 FAPECFT-PEC, expediente 25, CARRILLO PUERTO, Felipe, legajo 6/7, fojas 345–46, inventario 830. Calles to Carrillo Puerto, December 6, 1923; Calles to Carrillo Puerto, December 10, 1923.

86 FAPECFT-PEC, expediente 25, CARRILLO PUERTO, Felipe, legajo 6/7, fojas 347–48, inventario 830. Carrillo Puerto to Calles, December 10, 1923. It is possible that Carrillo Puerto sent this letter before receiving Calles' promise of an arms shipment, as both telegrams are dated on the same day.

87 FAPECFT-PEC, expediente 25, CARRILLO PUERTO, Felipe, legajo 6/7, foja 349, inventario 830. Sender and recipient unclear. The document does not specify that these guns were destined for Yucatán, but it was filed with Carrillo Puerto's correspondence at the time, probably by Soledad González, Calles' personal secretary (the FAPECFT retains González's original filing system).

88 The manuscript of Reed's memoir was discovered after her death, and published for the first time in 2007, meaning that many previous interpretations of Carrillo Puerto's downfall did not include Reed's partially insider account. All standard disclaimers about the historical value of memoirs published long after the facts in question apply; in using Reed's book as a source I have confined myself to details that are plausible, factual, and not available elsewhere. It is also worth noting that some of Reed's information seems to have been taken from sources that were published later. For instance, compare Reed's account of Carrillo Puerto's arrest with: Edmundo Bolio Ontiveros, *'De la cuna al paredon.' Anecdotario de la vida, muerte y gloria de Felipe Carrillo Puerto* (Mérida, Yucatán, México: Compañia Periodística del Sureste, 1932), 79–80.

who later protested that he did not comprehend the gravity of the coming attack on Yucatán.[89] Carrillo Puerto also ordered that all of the gunpowder and dynamite in the state be immediately inventoried, and decreed that it could not be sold without permission from his government. Lastly, Carrillo Puerto decided to send the loyal federal troops in the state to help fight the rebellion that had now reached Campeche, as a means of preemptively defending Yucatán.[90]

Despite his careful preparations, Carrillo Puerto believed his situation was extremely precarious. Many people familiar with Yucatán would subsequently lament that Carrillo Puerto was too trusting and too willing to take friendship and alliances at face value, thus overestimating the strength of his political position. Yet the governor was shrewder than his detractors assumed. He wrote to Reed: "At this moment we do not have confidence in anyone, because even the least of men may have a friend who is a traitor parading as a Socialist [. . .] we don't know from one minute to the next who is going to stab us in the back."[91] Reed recounted that Carrillo Puerto was convinced that the Catholic Church and disgruntled henequen planters were supporting the rebels in order to have his government overthrown.[92] A financial lawyer in Mérida further alleged in 1924 that in December, Carrillo Puerto was working to eliminate the middlemen who handled his government's henequen sales in the United States in order to maximize the state's profit margin, thus alienating the brokers who had made millions of dollars in commissions. According to this source, some of these men, including the powerful Tomás Castellanos Acevedo of the Yucatecan Sisal Sales Corporation, had funds at their disposal to help Carrillo Puerto defend his government and declined to do so on the assumption that they would be able to collect their accustomed fees from the rebel government that was poised to take over the peninsula.[93]

On December 12, General José Vallego defected to the rebels in Campeche, taking the troops under his command with him, and arming his soldiers with a shipment of weapons that had recently been sent by the federal government.[94] Word soon reached Carrillo Puerto that the troops he had sent to reinforce the garrison in Campeche had also joined the rebellion. According to Reed, Carrillo Puerto's new plan of action was to flee to the United States with his brothers, where he would procure the weapons necessary to return to fight the rebels. Carrillo Puerto told Reed that he

89 FAPECFT-PEC, expediente 9: MAGAÑA, Leobardo, legajo 1, fojas 12–13, inventario 3383. Leobardo Magaña to Calles, December 26, 1923.
90 Reed and Schuessler, *Peregrina*, 293.   91 Ibid., 293–94.   92 Ibid., 294–95.
93 FAPECFT-FPEC, fondo 12, serie 10500, expediente 1: CARRILLO PUERTO, Felipe, legajo 1, fojas 34040, inventario 79. Amado Cantón Meneses to Calles, August 8, 1924. On the career of Castellanos Acevedo, see Wells and Joseph, *Summer of Discontent*, 226–27.
94 *The New York Times*, December 14, 1923, p. 2. "Rebel Movements in Tamaulipas."

could count on the assistance of the labor unions in the United States, thanks to Haberman's efforts.[95] Instead, when the garrison in Mérida also rebelled, Carrillo Puerto and a small party of friends and supporters, including several of his brothers, escaped the city and attempted to cross Quintana Roo in order to flee to Cuba.[96] They were captured by rebel forces on December 21 and taken back to Mérida where the government had been taken over by rebel leaders.[97] The colonel who remained loyal to the state government was taken prisoner when he refused to join the rebellion, leaving the city defenseless. On December 27, an anxious Calles wrote to Castellanos Acevedo, the Yucatecan henequen financier who was in New York at the time, begging him for any information about Carrillo Puerto.[98] Meanwhile, as federal authorities got word of what was happening in Yucatán, the gunboat they hoped to dispatch to the peninsula was critically delayed.[99] On January 3 at 3:30 in the morning, Carrillo Puerto and his fellow prisoners were taken to the Mérida cemetery by rebel forces and executed.[100]

Calles knew how much he had lost when he received word of Carrillo Puerto's death. Calles had invested a great deal in their alliance over the previous years, and the de la Huerta rebellion and the presidential campaign made Carrillo Puerto's support all the more valuable to Calles. His alliances in the Socialist Southeast were one of the cornerstones of Calles' long-term national political strategies as he sought to consolidate his base of support and his political independence from Obregón, and Carrillo Puerto was by far the most important player on the field in the region. By one account Calles was so distraught by the news of the assassination that he was confined to his bed by his doctor.[101]

In a private letter to the sympathetic North American journalist Ernest Gruening a few months later, Calles explained that Carrillo Puerto had been killed by reactionary forces in Yucatán who had seen their own interests "mortally threatened" when Carrillo Puerto freed the Maya from slavery. It was a loss, Calles told Gruening, that he "profoundly lamented."[102] Beyond the short-term implications for his presidential

95   Reed and Schuessler, *Peregrina*, 301.
96   There are innumerable versions of this story. For another version, see Bolio Ontiveros, *De la cuna al paredón*, 75.
97   Reed and Schuessler, *Peregrina*, 296–99.
98   FAPECFT-FPEC, fondo 12, serie 10500, expediente 1: CARRILLO PUERTO, Felipe, legajo 1, foja 28, inventario 79. Calles to Tomás Castellanos Acevedo, December 27, 1923.
99   FAPECFT-PEC, expediente 9: MAGAÑA, Leobardo, legajo 1, fojas 12–13, inventario 3383. Leobardo Magaña to Calles, December 26, 1923.
100 Bolio Ontiveros, *De la cuna al paredón*, 84.
101 Luis L. León, *Crónica del poder: en los recuerdos de un político en el México revolucionario* (México, D.F.: Fondo de Cultura Económica, 1987), 168.
102 FAPECFT-PEC, expediente 64: GRUENING, Ernest (Dr.), legajo 1, fojas 10–11, inventario: 64. Calles to Gruening, February 7, 1924.

campaign, Carrillo Puerto's assassination at the hands of ostensibly loyal federal soldiers was an unspeakable object lesson for Calles and Obregón, and other politicians of the era, of the dangers of a political system that was still so thoroughly codependent on the army. It would not be an easy divorce.

Yet even in these dark days, Calles saw cause for hope, moving forward. "[The Indians] are asking for arms to avenge their apostle," he wrote to his brother, two days after Carrillo Puerto's murder.[103] Here was tangible evidence from the Southeast of the realization of Calles' stated hopes in the previous weeks that workers and campesinos across Mexico would unite in defense of Obregón's government, in recognition of their own best political interests.[104] Nor was it just popular forces whose will to support the government against the rebellion was crystallized by Carrillo Puerto's assassination. The Tabasco politician Justo A. Santa Anna wrote to Calles upon receiving the news, "this painful loss that we have suffered renews our energies and forces us to comprehend that all contemplation towards the traitors must stop and that we must combat them to the point of extermination."[105]

It has often been suggested that the Sonorans willingly allowed Carrillo Puerto's death as they diverged with him politically.[106] Yet it strains belief that a renowned military strategist like Obregón would willingly concede the whole of the Yucatán peninsula to rebel forces in order to rid himself of a wayward ally, particularly when he had no evident misgivings about ridding himself of political liabilities in much more straightforward and efficient ways. Furthermore, Carrillo Puerto's capture and execution were hardly foregone conclusions. Obregón's correspondence during the rebellion shows him to be hyperaware of the infrastructural and economic impacts of his war against the rebels. For instance, Obregón argued that to allow the Huasteca region to fall under rebel control for even a short time would be extremely disadvantageous because of the disruption it would cause to federal supply lines.[107]

It is yet harder to believe that Calles would have endorsed such a plan, given the lengths to which he had gone to build his alliances with the

103 FAPECFT-PEC, expediente: 53: ELIAS, Arturo M. (1919–1926), legajo: 9/22, foja: 362, inventario: 1717. Calles to Arturo M. Calles, January 5, 1924.

104 FAPECFT-PEC, expediente 17, SANTA ANNA, Justo (Dip.), legajo 1, fojas 52–53, inventario 5304. Calles to Justo A. Santa Anna, December 24, 1923.

105 FAPECFT-PEC, expediente 17, SANTA ANNA, Justo (Dip.), legajo 1, foja 60, inventario 5304. Justo A. Santa Anna to Plutarco Elías Calles, January 5, 1924.

106 See Joseph's arguments on this point, along with his analysis of several competing explanations. Joseph, *Revolution from Without*, 263–87.

107 AHSDN, XI/111/1-243, Serrano, Francisco R., Tomo 6, fojas 1461–63. Obregón to Serrano, February 11, 1924.

southeastern Socialists, and with Carrillo Puerto most of all. Calles praised his fallen ally: "for the Yucatecan reactionaries, Felipe [was] a scourge, for he and only he could rescue the poor from the clutches of the rich who insatiably profit from the worker."[108] Further, the de la Huerta rebellion was a moment in which Obregón was singularly willing to re-arm popular forces, and both of the Sonorans stood only to benefit from the mobilization of grassroots constituencies on their behalf. Lastly, scholarly consensus is that Carrillo Puerto was becoming relatively less politically radical by 1922–23, which would have obviated the Sonorans' alleged political repudiation of him.[109]

A simpler and more likely explanation is that Calles and Obregón simply did not have weapons and ammunition to send to Yucatán once they realized the gravity of the military situation there, and then events moved far too quickly for them to adequately correct their mistake. Calles was not able to make a concrete promise to send Carrillo Puerto a shipment of guns until December 10, by which time they almost certainly would have arrived too late to make a difference.[110] Further, a shipment of arms purchased in San Antonio was delayed because the company didn't receive the last payment due to them from the Mexican government.[111] These very well may have been some of the weapons that Calles intended to send to Yucatán. Meanwhile, the massive quantity of surplus arms and ammunition from the First World War that the US government sold to Obregón's government didn't arrive until January.[112] Even then, the government still didn't have sufficient ammunition for its troops; in some cases, federal troops had guns but not the appropriate bullets.[113] A much-needed shipment of ammunition from the US government didn't arrive until January 12, which Obregón ordered be sent preferentially to the front lines.[114] It was enough to arm thousands of federal soldiers, but it came over a week after Carrillo Puerto's death.[115]

108 FAPECFT-PEC, expediente: 53: ELIAS, Arturo M. (1919–1926), legajo: 9/22, foja: 362, inventario: 1717. Calles to Arturo M. Calles, January 5, 1924.

109 See, for example, Andrews, "Robert Haberman," 200–1.

110 FAPECFT, expediente 25, CARRILLO PUERTO, Felipe, legajo 6/7, foja 346, inventario 830. Calles to Carrillo Puerto, December 10, 1923.

111 León, *Crónica del poder*, 169–70.

112 AHSDN, XI/111/1-243, Serrano, Francisco R., Tomo 5, foja 1002. Obregón to Serrano, January 11, 1924.

113 AHSDN, XI/111/1-243, Serrano, Francisco R., Tomo 4, foja 942. Serrano to Obregón, January 9, 1924; foja 955. Serrano to Obregón, January 10, 1924. On problems with armaments, see foja 966. Serrano to Obregón, January 11, 1924.

114 AHSDN, XI/111/1-243, Serrano, Francisco R., Tomo 5, foja 1002. Obregón to Serrano, January 11, 1924.

115 AHSDN, XI/111/1-243, Serrano, Francisco R., Tomo 4, foja 974. Obregón to Serrano, January 11, 1924; foja 992. Obregón to Serrano, January 11, 1924.

In March of 1924, when the rebellion had been largely overcome elsewhere, President Obregón dispatched Secretary of War Francisco Serrano to the Southeast to oversee the remaining military cleanup of the region.[116] Serrano served as Obregón's representative in Yucatán, observing and reporting back to the president on the political reorganization of the state following Carrillo Puerto's death.[117] In mid-May, Serrano reported that the political situation in the state was "definitively resolved," and that the military there was once more subordinated to the state and federal governments. He added that with the assistance of federal troops, there had been no further disturbances in the state.[118]

Serrano's task also included political stabilization. On Obregón's orders, Serrano organized and directly participated in negotiations between Socialist governor José Iturralde's government and the henequen planters. These talks were "violent" at first, with recriminations on both sides. The planters threatened a general work stoppage, and the state government threatened to retaliate by seizing their plantations. Serrano reported to Obregón that after four or five days, he had successfully mediated between the state and the henequen producers, and that the planters had agreed to indefinitely suspend their plans for the stoppage, to allow fellow producers to continue to work with the Comisión Exportadora, and to take their case for a free henequen market to the courts.[119]

Obregón had his own ideas about how Yucatán's henequen market should be managed. He wrote to Serrano that he approved of a proposal made to him by a group of henequen planters that created a management committee for the henequen economy, comprising one representative from each of three cooperatives of large, medium, and small producers. The state government would also have a representative on the committee. Obregón did not favor continuing Carrillo Puerto's policies of strict state control and regulation of the henequen sector, or such extensive oversight of the state's economy more broadly. He explained to Serrano: "As far as I'm concerned, this is the best formula because it maintains control over sales without being an official institution, which by itself leaves room for many debates

---

116 AHSDN, XI/111/1-243, Serrano, Francisco R., Tomo 7, foja 1611. Obregón to Serrano, March 31, 1924.

117 In a rare case of explicitly documented federal interference in local politics, Obregón wrote to Serrano: "you are already aware of the agreement this Executive entered into so that the governorship of the state would be given to Mr. Iturralde." AHSDN, XI/111/1-243, Serrano, Francisco R., Tomo 5, foja 1154. Obregón to Serrano, May 7, 1924.

118 AHSDN, XI/111/1-243, Serrano, Francisco R., Tomo 4, foja 814. Serrano to Obregón, May 18, 1924.

119 AHSDN, XI/111/1-243, Serrano, Francisco R., Tomo 4, foja 804. Serrano to Obregón, May 25, 1924; foja 820. Serrano to Obregón, May 24, 1924; foja 805. Serrano to Obregón, May 26, 1924.

and protests." He ordered Serrano to stay in the state until "this delicate matter" was resolved.[120]

The de la Huerta Rebellion in Chiapas, 1923–1924

Chiapas was the least politically stable state in the Southeast when the de la Huerta rebellion arrived in the region. In 1920, Obregón empowered the leader of the Mapache rebellion, Tiburcio Fernández Ruiz as governor, and by 1923, he had been widely criticized as a corrupt dictator. At the same time, led by Carlos Vidal and Ricardo Alfonso Paniagua, the Chiapas Socialists had been expanding their political operation and growing their base of support both at the local level and in Mexico City, clearly with the 1924 gubernatorial election in mind. By that time, they enjoyed the strong support of Calles, Carrillo Puerto and the CROM. Yet in a rare instance of unanimity in a state notorious for its fractious politics, both the Mapache government and the Socialists supported the federal government during the rebellion.

Álvaro Obregón famously purchased the loyalty of many Mexican generals before and during the de la Huerta rebellion, and Carlos A. Vidal's promotion to General de Brigada in August of 1923 was almost certainly intended to preemptively secure his loyalty.[121] In spite of Obregón's favoritism toward his archrival Fernández Ruiz, it is doubtful that Vidal would have rebelled. A general's political outlook was not a reliable predictor of whether he could be counted upon to defend the government, as Salvador Alvarado's defection to the rebels demonstrated. Nevertheless, Vidal's politics were substantially to the left of de la Huerta's, particularly when it came to land and labor reform. More importantly, Vidal's most important political allies were Calles and Carrillo Puerto. Furthermore, in the years since his 1920 gubernatorial defeat, his loyalty to Obregón had already paid significant dividends, as he attained increasingly lofty positions within the Ministry of War. Whether Vidal intended to return to Chiapas to run for governor again, or to remain in Mexico City to pursue a career in administration or politics, remaining loyal to Obregón's government during the rebellion was his best option. It was the obvious choice for Fernández Ruiz, too, and the alliance that Obregón forged by favoring the Mapaches in 1920 in exchange for control of Chiapas' state government held fast. By that time, Fernández Ruiz was notorious in Mexico City, and Obregón's support was the only reason he was able to retain the governorship.

120   AHSDN, XI/111/1-243, Serrano, Francisco R., Tomo 5, foja 1249. Obregón to Serrano, May 26, 1924.
121   AHSDN, XI/111/3-1838, Vidal, Carlos A., Tomo 2, foja 470.

Even so, no political harmony was achieved within Chiapas. Led by Victórico Grajales of Chiapa de Corzo, a rebel faction allied with Vidal and the Socialists rose against both the de la Huerta rebels and the Mapache government. The rebellion was mediated by the federal commander in the state, General Donato Bravo Izquierdo, who protected the rebels from reprisals by Fernández Ruiz and then sent them to fight against the de la Huerta forces in Tabasco. He also armed Socialist battalions to fight against the de la Huerta-allied rebellion of Alberto Pineda, who briefly captured San Cristóbal and continued fighting in the highlands until his forces were defeated in July of 1924.[122] The paradoxical result of this confusing array of local and national alliances and enmities was that although it was internally rocked by the rebellion, Chiapas was the only southeastern state that never fell to the Delahuertistas.

Meanwhile, Carlos Vidal became an important player in the fight against the de la Huerta rebellion outside of Chiapas. He returned to active military duty several months before the rebellion began, initially stationed in Aguascalientes as Chief of Military Operations.[123] He led a campaign against rebel forces there, but was forced to flee when his troops defected to the other side.[124] When Calles returned to active duty in San Luis Potosí, he specially requested from Obregón and Serrano that Vidal be posted under his command, and ordered Vidal to Tampico.[125] Calles and Vidal were in near-daily communication for the next several months.

Vidal's work for Calles in Tampico was not strictly military. In addition to serving as Chief of Military Operations, he was put in charge of popular recruitment. In one instance, Obregón personally ordered Vidal to recruit a group of armed agraristas to fight for the government.[126] Vidal regularly wrote to Calles in these months to request arms for local factions and newly recruited soldiers and to inform him of the numbers of new recruits he could provide. At the same time, he was working for Calles' presidential campaign, and collaborating with the Calles campaign committee to arm popular forces to defend the government.[127] Vidal's dual commission makes especially clear that Calles' campaign and the military campaign

122 Benjamin, *A Rich Land, a Poor People*, 158–60.
123 AHSDN, XI/111/3-1838, Vidal, Carlos A., Tomo 4, foja 793. Sria. De Guerra to Vidal, September 28, 1923.
124 *The New York Times*, December 14, 1923, p. 2. "Evacuation of Puebla."
125 FAPECFT, APEC, expediente 118: VIDAL, Carlos A. (Gral.), legajo 1/4, foja 2, inventario 5886. Vidal to Calles, December 15, 1923.
126 AHSDN, XI/111/3-1838, Vidal, Carlos A., Tomo 4, foja 803. Obregón to Vidal, December 9, 1923.
127 FAPECFT, APEC, expediente 118: VIDAL, Carlos A. (Gral.), legajo 1/4, foja 8, inventario 5886. Vidal to Calles, December 19, 1923.

against the rebels were integral parts of the same project, undertaken by the same personnel.

Vidal's importance as Calles' ally and agent became even greater when Carrillo Puerto was killed. On the same days in early January of 1924 that Calles was receiving Vidal's updates about his progress with popular organizing in Tampico, he was also receiving ominous hints and rumors from Yucatán. With Carrillo Puerto's death, Calles lost his most important and powerful ally in the Southeast, and most of the region fell into the hands of the rebels for several months. There was no replacing Carrillo Puerto, but Calles still needed a trusted Socialist ally in the region. Ramón Félix Flores of Campeche had become less and less politically docile, and Tomás Garrido Canabal of Tabasco was a dedicated Obregonista who had not yet proven his reformist mettle. Carlos Vidal's credentials were solid and steadfast, and further proven by the work he did for Calles during the rebellion. What's more, the Chiapas Socialists had been campaigning for Calles' presidential candidacy since before the de la Huerta rebellion began. The agronomist Raymundo Enríquez, Chiapas Socialist Party cofounder, undertook the running of Calles' campaign in Chiapas. Part of this effort was the further consolidation of the Chiapas Socialist Party. Once the de la Huerta rebellion was defeated, the party, stronger than ever, rededicated itself to campaigning for Calles at the state level.[128]

The de la Huerta Rebellion in Tabasco, 1923–1924

Like Felipe Carrillo Puerto, Governor Tomás Garrido Canabal saw the de la Huerta rebellion coming well before it arrived in Tabasco, and by November of 1923 he was already attempting to replace any bureaucrats there who were rumored to be sympathetic to Adolfo de la Huerta.[129] Garrido had struggled to maintain his government as Tabasco's interim governor, and had significant difficulties in controlling the state once he was elected, too. As rumors of imminent military rebellion rippled throughout Mexico, Garrido had every reason to be concerned. Garrido helped to fuel some of these rumors, writing to Calles that he was certain that a rebellion in support of the old revolutionary leader Carlos Greene was unfolding in Tabasco, and that it would likely begin by December 1.[130] This time, Garrido's gossip was right.

128 FAPECFT, APEC, expediente 51: ENRIQUEZ, Raymundo E. (Ing.), legajo 1/9, fojas 9–11, inventario 1780. Raymundo Enríquez to Calles, April 4, 1924.
129 FAPECFT-PEC, expediente: 140, GARRIDO CANABAL, Tomás (Lic.), legajo 1/7, foja 58, inventario: 2312. Garrido to Calles, November 17, 1923.
130 FAPECFT-PEC, expediente: 140, GARRIDO CANABAL, Tomás (Lic.), legajo 2/7, foja 79, inventario: 2312. Garrido to Calles, November 26, 1923.

The difference in Calles' responses to Garrido and Carrillo Puerto's pleas for assistance as they worried about rebel threats to their state governments is striking. While Carrillo Puerto had been exhorting Calles to send him weapons to arm the ligas de resistencia in Yucatán for nearly a year and Calles did not do so, Calles was quick to send military assistance to Garrido in Tabasco. Over a week before Guadalupe Sánchez and his supporters declared themselves in rebellion against Obregón's government, Calles assured Garrido that loyal federal troops were on their way to defend Tabasco.[131]

At a moment in which Calles and Obregón were desperately in need of loyalty and support from all quarters, their emphasis on defending Tabasco and their decision to wait to defend Yucatán were almost certainly strategic, rather than an expression of ideological affinity or preference for Garrido over Carrillo Puerto. First, defending Tabasco was of greater military urgency, particularly in the early phases of the rebellion. It bordered Veracruz, where Calles and Obregón were well informed that the rebellion was likely to begin, making the military threat to Tabasco both greater and more imminent than the threat to Yucatán. Second, Tabasco had been much more politically unstable than Yucatán in 1922–23, again making the threat of rebellion appear greater there than in Yucatán, where Carrillo Puerto had long been touting the numbers of liga members who were prepared to defend the federal government. Carrillo Puerto had also been in power for longer than Garrido, and had consolidated his control of his state more fully, even if the political peace in Yucatán remained fragile. Lastly, the numbers support Obregón and Calles' decision: by the rebels' own count, there were 3,000 rebel soldiers in Tabasco over the course of the rebellion, and only 300 in Yucatán.[132]

Calles' correspondence with Garrido from the early days of the rebellion offers another clue as to why Calles and Obregón were so slow to send weapons and troops to defend Yucatán. Although Calles and Obregón were quick to dispatch troops to Tabasco before the rebellion had even begun, Calles expressed absolute confidence to Garrido that the rebellion would neither become a serious threat nor last for long. Even as Garrido sent him increasingly panicked reports of what was taking place in Tabasco and begged for further assistance, Calles calmly assured him that the situation would be resolved in short order.[133] If Calles and Obregón were as confident as they seem to have been that the rebellion would be defeated

131 FAPECFT-PEC, expediente: 140, GARRIDO CANABAL, Tomás (Lic.), legajo 2/7, foja 81, inventario: 2312. Calles to Garrido, November 28, 1923.

132 Martínez Assad, *El laboratorio de la revolución*, 160.

133 FAPECFT-PEC, expediente: 140, GARRIDO CANABAL, Tomás (Lic.), legajo 2/7, foja 84, inventario: 2312. Calles to Garrido, December 13, 1923; foja 98: Calles to Garrido, December 20, 1923.

quickly and easily, it makes sense that they would have rushed to defend Tabasco before Yucatán, for reasons of its proximity to the epicenter of the rebellion in Veracruz alone. If the Sonorans truly did not anticipate that Tabasco might fall to the rebels, they certainly could not have anticipated that Yucatán would.

It was a terrible miscalculation. Once the rebellion began, Tabasco was one of the first states targeted by the rebels.[134] "The situation is very bad," Garrido wrote to Calles in mid-December, as he repeated the reports that he had received that the rebels planned to occupy the southern part of the state.[135] Garrido was also vocal about his fears about what had taken place in Yucatán and Campeche after receiving word that the federal garrisons there had rebelled. A week before Carrillo Puerto's capture by rebel forces, Garrido pointedly asked Calles whether or not Carrillo Puerto was still alive.[136] Months earlier, Garrido met with Carrillo Puerto in Veracruz. Chronically suspicious of the federal military, Garrido warned Carrillo Puerto of the potential threat that Yucatán's Chief of Military Operations posed to his government.[137] It was the same colonel that sent Carrillo Puerto before a firing squad in early January.

The prolonged battle for Tabasco's capital city Villahermosa in late December of 1923 was one of the bloodiest episodes of the rebellion up to that point.[138] Garrido reported to Calles that he was on the front lines helping to defend the city, along with other prominent local politicians. He regretfully informed Calles that the civilian population had been largely unable to participate in the defense of the city for lack of weapons, but that he had armed eighty men with the guns he had been able to find.[139] That same day, Obregón wrote to the Mexican consul in New Orleans, requesting his help to acquire 500 guns with 300 cartridges each to be sent to Tabasco.[140] A few days later, as the battle for Villahermosa waged on, Garrido asked Calles if it was necessary to obtain legislative approval to arm workers and peasants to fight in support of the government. Months later, the state remained in rebel hands, and a group of workers wrote to Calles

---

134 Martínez Assad argues that because of its geography, and specifically, its relative isolation, that Tabasco became the most important piece of rebel territory in 1923–24. Martínez Assad, *El laboratorio de la revolución*, 160.

135 FAPECFT-PEC, expediente: 140, GARRIDO CANABAL, Tomás (Lic.), legajo 2/7, foja 82, inventario: 2312. Garrido to Calles, December 13, 1923.

136 FAPECFT-PEC, expediente: 140, GARRIDO CANABAL, Tomás (Lic.), legajo 2/7, foja 92, inventario: 2312. Garrido to Calles, December 15, 1923.

137 Canudas, *Tropico rojo, Vol. 1*, 1, 113.

138 *The New York Times*, December 20, 1923, p. 1. "Rebel Reinforcements Called Up."

139 FAPECFT-PEC, expediente: 140, GARRIDO CANABAL, Tomás (Lic.), legajo 2/7, foja 107, inventario: 2312. Garrido to Calles, December 23, 1923.

140 FAPECFT-PEC, expediente 5: OBREGON, Álvaro (Gral.), legajo 4/13, foja 191, inventario 4038. Obregón to Consul of New Orleans, December 23, 1923.

themselves, requesting to be armed in order to join Garrido to fight for the government and take revenge on the rebels.[141]

The memory of Garrido's personal leadership of workers in the battle for Villahermosa would win him admiration and loyalty from workers in Tabasco for years to come, but it was not enough.[142] After over a month of fighting, Villahermosa fell to the rebels on January 10, 1924.[143] Garrido was forced to flee and to briefly go into hiding as the rebels overtook the city, by his own account spending several days hiding behind a bed after refusing to sign his own resignation.[144] Carrillo Puerto had been executed the week before, and some rebel leaders evidently hoped to rid themselves of a second southeastern Socialist governor.[145] Once the rebels had taken control, Jorge Prieto Laurens personally named a governor to replace Garrido.[146]

The rebellion in Tabasco proved to be one of the most difficult for the government to rout, and it was the last part of the Southeast that federal forces recaptured. Several local rebel groups had arisen in the state, led by local dissidents.[147] As the rebellion wore on, an added difficulty was that rebels from other parts of Mexico fled to the Southeast, and to Tabasco in particular, as the tide of the rebellion turned in the government's favor.[148] This included Adolfo de la Huerta himself, who fled from Tabasco's port of Frontera to the United States in February. In March, Garrido was still pleading Obregón and Calles for assistance in the fight for Tabasco, now from exile in Veracruz.[149] By that time, Obregón had dispatched Francisco Serrano to the Southeast, suggesting to him that "the most vigorous campaign that you can wage against [the rebels] for the time being is to leave them to live in those states in the most distressing of conditions that they are experiencing, and it is the most practical way of destroying them without any great sacrifices on our part."[150] Obregón argued that the best strategy was to wait to embark on the campaign against the rebels in the

---

141 FAPECFT-PEC, expediente: 140, GARRIDO CANABAL, Tomás (Lic.), legajo 2/7, fojas 110 and 111, inventario: 2312. Garrido to Calles, December 28, 1923; Obreros Frontera de Tabasco to Calles, March 27, 1924.

142 AGN-TGC, caja 11, expediente: 3. Antonio del Valle Pardo to Garrido, March 3, 1926.

143 Martínez Assad, *El laboratorio de la revolución*, 160–61. Canudas, *Tropico rojo, Vol. 1*, 1, 122.

144 FAPECFT-PEC, expediente: 140, GARRIDO CANABAL, Tomás (Lic.), legajo 2/7, fojas 121–23, inventario: 2312. Garrido to Calles, April 10, 1923. Garrido spent part of his exile in Guatemala. AGN-TGC, caja: 5, expediente: 10. Alejandro Lastra to Garrido, March 6, 1924.

145 Canudas, *Tropico rojo, Vol. 1*, 1, 123.   146 Ibid., 122.

147 FAPECFT-PEC, expediente: 140, GARRIDO CANABAL, Tomás (Lic.), legajo 2/7, foja 121–23, inventario: 2312. Garrido to Calles, April 10, 1924.

148 Martínez Assad, *El laboratorio de la revolución*, 160–61.

149 FAPECFT-PEC, expediente: 140, GARRIDO CANABAL, Tomás (Lic.), legajo 2/7, foja 112, inventario: 2312. Garrido to Calles, March 29, 1924.

150 AHSDN, XI/111/1-243, Serrano, Francisco R., Tomo 5, foja 1350. Obregón to Serrano, March 24, 1924.

Southeast until all of the elements necessary for a decisive triumph were in place.[151] Finally, at the end of March, Obregón ordered a new federal advance against the rebels and sent 1,500 new troops to Tabasco.[152]

After several months of exile, Garrido personally participated in the military offensive to retake Tabasco.[153] He snidely dismissed Tabasco's politicians in Mexico City who did not show similar dedication to freeing their state from the rebellion, and invited them to join him.[154] He arrived at the port of Frontera in May with eight battalions and three regiments of federal troops to finally recapture Villahermosa.[155] Despite Obregón's confidence and planning and Garrido's angry determination to retake control of the state, the battle for Tabasco dragged on into June of 1924.[156] In July, federal forces were still pursuing suspected rebels who had fled across the Tabasco state line into Chiapas.[157]

In an ironic twist, one of the architects of southeastern Socialism met his gruesome end in the region, fighting for de la Huerta, long after de la Huerta himself was safely in exile. Salvador Alvarado returned to Mexico from his own exile in the United States in order to fight for the Delahuertistas. He was captured by the young General Lázaro Cárdenas in Colima in February of 1924, who allowed him to escape, eventually reaching safety in exile in Vancouver. In March, de la Huerta summoned Alvarado to New York and sent him back to the Southeast as his new military commander. Alvarado arrived in Tabasco shortly thereafter, where in addition to his military duties he advised on the rebels' efforts to export Yucatecan henequen in order to fund their war.[158] As the federal forces pushed southward in May, Alvarado fled Tabasco for Chiapas, hoping to unite his forces with Alberto Pineda's. He was betrayed by a fellow rebel commander en route, likely by arrangement with Obregonista forces, and

151   AHSDN, XI/111/1-243, Serrano, Francisco R., Tomo 7, foja 1585. Obregón to Serrano, March 25, 1924.

152   AHSDN, XI/111/1-243, Serrano, Francisco R., Tomo 5, foja 1133. Obregón to Serrano, March 31, 1924.

153   FAPECFT-PEC, expediente: 140, GARRIDO CANABAL, Tomás (Lic.), legajo 2/7, foja 133, inventario: 2312. Garrido to Calles, May 15, 1924.

154   FAPECFT-PEC, expediente: 140, GARRIDO CANABAL, Tomás (Lic.), legajo 2/7, fojas 118–19, inventario: 2312. Garrido to Calles, March 25, 1924.

155   Martínez Assad, *El laboratorio de la revolución*, 162.

156   AHSDN, XI/111/1-243, Serrano, Francisco R., Tomo 5, foja 1244. Serrano to Obregón, May 29, 1924. Canudas, *Tropico rojo*, Vol. 1, 1, 130.

157   FAPECFT-SGON, fondo: 1, expediente: 567: ORTIZ, Juan (Corl.), legajo 1, foja 1, inventario 497. Juan M. Ortíz to Soledad González, July 8, 1924.

158   FAPECFT, Colección Adolfo de la Huerta (hereafter ADH), Alvarado to Miguel Palacios Macedo, April 9, 1924. This effort reportedly netted the rebels over 500,000 pesos in one month. Miguel Palacios Macedo to Cándido Aguilar, April 7, 1924.

killed on June 9, shot in the head at point blank range.[159] Historian Enrique Plasencia de la Parra argues that Garrido almost certainly participated in Alvarado's betrayal and assassination, perhaps as retaliation against Alvarado for his interference with Garrido's political projects in Tabasco in the late 1910s, or perhaps to win favor with Obregón, who despised Alvarado.[160] Whether or not Garrido was involved, he, Vidal, and Carrillo Puerto had ended up on the other side of the war as the man from whom they all had taken significant inspiration. Not for the last time, leaders of southeastern Socialism found themselves at bitter odds over the matter of presidential succession, with mortal consequences.

Conclusions

The steadfast belief by so many politicians and soldiers that Calles and Obregón could be successfully overthrown in 1923–24 is powerful testimony to the precariousness of their grip on power that should not be overlooked or dismissed, in spite of their subsequent political successes. They both survived the de la Huerta rebellion (literally as well as politically), but this was by no means inevitable, nor was their ongoing domination of Mexican politics by any means guaranteed in 1924. Outside of Mexico, doubts about the Sonorans' political future ran rampant, even once the rebels had been defeated.[161] Calles' friend, the North American journalist Ernest Gruening, argued to him that the only way to ensure peace in Mexico in the long term was to eliminate the federal army, or at least to reduce it to a force that could be defeated by armed workers and campesinos.[162] Foreign commentators were not alone in zeroing in on potential weaknesses of the remaining Sonorans. Dissident politicians and generals, both in Mexico and in exile, continued to scheme against Calles and Obregón for the rest of the 1920s.

Calles and Obregón took different lessons from the de la Huerta episode that would decisively shape their respective political careers in the years that followed. Both recognized that a political system composed almost entirely of politically ambitious generals had to be reformed to survive. However, the transitions they envisioned from the Mexican Revolution to postrevolutionary political stability were quite different. For Calles,

159 Taracena, *Historia de la Revolución en Tabasco*, 1, 464–65.
160 Plasencia de la Parra, *Personajes y escenarios*, 266–69.
161 See, for example, an article in *Foreign Affairs* that suggested that Calles would not be able to stay in power without Obregón's support. "The Presidential Dilemma in Mexico," *Foreign Affairs* 3, no. 1 (1924).
162 FAPECFT-PEC, expediente 64: GRUENING, Ernest (Dr.), legajo 1, fojas 12–15, inventario: 64. Gruening to Calles, March 20, 1924.

political parties had become indispensable by the time he embarked on his presidential campaign. The support that parties lent to the government's cause during the de la Huerta rebellion further confirmed for Calles their importance for Mexico's political future. Calles paid tribute to the particular significance of the Socialist Party of the Southeast with a visit to Carrillo Puerto's hometown of Motul in July of 1924, where he praised the political and social mission of the recently fallen Socialist leader and attended the granting of an ejido to the community of Kaxatah.[163]

This was a new kind of Mexican political party. Following the model of the PLM and the Socialist parties in the Southeast, Calles recognized the advantages of including popular groups in national politics (at least nominally), and that political parties were the best means of connecting politicians with grassroots constituencies. After Calles failed to win sufficient support within the federal army, and at a moment in which the utter inadequacy of Mexico's electoral traditions was laid dramatically bare, he found new means of transforming himself into a viable presidential candidate. Although Calles had little to no direct contact with the southeastern ligas de resistencia, through his alliance with their leaders, their support for his candidacy gave him a new form of postrevolutionary political legitimacy that Adolfo de la Huerta never had. This moment was therefore an instrumental precedent for the mass politics that would take hold in Mexico in subsequent decades. During the rebellion, Calles' allies in the Southeast as well as in the PLM and the PNA demonstrated that popular organizations were now inescapably part of the balance of power, as armed workers and campesinos stepped in to support the federal government at a time when the military could not be counted upon to defend it.

In contrast, Obregón was more reluctant to arm popular groups and remained suspicious of political parties. The PCN's convincing challenge to him undoubtedly made him more so. The Cooperatists had demonstrated that an organized group of dissenting legislators could present a substantial challenge to a sitting president, in spite of Mexico's tradition of executive branch dominance. Obregonista legislators expelled their Cooperatist colleagues from the Chamber of Deputies during the de la Huerta rebellion to minimize the political risk to the president, setting another important precedent in the process.[164] Obregón's attitudes toward future political rebellions within the legislature were deeply colored by this experience. Following the de la Huerta rebellion, Obregón also sought to

163 FAPECFT-FEC, serie: 407, expediente: 10: LEON, Luis L. (Ing. y Dip.), legajo 1, foja 2, inventario 1317. Luis L. León to José Manuel Puig Casauranc, July 3, 1924.

164 On the purge of Cooperatist legislators, which was led by future interim president of Mexico and PNR party president Emilio Portes Gil, see Fowler-Salamini, "De-Centering the 1920s," 306–7.

reform the military, and thereby to eliminate further future coups and revolts from within its ranks.[165]

In sum, for Obregón, the solution was to remove individual sources of potential competition for power, rather than to definitively resolve long-term questions of presidential succession and the course of postrevolutionary political institutionalization more generally. Sometimes this was done through bribery, and the "cannon shot of 50,000 pesos" that Obregón famously quipped that no Mexican general could resist. Other times, it was accomplished through exile, as in the case of de la Huerta and many others. However, Obregón also occasionally eliminated rivals and potential rebels through arrest and/or assassination.[166] Obregón's reforms of the military were essential to the stabilization of the country and the long-term peace that future presidents were able to sustain. However, Obregón himself would prove to be one of the most problematic impediments to the creation of enduring political institutions, as shall be seen in later chapters.

The history of the de la Huerta rebellion demonstrates that state and national politics were deeply integrated in the 1920s. A local political crisis in San Luis Potosí helped to provoke a national political calamity, which in turn resulted in the downfall and death of Carrillo Puerto in Yucatán. This too had its own long-term influence, as it served to strengthen Calles' political bond with Carlos Vidal and the Chiapas Socialist Party, and with Tomás Garrido Canabal and the Radical Socialist Party of Tabasco. As shall be seen, this turn of events would have its own national political repercussions.

Lastly, the de la Huerta rebellion forced the postrevolutionary federal government to consolidate its military and political control over the whole of Mexico to a degree that none of the revolutionary factions had previously been able to accomplish. The Southeast had been an unanticipated front in the conflict, and was only recaptured with some difficulty, in spite of the Socialists' loyalty to the Sonorans and their government. The rebellion and its aftermath made clear the region's political and strategic significance to the nation, with decisive long-term consequences.

165 Plasencia de la Parra, *Personajes y escenarios*, 90–91. On postrevolutionary reform of the military, see Thomas G. Rath, *Myths of Demilitarization in Postrevolutionary Mexico, 1920–1960* (Chapel Hill: University of North Carolina Press, 2013).
166 Brush, "The de la Huerta rebellion in Mexico, 1923–1924," 155.

4

A Harder Line

Socialist Tabasco, 1920–1927

There is no triumph without struggle, nor glory without sacrifice.

Tomás Garrido Canabal

The Sonorans had no greater success in securing loyal Socialist allies than in Tabasco under governor Tomás Garrido Canabal in 1924–26. As governor, Garrido distinguished himself as one of the most radical politicians in Mexico thanks to the extreme implementation of his reform programs. He was one of the most adamant of Calles and Obregón's partisans during the de la Huerta rebellion, and even more so in its aftermath. In nearly all other respects, Garrido was notorious for his political independence. "He belongs to no political party," a Ministry of Government agent reported in 1924, "but his government's general politics have always been in agreement with General Obregón."[1]

Borrowing liberally from Salvador Alvarado and Felipe Carrillo Puerto, Garrido developed his own models of southeastern Socialism, political organizing, and political control. Although he hewed closely to Carrillo Puerto's basic concept of a statewide umbrella organization comprising many distinct and locally managed constituent groups, Garrido's political system was a less elegant and more authoritarian implementation of Socialist corporatism than the Yucatecan one. It was nevertheless grounded in many of the same political justifications.

Garrido's adaptations to the Yucatecan model helped him to stay in power for longer than almost any Mexican politician in any office in the postrevolutionary period. His government also set a high water mark for state-led anticlericalism in the years directly preceding the Cristero War of 1926–29. Garrido's political innovations also had far-reaching consequences for Mexico's political future. Above all, Socialist Tabasco provided critical precedents for employing the organizational structures of Southeastern Socialism in pursuit of less-than democratic goals, while adamantly maintaining a veneer of representative populism. By the

---

1 AGN-DGIPS, c. 171, exp. 12. Report on Garrido by Agent 18, October 15, 1924.

mid-1920s Mexico had long experience with authoritarianism, but never as managed and channeled through a political party as it was in Socialist Tabasco.

Socialism in Tabasco, 1923–1926

Even by his own estimation, Garrido's first months as Tabasco's governor were inauspicious, and that was before the de la Huerta rebels overthrew his government. Garrido had won the governorship in 1923 in a political dogfight, but he inherited a deeply divided and politically unstable state, and his election didn't put an end to any of that. He wrote to President Obregón in January of 1923 and expressed his frustration frankly. After so many years of violence and turmoil, the state government was in financial ruin and deeply in debt. As local rebellions continued to arise and citizens faced kidnapping and violent assaults by rebel forces, Garrido feared that he would not be able to govern effectively.[2] Tabasco's perennial insurgent Carlos Greene only agreed to a settled peace with the state government in June of 1923, but then joined the de la Huerta rebellion a few months later. Garrido's task of pacifying and rebuilding Tabasco was yet further complicated by General Luis T. Mireles, the chief of military operations in the state, who had wielded a tremendous amount of power there for several years and was loath to relinquish any of it to the new governor. Unable to work with a purported ally, Garrido eventually managed to have Mireles removed from the state.[3]

The de la Huerta rebellion was far worse. It left an enduring scar on the politics of Tabasco, on its particular brand of Socialism, and, it would seem, on Garrido himself. Garrido's support of the government during the rebellion cemented his alliances with Obregón and Calles, but his experience of the rebellion was also formative to his policies once he retook power.[4] In particular, the downfall and death of Felipe Carrillo Puerto was a powerful object lesson for Garrido. For the rest of the 1920s, he strove to make sure that the mistakes that he perceived had been made in Socialist Yucatán and had cost Carrillo Puerto his life were not repeated in Tabasco. In the short term, this meant the immediate, relentless purging of suspected rebels from the state. From Garrido's point of view, this was an opportunity that the Yucatecan Socialists had missed in the rebellion's aftermath in their state, as the arrest orders for Carrillo Puerto's killers were only issued months after his death.[5] The memory of Carrillo Puerto's

2   AGN-TGC, caja: 5, expediente: 4. Garrido to Obregón, January 9, 1923.
3   Canudas, *Tropico rojo, Vol. 1*, 1, 109–12.   4   See also Harper, "Revolutionary Tabasco," 71.
5   FAPECFT-SGON, expediente: 740: SIMON, Neguib, legajo 1, fojas 2–4, inventario 664. Neguib Simón to Calles, June 2, 1924.

execution shaped Garrido's decision making in more personal ways, too. Three years later, he requested that his chauffer and his groom be allowed to carry arms so that he would be protected from the kind of attacks by "disoriented soldiers" that Carrillo Puerto had suffered.[6]

In the long term, the rebellion and its consequences in Yucatán inspired Garrido's permanent mistrust of the federal military, his perennial efforts to arm Tabasco's ligas de resistencia, and when it came to politics, his substantially more disciplinarian approach to organizing his partisans. It also helped to fuel his sustained antagonism toward foreign capitalists and the Catholic Church, two of the forces that were widely perceived in the Southeast to have been behind Carrillo Puerto's overthrow and murder.[7] It is indubitable that the landed classes and their allies across the Southeast eyed Carrillo Puerto's unfolding reform project in Yucatán with significant trepidation. This included elites in Tabasco, although the Socialist Party of the Southeast had not made significant inroads there. Garrido understood that this was the general nature of the well-funded antipathy he faced from the elite of Tabasco who threw their lot in with the rebels. He mourned that organized workers and campesinos in Tabasco were being systematically targeted by a "retrograde capitalist army." As far as Garrido was concerned, the rebellion was not just an attack on his partisans, although it was certainly that, but also an attack on his fledgling political machine.[8] In sum, his bitterness in the long aftermath of the rebellion were formative to his politics in nearly every respect.

Upon reassuming power in 1924 Garrido was determined to unite, pacify, and govern the entirety of Tabasco once and for all. In doing so he hoped to leave an indelible imprint of reform, one that could not be so easily undone by an oppositionist or counterrevolutionary upsurge. He dedicated a tremendous amount of time and energy in subsequent years to identifying and weeding out rebels and suspected rebel sympathizers; "Delahuertista" became the ultimate political epithet in Tabasco for years to come, and a real liability for anyone designated as such. In his personal papers, Garrido kept a catalogue of alleged participants in the rebellion that remained in the state, organized by municipality and by profession.[9] Many people wrote to the governor to protest their innocence in the face of

6   FAPECFT-FFT, expediente "9"/114, GARRIDO CANABAL, Tomás (Lic.), legajo 1, foja 2, inventario 565. Garrido to Calles, December 30, 1926.

7   FAPECFT-SGON, expediente: 740: SIMON, Neguib, legajo 1, fojas 2–4, inventario 664. Neguib Simón to Calles, June 2, 1924.

8   FAPECFT-PEC, expediente: 140, GARRIDO CANABAL, Tomás (Lic.), legajo 2/7, fojas 121–23, inventario: 2312. Garrido to Calles, April 10, 1924. Martínez Assad found that some de la Huerta sympathizers had justified the rebel takeover of the Southeast as a means of extirpating the "bolshevism" that had taken hold there. Martínez Assad, *El laboratorio de la revolución*, 25.

9   AGN-TGC, caja: 8, expediente: 9. Undated list, marked in pencil as "1924 or 1925."

accusations of rebel sympathies, but they rarely received anything but chilly contempt in response.[10] As late as 1928, both Garrido himself and Tabasco Socialists were still denouncing former alleged collaborators and supporters of de la Huerta.[11]

In the midst of his concerted effort to definitively establish political control and to eliminate sources of opposition, Garrido also embarked on an ambitious program of reform. One of his first moves was to remake the Tabasco Radical Party, originally created in the 1910s, into the Radical Socialist Party of Tabasco.[12] This mirrored Carrillo Puerto's earlier transformation of Alvarado's Socialist Party of Yucatán into the PSS. Garrido also followed Carrillo Puerto's course with his creation of his own system of ligas de resistencia, presided over by the Liga Central de Resistencia, which soon became one of the most powerful political institutions in Tabasco.

This process had begun before the de la Huerta rebellion. By that time, Garrido estimated that nearly all of the urban and rural working class had been organized into ligas, 2,000 strong in Frontera, with another estimated 3,500 members in Villahermosa. Garrido lamented that had they been supplied with sufficient arms, the ligas could have defeated the rebellion.[13] But it was only after the rebellion that Tabasco's liga system was fully consolidated as a crucial part of a fearsome political machine. In the early 1930s, as the Ministry of the Interior sought to make sense of Tabasco's idiosyncratic political system, one of its agents explained that the Radical Party and the Liga Central were two political parties that were "completely in agreement in all of their decisions."[14] This assessment was not entirely accurate, but it is telling. Both inside and outside of Tabasco in these years, it was difficult at best for observers (and sometimes even participants) to distinguish between the state government, the party, and the liga system, all of which acted to support each other and frequently to pursue the same projects and goals.

Tabasco's liga system was a significant adaptation of the Yucatecan model in several important respects. First, in Tabasco the ligas de resistencia were not just institutions of political representation and labor organizing, but also served as the official, government-sanctioned labor unions in the state. This had important consequences. Because the Socialist

10   See, for example, AGN-TGC, caja: 8, expediente: 4. Garrido to Héctor Pérez Martínez, February 23, 1925.

11   For two such examples: AGN-TGC, c. 116, exp. 5. Dip. A. Medel Ramos to Garrido, February 4, 1928. AGN-TGC, c. 116, exp. 7. Garrido to Municipal President of Jalpa de Méndez, March 23, 1928.

12   Martínez Assad, *El laboratorio de la revolución*, 164.

13   FAPECFT-PEC, expediente: 140, GARRIDO CANABAL, Tomás (Lic.), legajo 2/7, fojas 121–23, inventario: 2312. Garrido to Calles, April 10, 1924.

14   AGN-DGIPS, c. 172, exp. 1. Report by Agents 5 and 18. August 21, 1931.

party in Tabasco had its own labor unions, it refused to collaborate with the CROM in organizing the workers of the state, a significant difference from the Socialist Party of Chiapas in the same period (as discussed in detail in Chapter 5). The local CROM affiliate in Tabasco frequently clashed with the Liga Central over the rights of its "free" (meaning non-liga) members to work, and finally petitioned for federal intervention on its behalf, which was ignored by the state government once it was granted.[15] The estrangement between Garrido and the CROM ran deep enough that Garrido accused the CROM's leader, Luis N. Morones, of conspiring to have him killed in 1926.[16] The isolation of most of Tabasco's workers from national organized labor, and the degree to which Garrido's near-total control over the ligas allowed him to control the economy of the state, further contributed to the high concentration of power in Garrido's hands.

Second, by unionizing workers and connecting them to the Socialist Party through their labor, Garrido was able to guarantee membership numbers in his party in a way that no other Southeastern Socialist was able to, via a more clientelist system than was developed elsewhere in the region. The unequivocal linking of labor and politics in Tabasco effectively meant that anyone who wanted a higher paying, unionized job in Tabasco also had to support Garrido and his policies, both within the state and at the national level.[17] Belonging to the ligas, and thereby also supporting the Radical Party, was optional in theory but less so in practice, and became effectively mandatory in 1927. Workers that did not join ligas were routinely harassed and threatened, and businesses owned by nonmembers were boycotted.[18] There were also clear benefits to joining ligas. Garrido's thorough integration of politics and organized labor helped to ensure that the unionized workers of Tabasco were earning the highest wages in Mexico by 1930. Workers within the system also enjoyed extensive workplace safety regulations and protections that were enforced by state officials.

There were also clear benefits for the state government in controlling labor to the extent it did. Tellingly, there were no strikes in Tabasco under Garrido or his handpicked gubernatorial successor, Ausencio Cruz.[19] The state also boasted a balanced budget, and in some years a surplus.[20] And although the political system he created functioned to concentrate political power in his hands, unlike other governors of the era, Garrido

15 Stan Ridgeway, "Monoculture, Monopoly, and the Mexican Revolution: Tomás Garrido Canabal and the Standard Fruit Company in Tabasco (1920–1935)," *Mexican Studies / Estudios Mexicanos* 17, no. 1 (2001): 156–57.

16 Martínez Assad, *Breve historia de Tabasco*, 179.   17 Harper, "Revolutionary Tabasco," 74.

18 Ibid., 77–79. See also Ridgeway, "Monoculture, Monopoly, and the Mexican Revolution," 155.

19 Dulles, *Yesterday in Mexico*, 615.

20 Martínez Assad, *Breve historia de Tabasco*, 178. Ridgeway, "Monoculture, Monopoly, and the Mexican Revolution," 166.

distinguished himself for not taking advantage of his undeniable power to dramatically enrich himself, although he was known to dip into the state treasury to send generous gifts to well-placed allies in Mexico City.[21]

The structure of Tabasco's liga system was far more elaborate and far-reaching than in other states with ligas de resistencia, beyond the near-total integration of labor and politics. It was a complex, sometimes redundant set of institutional structures that was designed to maximize the reach of the Radical Socialist Party into the lives of the largest possible number of people in the state, both where they worked and where they lived. By the mid-1920s, the party's base comprised thirty-one ligas that were organized by profession, from sailors to teachers to carpenters to banana growers. Each of Tabasco's seventeen municipalities also had its own liga, which was an umbrella organization of all of the local ligas de resistencia of particular professions and towns within that jurisdiction. Centla, on the northwestern coast of Tabasco and home to the port city of Frontera, was one of the largest municipalities in the state and had the largest municipal liga after Villahermosa's, with over 4,000 members. By 1925 the Liga of Centla confederated nearly thirty smaller ligas that were organized by profession, as well as ligas of campesinos of particular towns.[22] All of the subsidiary ligas under these various umbrellas were also constituent organizations of the Liga Central and the Radical Socialist Party. Each local liga elected a president, a secretary, a treasurer, a labor agent, a claims agent, and a commissioner.[23] By 1927, the ligas de resistencia claimed to collectively have 21,913 members statewide.[24]

New ligas were formed throughout the mid-1920s. They often began with an assembly of local workers, sometimes of a particular town and in other cases of particular professions or industries within a locality, convened by the leader of the larger, municipal liga, who explained to the gathered crowd all of the potential advantages of unionization and membership in the statewide organization of ligas. Those in attendance were then invited to give their opinions before voting on whether or not to form a new liga and then choosing its leadership. The Liga Central and the other ligas in the state were then officially notified of the creation of the new organization.[25] On other occasions, local ligas formed of their own accord

21   Dulles, *Yesterday in Mexico*, 614.
22   AGN-TGC, c. 114, exp. 3. Fernando Arauz to Garrido, December 25, 1925. AGN-TGC, c. 115, exp. 1. Liga Central de Resistencia flyer, c. 1927.
23   AGN-TGC, c. 115, exp. 3. "Relación de las directivas que forman el Partido Socialista Radical, con anotación de las agrupaciones, 1927."
24   AGN-TGC, c. 115, exp. 1. Liga Central de Resistencia flyer, c. 1927.
25   AGN-TGC, c. 114, exp. 4. Notification by Teodomiro Fabre et al. of the creation of the Liga Mixta de Artesanos of Paraíso, May 13, 1925 and of the Liga of Obreros and Campesinos of Paraíso, May 14, 1925.

and then petitioned the relevant municipal liga for recognition, including of the labor monopolies they intended to assert, one of the understood prerogatives of ligas de resistencia.[26]

Campesinos also formed ligas, although in lesser numbers than workers, usually on the particular haciendas where they worked and sometimes with the active assistance of agents of the Liga Central.[27] Land reform was not a centerpiece of Garrido's brand of Socialism. In part, this was because there was not the demand for land in Tabasco that there was in Yucatán, where Socialist state-led land reform was much more ambitious and extensive. Tabasco had a comparatively small and less dense rural population, which meant that the Socialists there focused a larger part of their attention on reforms that benefited workers, rather than campesinos. Although collectively held ejidos were created in Tabasco in this era, unlike his fellow southeastern Socialists, Garrido was a supporter of the individually held pequeña propiedad favored by Calles and Obregón.[28] Still, many rural working people were incorporated into the statewide liga system, if not on the same scale as their urban counterparts. This incorporation was further institutionalized in 1928, when the Liga of Banana Producers was founded as the rural counterpart of the Liga Central, by which time bananas had become the state's most important crop.[29]

Liga members all paid regular dues to their local organization, typically about one peso per month. Garrido himself paid as much as sixty pesos monthly to the Liga Central, and also paid smaller dues to various local ligas, evidently as a matter of solidarity.[30] There were limits on how much ligas could charge their members; in 1927, Garrido personally admonished liga leaders for charging their campesino members too much in monthly dues. Collected dues were supposed to be spent by the local ligas on services and support for their members, such as care for members who fell ill, or other expenses that could not be shouldered by individuals, and ligas were not permitted to spend any remaining funds as they saw fit.[31]

An accounting report for the Liga Central from the month of January 1928 provides some insight into the larger organization's income

26 AGN-TGC, c. 114, exp. 4. Ernesto Magaña et al. of the Liga de Alijadores, Balseros y Estibadores del Puerto to President of the Liga de Resistencia of Centla, July 14, 1925.
27 See, for example, AGN-TGC, c. 115, exp. 6. Cecilio Vázquez to Garido, September 10, 1927.
28 According to Canudas, Tabasco's population density was only 11 people/km² in this period. Canudas, *Tropico rojo, Vol. 1*, 1, 133.
29 Ridgeway, "Monoculture, Monopoly, and the Mexican Revolution," 150.
30 See receipts for these payments: AGN-TGC, c. 114, exps. 3 and 4.
31 AGN-TGC, c. 115, exp. 9. Tomás Garrido Canabal to presidentes de sucursal de resistencia, November 18, 1927. In this case, Garrido reminded the liga leaders that collected dues must not be spent on fiestas or fireworks.

and expenses. Dues and inscriptions constituted about 60 percent of the organization's monthly income; the rest was nearly evenly divided between the sale of print materials, and membership credentials. Its principle expenses were printing costs, salaries for its employees, renovations of facilities, general expenses, and night schools for workers, in that order. Printing cost the Liga Central nearly four times the revenue that the sale of printed materials generated. In this particular month, the organization operated in the red, spending over 1,300 more pesos than it earned; it did better in the previous month or months, judging by the balance of nearly 3,000 pesos that was carried forward.[32]

Individual members of the ligas were linked to the state government through an escalating series of memberships in multiple, overlapping organizations. A worker that belonged to a liga in Tabasco in this period was considered a member of his local liga, and of the larger municipal liga to which it belonged, and of the statewide Liga Central. The redundancy of simultaneous memberships was not just so that each level of the liga system could make a substantive claim to a robust constituency, although it achieved that. This arrangement formalized each member's allegiance to the Socialist political machine at the local, regional, and state levels simultaneously, and cemented clientelist relationships between citizens and the state via the institutional structures of the Socialist Party. Crucially, the ligas constituted new political constituencies, including at the micro-local level (such as on haciendas) and independent of geography (such as professional ligas), in many cases where none had existed before. It was an extreme and highly effective form of single-party gerrymandering that went beyond the organization of popular constituencies that Carrillo Puerto had achieved in Yucatán in his short time in power.

In practice, it was also a markedly less representative variation of southeastern Socialism, in spite of its dramatic successes in grassroots organizing. On paper, members of local ligas in Tabasco were empowered to choose their boards of directors. The Liga Central did likewise at a convention organized for that purpose, comprising two delegates from every liga in the state.[33] But Garrido himself exercised a high degree of control over who was chosen to lead the ligas de resistencia, even at the local level. This was power that went well beyond that which was formally granted to him in his dual role as governor and president of the Liga Central. In one typical case in 1926, as the municipal liga of Frontera prepared to elect new leaders, the liga president wrote to Garrido Canabal

---

32   I do not have sufficient data to assess how typical this month was. AGN-TGC, c. 116, exp. 5. Ana Santa María to Garrido, January 31, 1928.
33   AGN-TGC, c. 114, exp. 3. Homero Margalli to Garrido, December 7, 1925.

asking for guidance on which candidates they were to support. "We await your orders," he added.[34]

Many of the ligas were plagued by administrative problems, internal conflicts, and disappointments with their elected leaders. However, even when the liga system patently failed or disappointed its grassroots members, the idea that revolutionary redemption was to be found within the system proved to be strikingly resilient among Tabasco's working people. Rather than fueling widespread discontent with the liga system or with its architects and directors, complaints about liga mismanagement often served to facilitate control of the base by the leadership. When there were disagreements within ligas that the members could not resolve among themselves, they frequently reached out to the Liga Central, as was appropriate within the system, but also to Garrido himself in the hope that he would formulate a fair resolution. In one such case in 1924, the liga of porters and cart drivers of Villahermosa denounced their own president, treasurer, and labor agent directly to Garrido as drunks who were unable to fulfill their duties. They pleaded with Garrido to help them to "moralize" their liga, and to expel various troublesome members.[35] In other cases, Garrido participated in even smaller, more personal matters within ligas. In 1928, a woodcutter named Paulino Castro was suspended from his liga for two months; he pleaded his case with Garrido personally, promising to accept any punishment for future transgressions. Garrido overturned his punishment by the liga with the understanding that Castro would be banned from membership for life in the case of any future misbehavior.[36] Numerous such examples suggest that Garrido's power over the liga system effectively knew no bounds, no matter how it was delimited on paper.

In the Liga Central's propaganda materials in 1927, Tomás Garrido Canabal was described as the "Maximum Leader of Socialism in the state of Tabasco."[37] Yet, like their counterparts across the Southeast, the Tabasco Socialists infrequently documented their ideology. Still, this was a brand of politics that inarguably included a core set of principles. The flag of the Radical Socialist Party was emblazoned with the slogan "Effective emancipation and wellbeing for the Tabasco proletariat." Homero Margalli, the secretary of the Liga Central, elaborated that "with a herculean arm [the Radical Socialist Party] breaks everything that opposes its material, intellectual and economic improvement; with an iron fist it flogs anyone who is opposed to the clear light of reason and justice; it has cornered the damned

34 AGN-TGC, c. 114, exp. 6. C.A. Manuel to Garrido, December 2, 1926.

35 AGN-TGC, c. 114, exp. 2. Wilfrido León et al. to Garrido, September 17, 1924.

36 AGN-TGC, c. 116, exp. 7. Paulino Castro to Garrido, March 12, 1928 and Garrido to President of the Woodcutter's Liga of Frontera, March 13, 1928.

37 AGN-TGC, c. 115, exp. 1. Liga Central de Resistencia flyer, c. 1927.

Reaction that, with skeletal hands impotently succumbs and gives free passage to the gigantic wave of progress; and in a word, it has forever and ever broken with immoral and despotic slavery." Margalli also wrote that "the principle object [of the state government] is to achieve the establishment of a true equilibrium between all of the sources of production."[38] State law reflected these priorities. The state labor law mandated an "English" workweek (five days) for both workers and campesinos. No work was to be done after 2 PM on Saturday unless workers earned double their normal salary. Workers were to be paid in full at the end of each workday. Even businesses that were staffed by their owners had to conform to local dictates concerning opening and closing times.[39]

The liga system was a powerful tool for the Socialists' regulation and control of Tabasco's economy, and particularly the crucial agricultural export sector. The Liga Central urged producers of fruit, rubber, cacao, and coffee to form ligas and to nominate delegates to the central organization, declaring it to be "the best way to unify prices and to avoid the schemes of immoral commerce."[40] Agricultural ligas included unions of workers in all areas associated with the export of their particular crop. For instance, in Cárdenas in 1926, campesinos, merchants, and growers that produced and sold bananas joined a confederated liga with the workers who transported the crops for export.[41] Solidarity was inevitably neater on paper than in practice. Leaders of agricultural producers' ligas were supposed to realize the state government's goal of economic justice by equitably distributing work among their members, but they frequently failed to do so. A common complaint lodged with the Liga Central was that liga leaders who were either corrupt or inept were favoring some workers, leaving others without employment for months at a time.[42]

Similar to Socialist reforms of the henequen sector in Yucatán, one of the economic objectives of the Tabasco Socialists was to level the playing field for smaller producers of bananas, now the state's principal export.[43] It was not always effective in practice. Smaller producers complained that the favoritism the liga of producers showed toward larger operations allowed them to dominate the business. In July of 1925, the Union Alta Mezcalapa complained to the Liga Central that its members had not been allowed to

38 AGN-TGC, c. 114, exp. 7. Homero Margalli to José Gómez Ugarte (Director of *El Universal*), January 1926.

39 AGN-TGC, c. 114, exp. 4. Garrido to liga presidents. Undated. Filed as September 1927.

40 AGN-TGC, c. 114, exp. 3. Homero Margalli to Garrido, October 16, 1925.

41 AGN-TGC, c. 114, exp. 9. Memo by the Liga de Resistencia of Cárdenas, March 14, 1926.

42 See, for example (one of many), AGN-TGC, c. 115, exp. 11. Rómulo and Genaro Mendoza et al. to Garrido, November 6, 1927.

43 On the decline of mahogany and the rise of bananas in Tabasco, see Ridgeway, "Monoculture, Monopoly, and the Mexican Revolution," 151.

cut fruit for over two months, as other planters were systematically favored by their liga. The Liga Central took the complaint seriously, and ordered the liga to investigate the complaint and to protect its weaker members by insuring that all producers be given the opportunity to participate in the banana market. The Liga Central underscored that this was a matter of fairness, and necessary in order to maintain good relations between the larger liga and its aggrieved constituent organization.[44]

Nevertheless, these challenges persisted. The president of the liga of banana growers reported in 1926 that although growers had succeeded in dramatically increasing their annual production, they were exporting only slightly more than half of the total banana crop because of organizational challenges. He argued that if the total harvest were divided evenly between the unions that belonged to the larger liga, a good part of their problems would be resolved. Once more, practice was much more difficult. Fruit transporters and buyers predictably favored lowland plantations that were easier to reach, meaning that it was much more difficult for highland growers to get their crop to a port for export. They were able to do so infrequently enough that many highland growers reportedly could no longer afford to maintain their plantations.[45] As with political disputes, the Socialist leadership and Garrido himself shared little of the blame in any of these complaints. On the contrary, at least on paper, Garrido was consistently and effusively praised by grassroots liga members for his defense of the poor and working people, who laid all blame at the feet of local liga middlemen.[46]

One of the stated goals of state-led organizing of banana producers was to supplant US-owned companies, which had long dominated the business.[47] The Socialists' statewide liga organization enabled them to pressure foreign companies that were not following the state government's economic dictates. At least, this was the way the members of the banana growers' ligas understood it. When banana growers' Union of Highland Mezcalapa came into conflict with Guillermo de Witt of the Texas-based Southern Banana Company, a subsidiary of the Standard Fruit Company, they appealed directly to Garrido: "we believe that the Socialist ligas that you preside over with dignity will not permit a foreigner to impose his will on us . . . we are prepared to lose our fruit [crop] before bowing to the will of foreigners, as long as the corporatist system imposes equality for all."[48]

44 AGN-TGC, c. 114, exp. 4. Saul Rosique to President of Liga Central, July 20, 1925. President of Liga Central to Saul Rosique, July 29, 1925.
45 AGN-TGC, c. 114, exp. 9. S. Fernández to Garrido, June 18, 1926.
46 See, for example (one of many), AGN-TGC, c. 115, exp. 11. Rómulo and Genaro Mendoza et al. to Garrido, November 6, 1927.
47 AGN-TGC, c. 114, exp. 9. S. Fernández to Garrido, June 18, 1926.
48 AGN-TGC, c. 114, exp. 10. Francisco Vidal to Garrido, July 8, 1926. I have translated "societario" here as "corporatist." I am assuming that the person referred to as "Dewill" is De

For its part, Southern Banana claimed that it had tried to work with the ligas and within the system established by the Socialist Party, in which export firms took assigned turns buying crops from particular ligas. The company complained in May of 1926 that some exporters were jumping the line, and that other firms were buying bananas when and where they pleased, while Southern Banana suffered for doing as it was told by the ligas, and was only assigned to purchase crops from far-flung producers that were difficult and expensive to reach. The company requested authorization to buy the crops that were more convenient, as others had done, and wanted to know if their competitors had received special dispensation.[49] The producers' liga retorted that Southern Banana was not facing discrimination, that most shipping costs were paid by the producers, that the producers also absorbed the cost of any shipments that arrived late to the exporters' ships, and that there was no good reason to allow the company to buy whichever crops it pleased.[50] When Guillermo de Witt was subsequently accused by banana producers' ligas of trying to break up their organizations and of harming the interests of organized workers with the intent of influencing the state's gubernatorial election, Garrido ordered the liga to no longer sell to the company, and that they work instead with "another company that has nothing to do with that foreign Jew," at least until de Witt no longer worked for Southern Banana.[51]

None of these mutual recriminations and auto-exculpations on either side of the conflict addressed the heart of the matter. In seeking to circumvent the ligas de resistencia, DeWitt had allied with the CROM, which sought to organize the "free" workers of Tabasco in order to get its own foothold there, outside of the confines of the liga system and the Socialists' fierce labor regulations and protections for liga members.[52] By 1926, De Witt was seeking alternative sources of bananas, including from Pichucalco, just across the Chiapas state line. Those bananas were much harder for his ships to reach, but at least the Socialist party there had no ligas de resistencia.[53] In 1927 the Tabasco Socialists responded to the machinations of the CROM and the fruit companies operating in the state by passing a law that gave only liga members the right to work in Tabasco.[54]

Witt. Southern Banana was purchased and became a subsidiary of Standard Fruit in 1925. Standard Fruit sought to establish a banana export monopoly in Tabasco, but also in Mexico as a whole, with mixed results. Ridgeway argues that they were substantially thwarted by Garrido and the ligas de resistencia in this effort. Ridgeway, "Monoculture, Monopoly, and the Mexican Revolution," 152–53.

49 AGN-TGC, c. 114, exp. 10. Garrido to President of the Liga of Banana Producers, May 10, 1926.
50 AGN-TGC, c. 114, exp. 10. Bernabé Romero Priego to Garrido, May 3, 1926.
51 AGN-TGC, c. 114, exp. 8. Homero Margalli to Garrido, September 28, 1926. AGN-TGC, c. 114, exp. 10. Garrido to President of Liga de Productores de Roatán, October 2, 1926.
52 Canudas, *Trópico rojo, Vol. 1*, 1, 181.
53 AGN-TGC, c. 114, exp. 10. Francisco Gamas to Garrido, July 7, 1926.
54 Ridgeway, "Monoculture, Monopoly, and the Mexican Revolution," 159.

The liga system was also a valuable tool for implementing Garrido's social policies. This was another strategy borrowed from Yucatecan Socialist precedents, but in Tabasco it had substantially different goals and outcomes. Most notoriously, as the Cristero War of 1926–29 raged in other regions, Garrido and his allies undertook a campaign to expel the Catholic Church wholesale from Tabasco; this included forcing the bishop of Tabasco, Pascual Díaz Barreto, into exile in 1927.[55] Although the Southeast remained largely untouched by the violence of the conflict between supporters of the Church and the Mexican government, Garrido's campaign against the Church was tireless, and left Tabasco without a single priest for years on end, well into the 1930s.[56]

Prohibitions against Catholic practice and sanctions against priests began in Tabasco in 1925, before the church–state conflict boiled over into violence at the national level.[57] But anticlerical laws and regulations were only part of a broader effort by Garrido and his allies to secularize Tabasco and to supplant Catholicism with Socialism. At the grassroots, the Socialists' anticlerical campaign included replacing religious events with sponsored cultural events for liga members every Sunday. These commonly included the participation of students from public schools who were chosen by their teachers to present either literature or music, as a means of entertaining the attendees and also "developing the intellectuality" of the students themselves.[58] The ligas became mechanisms of social control of the rank and file, including (but not exclusively) in the anticlerical effort. In 1925, one liga requested that the Liga Central investigate rumors that one of its members covertly had one of his children baptized, in violation of the rules of the liga.[59] In another case, members of a liga of carters and day laborers requested the firing of a desk clerk in Macuspana who they claimed had participated in a religious festival.[60]

Garrido's anticlericalism was just one facet of his larger, stated goal of liberating Tabasco's citizens from numerous forms of oppression. Another central element of Garrido's plans to modernize the state was his perennial emphasis on public education, an ambitious reform program begun with limited success before the de la Huerta rebellion and then resumed afterward. These were related objectives: public education was intended to be

55 Canudas, *Tropico rojo*, Vol. 1, 1, 144.
56 Martínez Assad, *El laboratorio de la revolución*, 50–51.
57 Canudas, *Tropico rojo*, Vol. 1, 1, 143–44.
58 AGN-TGC, c. 114, exp. 3. Form letter from Homero Margalli to teachers, December 19, 1925. Attendance at these events was not always voluntary: In Frontera in 1928, dockworkers were required by their municipal liga to attend a cultural assembly. See AGN-TGC, c. 116, exp. 7. Cipriano Morales to Garrido, March 26, 1928. See also Harper, "Revolutionary Tabasco," 141.
59 AGN-TGC, c. 114, exp. 4. Unsigned copy of a telegram to Homero Margalli, October 28, 1925.
60 AGN-TGC, c. 114, exp. 5. Clemente Ocaña to Garrido, May 31, 1926.

a tool to "de-fanaticize" the population of Tabasco, and to enable everyday people to become active and modern revolutionary citizens.[61] The state was assisted in this effort by the federal government, which was making its own ambitious new commitments to public education in Mexico in this period, following the creation of the Secretariat of Public Education (SEP) in 1921. As Tabasco struggled to get its new public schools up and running, the SEP matched the state's funding for the project. The results were impressive: Between 1925 and 1926, Tabasco opened 185 new rural schools, licensed 95 new teachers, and dedicated more than 20 percent of its budget to education.[62] Once again, the liga system often became the institutional mechanism for putting policy into practice. The Liga Central installed schools for workers, and local ligas were expected to help to pay for their operations and upkeep.[63] Churches and cathedrals across the state were routinely seized and converted to "rationalist" schools for workers and campesinos.[64] In Garrido's words, rural education "will make campesinos into useful and capable men for the progress of the community."[65]

In the absence of a rural normal school, Garrido urged Tabasco's municipal leaders to set aside special funds for the education of one exceptional student each, who could all be specially trained for a year to work as teachers in their own communities.[66] Finding a sufficient number of teachers for all of the new schools was a challenge. In 1928, Garrido wrote to the head of the state Department of Education, Sarah M. de Castillo, that "all persons with significant knowledge" to teach should be allowed to do so, since there were not enough licensed teachers to cover the educational needs of the entire state.[67]

Garrido also broke new ground in Tabasco when it came to women's political rights, going well beyond precedents set by Carrillo Puerto and Alvarado in Yucatán. In March of 1925, Garrido's government formally recognized women's right to vote at the municipal level, making Tabasco one of the first states in Mexico to inscribe women's voting rights into law, twenty-eight years before Mexican women were granted the right to vote in federal elections. The enfranchisement of women was a telling example of

61 Mary Kay Vaughan argues that workers' rights, women's rights, and the attack on the Catholic Church were all part and parcel of Garrido's larger vision for the modernization and rationalization of the economy, society, and politics of Tabasco. Mary Kay Vaughan, *Cultural Politics in Revolution: Teachers, Peasants, and Schools in Mexico, 1930–1940* (Tucson, AZ: University of Arizona Press, 1997), 30.

62 Canudas, *Tropico rojo*, Vol. 1, 1, 118–20, 76–77.

63 See, for example, AGN-TGC, c.114, exp. 7. Marcelino Zamudio to Garrido, April 9, 1926.

64 See, for instance, AGN-TGC, c. 115, exp. 7. Crispín Pech G. to J. Medardo Rosado, December 2, 1927. See also c. 116, exp. 3, Espiridión Avalos to Garrido, January 20, 1928.

65 AGN-TGC, c. 115, exp. 9. Garrido to municipal diputados, December 9, 1927.   66 Ibid.

67 AGN-TGC, c. 116, exp. 7. Garrido to Sarah M. de Castillo, March 31, 1928.

Garridista Socialism's ambivalent approach to popular democracy. One the one hand, the enfranchisement of Mexican women in 1925 was inarguably radical for its time. On the other, yet again, Garrido's expansion of a particular constituency's political rights came along with provisions that facilitated the state government's control over the newly politically empowered and imposed limitations on their newly expanded political freedoms.

Tabasco's suffrage law explicitly circumscribed the political rights it extended to women. Although the state's suffrage decree justified the measure by recognizing women's equal intellectual capacity and argued that their participation in the political process was to society's benefit, women were only allowed to run for office at the municipal level, and the number of seats they were allowed to occupy was limited to a third of the total in any elected body. There were also further explicit restrictions on which women were allowed to participate in the political process. Only sufficiently educated Socialist women were given electoral rights by the 1925 decree; further, those women had to be of "irreproachable morality." This was a designation so vague that it could have been used as a loophole to exclude nearly anyone from participating in the political process. The limitations that Tabasco imposed on women's political rights were precedents for similarly limited suffrage measures proposed at the national level in Mexico in the 1930s, 40s, and 50s, particularly the 1946 enfranchisement of all Mexican women at the municipal level, which served as a test run for their full enfranchisement in 1952.[68]

For women as well as men in Tabasco in the 1920s, the liga system was the site of political empowerment and engagement, more than the ballot box. Although most of the ligas de resistencia were led by men, many women also joined and participated in their ranks, and occasionally held elected leadership posts.[69] Women also often led their own ligas, particularly of workers in professions dominated by women, including teaching.[70] In addition to some of the same protections offered to women workers in Socialist Yucatán, Tabasco's labor code required ligas to have special schools for the daughters of workers, as well as their wives: The latter were

68 For more details on the state level women's suffrage amendments in Tabasco and other states of the Mexican Southeast in the 1920s, see Sarah Osten, "A Crooked Path to the Franchise: The Historical Legacies of Mexico's Failed 1937 Women's Suffrage Amendment," *The Latin Americanist* 58, no. 2 (2014).

69 See, for example, a female regidora of a liga de resistencia: AGN-TGC, c. 115, exp. 3. Report by the Liga Socialista de Obreros y Campesinos de Macuspana, August 26, 1927. For the election of a woman as liga secretary, see AGN-TGC, c. 116, exp. 6. E. Graniel to Garrido, March 10, 1928.

70 See, for instance, AGN-TGC, c. 114, exp. 4. Price list published by the sub-liga de lavanderas of Centla, October 6, 1925. For one example of a teachers' liga led by women, see AGN-TGC, c. 115, exp. 11. Cármen C. de Santarelli et al. to Garrido, December 1, 1927.

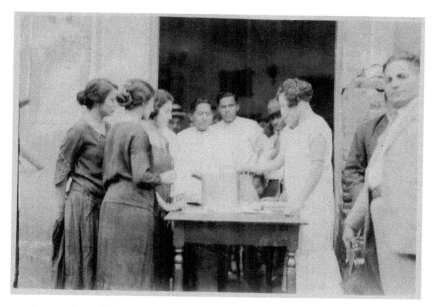

Photograph 4.1 Women voting in Villahermosa, December 1925
Source: Fideicomiso Archivos Plutarco Elías Calles y Fernando Torreblanca (FAPECFT)

to emphasize the teaching of Spanish, arithmetic, childcare, and home economics, as well as morality.[71]

Tabasco's 1926 Election: Test-Driving the System

When it came time for Tabasco to elect a new governor in 1926, no one doubted that Tomás Garrido Canabal had become one of the most powerful governors in all of Mexico, thanks to the successes of his political machine. But as Garrido prepared to undertake a campaign for the federal senate and to make the leap to the national political stage, it remained to be seen how his machine would operate under a new governor. As a result, numerous interested parties both inside and outside of the state were invested in and/or preoccupied by the outcome of the election. It was a tumultuous and violent year in Tabasco, in which Garrido survived two assassination attempts.

Garrido resigned from the governorship in April of 1926 to campaign for the senate seat. His chosen successor was Ausencio Cruz, one of his right-hand men during his own governorship, and a Socialist insider who had

71 Partido Socialista Radical de Tabasco, *Código obrero* (Villahermosa: Talleres de Redención, 1925), 39–40.

distinguished himself in terms of his loyalty to Garrido. He had also demonstrated his loyalty in his active participation in the fight against the de la Huerta rebels and the defense of Villahermosa.[72] As a Socialist yes-man, Cruz was the perfect foil for Garrido, who had no intention of relinquishing all of the immense political control he had amassed in Tabasco after leaving the governorship, as soon became clear and likely surprised very few. Cruz campaigned on promises of vindicating and motivating the proletariat of Tabasco, and the expansion of both agriculture and business in the state. He emphasized that he had been nominated by numerous Socialist organizations, as well as a large number of individuals, but there was no mistaking whose support was most important for his candidacy.[73]

Nevertheless, this was not an uncontested race, nor was Cruz the only Socialist who hoped to succeed Garrido. The negotiations and behind-the-scenes wrangling over the choice of a candidate within the Tabasco Socialist party in this first election after Garrido's first term offer insight into how informal and opaque processes of patronage and candidate selection determined political outcomes, in tandem with established electoral procedures. Crucially, as far as Garrido and his allies were concerned, the former did not obviate the latter. Nor was backroom political horse-trading perceived by the Socialists to undermine democratic processes, although many of their critics understandably felt otherwise.

In 1925, Garrido Canabal's uncle, legislator Manuel Garrido Lacroix, requested his nephew's permission to launch a gubernatorial bid in 1925, reminding him of a previous promise of support for his candidacy. Garrido Lacroix worried that the Liga Central would inevitably break apart if different ligas decided to support different candidates, and not necessarily those endorsed by Garrido Canabal. He also cautioned that the lack of free suffrage in Tabasco and the promotion of his nephew's personal favorites were liabilities that could be exploited by his enemies. Garrido Canabal breezily replied that it was well known that his position was that the people of Tabasco should be empowered to choose the leaders.[74] He did not offer further support for his uncle's candidacy.

Homero Margalli, the secretary of the Liga Central, also wanted to be governor, but he made clear to Garrido Canabal that he would not run without his permission. He conspicuously hedged a bit, claiming that it was his friends that were promoting his candidacy.[75] Garrido responded by sending a representative to Margalli to inform him that he would be

72 Canudas, *Tropico rojo, Vol. 1*, 1, 160–62. Harper, "Revolutionary Tabasco," 96–97.
73 AGN-TGC, c. 114, exp. 3. Form letter from Ausencio Cruz to Eusebio Pérez, July 25, 1925.
74 AGN-TGC, c. 114, exp. 3. Manuel Garrido Lacroix to Garrido, July 18, 1925. Garrido to Manuel Garrido Lacroix, August 14, 1925.
75 AGN-TGC, c. 114, exp. 7. Homero Margalli to Garrido, July 9, 1925.

backing Cruz's candidacy. If Margalli entertained any notion of running what would now amount to a doomed opposition campaign, it was only for a matter of hours. He wrote to Garrido the same day to renounce his candidacy, to pledge his support for Cruz, but above all, to reaffirm his loyalty to his mentor and patron. "I will be what you want me to be," Margalli vowed to Garrido. "The day that you don't want me to be anything, I will be nothing."[76] As a Socialist insider, Margalli knew better than anyone that while perhaps this would be a democratic gubernatorial election on paper, the voters would only have one viable candidate to choose from, and he had already been handpicked for them. Margalli soon transferred his energies to a campaign for a seat on the city council of Villahermosa.[77]

There were also formal legal challenges to candidates wishing to run for any office in Socialist Tabasco without Garrido's support. The state's legal and political systems were designed to make any "opposition" campaign or candidacy difficult at best, and the political rights and freedoms accorded to those working with and within Garrido's political machine were much more robust than those of anyone on the outside. Tabasco's electoral law gave political parties and their constituent organizations the right to organize demonstrations, publish manifestos and political programs, make political signs, edit newspapers, and produce any other form of propaganda, but it did not recognize the rights of individuals to do any of these things without the support of a party that was formally recognized by the state government.[78]

Further, electoral procedures that theoretically allowed the citizens of Tabasco to express their political wills were undertaken principally within ligas de resistencia. Liga members were convened to choose particular candidates for state and national offices, and to vote on slates of candidates proposed by liga leaders. There was no secrecy in voting, as members were called on to stand during these assemblies to show their approval of nominations. Unsurprisingly, unanimous results were not unusual. Indeed, electoral unanimity was the order of the day in Tabasco in the mid-1920s, or at least the desired result. If results were not unanimous, they were reported as such.[79]

Socialist electoral rhetoric in Tabasco strongly emphasized unity among the organized workers that belonged to the ligas. This was both an organizational strategy, and something that was offered as proof of its success. "Our

76   AGN-TGC, c. 114, exp. 3. Homero Margalli to Garrido, July 15, 1925.

77   AGN-TGC, c. 114, exp. 4. Form letter, the Comité Ejecutivo Electoral Pro-Margalli, November 10, 1925.

78   AGN-TGC, c. 114, exp. 5. Velentín Carrillo to Presidente Municipal, September 18, 1926.

79   See, for example, the report by the Liga de Montecristo on its electoral convention for federal senators and diputados. AGN-TGC, c. 115, exp. 11. Juan A. Reyes to Garrido, November 29, 1927.

unity can be seen from afar," a liga leader in Cárdenas reminded his members, in urging them to escalate their campaign for Ausencio Cruz's gubernatorial campaign in 1926. Liga members were urged to campaign for their candidates throughout their communities, not just among fellow Socialists. The stated objective was to demonstrate to all Socialist unity and solidarity of purpose, not only in campaigns for Socialist candidates, but also for the rights of workers in general. In other words, Socialist electoral campaigns were designed to promote particular candidates, but were also meant to be propaganda for Socialism itself.[80]

Conversely, lack of unity was considered a political liability. Socialist politicians and liga leaders viewed political "disorientation" by ligas at the local level with consternation, even when it came to electing municipal leaders, and all the more so when any candidate was rumored to have supported the de la Huerta rebellion. Liga leaders worried that former de la Huerta sympathizers (real or imagined) would be "dissolvent" elements within the Socialist ranks. They sought to prevent any such people from joining existing ligas, as well as from forming their own ligas. "We who today are willing to wage the honorable fight of the worker do not forget the dark, traitorous past of this same group of people," the liga of sailors and stokers of Centla declared, as one of their justifications for opposing the formation of a new liga.[81]

In some cases, there was little hesitation by Socialist leadership to impose its political will on the rank and file in order to achieve a desired political outcome, at least at the local level. Workers in Frontera complained to Garrido in 1925 that they had been threatened with being fired from their jobs and expelled from their ligas if they did not agree to support the gubernatorial candidacy of Homero Margalli, as demanded by the leaders of their ligas.[82] In 1928, a liga leader in Villahermosa reminded Garrido: "On one particular occasion, individuals who in every act and every word demonstrated their animosity and hatred of you were expelled [by you] from our Liga."[83] One frustrated liga leader in Cunduacán reported that his best efforts to organize campesinos to confront local employers and reactionaries had been in vain. He explained to Garrido: "Here, Socialism is still a tender child that needs much care and direction. Moreover, Socialism must be imposed here, not preached. [...] our campesinos do not understand."[84] In other cases, established procedure won out. In 1928, a liga leader in Tapijulapa complained that while the majority of liga members had

80 AGN-TGC, c. 114, exp. 9. Memo by the Liga de Resistencia of Cárdenas, March 14, 1926.
81 AGN-TGC, c. 114, exp. 4. Carmen Pérez et al. to Liga Central, July 4, 1925.
82 AGN-TGC, c. 114, exp. 3. Juan Mendoza et al. to Garrido. Undated (filed with documents from 1925).
83 AGN-TGC, c. 116, exp. 7. Angel Pérez P. to Garrido, February 17, 1928.
84 AGN-TGC, c. 115, exp. 11. A. Vazquez to Garrido, December 5, 1927.

supported one candidate for municipal office, the town council had imposed its own candidate; upon receiving word of this, Garrido made his own inquiries and wrote that the vote of the majority must be respected.[85]

By state law, liga members exchanged some political freedoms for the benefits of membership they received. Freedom of speech and political expression were explicitly restricted by Tabasco's labor code. This document prohibited liga members from speaking badly of any liga or subsidiary of a liga, any liga leaders or members of the party, and from criticizing or denouncing any of their acts, whether individual or collective. In March of 1926 leaders of a port workers' liga in Villahermosa used these clauses of the code to justify the expulsion of several of their own members, allegedly for multiple violations of these prescriptions. They added that the men had not been expelled after their first offense out of a spirit of comradeship and in the hope that they would "return to being friends of Socialism."[86]

The ligas played a pivotal role in state elections. Their members' votes cast on Election Day collectively served as crucial popular ratifications of decisions that had often already been made behind the scenes, within local ligas, and between the ligas, the Liga Central, and Garrido himself. Keeping up democratic appearances and some practices remained important to the Tabasco Socialists and were enshrined in their rhetoric. During the election of 1926, Garrido ordered Homero Margalli to remind all public employees in the state that they had to leave their jobs in order to participate in the political process, "so that it is clear that we don't need any government support to triumph."[87] Popular support for candidates did make a difference and truly mattered to many people in the state, although it was not always enough. In February of 1927, representatives of the bakers' liga of Frontera wrote to Garrido to announce its intent to support one candidate for municipal president over another in an upcoming election. Their chosen candidate, Juan Lugo, only agreed to accept their nomination if a majority of their members first requested (and presumably obtained) Garrido's approval. They underscored that they only ventured to ask because their candidate did indeed have more genuine popular support than his opponent.[88]

All of the formal and informal political arrangements in Socialist Tabasco were put to the test with the "independent" gubernatorial campaigns of Colonel Arturo Jiménez de Lara and state legislator Belisario Carrillo, who both challenged the Garrido-sponsored candidacy of Ausencio Cruz in 1926.

85 AGN-TGC, c. 116, exp. 3. Simón Méndez to Garrido, January 5, 1928, and Garrido to Simón Méndez, January 7, 1928.
86 AGN-TGC, c. 114, exp. 8. Andrés Pérez et al. to Garrido, March 17, 1926.
87 AGN-TGC, c. 114, exp. 6. Garrido to Homero Margalli, September 28, 1926.
88 AGN-TGC, c. 115, exp. 1. Rafael Suárez et al. to Garrido, February 10, 1927.

In spite of his credible claims to have a popular base of support for his political juggernaut, Garrido Canabal's brand of Socialism was not a system designed to deal with popular dissent gracefully. Both opposition candidates ran in spite of the state electoral commission's disqualification of their candidacies.[89] Both also came up against significant challenges to their candidacies by Tabasco Socialists, who used various means to justify their disqualification.[90] Predictably, both were smeared as former de la Huerta supporters. On Garrido's orders, Socialists also widely advertised an allegation that Jiménez de Lara, who was one of the earliest members of the Radical Party, had been a telegraph operator for Victoriano Huerta during his dictatorship in 1913–14.[91] Both candidates were blocked from registering their candidacies by the deadline, and on those grounds the state government declared them to be ineligible for the governorship.[92] Belisario Carrillo countered that it was Ausencio Cruz who was not legally able to hold the office, since he had already served as interim governor previously. Cruz replied that this was not prohibited by the state constitution.[93] Jiménez de Lara retorted that the state government of Tabasco was indistinguishable from a political party.[94]

The campaign likely confirmed the worst fears of observers across the political spectrum. As the election approached, violence broke out. At a late morning rally for Jiménez de Lara at a hotel in Villahermosa in September, his supporters clashed with partisans of Ausencio Cruz, and both groups threw rocks and pieces of masonry at each other. According to Cruz, federal troops arrived and fired shots into the crowd of his partisans. One member of a waiters' liga was killed.[95] This was just one incident of many in these months in which lives were lost in partisan confrontations. In November, Homero Margalli reported to President Calles that a Cruz supporter and his wife had been brutally murdered by supporters of the opposition candidates. He bitterly complained that the municipal police in the state, who had been disarmed along with everyone else in the state by the federal military during the election, were helpless to protect citizens from such attacks.[96] Margalli also accused the chief of military operations, General

89 Harper, "Revolutionary Tabasco," 98–99.
90 In the case of Jiménez de Lara, one justification was that he did not meet the state's legal requirement that candidates could not have served within the army within the previous three years. Canudas, *Tropico rojo*, Vol. 1, 1, 188.
91 AGN-TGC, c. 114, exp. 8. Garrido to Homero Margalli, September 17, 1926. Ibid., 16.
92 Martínez Assad, *Breve historia de Tabasco*, 170.
93 AGN-TGC, c. 114, exp. 5. Ausencio Cruz to Garrido, September 16, 1926.
94 Canudas, *Tropico rojo, Vol. 1*, 1, 192.
95 AGN-TGC, c. 114, exp. 5. Ausencio Cruz to Garrido, September 16, 1926.
96 FAPECFT-PEC, expediente: 58, MARGALLI G., H., legajo 1, foja 7, inventario 3432. Senator Homero Margalli to Soledad González, October 25, 1926. The statewide order to disarm exempted federal soldiers and employees, state and municipal police, and officials and public employees of the state government, with the understanding that they would be disarmed if they

Photograph 4.2 Rally in support of Jiménez de Lara, Villahermosa, September 14, 1926
Source: Archivo General de la Nación, Colección Carlos A. Vidal. Sección: Actividades militares, políticas y administrativas, serie: fotografías sobre eventos públicos y sociales y obras públicas en Chiapas, caja 3, sobre: 18, foto: 4.

Juan García Anzaldúa, of personally arresting and imprisoning a municipal president in Montecristo, and insisted that federal authorities punish him for overstepping the bounds of his commission and violating Tabasco's sovereignty.[97]

In part, the violence was symptomatic of the fact that numerous factions and interests believed that a great deal more than the governorship was at stake in this election. This was a time of marked growth and organization of "free" workers in Tabasco, many of them former liga members, some of whom formed their own organization, the Tabasco Federation of Workers. By one account, the election was as an opportunity for workers disaffected by Socialism to free themselves not only of Garrido and his chosen successor, but also of the ligas de resistencia, to which they no longer wished to belong.[98] The opposition candidates sought to take advantage of these circumstances.

used their weapons in any capacity outside of their regular duties. Licenses to carry arms that had been previously granted to individuals not belonging to any of these categories were temporarily suspended. See AGN-TGC, c. 114, exp. 8. Homero Margalli to Garrido, September 24, 1926.

97 FAPECFT-PEC, expediente: 58, MARGALLI G., H., legajo 1, fojas 9–10, inventario 3432. Homero Margalli and Alcides Caparroso to Soledad González, November 3, 1926.

98 FAPECFT-PEC, expediente 86: GOMEZ, Arnulfo R. (Gral.), legajo 7/7, fojas 357–60, inventario 2398. Manuel Pulido to Arnulfo Gómez, May 23, 1927.

In September, a liga president in Frontera reported rumors that Arturo Jiménez de Lara was due to arrive from Villahermosa with as many as three hundred "free" workers, with the intent of "disorganizing" the Socialist workers of the port. Ninety "enemy propagandists" had already arrived the day before, led by alleged former Delahuertistas, reportedly intent on killing unionized workers in order to avenge their defeat in 1924.[99]

The violence provoked by the campaign further reinforced the Socialists' perception that they were under attack from within and from without. Juan Lugo, the Secretary of the municipal liga of Centla, referred to the supporters of Belisario Carrillo's candidacy as rebels, bemoaning that they remained in possession of firearms even after the federal military order to disarm.[100] Opposition agents were routinely described as "enemy propagandists."[101] By 1926, there was no need to be explicit about whose enemies these were or what they stood for; in all of the Socialists' campaign rhetoric, it was made starkly clear that the opposition candidates and their supporters were staunch reactionaries driven by contempt for the Mexican Revolution and the working people of Tabasco, and hell-bent on destroying the hard-won gains that workers and campesinos had made through the Radical Socialist Party and the ligas de resistencia. The Socialists rarely if ever addressed or quoted the political proposals or positions of either Jiménez de Lara or Carrillo, but there was no need. In Tabasco in 1926, either you were with the Socialists, or you were against them.

Although Cruz's victory was likely never in doubt, the reaction of Tabasco's Socialists to a political challenge is revealing. As they confronted real political opposition, liga members and leadership expressed the sentiment that they had to protect what the Radical Socialist Party and the liga system had achieved at great cost, and not allow it to be lost or diminished. The leader of the Liga of Sailors and Stokers wrote to Garrido: "We see the hand of the capitalists who, in spite of the previous punishment [they received] persist in lifting their heads, but here, compañero, count on the fact that while we are heartened by your ideals we will not give up for a single instant and when the moment arrives, we will know how to give them what they deserve."[102] If it wasn't capitalists, it was dogged Delahuertista rebels, scheming at every turn to turn back the revolutionary clock, or both. There were also perceived counterrevolutionary threats within ligas de resistencia. In April of 1926, representatives of a liga of waiters and busboys wrote to Garrido to complain that the larger liga to

99   AGN-TGC, c. 114, exp. 6. C. A. Manuel to Garrido, September 30, 1926.
100 AGN-TGC, c. 114, exp. 7. Juan Lugo to Garrido, September 18, 1926.
101 See, for example, AGN-TGC, c. 114, exp. 8. Dionisio Morales and Pio Garrido to Garrido, September 13, 1926.
102 AGN-TGC, c. 114, exp. 7. Manuel Pérez to Garrido. 1926. Undated.

which they belonged had been taken over by reactionaries, and that they had been forced out of the organization and were not allowed to work. They added that the leaders of the liga were former Delahuertistas who were campaigning against Ausencio Cruz's gubernatorial candidacy. They offered to provide whatever proof was necessary and demanded that Garrido order the impeachment of the liga directors in question.[103]

The Socialists' perception that the opposition candidates not only threatened them at the ballot box but that they might also undermine the organization of Tabasco's workers was commonly expressed as the opposition campaigns gained ground. Liga leaders in Frontera complained that agents of Jiménez de Lara were attempting to propagate "dissolvent ideas" that were meant to undermine their liga and the work it did, and to organize "ignorant" campesinos outside of the liga system with "false promises" of work and other benefits, including jobs that were already guaranteed for liga members. When a group of these "free" workers attempted to board a ship in order to usurp work that was to be done by members of the Liga of Tropical Fruit Stevedores in Frontera, liga leaders described it not just as an affront to their members, but also as an attempt to "upset the legal order of the functioning of our Worker Institution."[104] In Centla, after a liga member was shot and killed by an agent of Jiménez de Lara, liga leaders referred to the opposition campaign as comprising "the dregs of delahuertismo," and as "based on crimes against organized workers."[105]

By construing opposition leaders and their supporters as rebels against the state government, just as they had used accusations of *delahuertismo* to disqualify, shun, and punish their political enemies for the past three years, the Socialists bypassed any of the otherwise obvious rhetorical contractions of their ongoing insistence that theirs was a democratic political system. The notion that the opposition candidates were transgressors of state law in one way or another was actively propagated by liga leaders to their members. This effort included public rallies to explain the various "legal impediments" of Jiménez de Lara's and Carrillo's campaigns to workers.[106] But some Socialists also went further than that, arguing that it was precisely the interference of reactionary forces, abetted by outsiders, that was preventing the people of Tabasco from resolving political matters democratically.[107]

They weren't wrong about the active role of outsiders in the state's election. First, from Mexico City, Luis Morones, Calles' Secretary of

103 AGN-TGC, c. 114, exp. 7. Manuel León et al. to Garrido, April 2, 1926.
104 AGN-TGC, c. 114, exp. 7. Liga de Resistencia of Frontera to Interim Governor, October 26, 1926.
105 AGN-TGC, c. 114, exp. 7. Undated and unsigned copy of a telegram from President of the Liga Central of Centla to Calles, Obregón and Joaquín Amaro.
106 AGN-TGC, c. 114, exp. 8. C. A. Manuel and Juan Lugo to Garrido, September 26, 1926.
107 AGN-TGC, c. 114, exp. 8. Homero Margalli to Garrido, September 15, 1926.

Industry and the leader of the CROM, actively supported the candidacy of Belisario Carrillo. The CROM had long been spurned by Garrido and the ligas in its efforts to make any inroads in organizing labor in Tabasco, and the national organization took this election as an opportunity to make its influence felt in the state. Guillermo de Witt of the Southern Banana Company collaborated with the CROM and allegedly helped to finance "free" workers who fought against the election of Cruz.[108]

Second, closer to home, the Socialist governor of Chiapas Carlos Vidal actively supported the candidacy of Arturo Jiménez de Lara, who had served as the head of propaganda for Vidal's gubernatorial campaign in Chiapas in 1924.[109] Both Garrido and Vidal borrowed amply from the innovations of Felipe Carrillo Puerto's model of Socialist government in Yucatán. However, the two southeastern Socialist governors who survived the de la Huerta rebellion soon became political enemies. Their dislike for one another was not merely grounded in competition for power and influence within the region, although that undoubtedly helped to fuel their mutual antagonism. Garrido and Vidal also had meaningfully different interpretations of what southeastern Socialism meant, and what it should be in practice. These differences ultimately translated into significantly different aspirations for Mexico's political future.

It is difficult to pinpoint the genesis of their mutual animosity.[110] In the early 1920s, their correspondence was cordial. Although Garrido would later repeatedly insist that Vidal had sympathized with the Delahuertistas, in the early days of the rebellion, he specifically requested Vidal's military assistance to defend the government of Tabasco.[111] To make matters more complicated between the two men, Vidal's father-in-law served as one of Garrido's representatives to banana companies in New Orleans in the mid-1920s, at the same moment as Vidal was waiting to take power in Chiapas.[112]

By 1925, trouble was brewing between the two southeastern Socialists. Garrido rebuffed requests for his support for Vidal's gubernatorial campaign, declaring that he had no intention of becoming involved in Chiapas

108 Canudas, *Tropico rojo, Vol. 1*, 1, 179–80, 95.
109 Harper, "Revolutionary Tabasco," 98. AGN-TGC, caja: 8, expediente: 8, Arturo Jiménez de Lara to Garrido, August 25, 1924.
110 Harper suggests that Vidal was disturbed by Garrido's anticlerical policies. However, it seems more likely that Garrido would have been more offended by Vidal's lack of anticlerical measures. Harper also suggests that Vidal was angered that Garrido thwarted his brother Luis' political aspirations in Tabasco. Ibid., 100–1.
111 FAPECFT-PEC, expediente: 140, GARRIDO CANABAL, Tomás (Lic.), legajo 2/7, foja 79, inventario: 2312. Garrido to Calles, November 26, 1923.
112 AGN-TGC, caja: 8, expediente: 3. Report written for Garrido by Don Ponciano Rojas, February 18, 1925.

politics.[113] Yet as Chiapas' election approached and Vidal's assumption of power appeared likely, Vidal's opponents turned to Garrido for support.[114] As Vidal prepared to take power, Garrido welcomed Mapache sympathizers to Tabasco, offering them whatever assistance he could, including help finding employment.[115] The growing polarization between Vidal and Garrido and their respective partisans only grew more bitter once Vidal finally became governor in May of 1925.[116] Seven months later, Garrido alleged that ex-de la Huerta rebels were being given refuge in Chiapas and Guatemala and volunteered to organize forces to root them out. He was likely disappointed by President Calles' assessment that the threat was not serious and that such an effort was unnecessary.[117] The following summer, municipal authorities in Chiapas near the state line reported that troops from Tabasco had been invading, causing disorder, and harassing citizens.[118]

The animus between Garrido and Vidal may have had national origins. Considering the strength of Garrido's alliance with Obregón over the years, it is possible that part of Calles' determination to see Vidal become the governor of Chiapas (as described in Chapter 5) following the death of Carrillo Puerto was because Calles wanted a political counterweight to Garrido in the region. The de la Huerta rebellion had shifted the balance of power in the Southeast. Before the rebellion, Calles indisputably had more connections and more influence in the region than any national politician had ever had, including Obregón. But Carrillo Puerto's death presented Calles with a serious problem. If Garrido gained control of the larger Southeast, as Carrillo Puerto had been attempting to do before him, Calles would lose an important base of regional support that he had been cultivating for some time. What's more, Vidal was poised to replace another staunch Obregonista in Chiapas, Fernández Ruiz, who was also an ally of Garrido's.

---

113 AGN-TGC, caja: 8, expediente: 8, Garrido to Arturo Jiménez de Lara, August 28, 1924.

114 AGN-TGC, caja: 7, expediente: 7. M. López Coronel to Garrido, February 1, 1925.

115 AGN-TGC, caja: 8, expediente: 5. Garrido to Juan F. Corzo, February 23, 1925. AGN-TGC, caja: 7, expediente: 6. Juan F. Corzo to Garrido, March 5, 1925.

116 Garrido's papers are full of allegations and conspiracy theories about Vidal's intentions in regards to him personally and to Tabasco. No equivalent documents exist among Vidal's papers (however, Vidal's papers are also far less extensive). Vidal rarely mentioned Garrido in any of his personal or political correspondence. Vidal's support of Jiménez de Lara is well documented, but I have not been able to substantiate any of Garrido's other accusations against Vidal.

117 FAPECFT-PEC, expediente: 140, GARRIDO CANABAL, Tomás (Lic.), legajo 3/7, foja 160, inventario: 2312. Garrido to Soledad González, January 13, 1926.

118 Archivo Histórico del Estado de Chiapas, Universidad de Ciencias y Artes de Chiapas (hereafter AHECH) Gobernación: 1926, vol. 5, exp. 62. Presidente Municipal of Catazajá to Vidal, July 31, 1926.

If Calles indeed helped to bring Vidal to power in part to check Garrido's influence in the region, the animosity that Garrido felt toward Vidal is substantially clarified. It would also help to explain why Garrido seems to have regarded Vidal as an ally before the de la Huerta rebellion and an enemy after. Likewise, if Calles was playing the two southeastern Socialists against one another in order to maintain his own sound political footing in the Southeast, it would go far to explain why Garrido and Vidal had so many political mentors, friends, and allies in common over the years, as well as numerous political goals in common in their respective states, and yet came to be enemies rather than allies.

After months of political turmoil, Ausencio Cruz was elected governor, and Garrido became one of the state's federal senators, but kept his position as president of the Liga Central.[119] Cruz's supporters dismissed any suggestion that he had been imposed by the Socialist government. One liga leader pointedly suggested to Calles that Cruz had been imposed on Tabasco no more than Calles had been imposed on Mexico in 1924, but that the same justification was used in both cases to de-legitimate perfectly democratic elections.[120] Democratic or not, the election did not bring peace. For weeks after Cruz's triumph, Tabasco Socialists continued to vociferously complain of violent attacks against them by partisans of the defeated opposition candidates, including the outright murder of their partisans.[121] They also complained of schemes to invalidate the election, and requested federal intervention on their behalf.[122] In Chiapas, a supporter of Jiménez de Lara was assassinated by a police inspector sympathetic to Garrido.[123] An exasperated President Calles wrote to Tabasco's federal senators in late November that he considered the election over and Cruz elected, and he ordered the Chief of Military Operations in the state to support the civil authorities and permit no further political agitation.[124]

Garrido's absence from the state, particularly when he was in New Orleans for a time during the gubernatorial campaign, posed a challenge

119   Canudas provides an in-depth examination of the 1926 election in Tabasco. Canudas, *Tropico rojo*, Vol. 1, 1, 159–220.
120   FAPECFT-PEC, expediente: 10, LIGAS DIVERSAS, legajo 4/16, foja 160, inventario: 3199. Antonio del Valle Pardo to Soledad González, November 21, 1926.
121   FAPECFT-PEC, expediente: 58, MARGALLI G., H., legajo 1, fojas 30–31, inventario 3432. Homero Margalli, Alcides Caparroso and Alejandro Ruiz to Soledad González, November 24, 1926.
122   FAPECFT-PEC, expediente: 58, MARGALLI G., H., legajo 1, fojas 21–22, inventario 3432. Homero Margalli and Alcides Caparroso to the Supreme Court of the Nation, November 18, 1926.
123   AHECH, Gobernación: 1926, vol. 1, exp. 21. Unsigned copy of a telegram to Mariano Lara, November 22, 1926.
124   FAPECFT-PEC, expediente: 58, MARGALLI G., H., legajo 1, fojas 34, inventario 3432. Calles to Homero Margalli, Alcides Caparroso and Alejandro Ruiz, November 25, 1926.

for the Tabasco Socialists. Some local politicians questioned his political dictates, doubting that he could possibly understand what was happening on the ground in their districts from so far away.[125] Confidence in the liga system among its members also seemed to wane the longer Garrido was not officially in charge of the state government. In January of 1927, a Socialist in Villahermosa wrote to Garrido: "I don't know if it's because of neglect by the leaders or apathy of the Government that haven't known how to energize [the base] like you did, but I have noticed that only a fraction of the liga comrades from last year are sticking around, and the number of allies of those that are unhappy with the government has grown because they don't even remember that we truly fight for it [the government]." He added: "For the presidential campaign that approaches, it is urgent that you are here among us to set these matters on the right path."[126] Doubts also emerged among Socialists in the state about Ausencio Cruz's ability to fill Garrido's shoes as governor.

Garrido's departure for Mexico City in 1926 was fitting. The conflict over the governorship in Tabasco in 1926 closely mirrored what was taking place in Mexican national politics at this time, as Álvaro Obregón made it increasingly clear that he was pondering a bid for a second presidential term in 1928. Politicians in Tabasco and Mexico City alike questioned and debated whether it was advisable to allow an individual to accumulate so much power, and to hold it for so long. Tomás Garrido Canabal would be one of the most active participants in this polemic.

Conclusions

The de la Huerta rebellion of 1923–24 had more of a political impact in Tabasco than perhaps anywhere else in Mexico. It also left its mark on Tomás Garrido Canabal himself. In particular, the death of Felipe Carrillo Puerto was a watershed event for Garrido. In the months and years following the rebellion, Garrido sought to fill Carrillo Puerto's shoes as the leader of southeastern Socialism, as did his counterpart and rival in Chiapas, Carlos Vidal. But perhaps more importantly, Garrido had witnessed the failure of the ligas de resistencia in Yucatán to protect the governor and their party's leader; for Garrido, Carrillo Puerto's death laid bare all of the weaknesses of his political creation. Six months after Carrillo Puerto's assassination, a prominent Yucatecan Socialist assessed that the turncoat federal officers in Yucatán had found a substantial base of popular support in the state because of a "lack of consistency in the political judgment" of the Socialists

---

125   AGN-TGC, c. 114, exp. 8. Letter to Garrido from the Liga of Centla. Indecipherable signature. November 8, 1926.

126   AGN-TGC, c. 115, exp. 1. Juan Hernández to Garrido, January 2, 1927.

there.[127] Surely, Garrido's personality, the particularities of Tabasco and the particular challenges of governing it also contributed to the Tabasco Socialists' variations on Carrillo Puerto's organizational model. But all of Garrido's innovations on the Yucatecan blueprint also have in common his determination not to meet Carrillo Puerto's fate, rendered helpless in the face of a counterrevolutionary assault, with partisans too disorganized and ill-equipped to come to the government's defense.

When Garrido returned home to Tabasco in the spring of 1924 he was determined to take control of the state, and to keep it. This nearly single-minded objective profoundly influenced the shape of the political system he developed there from that point forward. Whereas Carrillo Puerto had created the ligas de resistencia as a means of building substantive connections between political leaders and grassroots constituents in Yucatán, Garrido also used his own liga system to dramatically concentrate political power in his own hands. From 1924 onward, the de la Huerta rebellion was explicitly cited as both the impetus and the justification for Garrido's political extremism as well as his authoritarian tendencies.

With the benefit of nearly a century of retrospect, in the Radical Socialist Party of Tabasco we find what is arguably the most important precursor to the Institutional Revolutionary Party (PRI). Like the PRI's adaptations to the reformist corporatist system established by Lázaro Cárdenas when he reorganized the party into the Party of the Mexican Revolution (PRM) in 1938, Garrido took Carrillo Puerto's more popular and more democratic version of Socialism and adapted it to make it a powerful mechanism of political control and a highly effective means of mustering and managing political patronage. Through the ligas de resistencia, Garrido offered Socialist partisans representation of their interests and a collective political voice, but he gave them less political agency and less political power. This was not a purely authoritarian system, but it was profoundly clientelist, and remarkably effective at concentrating power in the hands of the man in charge. It was also wildly successful. Like the PRI itself, Socialism in Tabasco significantly outlasted peers, predecessors, and antagonists alike.

The long-term, national influence of Garrido's adaptations of Carrillo Puerto's Socialist model should not be overstated, but nor should it be underestimated. Garrido, more than any other individual, demonstrated that even as the southeastern Socialist model succeeded in building substantive relationships between the political class and its previously disen-franchised constituents, often to the benefit of both, it could also be used to empower a small handful of individuals at the expense of transparency, democracy, and the ability to reform the system once it was in place.

---

127 FAPECFT-SGON, expediente: 740: SIMON, Neguib, legajo 1, foja 1, inventario 664. Neguib Simón to Soledad González, June 18, 1924.

5

The Forgotten Revolution

Socialist Chiapas, 1924–1927

> The Revolution has triumphed for the first time in Chiapas, along with all of its principles, and it fills those of us who fought to achieve it for so many years with satisfaction.
>
> Letter from a constituent to Governor Carlos A. Vidal of Chiapas, 1925

Thanks to Lázaro Cárdenas' famous description of Tomás Garrido Canabal's political project, Tabasco is remembered as Mexico's "laboratory of revolution." By contrast, neighboring Chiapas, which also conducted an experiment in Yucatecan-style Socialism in the same period, does not share the same reputation for radicalism and political innovation. Instead, Chiapas is commonly described in national histories of this period as an isolated backwater that, thanks to the counterrevolutionary Mapache rebellion, effectively had no revolution at all.

Chiapas is the last case study of southeastern Socialism in this book. In terms of understanding the larger regional Socialist movement in the 1920s and its long-term national significance, the lesser-known history of Socialism in Chiapas provides crucial data points. Carlos Vidal, Ricardo Alfonso Paniagua, and the other leaders of the Chiapas Socialist Party took a different set of political lessons from Felipe Carrillo Puerto's bold experiment in Yucatán than Garrido did in Tabasco. It was a brand of Socialism that was not less ambitious than its counterparts but in practice was relatively less radical, for various reasons. Its leaders were also less successful in incorporating Chiapas' large indigenous population into the political system than the Socialists were in Yucatán. Even when the will to do so existed, Socialist organizers in Chiapas were faced with daunting logistical hurdles when it came to outreach to indigenous people. These included limited transportation infrastructure across an especially challenging terrain (a limiting factor in all of their grassroots work), as well as the ethnic and linguistic diversity of Chiapas, where numerous Mayan languages are widely spoken by distinct ethnic groups, whereas in Yucatán,

Yucatec Maya overwhelmingly predominates.[1] Socialism in Chiapas was also less overtly designed to concentrate power in the hands of a few than Socialism in Tabasco. Lastly, it was different from all of its counterparts in that it had no ligas de resistencia, at least not in name. It was also the shortest-lived Socialist government in the Southeast.

Some of these differences may indubitably be attributed to a difference of personalities, abilities and the collective political will of Socialist leadership in Tabasco versus in Chiapas. Other differences must be considered in light of the particular, acute political challenges that the Chiapas Socialists faced in reforming their state. On all counts, the Socialist experiment in Chiapas is most significant because it was an ancestor of the modern Mexican political system that quickly went extinct. Its rise and then its rapid undoing, described in Chapter 6, offer important insights into the political descendants of southeastern Socialism that survived the 1920s, and why one variation on Carrillo Puerto's Socialist model thrived in the region while the other failed.

Socialism vs. the Chiapas Counterrevolution, 1923–1925

Álvaro Obregón empowered the counterrevolutionary Mapache faction in Chiapas in 1920 in exchange for their support of his rebellion against Venustiano Carranza, and as the surest means of pacifying the state after six years of civil war. It worked, but it also meant an indefinite deferral of revolutionary reform in the state. The Mapache government spent much time and energy in the years that followed attempting to stamp out any and all political opposition, and to ensure that any reform in Chiapas was limited, at best. Above all, the new state government hoped to curtail the political activities of the Socialist movement there, which had risen out of the failed gubernatorial campaign of Carlos Vidal, and took particular inspiration from Felipe Carrillo Puerto's ambitious political experiments in nearby Yucatán.

In spite of the political repression Socialists and their sympathizers faced in these years, by 1923 the Chiapas Socialist Party was coalescing as a political force with which to be reckoned, with strong presence both at home and in Mexico City. Two Chiapas Socialists won seats in the Chamber of Deputies in 1922, gaining political ground in the national legislature even as their party remained under attack by state government.[2] The persecution of Socialist party members by the Mapaches only intensified as the Socialists became an increasingly credible political threat to their monopoly of power. In 1923, eighty campesino supporters of the Socialist Party were arrested in Motozintla, and four were executed.[3] In another case, police attempted to arrest the Socialist party president, Ricardo Alfonso Paniagua, at a movie theater in Tuxtla Gutiérrez and shot at him when he resisted, leaving him seriously injured.[4]

In Mexico City, the Chiapas Socialists and their allies regularly turned to their most important ally, Secretary of the Interior Plutarco Elías Calles, for support and protection. Chiapas' federal legislators, Jaime Solís and Luis Espinosa, wrote to Calles at length about the abuses of the Mapache government, including a scathing condemnation of Governor Tiburcio Fernández Ruiz. Their allegations included violations of both state and federal laws by the Mapache government in its interference with the state's municipal elections of 1923, and denunciations of the ongoing abuses suffered by members of the Socialist party. "Individual rights in Chiapas are a dead letter," Espinosa and Solís declared. "We put our hope in your firm revolutionary convictions and your irrefutable patriotism, that with your invaluable help the President of the Republic will put a stop to the arbitrary acts of the government of Chiapas and save our beloved state from the desperation and ruin in which it finds itself."[5]

Calles was already convinced that Fernández Ruiz should be removed from power, but Obregón continued to resolutely support the governor that he had empowered. Even so, the unrest that Fernández Ruiz's government was provoking was becoming too much of a political liability for the president to ignore. In February of 1923, Obregón dispatched Calles himself to investigate what was happening on the ground in Chiapas. After meeting with various factions and the governor, Calles telegraphed Obregón that he believed that the prevailing political instability in the state would only worsen under Fernández Ruiz's leadership.[6] Obregón took this warning seriously enough that he temporarily recalled the governor to Mexico City in the hope that it would allow tempers to cool in Chiapas, but two months later he bitterly disappointed opposition factions when he allowed Fernández Ruiz to return and reassume his office. An incensed Luis Espinosa fumed to Calles: "This is the way that General Obregón has repaid everything that my allies and I have done for him in the days of struggle and trial."[7] In a further

3 Antonio García de León, *Resistencia y utopía: memorial de agravios y crónicas de revueltas y profecías acaecidas en la Provincia de Chiapas durante los últimos quinientos años de su historia*, 2nd edn. (México, D.F.: Ediciones Era, 2002; repr., 3), 380.
4 Rébora, *Memorias de un chiapaneco*, 140.
5 FAPECFT-APEC, exp. 68: ESPINOSA, Luis (Dip.), legajo 1/1, fojas 8–18, inventario 1899. Luis Espinosa and Jaime Solís to Calles, February 15, 1923.
6 FAPECFT-APEC, expediente 5, OBREGON, Álvaro (Gral.), legajo 2/13, fojas 85–87, inventario 4038. Calles to Obregón, February 21, 1923.
7 FAPECFT-APEC, exp. 68: ESPINOSA, Luis (Dip.), legajo 1/1, fojas 28–32, inventario 1899. Espinosa to Calles, August 21, 1923.

blow to the Socialists, Obregón also had party president Ricardo Alfonso Paniagua removed from his position as Procurador de Pueblos for the federal Ministry of Agriculture in Chiapas. "Although Señor Paniagua is honorable, and his political affiliation is well known, he has very serious conflicts with the state authorities, and his work is not as efficient as is required," Obregón explained to one citizen who wrote him to protest.[8]

Obregón showed what was, arguably, extraordinary patience with the embattled Mapache governor, but Calles believed that there were better alliances to be made in Chiapas. By 1924 Calles could rely on the Socialists there as a cohesive and well-organized political force, and one that was eager for his patronage. Better yet, they were steadfast allies who had demonstrated their loyalty during the de la Huerta rebellion and were dedicated to carrying on the reformist project of Felipe Carrillo Puerto in the Southeast once it was over. What's more, the Chiapas Socialist Party was politically battle-hardened. "The Chiapas Socialist Party is the only [opposition party] that has endured," wrote one of the several agents reporting confidentially back to Calles' Minister of the Interior, "and that is only because some of its members are in the Capital, and some were able to escape the state when Governor Fernández Ruiz initiated the persecutions of the people that led and comprised [opposition] parties."[9] For the first time, there was a political organization in Chiapas, complete with a well-organized grass-roots base, that could credibly compete with the Mapaches for power.

By allying with the Chiapas Socialists, Calles was also able to continue to consolidate his influence across the larger Southeast, even without Carrillo Puerto. Venustiano Carranza tried to impose his will on the Southeast in 1915–20 and alienated nearly every faction in every state in the process. Obregón supported the Mapaches in 1920–24 in order to stabilize and pacify Chiapas by coopting the counterrevolution that Carranza had provoked, and ended up with allies of dubious reputation and limited political skill.[10] Calles sought a new and different means of bringing Chiapas and the whole of the Southeast into a closer, more productive working relationship with the federal government, through alliances with the Socialist parties across the region. In Chiapas, the ties that Calles forged to this end were close enough that by 1923, he declared that he considered the Chiapas Socialist Party to be his own political party.[11]

8   AGN, O/C, c. 352, exp. 818-P-50. Obregón to H. Vásquez, April 7, 1923.
9   AGN-DGIPS, c. 175, exp. 5, fojas 2–5. Report by Manuel Cervantes, May 26, 1924.
10   Georgette José Valenzuela argues that in the wake of the political fragmentation caused by the armed phase of the Mexican Revolution, Obregón was able to consolidate his power through a series of clientelistic relationships with regional caudillos, and that, in the end, it was Calles who benefited, as President, from the stabilizing effects of these political deals. Georgette José Valenzuela, "1920–1924: ¡ ... Y Venían de una Revolución! De la Oposición Civil a la Oposición Militar," in Meyer, "La diarquía (1924–1928)," 181–82.
11   Rébora, *Memorias de un chiapaneco*, 143.

As the dust settled in Chiapas after the de la Huerta rebellion, Carlos Vidal prepared to launch a new gubernatorial campaign. The Mapaches were so determined to hold on to power in the state that historian Manuel B. Trens, a Vidal apologist, believed that Vidal knowingly risked his life by running for the governorship again. Indeed, Vidal survived an assassination attempt in August of 1924 during a campaign stop, and the gunman was allegedly protected by the Mapache government. In a separate incident the same month, his campaign office in Tuxtla was riddled with bullets by Mapache partisans. As violence continued into the fall, President Obregón ordered that all forces in the state be disarmed except the police and a fifty-man guard detachment at the government palace.[12]

As he and his supporters came under attack at home, Vidal could count on strong support in Mexico City, and not just from Calles. By that time, the Chiapas Socialists had secured another powerful ally: Luis Morones of the Mexican Regional Labor Confederation (CROM) and the Mexican Labor Party (PLM). Like many of the southeastern Socialists, Morones had been a staunch supporter of Obregón who progressively shifted further toward Calles by the mid-1920s. For his part, Calles built his relationships with Morones and the southeastern Socialists in order to establish a popular base of support for himself among workers and campesinos that was independent of Obregón.[13] Shut out of participating in Garrido's state-led organized labor movement in Tabasco, the CROM cultivated its relationships with pro-labor organizations in Chiapas as a means of staking out political territory in the Southeast. In the process, it became another conduit of influence between Calles and the Chiapas Socialists.

Morones was in contact with the leaders of the Chiapas Socialist Party well before his endorsement of Vidal's 1924 gubernatorial candidacy. The CROM was formally affiliated with the Socialists in Soconusco and their Workers' and Peasants' Union, which was led in part by Ricardo Alfonso Paniagua's father.[14] The PLM was therefore well on its way to establishing its own operation in Chiapas, in collaboration with the Socialists there. In the short-term, this meant collaborating to campaign for Calles as president, and for Vidal as governor. Morones personally assured the Chiapas Socialists that he considered Vidal's election to be inevitable.[15] When Vidal returned to the state five months after his gubernatorial nomination, he was greeted by a Laborista demonstration in his honor (see Photograph 5.1).[16]

12 Trens, *Vidal y Chiapas*, 54, 60, 73–74, 87.
13 Buchenau, *Plutarco Elías Calles*, 98–99, 107–9.   14 Lewis, *The Ambivalent Revolution*, 29.
15 AGN-CAV, c. 6, f. 5. Paniagua to Vidal, February 13, 1924.
16 Rébora, *Memorias de un chiapaneco*, 156.

Photograph 5.1 Laborista Party rally in support of Vidal. Huixtla, Chiapas, December 1924
Source: Archivo General de la Nación, Colección Carlos A. Vidal. Sección: Actividades militares, políticas y administrativas, serie: fotografías sobre eventos públicos y sociales y obras públicas en Chiapas, caja 3, sobre: 8, foto: 10.

The Mapaches were undeterred by the favoritism that the president-elect and the CROM showed toward Vidal and the Socialists. Tiburcio Fernández Ruiz chose the federal legislator Luis Ramírez Corzo as his successor, and dedicated all of the power, influence, and resources available to him as governor to helping Ramírez Corzo to defeat Vidal.[17] But Mexico had changed since Fernández Ruiz took power in 1920. Demonstrating political strength at the local level was no longer reliably sufficient for state-level politicians to win the support of powerful allies in Mexico City, particularly if they had other, better options to choose from. The Mapache movement began as an adamant, armed refusal to tolerate any interference of outsiders in Chiapas' politics. Now, just four years later, they worked to adapt to new political realities. The result was that as the gubernatorial campaign began, both the Mapaches and the Socialists actively courted the support of the same patrons in Mexico City. In nearly identical language, both factions described the crimes and offenses perpetrated against them by their opponents. Both sides also bitterly complained of the perceived lack of impartiality of the federal military in the state, in favor of the other side. "I receive the same complaints from Vidalistas," a frustrated Obregón responded to two Mapache complainants. "I can assure you that the military chiefs have concrete instructions not to become involved in electoral matters."[18]

As in Tabasco, one of the chief lines of argument made by both sides of the ever-widening political divide in Chiapas was that their opponents had supported the de la Huerta rebellion (or conversely, that false accusations of Delahuertista sympathies were the principal rhetorical weapons that their opponents were using against them). These allegations were almost entirely spurious. While a few prominent citizens of Chiapas had joined the rebellion, most notably General Alberto Pineda, and some members of all of the contending political factions in 1924 seem to have briefly allied themselves with the rebels, both the Socialists and the Mapaches had stayed loyal to the federal government.[19] As a Mapache state legislator reminded the president in September, Chiapas was the only southern state to remain loyal during the rebellion.[20] Obregón and Calles were already well aware that neither faction had any substantive ties to the rebels. When Fernández Ruiz rather desperately wrote to Obregón in the thick of post-electoral chaos that Fall that he had heard that Vidal had been meeting with known Delahuertistas, Obregón replied sharply: "Since some of your previous reports have proven to be false, I would greatly appreciate it if in the future you would not send me any piece of information without first being certain

17 Ramírez Corzo was trained as a lawyer, and worked for a time as a journalist. He also served as both a representative and a senator from Chiapas. Octavio Gordillo y Ortiz, *Diccionario de la revolución en el estado de Chiapas* (San Cristóbal de Las Casas: Programa de Investigaciones Multidisciplinarias sobre Mesoamérica y el Sureste, UNAM, 1999), 65–66.
18 AGN-OC, 408-Ch-10, leg. 3, c. 142. Obregón to S. Orantes and S. M. Araujo, September 6, 1924.
19 On Pineda's rebellion, see Plasencia de la Parra, *Personajes y escenarios*, 270–74.
20 AGN-OC, 408-Ch-10, leg. 3, c. 142. Secundino Orantes Z. to Obregón, September 1, 1924.

of its veracity."[21] Calles and Obregón also did their own research. Secret agents stationed in Chiapas by the Ministry of the Interior conducted detailed research on the political character and affiliations of numerous Chiapas politicians in this period, nearly always specifying the nature of their involvement (or the lack thereof) with the de la Huerta rebellion.

Chiapas' election was held on September 7, 1924. Both Vidal and Ramírez Corzo claimed to have been elected, along with their respective legislative slates. Neither side was willing to concede, and a chaotic and violent political impasse ensued. A Ministry of the Interior agent, undercover in Chiapas as a journalist, reported that the governor was largely to blame for the electoral fiasco because he had used his office to try to impose Ramírez Corzo.[22] The Mapaches claimed that their candidate had won nearly the entire state except the Socialist stronghold of Motozintla and Vidal's hometown of Pichucalco, and that the Socialists' refusal to admit defeat was intended to cause further conflict.[23] Vidal and his supporters countered that it was the Socialists that had won thirty of the thirty-four districts in the state, with three districts' elections nullified and the Mapaches carrying only one.

Many municipalities across the state protested to the federal Senate that they had freely and fairly elected Vidal, as that body pondered how to handle Chiapas' political mess. The municipal president of San Diego Reforma elaborated that Vidal had offered his community a road and a school, while the Mapaches had stolen livestock and burned down his house. The municipal officials of Agua Tenango wanted the senators to know that the Tzeltal members of their community didn't want another Mapache governor, and that Vidal had many friends among the poor there. Seemingly, only Mapache politicians spoke up to claim a victory for Ramírez Corzo. "[His] election suffers from some flaws, and no one doubts that," they conceded, "but no one is to blame for it, since it is the result of our incipient democratic practices, whose best fruits have been the elections of Madero, of Obregón, and of our current president."[24]

Following the inconclusive election, the political climate in Chiapas grew yet more uneasy, exacerbated by Obregón's ongoing refusal to take any decisive action to resolve the state's electoral crisis beyond urging all sides to remain calm while a resolution was formulated. However, there is no evidence that the president ever actively participated in arranging any

21   AGN-OC, 408-Ch-10, leg. 6, c.142. Obregón to Fernández Ruiz, November 20, 1924.
22   AGN-DGIPS, 311.1 (7.4)-1, c. 192, exp. 17, fs. 1–3.
23   AGN-OC, c. 142, 408-Ch-10, leg. 2. Unsigned memorandum, received by the office of the President, October 27, 1924.
24   Congreso de la Unión, "Diario de los Debates de la Cámara de Senadores." Año I, XXXI Legislatura. Tomo I, núm. 48. December 9, 1924. Ibid. Año I, XXXI Legislatura. Tomo I, núm. 54. December 18, 1924.

such resolution. In his persistent support of the Mapaches for the previous four years, Obregón had painted himself into a political corner. In the face of the overwhelming evidence of corruption and abuse by the government he had helped to install, throwing his support to the Mapaches for a second term in Chiapas was surely not an appealing option, nor one that Calles, now president-elect, would have endorsed. At the same time, throwing his support to the Socialists would have contravened his long-standing alliance with the Mapaches. Faced with these choices, Obregón opted to run out the clock.

Law and order rapidly disintegrated in Chiapas. Vidal was fearful for his safety, and with good reason: Some of his associates and supporters had already been assassinated during the campaign.[25] On October 5, a heavily drinking crowd at a Mapache rally in the state capital of Tuxtla Gutiérrez turned rowdy and then violent, leaving two people dead.[26] Then, a week later, all of the unresolved political tensions in the state finally boiled over. As Vidal made his way through a crowd of supporters in Tuxtla on October 12, passing under floral arches built to celebrate his arrival, a gunman shot at him, taking advantage of the cover of noise provided by celebratory fireworks. Moments later, another man pointed a pistol at Vidal at close range but didn't fire, and then was lost in the crowd. Once Vidal arrived at the main plaza, gunmen positioned on the roof of the government palace and in the towers of the cathedral opened fire on the gathered crowd of his supporters, which included many women and children. From the balcony where he stood, Vidal tried to calm the panicked crowd as people attempted to flee the plaza. Meanwhile, some of his partisans returned the attackers' fire and charged the government palace. The shooting stopped only with the arrival of federal soldiers on the scene.[27]

Vidal later claimed that several of the shooters were Mapache state legislators.[28] Several of his associates were killed, and many others were injured. In a letter to his wife, Vidal described the scene:

... they started to fire shots into the crowd, which caused terror and confusion among the families and the most just indignation among the rest of the crowd. The garrison of the plaza had to impose order, as there were about twelve casualties and many injured. I don't even know how I saved myself, because there were infinite bullet holes in the balcony where I was standing, and where I stood for a good while, believing that I could calm the confusion there. Only good luck could have been

25 AGN-CAV, c. 6, f. 1. Carlos A. Vidal to José Bustamente, September 14, 1924. AGN-CAV, c. 6, f. 1. Vidal to Luis Ramírez Corzo, July 28, 1924.

26 Trens, *Vidal y Chiapas*, 116.

27 Ibid., 123–41. Trens was present at the scene, and published this account three years later.

28 Congreso de la Unión, "Diario de los Debates de la Cámara de Senadores." Año I, XXXI Legislatura. Tomo I, núm. 54. December 18, 1924.

what saved me from that catastrophe, since they were shooting at me from the palace and from the towers, as the principal object was to kill me.[29]

In a report to President Obregón, one of the military commanders catalogued the startling collection of weaponry that he and his men had confiscated from the attackers, whom he described as "police and officials at the service of the governor": forty-two rifles, five cases of ammunition, forty-five cartridge belts with forty cartridges each, and two cases of hand grenades.[30]

Still, President Obregón continued to protect his Mapache allies. When the commander of the army garrison in Tuxtla attempted to get the situation in the plaza under control by arresting the Mapache legislators who had taken possession of the government palace, Obregón ordered their release, declaring it an inappropriate intervention by the federal military in a local political struggle. He then removed the colonel who had given the order and sharply reprimanded his subordinates who had been involved in the arrest, while simultaneously assuring Vidal that the guilty parties would be remanded to the appropriate authorities.[31] When a group of women wrote to the president to insist that the arrest of the legislators was entirely justified, Obregón reminded them that as legislators they were protected by *fueros*, and could not be arrested.[32]

The political impasse continued. Two rival state legislatures operated: the Mapache one out of the office of the legislative palace, while the Vidalistas met in the legislative chamber, which they were only able to enter after a janitor left a door unlocked.[33] Both factions continued to insist on the legitimacy of their respective governors-elect.[34] For lack of other options, the federal government continued to recognize Fernández Ruiz as acting governor.[35] Subsequently, both the Mapaches and the Vidalistas also named their own interim governors. The result was four governors claiming some degree of legitimacy in the state at the same time: two who claimed to have been elected in September, and two who claimed to be standing in for them. The Mexico City daily *Excélsior* marveled: "The situation that prevails in the

29 AGN-CAV, c.6, f. 11. Vidal to Dévora Rojas de Vidal, October 17, 1924.

30 AGN-OC, 408-Ch-10, leg. 2, c. 142. Pascual Fuentes to Obregón, October 13, 1924.

31 AGN-OC, 408-Ch-10, leg. 2, c. 142. Obregón to Jefe Guarnición, October 13, 1924. Obregón to Vidal, October 13, 1924. Obregón to Pascual Fuentes. October 14, 1924.

32 AGN-OC, 408-Ch-10, leg. 1, c. 142. Obregón to Dolores López Castillejos et al., October 20, 1924.

33 Trens, *Vidal y Chiapas*, 152.

34 *Excélsior* (Mexico City), November 7, 1924, 1. "En el Estado de Chiapas hay Fungiendo dos Gobernadores."

35 *Excélsior* (Mexico City), November 13, 1924, Section 2, p. 8. "Nada se ha Resuelto en el Caso Chiapas."

state of Chiapas is unusual in the extreme, like nothing that has been seen before in any state in our nation."[36]

Plutarco Elías Calles had other plans for Chiapas that did not involve further protection of the Mapaches, nor further delays in seating a governor. Once he was inaugurated as president of Mexico on December 1, 1924, Calles immediately ordered the Ministry of the Interior to study the situation and to determine which governor had been elected.[37] Even this inspired controversy in Chiapas, as Socialist legislative hopefuls accused the Mapaches of attempting to mislead the federal investigators.[38] The final report found that rampant fraud had occurred on both sides, effectively rendering the election void.[39] On December 3, just two days into his presidency, Calles announced that he would not recognize either Ramírez Corzo or Vidal as governor of Chiapas because the people of the state had not been able to express their political will at the ballot box, and he referred the case to the federal Senate for resolution.

As the Senate took up the case, Vidal bluntly offered the bullet holes in the wall behind where he had stood in Tuxtla at the rally in October as evidence of the kind of politics practiced by the Mapaches. Observers in the Senate gallery grew so unruly during the proceedings that the president of the chamber threatened to throw them out.[40] The exasperated senators finally found that Chiapas effectively had no election, and declared that the state "deserves the true and effective protection of the federal powers, to seize it from the state of tyranny in which its former caciques have sunk the unlucky people of Chiapas."[41] As mandated by the 1917 Constitution when a state's powers were declared to have "disappeared," Calles gave the Senate a list of three candidates for provisional governor.[42] The president also pointedly reminded the federal military commander in the state that while the Senate considered the case, neither of the feuding candidates was to be empowered as governor.[43]

---

36   *Excélsior* (Mexico City), November 23, 1924, Section 2, p. 3. "Cuatro Son los Ejecutivos que Hay en Chiapas."

37   AGN-OC, c.172, 428-Ch-8. Calles to Raúl García, et al., December 3, 1924. See also *Excélsior* (Mexico City), December 3, 1924, 1. "El Conflicto de Chiapas Va a Ser Resuelto Muy Pronto."

38   AGN-OC, c. 172, 428-Ch-8. Alfredo Marín and Dr. Galileo Cruz Robles to Calles, December 3, 1924.

39   Gruening, *Mexico and Its Heritage*, 408–9. I am assuming that Gruening is referring to the same Ministry of Government report which Calles commissioned at this time.

40   Congreso de la Unión, "Diario de los Debates de la Cámara de Senadores." Año I, XXXI Legislatura. Tomo I, núm. 54. December 18, 1924.

41   Ibid. Año I, XXXI Legislatura. Tomo I, núm. 54. December 18, 1924. On this election and other failed state elections like it, see Osten, "Trials by Fire."

42   *El Universal*, December 6, 1924, p. 1. "Terna Para Gobernador de Chiapas."

43   AGN-OC, c. 172, 428-Ch-8. Calles to General Benecio López, December 11, 1924.

In one of its last sessions of 1924, the Senate selected the lawyer César Córdoba as interim governor, who was widely understood to be Calles' choice.[44] This amounted to bolstering the position of Vidal and the Socialists. Córdoba was an associate of Vidal's from his hometown of Pichucalco. He had worked as a journalist and a lawyer before attaining several offices of note in the federal government. In addition to serving as Mexico's ambassador to several European countries, he was a bureaucrat who had helped to implement land and labor reform at the federal level, briefly serving as the director of the Department of Industry and Commerce, and as the sub-director of the Ministry of Agriculture.[45] He was still working for Agriculture when he was named as provisional governor, and was granted a leave from his position there to accept the post.[46] With an ally in the governor's office and a supportive president, the months that followed were taken by the Socialists and their allies as an opportunity to lay the ground-work for Vidal's presumed assumption of the governorship in May of 1925, following a new election.

The Socialists' allies in Mexico City also began to prepare, as the leaders of the CROM took it upon themselves to groom Vidal for the new electoral battle ahead. Juan Rico sent several sharply worded letters to Vidal, reprimanding him for political acts and affiliations that the Laboristas believed could be prejudicial to his candidacy and to his public image in Mexico City. Yet Rico also repeatedly assured Vidal of the unwavering support he enjoyed from the CROM and from Luis Morones. This was all the more important for Chiapas Socialists now that Morones had been given a cabinet post, as Calles' Minister of Industry. "It has given us much pleasure, despite everything, that we have been given another opportunity to demonstrate that the people of Chiapas are with us, because with the latest events, the naming of a Provisional Governor by the Senate is nothing more than delaying your assumption of power," Rico wrote to Vidal in January of 1925.[47]

Laborista support was also decisive at the local level as the Socialists prepared for a new gubernatorial campaign. With Calles' and the CROM's support, the Socialists were able to take over Chiapas' Agrarian Commission in December of 1924 and to reinstate Ricardo Alfonso Paniagua as Procurador de Pueblos. In that capacity, he threatened Mapache landowners

44 *Excélsior* (Mexico City), December 25, 1924, Sec. 2, p.1. "Labor de Acercamiento y Progreso de Chiapas." See also Benjamin, *A Rich Land, a Poor People,* 161.

45 Camp, *Mexican Political Biographies, 1884–1935,* 53. Edgar Robledo Santiago, *Valores Humanos de Chiapas* (Tuxtla Gutiérrez: Universidad Autonoma de Chiapas, 1992), 302–3.

46 *Excélsior* (Mexico City), December 25, 1924, Sec. 2, p.1. "Labor de Acercamiento y Progreso de Chiapas."

47 AGN-CAV, c. 2. Rico to Vidal, January 10, 1924.

with the redistribution of their lands.[48] His reinstatement was part of a larger collaboration between the Chiapas Socialists and the CROM to have friends and allies of the Socialists appointed to federal offices, including in Morones' Ministry of Industry.[49] The PLM also collaborated with the Chiapas Socialists in the production of propaganda materials and preparation of manifestos for Socialists candidates for state office in the new election.[50] It was a mutually beneficial exchange of power and influence – and also of money, as the Socialists counted on financial contributions from Morones and his collaborators in their ongoing struggle against the Mapaches.[51] In their extensive correspondence with the federal government in this period, Vidal's agents commonly described their party affiliation as Laborista, rather than Socialist.

The strategic exploitation of the Chiapas Socialists' grassroots organization for its own purposes was characteristic of the CROM under Morones' leadership, which made a habit of coopting preexisting unions and organizations into its ranks, sometimes forcibly so.[52] But tensions soon began to brew between the Socialists and the Laboristas in Chiapas. Even as the Laboristas escalated their organizing for Vidal's candidacy, they also began to differentiate themselves from the Socialists. By 1925, Laboristas had begun to establish their own local political parties in Chiapas, independent of the Socialist Party.[53] The Socialists and the Laboristas also sometimes disagreed on the slates of candidates they each supported for local offices. A partisan from Tapachula wrote to Vidal shortly after Córdoba was imposed as interim governor that "in Chiapas there is only the Labor Party, including in the last corners [...] the Socialist Party is just a little group there, and they say that it is in Motozintla."[54] But another supporter assured Vidal that regardless of his own Laborista affiliation, "we are all Vidalistas, first and foremost."[55]

The growing friction between the Chiapas Socialists and the PLM over candidates for municipal offices reflected a fundamental difference in their respective priorities and perspectives. For the Socialists, these differences were symptomatic of the Laboristas' lack of experience and knowledge of local politics. One of Vidal's collaborators expressed his contempt for the candidate that the Laboristas backed for municipal president in Tapachula, and his shock that they would back an opposition campaign against

48 García de León, *Resistencia y utopía*, 383.
49 AGN-CAV, c. 6, f. 5. Paniagua to Vidal, February 22, 1925.
50 AGN-CAV, c. 6, f. 13. Paniagua to Vidal, January 28, 1925.
51 AGN-CAV, c. 6, f. 5. Paniagua to Vidal, February 22, 1925.
52 Buchenau, *Plutarco Elías Calles*, 116.   53 Spenser, *El partido socialista chiapaneco*, 137.
54 AGN-CAV, c. 6, f. 13. Onésimo Barrientos to Vidal, February 8, 1925.
55 AGN-CAV, c. 6, f. 5. Partial letter missing attribution to Vidal, February 15, 1924.

a candidate who was well known and well-loved in the community.[56] Yet at least in the short term, both sides remained determined to smooth over these differences in the name of their shared interest in defeating the Mapaches. "Here the Laborista and Socialist parties are divided over municipal elections, but not so for the elections for Governor and Representatives," an associate in Tapachula assured Ricardo Alfonso Paniagua.[57]

With the collapse of Chiapas' political institutions and a crisis of legitimacy in 1924–25, it was logical that local politicians and power brokers across the political spectrum turned to the federal government and military, and in the case of the Socialists, also to the CROM. If Chiapas' reputation for isolation and isolationism within Mexico was deserved in the 1910s, this was no longer the case by the mid-1920s. Yet arguments over political details at the local level between allied factions underscore the complexity of the links that were forged between local and national political blocs. It was to be expected that this process would not be as smooth or straightforward as Obregón's opportunistic alliance with the Mapaches four years earlier, particularly as state-level parties and their national patrons became increasingly reliant on each other to achieve their respective political objectives, but inevitably failed to see eye to eye in every case. The differences between the Chiapas Socialists and the PLM could be papered over for the sake of the new state election, and they were, because it was to the short-term benefit of both organizations. But their disagreements were not erased or resolved as a result.

The electoral impasse was a setback for the Socialists, but César Córdoba's interim governorship was a significant opportunity. In the absence of a confirmed legislature, Córdoba was empowered to govern by decree. In his short time in the governor's office, he was able to push through laws and reforms that laid important groundwork for Vidal after his presumed triumph in the new election. The Mapaches could protest, but they had no leverage unless they recaptured the government, which would have required Calles' support. Córdoba worked to put the state government's affairs in order. In an interview with the Mexico City daily *Excélsior*, Córdoba said that his three top priorities were to review the state budget and tax collections, to reorganize new state and municipal elections, and to "minutely" review land grants, and to give new grants to communities in need.[58] Within weeks of taking office, he also announced a new tax on coffee exports.[59] All of these

---

56   Rébora, *Memorias de un chiapaneco*, 168. Tapachula was a particular hotbed of tensions between Socialists and Laboristas, perhaps as a result of this electoral engineering. For details on Tapachula's contested election in 1925, see Spenser, *El partido socialista chiapaneco*, 137–39.

57   AGN-CAV c. 6, f. 5. Paniagua to Ernesto C. Herrera, March 20, 1925.

58   *Excélsior* (Mexico City), December 25, 1924, Sec. 2, p.1, 6. "Labor de Acercamiento y Progreso de Chiapas."

59   Trens, *Vidal y Chiapas*, 228.

measures would assure that Vidal would take power under the best possible circumstances.

Communities across Chiapas understood Córdoba's brief time in power as a window of opportunity to advance their interests. Numerous local leaders reached out to the state government in these months for help reestablishing law and order. They frequently explained to Córdoba that after four years of Mapache government, they were eager for the advent of a more lawful and democratic era. Such requests began immediately. Weeks before Córdoba took office, residents of Chicoasén wrote to him to decry the abuses and electoral corruption their community had suffered at the hands of a local hacendado and his armed thugs, and to request new local elections. "Today things are taking on a different character," they wrote. " ... in our demand for Justice many years have passed [...] Convoke new elections so that the vote may be free and thereby bring about peace and the advancement of this poor town that has suffered so greatly." The governor's office responded that their rights would soon be guaranteed by the naming of new municipal councils.[60]

Córdoba's political reorganization efforts were comforting to some, but they were also the source of widespread preoccupation. Mapaches and Socialists alike fretted over the legality of the laws passed during the interim governorship, a period in which lawmaking procedures were rendered murky by the revocation of state powers and the dissolution of the state legislature. There were good reasons for concern, depending on which political faction one belonged to. In 1923, as the Mapaches and their allies sought to re-exert control over indigenous labor following the disruptions of Constitutionalism in the state to the old ways of doing things in Chiapas, indigenous municipalities routinely had their legal statuses downgraded to "municipal agencies" that were subject to the political control of the closest nonindigenous (ladino) town, and governed by a municipal agent imposed on them by that town.[61] This was part of a larger pattern of political manipulation across the state by the state government, which rewarded communities loyal to the governor with elevated political status, and demoted towns that didn't support him, including ones that petitioned the state for land grants.[62]

This was understandably one of the chief political grievances of indigenous communities, and Córdoba prioritized its reversal. In a series of early decrees, the interim governor changed the legal statuses of numerous localities. For example, Córdoba recognized the Zoque community of Copainalá as a city instead of a village. The decree specified that this was

60 AHECH, Gobernación 1925, vol. 3. Teófilo Santiago et al. to César Córdoba, 20 December 1924. Srio. Gral. to Teófilo Santiago et al., January 6, 1925.
61 Rus, "Revoluciones contenidas," 78–79.   62 Benjamin, *A Rich Land, a Poor People*, 154–55.

a corrective to the preceding period of chaos there, and that "this period of transition inarguably has to end, for the era of peace that the Republic has now entered."[63] This effort continued throughout Córdoba's brief time in office and into the early days of Vidal's elected term. In some cases, communities had their status downgraded multiple times by the Mapache government (in one case, from municipality in 1878 to delegación in 1920 and to agencia in 1922). This downgrading happened in several towns in Mariscal and Motozintla, longtime centers of Socialist organizing. In the case of the Mam community of San Pedro Remate in Mariscal, local political leaders had ignored the downgrading of their political status and the town had continued to elect its own leaders, with the approval of the local ayuntamiento.[64] However, even after the Socialist reforms, indigenous majority towns that were restored to the status of municipalities in 1925 were still saddled with ladino political overseers.[65]

Meanwhile, some towns that were never downgraded in status were elevated to the status of municipality, such as El Edén in the district of Soconusco, another Socialist stronghold.[66] It seems likely that at least in some of these cases, Córdoba strategically manipulated the relative political strength of various communities in ways favorable to the Socialists. Other cases of electoral manipulation by Córdoba were less subtle. When he and Vidal disapproved of the outcome of a municipal election in Tapachula, Córdoba nullified the results and ordered the state legislature to impose an interim municipal president of his choosing. Citing this case, historian Daniela Spenser argues that as governor, Vidal was no more democratic in practice than his Mapache predecessor, in terms of his willingness to impose the candidates he chose for local offices.[67]

In other cases, Córdoba's work on behalf of the incoming Socialist administration had more clearly ideological objectives. The most famous instance is one of Córdoba's very last decrees as provisional governor, in May of 1925, which declared women to be full citizens of Chiapas. Women's suffrage in the Southeast provides useful insight into the spread of Alvarado's and Carrillo Puerto's influence across the region. It also demonstrates the progressively greater institutionalization of Socialist ideas and policies in the Southeast, as well as the different approaches that Socialist state governments took to the same political question. Salvador Alvarado had first made some of the most

---

63   AHECH, Gobernación 1925, vol. 4, exp. 241: Decree 18, March 5, 1925.

64   AHECH, Gobernación vol. 4, exp. 241: Decreto 16, June 3, 1925 restored San Pedro Remate to the status of a municipality.

65   Rus, "Revoluciones contenidas," 81.

66   AHECH, Gobernación vol. 4, exp. 241: Decreto 17, June 8, 1925.

67   Spenser, *El partido socialista chiapaneco*, 138–41. See also the account of what happened in Tapachula by Hipólito Rébora, on which Spenser bases much of her analysis: Rébora, *Memorias de un chiapaneco*, 169–75.

significant gestures toward the political enfranchisement of women in Mexico up to that point with his organization of two feminist congresses in Yucatán in 1915 and 1916. Carrillo Puerto took up the cause of women's political rights as governor there in the early 1920s, enabling women to vote but never committing their enfranchisement to state law. Tomás Garrido Canabal, as discussed in Chapter 4, sponsored a reform that allowed at least some women to vote in municipal elections in 1925. But it was Chiapas, later that same year, which became the first state in Mexico to permanently and fully recognize women as citizens, with the same political rights as men.[68] This can be explained in part by timing and circumstances, but it was also the result of larger differences between Socialism in Tabasco and Socialism in Chiapas.

Women's rights had been one of the central tenets of the Chiapas Socialist Party's platform since the beginning. The party's constitution, drafted in January of 1920, described women's equality as chief among Socialism's goals. Like many feminists and supporters of women's rights in Mexico in this period, the Chiapas Socialists understood feminism in terms of the precedents set by other nations, particularly the United States and England. Suffrage was described as not only a means to attain a more just social order, but also to attain modernity and join the "vanguard of civilization." The Socialists contextualized their goal of attaining equality between the sexes as part of a larger campaign for social justice: the end of worker exploitation, the attainment of class equality, and communism as the "superlative" of Socialism, and the means of bringing about "the reign of justice in the world."[69]

For Vidal, the enfranchisement of women represented a dramatic public acknowledgment of his Socialist identity. It was also a visible nod to Paniagua, who was the principle grassroots organizer for the party and was likely the author of the suffrage decree.[70] Vidal was also progressive for the time on women's rights at a more personal level. He was adamant that his daughter Noya be educated and independent from the time she was very young. When she was fourteen, her father encouraged her to learn English and to take business and finance courses so that she would always be able to support herself, and advised her to never allow herself or her affairs to be dominated by a husband.[71]

The most significant effect of the Chiapas suffrage decree was that it led to one of the first elections of a woman to state-level office in Mexico, if not

---

68 On Socialism in the Southeast and women's suffrage, see Osten, "Crooked Path to the Franchise."
69 Spenser, *El partido socialista chiapaneco* 181–82.
70 Robledo Santiago, *Valores Humanos de Chiapas*, 502.
71 AGN-CAV, c. 6, f. 11. Vidal to Noya Vidal, July 3, 1918; Vidal to Noya Vidal, February 25, 1927.

the first. Florinda Lazos León won a state legislative seat as a Free Workers' Party candidate in 1926. Lazos was a Socialist operative and organizer and a Laborista who worked for Vidal's gubernatorial campaign, delivering speeches and publishing manifestos on his behalf. She also published her own Laborista newspaper in San Cristóbal, *La Gleba*. In it, in addition to lengthy treatises on the global, historical significance of Socialism, Lazos praised Vidal's government for its progress in reforming the state.[72] The Chiapas Socialist Party was pleased to count Lazos as one of its members, and proudly touted her election. Socialist legislator Raymundo Enríquez cited Lazos' election in the state as one of the great accomplishments of Socialism in Chiapas in a passionate defense of the party that he gave in the Chamber of Deputies in 1926.[73]

It bears underscoring that the Socialists of Chiapas could have made a dramatic public gesture toward women's rights in the same ways that Carrillo Puerto's and Garrido Canabal's governments did previously, without committing women's full, equal citizenship to law. Considering the relatively low levels of political enfranchisement and voter participation in the state in this period, it is doubtful that women's suffrage greatly increased voter turnout for Socialist candidates; in any case, it came too late to help Vidal, who was already the governor-elect by the time Córdoba decreed women's political equality. Rather, women's suffrage was a fulfillment of a long-term ideological objective that also contributed to the Chiapas Socialists' project of political reorganization, enfranchisement at the grassroots, and a marked emphasis on fortifying electoral laws and procedures in the period following the failed 1924 election.

This was also a time in which the Socialists put a great deal of effort into recruiting popular support for Vidal among Chiapas' indigenous communities, as the Socialists sought to bolster Vidal's grassroots base leading up to the new election. After elite-led factions had all long eschewed recruitment of indigenous people, this was a notable shift in political practice in Chiapas.[74] The Socialists worked to establish a presence in numerous indigenous-majority towns, to win popular support for Vidal's gubernatorial campaign and then his government, and to strengthen their position in the case of future conflicts with the Mapaches. They also sought to counteract the Mapache government's previous manipulation and coercion of campesino voters in both state and municipal elections, and requested Calles' support in that effort.[75]

72 *La Gleba* (San Cristóbal de Las Casas), July 30, 1926.
73 "Diario de los Debates de la Cámara de Diputados," H. Congreso de la Unión, http://cronica .diputados.gob.mx/DDebates/index.html. Legislatura XXXII – Año I – Período Ordinario – November 3, 1926 – Número de Diario 29.
74 Rus, "Revoluciones contenidas," 59.
75 AGN-OC, c. 142, exp. 408-ch-10, legajo 5. Raquel García to Calles, March 3, 1925.

This outreach effort went both ways in 1924–25. As ethnohistorian Jan Rus has emphasized, indigenous communities of highland Chiapas were neither passive nor united in their response to revolutionary movements in the state, nor did ethnicity necessarily determine their politics.[76] Rival factions of ladino elites had long struggled over who would control and have access to the supply of indigenous labor in the highlands surrounding San Cristóbal de Las Casas. For this reason, no local revolutionary faction sought to mobilize indigenous partisans. Instead, Rus has found, they all largely discouraged Maya political organization, making Chiapas' political landscape quite different than Yucatán's. This continued into the 1920s with Obregón's empowerment of the Mapaches. When the Mapaches took power, they undertook a political reorganization of the highlands that included the imposition of municipal authorities on indigenous towns as a means of controlling residents' labor.[77] Now some of these same towns reached out to the Socialists in the hopes of freeing themselves from ongoing interference in local governance, and laid the blame for the political subjugation they had long faced at the feet of the Mapache government that had perpetuated it.

In the highland Tzotzil town of Zinacantán, which enjoyed relatively more political independence during the Porfiriato than some of its neighbors, local representatives wrote to Obregón that they were outraged by electoral abuses and impositions by the Mapache government during the failed state election of 1924.[78] Leaders of the Tzeltal town of Bachajón complained that local authorities had been imposed on them a year earlier and had proceeded to extort them for sums they could not possibly afford. This money was allegedly in part to pay the salary of a teacher that according to the complainants had never so much as opened the door of the local school. They also alleged that the municipal agent imposed on them demanded that he be provided with access to young women from the community, which understandably outraged them. "Señor Flores has declared himself to be a true cacique, converting the poor Indians into beasts of burden," they wrote.[79] San Juan Chamula, with 20,000 Tzotzil residents, was another town that was restored to the status of a municipality in Vidal's first weeks in office after being downgraded to a political subsidiary of the smaller San Andrés by the Mapache government. In their petition for this restoration in January of 1925, Chamula's representatives praised the new government as one that

---

76 Rus, "Revoluciones contenidas," 57–59.   77 Ibid., 61.
78 Ibid., 67. AGN-OC, c. 142. 408-ch-10. Leg. 3. Pedro Pérez et al. to Obregón, August 31, 1924. On the history of Zinacantán, see also Wasserstrom, *Class and Society in Central Chiapas*, chapter 7.
79 AHECH, Gobernación: 1925, vol. 1. Eusebio Díaz et al. to Secretario General de Gobierno, February 15, 1925.

was dedicated to the moral and material improvement of all of the pueblos of the state.[80]

One Socialist agent was surprised and pleased to report that Vidal's promises of improvements for all social classes of Chiapas had been so successful that he had received messages of support from the leaders of various indigenous communities who hoped that the Socialists might help them to recover lands from which they had been evicted. He assured them that Vidal would attend to their petitions as soon as he was elected.[81] In some cases Socialist organizers were also able to meet with indigenous workers on fincas (plantations), to try to win their support for Vidal's campaign. "Our enemies have wanted to take advantage of the good faith or the ignorance of the Indians with infinite lies, but I convinced them that it is all to deceive them," one organizer reported from the fincas of Comitán.[82]

This was the first time a revolutionary movement had sincerely sought to ally itself with the Maya of Chiapas. It was a far cry from the so-called Pajarito rebellion of 1911, when conservatives in the highlands organized an army of Tzotzil men from Chamula to fight against their elite rivals in the lowlands, nominally in support of Madero. In the process, the Tzotzil men who joined the rebellion turned on members of their own communities who had participated in taxation and labor recruiting on behalf of the state. Hundreds were killed. Tzotziles and Tzeltales in neighboring areas also purged members of their communities, in a few cases also targeting and killing ladinos. This was later reimagined by highland elites as an indigenous uprising against ladinos, and incontrovertible evidence of the dangers of politically mobilizing Indians. For the Maya communities involved, particularly Chamula, the long-term result was political disillusionment and an enduring legacy of suspicion of proposed alliances with ladinos of any political persuasion. To make matters worse in Chamula, Carrancistas executed the insurgent leader Jacinto Pérez "Pajarito" in 1914.[83] While some highland indigenous communities fared far better than Chamula during the armed phase of the revolution, this disillusionment and collective memory of betrayal significantly complicated Socialists' efforts to win highland indigenous support for their cause thirteen years later.[84]

Socialist organizers promoted Vidal's election as an unprecedented window of opportunity for wrongs committed against indigenous communities

80 AHECH, Gobernación: 1925, vol. 4, exp. 241: Vidal to Presidente de la Legislatura Local, June 29, 1925. Manuel Pérez et al. to César Córdoba, January 26, 1925.
81 CAV c. 2. José Castellanos to Vidal, January 17, 1925.
82 CAV, c. 6, f. 15. Emilio Esponda to Vidal, April 1, 1925.
83 Rus, "Revoluciones contenidas," 68–74, 80.
84 See Rus' discussion of the contrasting experience of the town of Chenalhó, where some men enlisted in the Constitutionalist army. Ibid., 75–76.

to be made right, and some towns in the highlands came to see the triumph of Socialism as their best hope. Representatives of the Tzeltal town of Cancuc, thirty miles northwest of Chamula, wrote to César Córdoba to decry years of extortion by local officials and the decimation of their community as many people fled the depredations they faced there, and expressed their hope that the Socialists might win their community "a few years of freedom." They requested that the interim governor restore Cancuc to its previous status as an independent municipality and empower it to elect its own authorities. They wrote: "Sir, we want to live united, to be brothers and to enjoy the blessings of humanity, of properly understood Socialism, of the lands that we possess and that have cost us the sweat of our brows and the labor of our ancestors and that we benefit from even today as a community." They also requested that the government send them a teacher to teach them and their children to read and write, offering a place for the teacher to live, and a small stipend either in cash or kind. Invoking the promises of the 1917 Constitution, they implored: "we want to be considered men, not beasts of burden, like honest and hardworking farmers, and that the principles enshrined in our Magna Carta be made effective after it has cost our Nation so much blood to be able to achieve these rights of man."[85] A Socialist agent in Cancuc reported that when he first started organizing there in 1921, his progress was slow at best. The people there unconditionally supported the authorities, in spite of significant abuses and violence suffered by their community under the Mapache government. By 1925, the town was committed to supporting the Socialists and had been able to elect its own municipal secretary. He concluded: "Happily, we have taken a step that will destroy yesterday's mandarins."[86]

The Socialists' understood their campaign for indigenous support to be crucial to Vidal's defeat of the Mapaches in the new election in April of 1925. It paid off in some places. When the new election took place, Vidal received an estimated 2,500 votes in San Juan Chamula, and overwhelmingly carried the entire highland district of San Andrés.[87] In other towns, the results were less favorable. Although the Socialists had helped the leaders of Cancuc to organize and to make their demands of the state government, their political empowerment proved more difficult. When the new state election took place in April, indigenous people in many towns were prevented from voting by local authorities, and the citizens of Cancuc and Zinacantán were prevented from casting ballots for any candidate.[88]

85 AHECH, Gobernación: 1925, vol. I. Lorenzo Martínez to César Córdoba, January 18, 1925.
86 CAV c.2. José A. Mijangos to Vidal, January 13, 1925.
87 CAV c. 3. Joaquín M. Suárez to Vidal, April 6, 1925.
88 CAV c. 3. On Cancuc: José Castellanos to Vidal, April 9, 1925. On Zinacantán: Joaquín M. Suárez to Vidal, April 6, 1925.

A year and a half later, as governor, Vidal requested that a federal garrison be established in Cancuc and surrounding areas in the district of Chilón, to provide support and protection for indigenous residents (Tzotzil and Ch'ol) from repeated robberies and assaults.[89] Incidents like these underscore how difficult and sometimes ineffective the Socialists' outreach effort to indigenous communities was in practice. Municipal authorities accustomed to abusing their power over indigenous towns often continued to do so. It was also a time in Chiapas when ladinos in some parts of the state resented or even actively feared the empowerment of indigenous people by the Socialists. In February of 1925, ladinos of Chilón requested federal troops to protect them from hundreds of their indigenous neighbors, who were rumored to have recently armed themselves.[90] In spite of their extensive stated commitments to organize and collaborate with indigenous communities, popular fears among ladinos of race wars and powerful, long-entrenched powers in the state continued to work against the Socialists in their effort to politically organize among indigenous communities, even

Photograph 5.2 Vidal's supporters in Tuxtla Gutiérrez on Election Day, April 4, 1925
Source: Archivo General de la Nación, Colección Carlos A. Vidal. Sección: Actividades militares, políticas y administrativas, serie: fotografías sobre eventos públicos y sociales y obras públicas en Chiapas, caja 3, sobre: 15, foto: 10.

89   AHECH, Gobernación: 1926, vol. 1. Vidal to Regino González, November 17, 1926.
90   AHECH, Gobernación: 1925, vol. 1. Copy of a report by the President of the Municipal Council of Chilón, February 19, 1925.

as they took control of the state government in May of 1925. Members of the landholding class strongly resisted relinquishing their accustomed power over their campesino neighbors and employees. Although workers inspired by Socialist promises of reform expected a great deal of the new state government, many elites in Chiapas continued to expect no significant change to the status quo and to carry on with timeworn practices of asserting economic and political control over campesinos, indigenous or otherwise.[91]

The new election in Chiapas was held on April 4, 1925. The Tuxtla paper *Reconstrucción* estimated that there were three times as many people lined up to vote for Vidal in the central plaza of Tuxtla as there were for his Mapache-aligned opponent in this new round, Fausto Ruiz.[92] "We did not count them, as the task would have been never ending," the paper declared.[93] Buoyed by the local constituent base organized by the Chiapas Socialist Party and numerous other anti-Mapache factions and parties, and supported by Calles and the CROM in Mexico City, Carlos Vidal was finally elected governor, and took office in May of 1925.

Socialist Chiapas, 1925–1927

As Vidal took power, US military intelligence described him as a "furious Agrarista" and "ultra-rojo," and a puppet of Calles and Morones who only came to power with their assistance.[94] This was an overstatement by a foreign government that was increasingly paranoid about the spread of Bolshevism in Mexico. Still, the report contained some kernels of truth. Vidal consistently stressed the closeness of his relationship with Calles, and emphasized its importance as he now embarked on his effort to reform Chiapas.

Land and labor reform, which had been indefinitely deferred by the Mapaches, were Vidal's first priorities. The Socialists described their assumption of power as the long overdue arrival of revolutionary politics to Chiapas,

91 See, for example, the case cited by Spenser of campesinos threatened at gunpoint by their employers in Tapachula if they did not support a particular candidate for municipal office. Spenser, *El partido socialista chiapaneco*, 138. See also Nolan-Ferrell's case study of the Soconusco region of Chiapas, and how difficult it was to implement revolutionary reforms there in the 1920s. Nolan-Ferrell, *Constructing Citizenship*.

92 On the gubernatorial campaign of Fausto Ruiz, see Óscar Janiere Martínez, *General Fausto Ruiz Córdoba: Apuntes biográficos* (Tuxtla Gutiérrez, Chiapas, México: Consejo Estatal para las Culturas y las Artes de Chiapas, 2011), 42–48.

93 *Reconstrucción* (Tuxtla Gutiérrez), April 7, 1925, 1. "En el Plebescito de Ayer Triunfó el Gral. Vidal."

94 CDEEUM, serie: 1925, expediente: 100203: AGREGADO MILITAR DE ESTADOS UNIDOS: Informes, legajo 6/7, fojas 336–38, inventario 40. Report: Mexico. Political. State Governments. November 23, 1925.

and Vidal envisioned Chiapas' revolutionary redemption as resting on his and the Socialist Party's shoulders. He opened his first gubernatorial address to the state legislature in the Fall of 1925 by emphasizing the disastrous state of the government that he inherited from the Mapaches: "Our task has been arduous, because our work has not even been that of reconstruction, but rather we have had to come to construct [...] in only five months of a respectable Administration, we have done what our predecessors were unwilling to do, even in favorable circumstances."[95]

Communities across the state wrote to Vidal and Socialist party president Ricardo Alfonso Paniagua with various complaints and concerns, and commonly described the new Socialist government as their most important source of hope for political redemption after years of "bad administration" by the Mapaches.[96] Vidal's first acts in office were conspicuously designed as correctives to the corruption, mismanagement, and abuses by the Mapache government decried by his base. Many of these were reforms of the state government, and the attempted amelioration of tense relations between government officials and the general public. This included a purge of Mapache officials and their replacement with Vidal's loyal subordinates.[97] Vidal made starkly clear that Mapache politicians were not welcome in his government, even ordering the arrest of the Mapaches who had tried to claim legislative seats during the electoral chaos of the preceding months. Some were arrested and tried on charges of betraying the nation, and advocating the separation of Chiapas from Mexico.[98] Other reform initiatives Vidal pursued in the early days of his governorship were less overtly political, and meant remediating legacies of corruption, violence, and perceived lawlessness. He bolstered the state police force with new uniforms and weapons supplied by the federal government. Judges without law degrees were dismissed and replaced.

Once political reform and reorganization was underway, Vidal and the Socialists turned their attentions to social reforms. Many of these were consistent with programs undertaken by his counterparts in Yucatán and Tabasco, and some were also conspicuously influenced by the US-style progressivism of Salvador Alvarado in Yucatán in the 1910s. In the progressive mold, many of Vidal's first reform projects were dedicated to the betterment of the lives of women and children. In addition to the women's

95 AHECH, Gobernación: 1925, vol. 2, exp. 248. "Informe del Ejecutivo Ante la H. XXX Legislatura," November 1, 1925.
96 See, for example, AHECH, Gobernación: 1925, vol. 1. Carlos Flores Tovilla to Vidal, June 2, 1925.
97 AHECH, Gobernación: 1925, vol. 2, exp. 248. "Informe del Ejecutivo Ante la H. XXX Legislatura," November 1, 1925.
98 Secessionism was a very common allegation that was made by Chiapas politicians against one another in this period, irrespective of their political affiliations, or the circumstances and substance of their argument.

suffrage decree issued under Córdoba, this included the reform of the state's divorce law, and a law prohibiting the presence of minors in any establishment where alcohol was served. Vidal also increased the budget of the Civil Hospital in the state by 50 percent, undertook a child vaccination campaign, and made new supply and education provisions for the orphanage of Tuxtla.[99]

The Socialists had put significant effort into recruiting indigenous support for Vidal's candidacy, and Vidal advocated for new protections of the rights of indigenous people once he was governor. A new agency of Indigenous Peoples, Rights, and Labor, directly dependent to the state's Ministry of Government, was created during Córdoba's interim governorship. Once he took office, Vidal forged new policies to regulate the contracting of indigenous campesinos in the highlands, to protect them from abuses and to ensure that their hiring followed clearly defined legal procedures. This was, he underscored, something that had been ignored by all Chiapas state governments up to that point. He condemned previous state governments, under which "indigenous individuals were treated like cargo animals, instead of treating them like men, and as fellow workers."[100]

As a means of addressing a long history of the abuse of indigenous people in Chiapas, Vidal dispatched a special inspector to the Las Casas district "in order for the government to become aware of the ways the authorities treat the [indigenous] pueblos." Vidal warned state officials that they were to "adjust" their conduct in accordance with the law, and to abstain from abusive behavior, particularly in their treatment of indigenous people. As part of this project, municipal presidents were to solicit reports of any abuses against Indians so they could be addressed. Tzotzil residents of San Andrés complied, detailing the corruption and abuses committed by the government-appointed municipal secretary that had been imposed on them. Fearful of the consequences of openly complaining about a government official, they opted not to sign their names on their letter. Vidal personally ordered an investigation of their complaints.[101] The outcomes of all of these efforts and programs are much harder to assess from extant archival sources. It is safe to assume that practice never came close to living up to the Socialists' laws as written, nor could the Socialists have possibly expected to overcome a long history of injustice, racism and exploitation through a few months of outreach and legislation. Nevertheless, Vidal was pleased. In his first gubernatorial address, he proudly reported that his

99 AHECH, Gobernación: 1925, vol. 2, exp. 248. "Informe del Ejecutivo Ante la H. XXX Legislatura," November 1, 1925.
100 Ibid.
101 AHECH, Gobernación: 1925, vol. 1. Unsigned letter from San Andrés to Vidal, July 7, 1925. Oficial Mayor Encargado to Alfredo Marín, August 1, 1925.

Photograph 5.3 Governor Carlos Vidal with constituents from Tenejapa and San
Andrés Larráinzar, 1925
Source: Fideicomiso Archivos Plutarco Elías Calles y Fernando Torreblanca (FAPECFT)

government's outreach effort to indigenous communities had yielded
a "greatly moralizing effect."[102]

At the very least, many indigenous communities in different parts of
Chiapas regarded Vidal's governorship as an opportunity to get out from
under the longstanding political and economic domination of local officials
and landowners. In some cases, they also took it as an impulse to organize.
In the same week that Vidal took office, he received word that a new "Union
in Defense of Indians" (Sindicato Defensor de los Indios) had been formally
installed in the Zoque town of Amatán, on the Tabasco border, near Vidal's
hometown of Pichucalco. The union's organizers explained: "It is finally
time to put an end here to the attacks that we have been suffering by past
Authorities and now that the time is coming or the first time in our lives to
put our legitimate rights to use, in accordance with the program of our
future Governor [...] we consider him to be a faithful friend and the
protector of the humble classes." They swore to uphold and pursue the
principles of Socialism.[103]

102 AHECH, Gobernación: 1925, vol. 2, exp. 248. "Informe del Ejecutivo Ante la H. XXX
Legislatura," November 1, 1925.
103 AHECH, Gobernación: 1925, vol. 3. Alejandro Gómez to El C. Secretario General del Gobierno,
May 15, 1925.

Labor reform went hand in hand with the Socialists' grassroots organizing, and was another critical priority for the new government. Following the Yucatecan blueprint closely, Vidal quickly established new bureaucracies that were intended to more closely link his constituents to both his government and to the Socialist Party. In order to organize workers, Vidal established the Socialist Workers' Confederation of Chiapas.[104] Its task was to mobilize the Socialist base, but also to finally begin to implement the 1917 Constitution in Chiapas. Led by Paniagua, the Confederation was designed to put an end to the chronic violations of constitutionally guaranteed labor protections by owners and managers of fincas in the state, and as a mechanism for the government to offer workers meaningful protections of their rights.[105] This included the establishment of a minimum wage, set maximum workdays and workweeks, and required indemnification for workers who were injured or took ill. Workers were also to be guaranteed hygienic medical care.

The workers' confederation operated in ways very similar to the Ligas Centrales in both Tabasco and Yucatán, and its purview was similarly broad, extending well beyond labor organizing. Its stated mission was to maintain just relations between labor and capital, to ensure the rights of all workers, including smallholders, sharecroppers, tenant farmers, or any other type of citizen, via unionization. The confederation was also to oversee social projects of the Socialist government, as well as land reform and political mobilization of Confederation members. Reminiscent of Garrido Canabal's take on Socialism were the Confederation's goals to limit the production and consumption of stimulants, and its extensive commitments to the creation of rationalist schools, night schools, and public libraries for workers, who were also to participate in demonstrations, conferences, and the production of propaganda.[106]

Like its counterpart organizations in Yucatán and Tabasco, Chiapas' Socialist Confederation of Workers was composed of committees that were tasked with pursuing particular reform objectives, such as labor, education, social organization, propaganda, development, finance, and justice. The state-level leaders of the Confederation were to meet weekly, and were charged with representing members in all official matters, both inside and outside of Chiapas. They were to ensure the observance of all labor laws in the state, and to support workers in conflicts that arose with employers, as well as in any conflicts between workers and state authorities. Further, they

104 AGN-DGIPS, c. 2046-c, exp. 5. "Confederación Socialista de Trabajadores de Chiapas: Programa y Reglamento con Reformas." July 5, 1925.
105 *El Palenque* (Tuxtla Gutiérrez), September 3, 1925.
106 AGN-DGIPS, c. 2046-c, exp. 5. "Confederación Socialista de Trabajadores de Chiapas: Programa y Reglamento con Reformas." July 5, 1925.

were tasked with supporting all members of the confederation in achieving better contracts, whether collective or individual. They were also mandated to report any employers that harmed employee interests, either by fault or omission. They were responsible for forming new unions among all trade associations in the state, and to assist all workers who wished to unionize. They were also to lead the charge to found both producers' and consumers' cooperatives.

Like the Liga Central in Tabasco, the Confederation included committees from particular districts, whose representatives also served on thematic committees. At least on paper, these local committees organized across the state very closely resembled ligas de resistencia. The Workers' Confederation charter mandated that a committee was to be organized in each district across the state, with every municipality sending a representative to the district committee. Districts were defined as any locality large enough to have its own state legislative representative. The municipal committees were to be organized along nearly identical lines, with a representative from every union or syndicate within that municipality. Members of municipal committees were to meet monthly and to be elected annually, while district committees were to meet every fifteen days and to be elected every two years, with their leaders nominated by three representatives from each of the municipal committees. Leaders of the general commission of the confederation were to be chosen every two years by three representatives of each of the district committees. All unionized workers, whether male or female, were eligible for membership in the Confederation; the only exception to this was workers who lived in places with no unions in their respective professions.

All members of the Confederation were entitled to attend meetings of their committees, but they were to "have a voice, but not a vote," a privilege that was limited to elected committee members. By belonging to unions that were part of the confederation, workers assumed all rights and responsibilities of members of the confederation, as did individuals who joined the confederation independently of unions. All members paid dues to the Confederation, based on their labor; salaried employees paid the most (one peso per month), workers paid sixty cents every three months, and campesinos and day laborers paid thirty cents every three months. Members were also responsible for making emergency contributions that the Confederation's leaders deemed necessary. All collected dues were to be spent on the organization's operational expenses, divided evenly between the Socialist Party and the committees that comprised the Confederation.

Like the ligas de resistencia of Tabasco, the members of the Workers' Confederation in Chiapas were also to serve as Socialist agents and organizers at the local level. These duties included propaganda activities in favor of labor organizing, as well as "being in all cases an exponent of integrity, seriousness and the spirit of justice that should guide all acts of all confederated workers." Members could be expelled at the Confederation's discretion; grounds for expulsion included failing to pay dues, failing to fulfill assigned duties, having been justly imprisoned, or "any act in defiance of morals and good customs." By 1926, Vidal was submitting slates of candidates for federal offices to the federal Ministry of the Interior in the name of the Confederation. At the local level, these selected individuals were regarded to be the sole "popular candidates" for these offices.[107]

As with liga systems in the rest of the Southeast, both the strengths and the weaknesses of Socialism in Chiapas lay with the Workers' Confederation. In practice, Vidal's government saw to it that only Confederation members attained local political office, as a means of expanding the Socialist presence at the local level across the state. The problem with this, much like in Tabasco, was that the best avenue to political power in the state became declaring one's self to be a Vidalista, or a Socialist, and not all of those who did were especially invested in Vidal's political programs or ideals. Many used the empowerment that the opportunistic assumption of the mantle of Socialism afforded them to enrich or empower themselves, first and foremost.[108]

Considering how closely the Chiapas Socialists adhered to the precedents established in Yucatán in so many other respects, it is curious that they did not choose to refer to their syndicates and local workers' organizations as ligas de resistencia. Tomás Garrido Canabal is the likely reason. By the time Vidal finally became governor, Socialism in Tabasco was well developed and taking the Yucatecan model in a decidedly new and different political direction, and the ligas de resistencia were very much the centerpiece of that project. Perhaps more importantly for the Chiapas Socialists, Garrido offered his support to their political opponents and was closely allied with the Mapache leader, Tiburcio Fernández Ruiz. In other words, in spite of their common political ancestry, the Chiapas Socialists were likely loath to adopt a political idiom so closely associated with Socialism in Tabasco, even while they applied very similar principles to the organization of their respective partisans and members.

The Chiapas Socialists' Workers' Confederation charter also included provisions that were designed to reform land tenure in Chiapas. These stated objectives were a hybrid of goals pursued by their counterparts elsewhere in the Southeast, such as the restitution of lands, the expansion of ejidos, the "extinction" of latifundia, the creation of agricultural cooperatives, and the creation of rural credit banks. Yet the creation of pequeñas propiedades was also included on their list of priorities, perhaps in a nod to

---

107 AGN-G3, 408-C-54. Rubén Culebro to Calles, February 19, 1926.
108 Spenser underscores that even as the Socialist government created this dilemma, it was also quick to prosecute offenders whenever it was able. Spenser, *El partido socialista chiapaneco*, 145–46.

their allies in Mexico City who were more dubious about the kind of land reform undertaken by Carrillo Puerto in Yucatán.[109]

Vidal's government acted very quickly when it came to land reform and redistribution. Under the Mapache government, land reform was all but non-existent in Chiapas.[110] By contrast, Vidal and his allies actively encouraged campesinos to request land grants from the government. From the pages of the Socialist Party's newspaper, *Alba Roja* ("Red Dawn"), the government published announcements urging citizens to request land grants: "Campesino: 55,000 hectares have been granted by the Governor of the State to lift your brothers out of misery. You also have the right to your parcel. Ask for it. The land is yours. Send a request in a simple letter to the Local Agrarian Commission, or to the Procurador de Pueblos in Tuxtla Gutiérrez."[111]

The results were dramatic: petitions for ejido grants increased from only ten per year during the Mapache regime (1920–24), to sixty-eight in 1925 and thirty-four in 1926, overseen by a reorganized Agrarian Commission. Vidal's government made its first ejido grant only seven days after he took office.[112] He took evident pride in all of the land grants, restitutions, and formations of ejidos by his government. By the numbers alone, it was an aggressive start to a long-overdue process. By Vidal's own calculations, within his first six months in office, his government had distributed, or was in the process of distributing 32,558 hectares of land.[113] The majority of these were in Soconusco and Mariscal: the coastal coffee region of the state, where his base of support was historically the strongest.[114] By the end of his two years in office, Vidal's government distributed 81,344 hectares to 6,634 families via thirty-nine successful petitions for land, nearly

---

109 AGN-DGIPS, c. 2046-c, exp. 5. Program of Regulations and Reforms of the Socialist Confederation of Workers of Chiapas. July 5, 1925.

110 Reyes Ramos, *El reparto de tierras*, 30.

111 *Alba Roja* (Tuxtla Gutiérrez). Año 1, Vol. 6. June 6, 1926, p. 5.

112 Spenser, *El partido socialista chiapaneco*, 142.

113 AHECH, Gobernación: 1925, vol. 2, exp. 248. "Informe del Ejecutivo Ante la H. XXX Legislatura," November 1, 1925. For a fuller accounting of the land grants recorded in Chiapas in this period, see Reyes Ramos, *El reparto de tierras*, 51, 133–34. Spenser underscores that most of the land that Vidal redistributed was either federal, or idle, evincing a reluctance to expropriate productive haciendas. Spenser, *El partido socialista chiapaneco*, 142. This was another way in which Vidal followed Alvarado's example in Yucatán.

114 Reyes Ramos, *El reparto de tierras*, 52. Reyes Ramos argues that the concentration of land grants in this part of the state was a strategic maneuver to create ejidos in the coffee zone, the increased population of which would in turn provide labor to the coffee plantations. A nonmutually exclusive explanation for this regional concentration of land grants is that Soconusco was the heartland of the Chiapas Socialists, Vidal's most dedicated grassroots base, which he sought to reward with new ejidos.

quadruple the amount of land redistributed by his Mapache predecessor.[115] Rus found that none of this land went to highland indigenous communities. Zinacantán was the first Tzotzil town to petition for land, in 1925, and it was not granted.[116]

As in neighboring Socialist states, the Socialists' Agrarian Commission, led by Paniagua, worked to uphold the rights of rural workers and citizens, particularly in the face of years of mistreatment by local officials and landowners that predated the Revolution and continued through the Mapache period, unabated.[117] The Agrarian Commission worked in tandem with the Socialist Workers' Confederation, which was responsible for many of the bureaucratic processes of the land reform. Confederation leaders were charged with guiding campesinos through the process of petitioning for both grants and restitutions of lands. They were also responsible for assisting all Confederation members with any lawsuits concerning landholding, for the creation of agricultural cooperatives for both production and consumption, and for the founding of agricultural colonies.[118]

When it came to social reform, the Chiapas Socialists were much less invested in the anticlerical project of President Calles than their counterparts in Tabasco, where Garrido set the Southeast's high water mark for antagonism toward the Catholic Church. Governor Vidal carefully cited his compliance with the Calles Law and article 130 of the federal constitution, which prohibited the activities of foreign priests in Mexico, but in practice he erred on the side of leniency. In September of 1925, he ordered the deportation of just three foreign-born priests from Chiapas.[119] Even the governor's relatively mild anticlerical enforcement efforts precipitated protests from the religious faithful in the state, to which officials of the state government repeatedly responded that it was a federal constitutional matter that was out of their hands. Numerous residents of Chiapa de Corzo acknowledged that their Spanish priest could no longer minister to them, but pleaded with the state government that he at least be able to continue living among them.[120] A group of citizens in Ocozocuautla reiterated their loyalty to Vidal's government, and emphasized their priest's dedication to

115 Spenser, *El partido socialista chiapaneco*, 142; Nolan-Ferrell, *Constructing Citizenship*, 84, table 3.1. Thomas Benjamin's numbers for hectares distributed by Vidal are slightly higher, but in the same range. Benjamin, *A Rich Land, a Poor People*, 208, table 5.
116 Rus, "Revoluciones contenidas," 83.
117 See, for example, AHECH, Gobernación: 1925, vol. 2, exp. 248. Paniagua to Vidal, July 15, 1925.
118 AGN-DGIPS, c. 2046-c, exp. 5. Program of Regulations and Reforms of the Socialist Confederation of Workers of Chiapas. July 5, 1925.
119 AHECH, Gobernación: 1925, vol. 4, exp. 242. Vidal to Gobernación, September 11, 1925.
120 AHECH, Gobernación: 1925, vol. 4, exp. 242. Safonia Moreno et al. to Vidal, September 8, 1925.

democratic and liberal ideas, in their request that he be spared from deportation.[121] In the end, Vidal's efforts to expel non-Mexican clerics were not particularly extensive, and were positively mild compared to the sweeping expulsions of priests that took place in Tabasco.

The relationship between the Socialist state government and the Chiapas Socialist Party was nearly seamless in practice. As in both Tabasco and Yucatán, the leaders of the Socialist Party of the state, and of the Socialist state government were the same: in this case, Carlos Vidal and Ricardo Alfonso Paniagua. This was an obvious emulation of Carrillo Puerto's organization of the PSS and the state government of Yucatán, and mirrored both Carrillo Puerto and Garrido Canabal's redundant leadership of multiple new Socialist bureaucracies. Vidal and Paniagua both maintained their leadership roles within the Chiapas Socialist Party once they had taken office as governor and president of the state legislature, respectively, and both were commissioners of the Workers' Confederation. Paniagua also maintained his position as the president of the Agrarian Commission. Some of their partisans recognized this redundancy. In October of 1926, Miguel Sánchez, the president of a municipal branch of the Socialist Party, sent Vidal a copy of a petition he had already sent Paniagua. He added in a wry postscript: "we understand perfectly well that all of the [Socialist] municipal centers belong to the Chiapas Socialist Party which is united with the Socialist Workers' Confederation to which we also belong, so in one way or another, we address ourselves to you."[122]

The tendency of Socialist politicians in the Southeast in this period to maintain their positions of party leadership even once they attained elected offices, and to insist on the distinctions between the different positions that they simultaneously occupied, is testimony to the transitional nature of this moment in Mexican politics. Even though parties and governments might have been led by the same individuals as they were in Chiapas, Tabasco, and Yucatán in this period, that Ricardo Alfonso Paniagua and Felipe Carrillo Puerto both went so far as to have separate letterheads for their correspondence from the separate offices that they held speaks to the importance that they understood these distinctions to have. Paniagua was far from the only Socialist party leader to be given lofty positions in Vidal's bureaucracy, as numerous longtime allies lost no time in petitioning Vidal for government posts.[123] Vidal's desire to replace Mapache officials at all levels with his own loyal agents fortuitously coincided with his ability to repay his local operatives for years of service to his various campaigns. For all intents and

121   AHECH, Gobernación: 1925, vol. 4, exp. 242. Enoch Espinosa et al., to Vidal, September 18, 1925.
122   AHECH, Gobernación, 1926: vol. 6. Miguel Sánchez to Vidal, October 13, 1926.
123   See, for example, AGN-CAV, c. 6, f. 2, Pablo Quiñones to Vidal, April 15, 1925.

purposes, the party became the new state government, much as its counterparts did in Tabasco and Yucatán. At this time in the Southeast and in Mexico as a whole, the lines between political parties and governments, as well as the accepted norms of interactions between them, were still very much in the process of being defined.

The Socialists' rise to power inevitably caused strife within some communities. In 1926, petitioners from San Gabriel in Chiapa de Corzo asked the state government (perhaps rhetorically) if Socialists had the right to strong-arm non-Socialists, since local Socialists were wandering about heavily armed, declaring that Governor Vidal had given them guns and authorized them to do as they pleased. The state government responded by ordering the municipal government to disarm the offenders.[124] More often, reform initiatives were simply never undertaken by municipal authorities that were sympathetic to the Mapaches and likely hoped that they would return to power. In December of 1926, numerous residents of Las Margaritas wrote to Vidal to complain that the same men had been in power in the municipal government since the governorship of Tiburcio Fernández Ruiz. "They support in absolutely no way the ideals of progress and wellbeing of the state," they wrote. They went on to complain that while neighboring municipalities were benefitting from new schools, road construction, new telephone lines, and health and development initiatives, in Las Margaritas they had enjoyed none of these benefits because the local authorities refused to support Vidal's government. "Our present municipal council dedicates itself only to completely abandoning its obligations," they wrote, pleading for justice and the governor's assistance in achieving it.[125]

Conclusions

All attempted impositions of revolutionary politics on Chiapas from the outside in the 1910s proved significantly counterproductive, finally sparking one of the most tenacious counterrevolutions in Mexico in those years. The Mexican Revolution only took root in Chiapas once it was led by a native-born son who carefully constructed alliances and networks of support at the local, regional, and national levels over the course of numerous years. When it finally arrived, Chiapas' revolution came along with an established set of ideas about how to bridge the longstanding gaps between Mexican politicians and grassroots constituencies, thanks to the

---

124 AHECH, Gobernación: 1926, vol. 1, exp. 12. Nicanor Pérez to Secretario General de Gobierno del Estado, March 2, 1926, and Oficial Mayor to Presidente Municipal, April 6, 1926.

125 AHECH, Gobernación: 1926, vol. 1, exp. 22. Jerónimo Domínguez et al. to Vidal, December 4, 1926.

precedents set by Felipe Carrillo Puerto, and buoyed by a loosely defined Socialist zeitgeist that he inspired across the Southeast in the 1920s.

Socialism in Chiapas also benefited from the patronage of the most powerful man in Mexico. Albeit for their own reasons, Plutarco Elías Calles and the Chiapas Socialists shared a desire to integrate Chiapas and the larger Southeast into national political life, a true feat in light of Carranza and Obregón's failed efforts to the same end. Calles and Vidal were able to accomplish this in 1925 via a series of strategic compromises. During the gubernatorial interim period, Calles allowed the Vidalista Socialists to experiment with progressive social reforms such as women's suffrage, and more generally gave them freedom to govern as they saw fit. Vidal meanwhile allowed for a degree of outsider control of his grassroots base, such as the CROM's attempted cooptation of the Chiapas Socialist Party, and abandoned some of the more radical tenets of the Socialist platform once he came to power. As Vidal would subsequently discover, exercising that power would require a new set of compromises and understandings with his powerful national allies, particularly as Calles' strategies and objectives changed over the course of his presidency.

It is hard to imagine a governor who came to power in Mexico in this period who can be said to have had more of a political mandate than Carlos Vidal did in Chiapas in 1925, at least on paper. He had an enviable set of alliances in Mexico City, and a relatively well-organized and mobilized base of grassroots partisan support at home, something that was equally enviable for most Mexican politicians of the era. What's more, he and his fellow Socialists were implementing political and organizational strategies that they had every reason to believe would work, based on precedents established in Yucatán and Tabasco. Carrillo Puerto's death at the hands of rebel federal troops during the de la Huerta rebellion was not clearly the result of a particular political failure, and Garrido's political machine still appeared to be unstoppable. Yet the story of Socialism in Chiapas is not one of sustained reform. Nor is it one of devout adherence to the political program(s) of Plutarco Elías Calles, as the means by which Vidal finally attained the governorship might have implied. Nor did it prove to be especially durable, in spite of the political and programmatic precedents upon which it was built, or the strategic and ideological compromises the Chiapas Socialists made in the interest of maintaining their networks of alliances. The rapid undoing of Chiapas' Socialist government is explored in Chapter 6, but it can only be fully understood in light of the nature of the Socialists' rise to power there, and the deals and concessions it required.

6

Closing Ranks

Socialism and Anti-Reelectionism, 1925–1927

> We don't want experiments that disturb the nation, we don't want experiments that hurt it, we want to implant in our country the good results of Mexico's social laboratory.
>
> Luis Torregrosa, on behalf of the Alliance of Socialist Parties of the
> Republic, 1926

By 1926 it was clear that Álvaro Obregón intended to return to the presidency for a second term. This eventually provoked another crisis over presidential succession in which the Socialists of the Southeast were deeply implicated. Tomás Garrido Canabal of Tabasco was one of the first politicians of note to nominate Obregón for reelection, while Governor Carlos Vidal and many of the Chiapas Socialists helped to run the national anti-reelectionist movement.

As a result, the southeastern Socialist models of political organization and party formation received unprecedented levels of national attention. Plutarco Elías Calles had been a close observer and sometimes an active supporter of the region's Socialists and their political projects since 1920, but now politicians across the political spectrum began picking and choosing elements of southeastern Socialism and applying them as they saw fit. Nearly all politicians of the postrevolutionary generation found something to like in the Socialists' basic framework for building a centralized political party with strong ties to a well-organized, disciplined popular constituent base. In these years, "Socialism" became the standard model of political institutionalization in Mexico and synonymous with the formation of political parties, irrespective of their programs or ideologies. Thus, the bitter fight over presidential reelection in 1926–27 was led by politicians on both sides who all described themselves as Socialist.

Socialism and Anti-Reelectionism, 1926–1927

Even in the early days of Calles' presidential term (1924–28), the question of presidential succession for the next term was on the minds of many Mexicans. Francisco I. Madero's slogan of "effective suffrage, no reelection" became the nearly sacred precept of the entire political class in the years that followed the Mexican Revolution. It was also inscribed in Articles 82 and 83 of the 1917 Constitution, which in conjunction prohibited presidents from serving more than a single term. Nevertheless, scarcely more than a decade and a half after Madero's rebellion against the repeated reelections of Porfirio Díaz, a new fight over presidential reelection loomed.

Obregón returned to his ranch in Sonora when his presidency ended in 1924, and claimed that his political career was over.[1] Still, as rumors circulated about who would and would not run as Calles' successor, Obregón's potential return to the presidency was always part of the conversation. Some credible contenders such as Luis Morones of the CROM and Secretary of War Joaquín Amaro reportedly declined to run based solely on rumors that Obregón aspired to return to the office. Others were undeterred: The prominent generals Arnulfo Gómez of Sonora and Francisco R. Serrano of Sinaloa each launched presidential campaigns in 1926.

Both Gómez and Serrano were longtime allies and defenders of Calles and Obregón, but Serrano was also a close personal friend of Obregón's and had served as his chief of staff for many years. He was also related to Obregón by marriage. For all of these reasons, many observers saw Serrano's presidential candidacy as a natural continuation of the successive presidencies of the Sonorans.[2] The good will and collaboration between Serrano and Obregón did not last once Serrano made clear his intentions to run for president. Obregón allegedly promised his old friend that he would support his candidacy to succeed Calles in 1928. Obregón's formal announcement in 1927 that he would run for reelection was an embarrassing surprise to Serrano, who had widely repeated Obregón's promises of support for his own campaign.[3] Both Gómez and Serrano chose to press on. Both grounded their campaigns in the assertion that presidential reelection was fundamentally contrary to the most basic and most vaunted principle of the Mexican Revolution. Obregón and his supporters countered that the former president and hero of the revolution was the best man to lead Mexico, again. The stage was set for a pitched political battle between Obregón and both anti-reelectionist candidates, and what eventually came to be known as the Gómez-Serrano rebellion of 1927.

The anti-reelectionist movement against Obregón was led in part by Socialists from Chiapas. After spending much of his political career campaigning for the governorship, Carlos Vidal's time in the office was brief. He formally left it in July of 1927 to serve as Francisco Serrano's campaign

1 Buchenau, *Plutarco Elías Calles*, 137.
2 Pedro Castro Martínez, *A la sombra de un caudillo: Vida y muerte del general Francisco R. Serrano* (México, D.F.: Random House Mondadori, 2005), 22, 127–28.
3 Rébora, *Memorias de un chiapaneco*, 202–3.

manager, by which time he had already been deeply involved in leading the campaign for at least a year. He was regarded by many participants in the movement as the heart and soul of Serrano's campaign, and by extension, of the national anti-reelectionist movement.[4] "You have known to set an example for the other leaders, showing them which is the path they must take," an anti-reelectionist worker from Oaxaca wrote to Vidal.[5]

By 1926, Vidal was confident that Serrano would be the next president of Mexico and that he would be given a lofty cabinet post.[6] He had already worked with Serrano in the early 1920s in Serrano's Ministry of War, where Vidal served as Chief of the Department of Staff. Vidal's anti-reelectionist fervor was possibly also fueled by a grudge against Obregón. Obregón had slighted Vidal by choosing to support the Mapaches in Chiapas in 1920, and he had continued to support the Mapache leader Tiburcio Fernández Ruiz in his attempted suppression of the Chiapas Socialists and other Vidal allies in the years that followed. Vidal was well aware that he became governor of Chiapas in 1925 in spite of Obregón's ongoing support for his political enemies and evident antipathy toward the Chiapas Socialist Party.

Tomás Garrido Canabal moved in the opposite direction and allied himself more closely to Obregón after he left the presidency. Garrido's natural tendency toward suspicion and even paranoia, his tireless quest to ferret out disloyalty and counterrevolution, and his dislike of Vidal all found fertile ground in Vidal's anti-reelectionist stance. In a telegram to the Chamber of Deputies in November of 1926, Garrido shrilly reminded the legislators that Vidal had supported Carranza's chosen candidate, Ignacio Bonillas, for president in 1920 against Obregón (which was true) and that he had been a Delahuertista (which was not). More inflammatory still, Garrido openly accused Vidal and the Chiapas Socialist Party of "preparing a war." He insisted that Vidal resign his governorship in order to campaign for Serrano. Representative Raymundo Enríquez of Chiapas, a longtime collaborator of Vidal's, responded with a passionate defense of Vidal and the Chiapas Socialists, before dramatically ripping up Garrido's telegram on the chamber floor.[7]

The fact that Vidal's political rebellion against Obregón in 1926 was understood (or at least ungenerously interpreted) by his critics to have military implications (whether or not this was the case) underscores that all postrevolutionary politicking in this period was carried out in the long

4 See, for example, Francisco Javier Santamaría, *La tragedia de Cuernavaca en 1927 y mi escapatoria célebre* (México, D.F.: F.J. Santamaría, 1939), 23, 65.

5 FAPECFT-FFT, fondo: 13, serie: 10212, expediente: "55"/71: GARCIA, Inocente, legajo 1/1, foja 3, inventario: 927. Inocente García to Vidal, August 9, 1927.

6 Rébora, *Memorias de un chiapaneco*, 190.

7 "Diario de los Debates de la Cámara de Diputados." Legislatura XXXII – Año I – Período Ordinario – November 3, 1926 – Número de Diario 29.

The Mexican Revolution's Wake

shadow cast by the still-credible fear of a military overthrow of the government. But the anti-reelectionist movement was political rather than military, at least in the beginning. It was composed of two significant and related political components: first, activism and debate within the federal legislature, and second, the attempted marshaling of scattered, sympathetic local political parties across Mexico into a coherent national political organization.

The latter project was spearheaded by Vidal, who attempted to build a national opposition movement in support of Serrano. Both Gómez and Serrano had their own political parties (the National Anti-Reelectionist Party and the National Revolutionary Party, respectively).[8] Like most other parties of the era, these were principally electoral vehicles with little staying power or substantive ties to popular constituencies. Vidal's efforts constituted something different. As the head of the Comité Pro-Serrano ("Pro-Serrano Committee"), which oversaw all of the administrative aspects of Serrano's campaign at the national level, Vidal worked toward building a cohesive, centralized network of preexisting local anti-reelectionist political parties across Mexico. The creation of an umbrella organization to mobilize a grassroots base through proxy organizations administered at the local level reflected the structure of all of the Socialist parties of the Southeast, but particularly the design of the Chiapas Socialist Party, which relied heavily on collaboration with preexisting local parties and organizations.

In Mexico in 1926, strong and effective national political parties as such were yet to emerge. Presidential campaigns still involved lengthy processes of coalition building between politicians and generals, who agreed to support a candidate who they believed could best advance their collective and/or individual interests. Much of the required negotiation took place in the federal legislature, where legislative blocs in both the Senate and the Chamber of Deputies behaved much like parties. The political positions of these blocs were contested internally, while externally they were frequently in conflict with one another. It was in this volatile legislative environment that the new debate over presidential reelection took place, as Obregón's supporters led the reelectionist charge within the Chamber of Deputies.

Like Vidal's work for the Comité Pro-Serrano, the reelectionists also worked to build a national organization, also taking inspiration from the Socialists. In May of 1926, some of Obregón's most powerful and dedicated allies gathered in Mexico City for a convention at which they founded the Alliance of Socialist Parties of the Republic. Its slogan was "Unity, Land and Liberty," and its stated purpose was to see that political parties managed electoral politics in order to sustain and realize the social

8 Serrano's National Revolutionary Party should not be confused with the National Revolutionary Party (PNR) that Calles would subsequently found in 1928.

principles of the Mexican Revolution. Each allied local Socialist party sent one representative to the convention; over eight hundred delegates attended. Among the delegates were prominent Socialists from all of the states of the Southeast, including Chiapas, which was represented by Luis Espinosa and Dr. Ulises Vidal, one of the governor's brothers, who had also been a delegate to the constitutional convention of 1916–17. Both the Radical Socialist Party of Tabasco and the Socialist Party of the Southeast of Yucatán sent representatives. Gonzalo N. Santos of San Luis Potosí was president of the Alliance and opened the convention by arguing that its formation was a necessary corrective to the tendency of national parties based in Mexico City to send their mandates and candidate lists to the regions. By contrast, a central goal of the Alliance was to respect regional variation and differences among its constituent organizations.

Yet the Alliance's strength was to be in its unity. Delegate Luis Torregrosa of Yucatán emphasized during a later debate that the Socialist parties represented at the convention would no longer be isolated regional or state-based organizations, and that the Alliance would represent Socialists in all of Mexico, and that their enemies would inevitably be frightened by that prospect. The shorter-term goal of the convention was to bring together Socialist parties from across the country to draft a unified political program and plan of action for the upcoming national election in 1928. The leaders of the convention described their larger project: "this will translate into the ideological unification of revolutionary Mexico and the immediate and everlasting union of the molecules of the nation that have been dispersed by false apostles who have fabricated anarchic and destructive socialisms at will [...] to produce the force capable of reconstructing the nation."[9]

Throughout the proceedings and debates among the delegates in the days that followed, the strong influence of southeastern Socialism on both the program and structure of this new organization was clear, and sometimes referenced. Yet what the Alliance always lacked, even as it broke important new ground when it came to the formation of a national organization of like-minded politicians on this scale, was the substantive relationship with popular constituencies that was so integral to the political mission, activities, and successes of the Socialist parties of the Southeast. This was, after all, an alliance of parties and their national representatives in the federal legislature. For all of the talk of principles and ideals that the

9   All information about the convention of the Alliance of Socialist Parties of the Republic is taken from a volume the Alliance itself assembled of transcriptions of the debates and accords, along with several press clippings about the Alliance and its significance. Alianza de Partidos Socialistas de la República, *Alianza de Partidos Socialistas de la República, primera convención, "unión, tierra y libertad"* (México, D.F.: La Alianza, 1926).

founders of the Alliance engaged in at their first and only convention, it never became more than that.[10]

Nevertheless, the convention's delegates spent a great deal of time discussing its foundational principles. The leaders of the Alliance recognized that "Socialism" was a term used in numerous ways both inside and outside of Mexico and nominated a special commission that sought to define it concretely. In the first draft, the commission emphasized that Socialism included: "the absolute application of the principles of justice to the organization of society in order to obtain a maximum of liberty with a maximum of order," "to organize and consolidate the postulates of the 1917 Constitution," "to fight for the economic, moral and intellectual elevation of all Mexicans, and especially the working classes and campesinos," "to not threaten the well-intentioned capitalist who is dedicated to evolving and modernizing his system of labor and exploitation of wealth and who treats his workers as collaborators rather than slaves," "to foment the formation of Ligas de Resistencia or any form of labor organization that has as its goal the liberation of labor from unfair capitalist exploitation," and "to sustain the principle that the land and other natural resources are the sacred and inalienable patrimony of the nation." Led in part by delegate Luis Torregrosa of Yucatán, these principles were derived from a study of local and regional Socialist parties in various states, including Yucatán, as well as Aguascalientes, Tamaulipas, and the state of Mexico.[11] Some of the foremost sources consulted by the commission were the accords of Felipe Carrillo Puerto's Socialist conventions of Motul and Izamal.

Once drafted, the commission's definition of Socialism was taken up for debate. In their efforts to define the meaning of Socialism, the convention's delegates left behind a rare glimpse into contemporary understandings of the meaning of a political designation that has been used in myriad ways in Mexico's political history. The most heated discussion was over the extent to which the convention's definition of Socialism would enshrine and commit to upholding individual liberties. Alejandro Cerisola of Veracruz argued that Socialism and maximum individual liberty were inherently incompatible and, further, that the restriction of individual freedom in the interest of the collective good was fundamental to Socialism in practice. Luis Espinosa offered the Chiapas delegation's proposed definition of Socialism as "the organization of society according to the principles of justice, that pursues as its goal the wellbeing of each and every of its

---

10 On this point, and for a detailed analysis of the formation and significance of the Alliance, see Javier MacGregor Campuzano, "Partidos nacionales y programas políticos en México, 1918–1928" (Ph.D. dissertation, El Colegio de México, 2005), 246–49.

11 On the Partido Socialista Fronterizo of Tamaulipas, see Fowler-Salamini, "De-Centering the 1920s."

associates, definitively consolidating an organic peace that is based in liberty, equality, and fraternity." The allusion to the French Revolution was purposeful, Espinosa explained, adding that it was "the most humanitarian of sentiments." Fernando Moctezuma of San Luis Potosí argued that any definition of Socialism would be incomplete without an economic element, and proposed that economic emancipation be added to the definition, along with subordination of individual interests to that of the collective. But when Manuel S. Hidalgo of the Federal District proposed a definition of Socialism that included the abolition of private property and collective control of production and distribution, he was shouted down by delegates in the audience that what he was describing was communism.

As the debate devolved into lengthy semantic disagreements, delegate C. Zavala Jesús argued that if Proudhon, Lenin, and Trotsky could not agree on a definition of Socialism, the gathered delegates had no hopes of doing so either. Gilberto Fábila of the state of Mexico concurred, arguing that the task at hand was not to define a universal Socialism, but a specifically Mexican one that would be unmistakable from other forms of politics that emphasized collective wellbeing. The final definition ratified by the delegates was: "Socialism is the organization of society according to the prescriptions of justice, in order to assure the wellbeing of each and every person, based on the preeminence of collective rights and definitively consolidating social peace." This working definition, based heavily on the Chiapas delegation's proposed text, could have applied to any of the Socialist governments of the Southeast.

Above all, the Alliance of Socialist Parties was meant to be a more institutionalized counterpart to an alliance that already existed within the legislature as the Allied Socialist Bloc.[12] Leaders of the Alliance presented the delegates with a draft of the organizational principles of the new body for their consideration. They proposed that the Alliance would collaborate with all political parties that pursued the same political goals and principles as it did, and that it would support the candidates put forward by all regional affiliates. The proposed structure of the organization was nearly identical to the southeastern Socialist parties. It would be composed of individuals, political organizations, ligas de resistencia, and cooperative societies, all of which would commit to supporting the Alliance's national political program, which would be determined at conventions of delegates. Delegates would also nominate presidential candidates at conventions. The larger organization would be led by a board of directors that would be elected for one-year terms. Yet Luis Torregrosa

12 The Allied Socialist Bloc was preceded by two other "Socialist" legislative blocs: the Bloque Socialista Reconstructor, led by Agustín Arroyo Ch., and the Bloque de Izquierdas Socialistas, led by Carlos Riva Palacio. Medina Peña, *Hacia el nuevo estado*, 66.

emphasized that the Alliance would not be a national political party. It would only support candidates that already had strong support at the regional level, and would refrain from imposing candidates on regions. In his words, "in places where we do not have a majority of votes [. . .] we will respect the popular will."

At least on paper, the Alliance sought to build productive, collaborative relationships with popular constituencies, particularly via alliances with organized workers and campesinos, and thereby to put the ideals of the Mexican Revolution into practice. Like its regional counterparts, the Alliance declared its intent to aid in the formation of new unions and ligas de resistencia. As often as possible, local workers' organizations would be united and represented by a Liga Central, which would be responsible for advancing its members' interests and, during elections, for organizing campaigns for candidates that would best serve them. Representatives from each Liga Central would form a board of directors in Mexico City. The Alliance also stipulated that it would maintain respectful relationships with all workers' and campesinos' organizations, as well as student and intellectual groups, whether or not they were members.

In sum, this was an ambitious and unprecedented proposal to apply Felipe Carrillo Puerto's model of party organization at the national level. Yet, for all of the delegates' talk of respecting the popular will and collaborating with local workers' organizations, the Alliance was above all dedicated to supporting Álvaro Obregón's return to the presidency. In October of 1926, it was Gonzalo N. Santos, the president of both the Alliance and the leader of Allied Socialist Bloc, who submitted proposals to the Chamber of Deputies to reform Articles 82 and 83 of the 1917 Constitution in order to legalize presidential reelection.[13] This met the second goal articulated at the Socialist convention, which was to support the 1917 Constitution in all points, but also to support its reform when "genuinely revolutionary" public opinion called for it. The delegation from Tabasco had immediately raised the subject of Obregón's reelection at the Alliance convention in May, as soon as constitutional reform was tabled for discussion. While the convention did not move to formally nominate Obregón, even the mention of his name invariably precipitated applause from the gathered delegates.

By that time, Allied Socialist Bloc was the most powerful faction in the legislature.[14] Its members described their mission as putting the Mexican Revolution into political practice, but did not consider the Constitution of

13   A previous attempt to amend the constitution to allow for presidential reelection failed in 1925. Jürgen Buchenau, *The Last Caudillo: Álvaro Obregón and the Mexican Revolution* (Chichester, England: Wiley-Blackwell, 2011), 153.
14   For an explanation of the way that these legislative blocs formed and operated in this period, particularly the Socialist Alliance, see Meyer, "La diarquía (1924–1928)," 202–5. See also Medina Peña, *Hacia el nuevo estado*, 63–70.

1917 to be a sacrosanct, untouchable charter. In his proposed constitutional reform on behalf of the Alliance, Santos described anti-reelectionism as an inappropriately zealous interpretation of Madero's famous principle of "effective suffrage, no reelection," and argued that it was an effort by reactionaries to disorient the Revolution via the misapplication of its own core principles. The Alliance's proposed reform removed the prohibition of Article 82 that disqualified any presidential candidates that had participated in any coup or uprising against the government. The justification Santos gave was that this prohibition effectively disqualified all potential candidates in Mexico following the Revolution, in which they had all participated. The proposed reform of Article 83, which prohibited presidential reelection, was to allow former presidents to be reelected to a single, nonconsecutive term. According to the proponents of the reform, this was merely "a small and simple clarification" of the law as it already existed. Santos argued that there was no reason to "incapacitate" good revolutionary leaders by preventing them from running for reelection, as long as it was not for consecutive terms, particularly a man beloved by the people, who desired his return to power.[15] He added that he and the other legislators that were in favor of the amendment were also anti-reelectionists, but in favor of definitively clarifying the anti-reelection prohibitions of the constitution.

Anti-reelectionist legislators scoffed at this notion, arguing that it was an utter distortion of Madero's principle of "no reelection," and maintained that their opposition to the reform was founded in their desire to uphold the most fundamental tenet of the Mexican Revolution. Eugenio Mier y Terán of Morelos was the first to defend the anti-reelectionist position. "I come here in extreme rebellion, so that my humble name will not be inscribed nor have the historical responsibility [for what] this Assembly is attempting to bring about, and surely will bring about. The basic principles of the revolution, as I understand them from my point of view, are two: effective suffrage, and no reelection," he informed his colleagues in the Chamber. He went on: "I want you to know that if the revolution shatters, it will be your fault." Many anti-reelectionist legislators struck similarly apocalyptic tones in describing the fate that would befall Mexico should Álvaro Obregón be permitted to return to power. Despite their protests, the amendments passed easily through the Chamber of Deputies, with only seven legislators dissenting. They hailed from the states of Chihuahua, Guanajuato, Morelos, Puebla, Veracruz, and the territory of Quintana Roo, collectively representing nearly every region of Mexico.[16]

15 "Diario de los Debates de la Cámara de Diputados." Legislatura XXXII – Año I – Período Ordinario – October 19, 1926 – Número de Diario 25.

16 Ibid. Legislatura XXXII – Año I – Período Ordinario – October 20, 1926 – Número de Diario 26. Camp, *Mexican Political Biographies, 1884–1935*, 393–98.

Although Socialist Chiapas was already a center of anti-reelectionism, the legislators from Chiapas voted for the reelectionist reforms. Their decision to do so provides rare and valuable insight into the dynamics of power within the legislature, the way legislative blocs operated, and the pressures that were increasingly felt by opposition politicians in this period. Raymundo Enríquez, Chiapas Socialist Party co-founder and one of Chiapas' legislators, wrote Governor Vidal a long letter the next day to explain the decision of the Chiapas delegation to support the reforms. As members of the Allied Socialist Bloc, the Chiapas legislators' voting loyalties were divided between maintaining bloc discipline and the directives they received from Vidal, as the leader of the Chiapas Socialist Party. Enríquez explained to Vidal that by the afternoon before the vote, many legislators from other states who had initially agreed to oppose the reform had nevertheless signed on to support it, and the Chiapas legislators were wary of potential consequences of being the sole dissenters.

Perhaps more significantly, before the vote, Enríquez consulted with Luis L. León, Calles' friend and Minister of Agriculture. León pressured Enríquez to support the constitutional reform, telling him that "all of the good revolutionaries" were in favor of it. He assured Enríquez that if the Chiapas delegation supported the reform, it would not mean that they would have to give up their support of Serrano's candidacy. León also gave Enríquez some warnings, some more veiled than others. He told Enríquez that he needn't worry about the Mapaches, despite their agents' ongoing machinations to turn Calles and Obregón against the Chiapas Socialists. He assured Enríquez that the Sonorans had no intention of lending support to Vidal's enemies, particularly because they regarded Vidal's government to be successful in maintaining law and order in Chiapas.[17] But León also suggested that it would be unwise to antagonize Calles and Obregón by refusing to support the reforms, and emphasized that opening the door to Obregón's return was a means of blocking the Reaction's nefarious plans to continue to soak Mexico in the blood of fratricidal war. "You are the only ones who show yourselves to be oppositionist, and your enemies take advantage of that to attack you as anti-Obregonista," León cautioned.

Enríquez reported back to his fellow Chiapas legislators about his meeting with León just before the Allied Socialist Bloc met to prepare for the final vote on the proposed amendments. Without adequate time to come to a consensus, the Chiapas delegation split in the Bloc's internal vote. Still divided and uncertain as to what to do in the final vote in the Chamber, the delegation met with Serrano, who encouraged them to vote for the reelectionist amendments. Serrano told them that he considered himself to be Obregonista, that all revolutionaries ultimately pursued the same cause,

17   Ibid.

and that "the camps would become defined" once Obregón returned to Mexico City. Serrano thus dissuaded his most passionate partisans from rocking the political boat too significantly, or at least from doing so on the floor of the legislature.[18]

Taking the hints from Serrano and León to heart, Enríquez counseled Vidal to tread carefully. He urged him to appoint a special representative to meet with Obregón to assure him that the government of Chiapas continued to support him, "along with the other true Revolutionaries." Vidal was unmoved by arguments for compromise and caution by his friends and allies. Once the reelectionist amendments were passed by the Chamber of Deputies, they were unanimously passed by the Senate in November of 1926, and were sent to the states for ratification. On Vidal's orders, the Chiapas legislature was the only one in Mexico that refused to ratify the reforms. Vidal had not been able to control the votes of the state's federal legislators, but this act of defiance was within the scope of his gubernatorial power. In an open letter that he wrote to Calles and to the Mexican military the following summer, Vidal proudly flaunted Chiapas' intransigence: "It has only been the government of Chiapas that categorically and honorably rejected the reelectionist reforms that threatened to bury all of the lives and all of the blood that it has cost our people to achieve one of their most costly revolutionary principles."[19]

Vidal was becoming increasingly politically isolated. The reelectionist victory by the Allied Socialist Bloc meant, among other things, that Obregón was now touted by his supporters as leader of Socialism in Mexico. Conversely, in their refusal to accept Obregón's return to power, the Chiapas Socialists and other anti-reelectionists were now cast as reactionaries and counterrevolutionaries. The Obregonista dilution of the Socialist classification was even more extreme than in the Southeast, where it had been used to describe heterogeneous political projects that were nevertheless recognizably related in both intent and outcome. As "Socialism" as a political brand was commandeered by the Obregonistas and was increasingly equated with general support for the Mexican Revolution, Vidal and the Chiapas Socialists, along with other Mexican politicians who refused to abandon Madero's vaunted principle, had their revolutionary bona fides widely undermined.

This was not just a matter of semantics, but a political turn with real consequences, driven by the exigencies of the moment. Increasingly

18 FAPECFT-FFT, fondo: 13, serie: 10207, expediente: "246"/97: ENRIQUEZ, Raymundo E. (Ing.), legajo 1/1, fojas 1–7, inventario 458. Raymundo Enríquez to Vidal, October 20, 1926.
19 FAPECFT-FFT, fondo: 3, serie: 010212, expediente: 24: BOLETINES DE PRENSA, legajo 1/2, fojas 43–6, inventario: 880. "Protesta ante el C. Presidente de la República y ante el ejército nacional, el General Carlos A. Vidal," August 16, 1927.

draconian lines were being drawn in Mexican political rhetoric as the concept of an official "Revolution" was crystallizing, largely negatively defined by an equally abstract "Reaction." In large part, this was a consequence of the Cristero uprising, which was ongoing at the time, with no end in sight.[20] For the first time, Mexico's diverse revolutionaries were confronted with a real and sustained counterrevolution; worse, it was one with significant popular support. As Calles faced a popular uprising of enraged Catholics willing to take up arms in defense of the Church and their censured priests, his tolerance for grassroots political organizing seems to have correspondingly waned. In 1927, all defections and rebellions against the federal government, whether or not they were religiously driven, were commonly conflated by Calles and Obregón and their allies as the work of reactionaries.[21] Thus, even two longtime Sonoran loyalists like Arnulfo Gómez and Francisco Serrano were now readily identified by the Obregonistas as counterrevolutionaries, with little rhetorical contortion required. After a highly heterogeneous revolution and an equally politically fragmented postrevolutionary period, unity was now the nonnegotiable order of the day. You were either with the "Revolutionary Family," or you were against it.[22]

These mounting political pressures took a heavy toll on the Chiapas Socialists. In the months that followed the reform of the constitution, discord grew within their ranks. By the spring of 1927, only five of Chiapas' seven federal representatives continued to support Serrano's presidential candidacy.[23] Other Chiapas Socialists also began to reconsider their opposition to Obregón's reelection, particularly as the mood in Mexico City seemed to increasingly favor his return. Luis Espinosa, a Socialist senator and a longtime ally of Vidal's, was one of the first to openly support Obregón's reelection.[24] If Vidal could not see which way the political winds were

20 On the Cristero War of 1926–29 see in particular Matthew Butler, *Popular Piety and Political Identity in Mexico's Cristero Rebellion: Michoacán, 1927–29* (Oxford, England: Oxford University Press, 2004); Jean A. Meyer, *The Cristero Rebellion: The Mexican People Between Church and State, 1926–1929* (New York, NY: Cambridge University Press, 1976); Jennie Purnell, *Popular Movements and State Formation in Revolutionary Mexico: The Agraristas and Cristeros of Michoacán* (Durham, NC: Duke University Press, 1999); Julia G. Young, *Mexican Exodus: Emigrants, Exiles, and Refugees of the Cristero War* (New York, NY: Oxford University Press, 2015).

21 "Diario de los Debates de la Cámara de Diputados." Legislatura XXXII – Año II – Período Ordinario – October 4, 1927 – Número de Diario 15.

22 Thomas Benjamin argues that this construction of the concept of a unitary revolutionary family had been increasingly rhetorically consolidated by the Sonorans over the course of the 1920s in Mexico, as Calles and Obregón repeatedly laid claim to a singular, legitimizing revolutionary legacy. Thomas Benjamin, *La Revolución: Mexico's Great Revolution as Memory, Myth and History* (Austin, TX: University of Texas Press, 2000), 68–69.

23 The other two, both longtime Vidal allies, dissented: Evaristo Bonifaz supported Obregón, and Jaime Solís supported Gómez. Rébora, *Memorias de un chiapaneco*, 198.

24 Ibid., 196–97. Espinosa was killed a few months later in a duel in with Senator Enrique Henshaw of San Luis Potosí. Camp, *Mexican Political Biographies, 1884–1935*, 275.

blowing by mid-1926, this was not the case for some of his former partisans. Nor was it the case for his old Mapache antagonists, who gladly found new political relevance as Obregón's longtime, steadfast allies in the state. By all accounts, Vidal resolutely believed that Calles would continue to diverge from Obregón in his politics and policies, while other members of the Chiapas political class seem to have correctly surmised that the Sonorans simply had too much to lose by abandoning one another politically, in spite of their political differences.

Garrido vs. Vidal: The Southeastern Socialists Clash over Presidential Reelection

While Carlos Vidal drew closer to Calles in the aftermath of the de la Huerta rebellion, Tomás Garrido Canabal bet everything on what became a near-fanatical allegiance to Álvaro Obregón. By 1926, the Southeast was politically polarized between Garrido, who worked fervently to see Obregón reelected, and Vidal, who insisted that Obregón's reelection would contravene the most central principles of the Mexican Revolution. Over the years, Garrido had grown increasingly suspicious of Vidal, and of his brother, General Luis P. Vidal. Garrido received reports in March of 1926 that suggested that both Vidal brothers were conspiring against him and leading a group of his enemies in accusing him of having joined the Delahuertistas during the rebel takeover of Tabasco, or of having surrendered Villahermosa willingly.[25] A short while later, Garrido and his allies turned the tables and accused Vidal of having been a Delahuertista, a traitor, and a reactionary, and of masterminding an assassination attempt against Garrido.[26]

Battling against the "Reaction" by attacking Vidal was an integral part of Garridista efforts to establish an Obregonista movement on the ground in Tabasco.[27] By extension, this was a confrontation between schools of southeastern Socialism, as Garrido repeatedly condemned Vidal and his supporters as scheming reactionaries while praising his own Socialist party for its patriotism. At a time when Obregón and his supporters were also staking a claim to the "Socialist" label in Mexico City, and "Socialism" was becoming rhetorically indistinguishable from "revolution" in national politics, Garrido conspicuously strove to make it unmistakably clear who the real southeastern Socialists were. If Obregón was to embody and lead

25   AGN-TGC, caja: 11, expediente: 3. Pablo Sevilla Oliver to Garrido, March 3, 1926. AGN-TGC, caja: 9, expediente: 5, S. Córdoba to Garrido, March 5, 1926. See also various telegrams to Garrido in the same expediente, all dated March 3, 1926.
26   AGN-TGC, caja: 11, expediente: 2, Garrido to David Camacho Silva, April 26, 1926 and S. Ruiz S. to Garrido, April 26, 1926.
27   AGN-TGC, caja: 10, expediente: 5. José J. Ruiz to Garrido, December 7, 1926.

the ever more singular "revolution," Garrido was determined to make sure that Carlos Vidal had no place in it. His efforts to this end included an ever-closer collaboration with Tiburcio Fernández Ruiz, now a federal senator. Eager to capitalize on an opportunity to regain his lost power and avenge himself on the Chiapas Socialists, the Mapache leader was quick to offer his assistance to Garrido in his attacks against Vidal and to counter Vidal's anti-reelectionist activities in the Southeast. He also led an unsuccessful effort to have Chiapas' powers disappeared, based on yet another allegation that Vidal's electoral victory was illegitimate.[28]

In June of 1926, just weeks after the Socialist Alliance's convention, a group of Garridistas gathered in Mexico City and founded the Radical Socialist Party of the Southeast. Unlike the Alliance, this new, Tabasco-led organization did not hesitate in its open support for Obregón's reelection, nor to describe itself as a party. Its stated goal was:

... to found in Mexico City a great political party with clearly Socialist tendencies that extends its sphere of activity to the states of the Southeast of our Republic, including Yucatán, Campeche, Tabasco, Chiapas and Veracruz such that linked as they are in their political, economic and social lives, they unite in their activities to work for and support the candidacy of General Álvaro Obregón as President of the Mexican nation in the next presidential term that now approaches.[29]

Although the new party seems to have never gained much traction, the intent was also clearly to formalize Garrido's claim to Carrillo Puerto's legacy as the leader of a broader, multistate Socialist movement in the Southeast.

In 1927, Garrido tried again, helping to found the Pro-Obregón Socialist Party of the Southeast in Mexico City. Like Carrillo Puerto's Socialist Party of the Southeast (PSS), the Pro-Obregón Socialist Party of the Southeast was an umbrella organization for a network of local affiliate parties across the region. Unlike the homegrown PSS, however, this party was a creation of politicians at the center, and exported to the region. It also lacked any affiliation with southeastern Socialist parties that already existed, other than Tabasco's. Led by Garrido and supported by Fernández Ruiz in Chiapas, the new Obregonista Socialist party was intended to counter the influence of Carlos Vidal in the Southeast and beyond. Garrido had little hope of winning the support of the Chiapas Socialists,

28	In June of 1926, Fernández Ruiz sent the Mapache politician Juan F. Corzo to Tabasco to work with Garrido. Corzo had been one of the leaders of the opposition campaign against Vidal in the previous election. AGN-TGC, caja: 9, expediente: 1. Fernández Ruiz to Garrido, June 10, 1926. AGN-TGC, caja: 8, expediente: 7. Juan F. Corzo to Garrido, October 20, 1925. On the attempted disappearance of Chiapas' powers, see Castro Martínez, *A la sombra de un caudillo*, 160.

29	AGN-TGC, caja: 9, expediente: 1. Manifesto of the Radical Socialist Party of the Southeast, June 12, 1926 (attached to letter: Garrido to Ramón Ross, June 30, 1926).

and so he created an alternative regional "Socialist" organization out of Mapache-supported affiliate parties there.[30] Garrido seems to have hoped that with Carrillo Puerto dead and Vidal immersed in the fight against reelection, he could position himself as the leader of southeastern Socialism as a regional movement.

Garrido's support of Obregón in 1926–27 was fervent and seemingly tireless. However, it bears underscoring that his support of Obregón's reelection may have had as much to do with his own long-term political aspirations as his desire to see Obregón return to power. On the one hand, his alliance with Obregón (and secondarily with Calles) had allowed Garrido to accomplish much of what he had in Tabasco once he returned to the state in 1924 after the de la Huerta rebellion. On the other hand, Garrido undoubtedly had more personal reasons for supporting the return of reelection to Mexican politics. Once the federal legislature succeeded in reforming the 1917 Constitution to allow for presidential reelection, the Tabasco state legislature followed suit, legalizing gubernatorial reelection.[31] In 1926, no one was better positioned to benefit from this reform than Garrido himself. He was reelected to the office in 1931.

The Gómez-Serrano Rebellion of 1927

In the summer of 1927, the battle over presidential reelection took a new shape and direction as Arnulfo Gómez and Francisco Serrano joined forces in a shared campaign against Obregón's reelection, although neither abandoned his own candidacy. The leaders of the anti-reelectionist movement were both candid and vocal about their opposition to Obregón's return to power with both the press and the government. While both anti-reelectionist candidates and their representatives were adamant that theirs was a principled and legitimate opposition political movement, the merger of their respective campaigns inevitably provoked speculation of a brewing coup, particularly in light of the political class' recent and bitter experience of the de la Huerta rebellion just three years before.

In the summer and fall of 1927, Carlos Vidal worked tirelessly to build a national base of support for Serrano and the anti-reelectionist cause, through a campaign to win the support of preexisting local parties across Mexico.[32] Vidal asked local organizations to adopt an anti-reelectionist platform that

---

30   This is not to say that Garrido did not attempt to win the support of Vidalista Socialists in 1926. See AGN-TGC, caja: 11, expediente: 1. Garrido to Amet Ramos [Cristiani], June 7, 1926.

31   Enrique Canudas, *Trópico rojo: historia política y social de Tabasco los años garridistas 1919/1934*, vol. 2 (Villahermosa, Tabasco: Gobierno del Estado de Tabasco, Instituto de Cultura de Tabasco, 1989), 10.

32   See numerous examples: FAPECFT-FFT, fondo: 13, serie: 10212, expediente: 24, BOLETINES DE PRENSA, legajo 2/2, fojas 129–30, 138–39, inventario 880.

conformed to the dictates of the Comité Pro-Serrano. In a letter sent to local party presidents, Vidal outlined the nature of their future collaboration. He explained that because each local party would remain autonomous, and because each faced a unique situation in their respective locations, they were responsible for funding themselves, but were authorized to conduct fundraising on behalf of Serrano. The organizing committee reserved control over the "political and intellectual leadership" of the campaign, but the design of demonstrations, rallies, and other propaganda efforts tailored to local circumstances were left to the discretion of local party leaders.[33] The Comité Pro-Serrano also recruited individuals, requesting details from potential supporters on what they might be able or prepared to do to advance the anti-reelectionist cause where they lived.[34]

Many of these local organizations had the political will but lacked the means to campaign for Serrano. Despite Vidal's caveats about local fundraising, the Comité Pro-Serrano funded some local groups to aid them in their anti-reelectionist activities. These grants were typically small, of several hundred pesos each, in addition to supplied propaganda materials, such as flyers and campaign buttons.[35] Even these small contributions were undoubtedly meaningful to small local organizations, particularly in places where Obregón's campaign events were allegedly paid for with public funds and obligatory contributions from local businesses.[36] Their requests for assistance were often very humble, such as the anti-reelectionist party in Hidalgo that requested six thousand pieces of paper for its written correspondence that it could not otherwise afford, and a party in Oaxaca that requested a customized stamp for its campaign documents.[37] In other cases,

33 FAPECFT-FFT, fondo: 13, serie: 10212, expediente: "26"/33: CIRCULARES DEL COMITE PRO-SERRANO, legajo 1/1, foja 7, inventario: 889. Form letter to party presidents, August 24, 1927.

34 FAPECFT-FFT, fondo: 13, serie: 10212, expediente: "91"/126: OFICIALIA MAYOR, legajo 1/1, foja 15, inventario: 982. Unsigned, undated form letter.

35 See, for example, the correspondence between Vidal and Julio García, president of the Gran Partido Socialista Occidente (Guadalajara), regarding the receipt of a 500-peso grant from the Serrano campaign. FAPECT-FFT, fondo: 13, serie: 10212, expediente: 73: GARCIA, Julio, legajo 1/1, foja 1, inventario: 929. Julio García to Vidal, August 21, 1927. See also FAPECFT-FFT, fondo: 13, serie: 10212, expediente: "11"/14: ARENAS, Everardo (Gral.), legajo 1/1, foja 4, inventario 870. Everardo Arenas to Vidal, September 5, 1927. FAPECFT-FFT, fondo: 13, serie: 10212, expediente: "52"/84: GONZALEZ, Rodolfo C., COMITE UNIFICACIÓN REVOLUCIONARIA, legajo 1/1, fojas 3–4, inventario 940. Rodolfo González to Comité Pro-Serrano, August 13, 1927.

36 FAPECFT-FFT, fondo: 13, serie: 10212, expediente: "96"/148, PIÑON B., Federico; Rafael CHAVEZ MORENO. PARTIDO NACIONAL DE TRABAJO, legajo 1/1, fojas 8–11, inventario 1004. Informe del Presidente del Partido "Nacional del Trabajo" y Presidente del Partido "Michoacano Unión," August 10, 1927.

37 Hidalgo: FAPECT-FFT, fondo: 13, serie: 10212, expediente: "92"/138: PARTIDO NACIONAL REVOLUCIONARIO, legajo 1/1, foja 371, inventario: 994. Ing. José Laguardia to Gral. Arturo

local parties requested that the Serrano campaign dispatch political organizers and propagandists to assist them.[38]

Vidal brought the Chiapas Socialists' experience at the local and regional levels to bear on the national political stage in his work for Serrano's campaign, but by that time it was becoming standard practice. As the Obregonistas sought to unite all of the Socialist parties of Mexico, Vidal worked on Serrano's behalf to create a competing national alliance of political parties and to instill party-like discipline among the diverse and scattered affiliates of the anti-reelectionist movement. This brand of organizing by both campaigns was strikingly similar to the work that Vidal and Ricardo Alfonso Paniagua had carried out in Chiapas in the early 1920s. Without ligas de resistencia, and facing an entrenched counterrevolutionary movement that had support of the sitting president (Obregón, more specifically), Socialism in Chiapas was always reliant on alliances with preexisting organizations. This was unlike its counterparts in Yucatán and Tabasco, which built their organizations from the ground up. The only other comparable precedent for this kind of political organizing at the national level in this period was the network of local affiliates belonging to the Mexican Labor Party (PLM).

As Paniagua and Vidal had done in carefully appointing Socialist delegates and proxies in local communities across Chiapas, and as the PLM did in building alliances with preexisting local parties sympathetic to its national political program, Vidal empowered a network of local party leaders across Mexico to work for a larger, common political cause at the grassroots, coordinated by a central organization.[39] He also organized a national convention of local parties that supported Serrano, held in August of 1927. Like Carrillo Puerto had done when he organized the workers'

Lasso de la Vega, August 25, 1927. Oaxaca: FAPECFT-FFT, fondo: 13, serie: 10212, expediente: "34"/47, DIAZ, Jesús C. PARTIDO OBRERO INDEPENDIENTE Y CAMPESINO. UNION REVOLUCIONARIO NACIONAL, legajo 1/1, foja 3, inventario 903. Jesús C. Díaz to Comité Pro-Serrano, August 25, 1927.

38   See, for instance, the Socialists of Michoacán: FAPECFT-FFT, fondo: 13, serie: 10212, expediente: "96"/148, PIÑON B., Federico; Rafael CHAVEZ MORENO. PARTIDO NACIONAL DE TRABAJO, legajo 1/1, foja 28, inventario 1004. Federico Piñón B. to Secretario General del Comité Pro-Serrano, September 10, 1927. See also the anti-reelectionists of Oaxaca: FAPECFT-FFT, fondo: 13, serie: 10212, expediente: "34"/47, DIAZ, Jesús C. PARTIDO OBRERO INDEPENDIENTE Y CAMPESINO. UNION REVOLUCIONARIO NACIONAL, legajo 1/ 1, foja 2, inventario 903. Jesús C. Díaz to Comité Pro-Serrano, August 21, 1927.

39   See, for example, Vidal's naming of an official propaganda agent in the state of Puebla in this period (September 5, 1927). FAPECFT-FFT, fondo: 13, serie: 10212, expediente 78: GAVIÑO, Adampol (Gral.), legajo 1/1, foja 1, inventario 934. A day later, he named another propaganda agent and "Delegado General" in Tamaulipas. FAPECFT-FFT, fondo: 13, serie: 10212, expediente 85: GONZALEZ RUBIO, Arnulfo, legajo 1/1, foja 1, inventario 941. These are but a few instances of numerous such formal authorizations of local propagandists and agents by Vidal and the Comité Pro-Serrano.

congresses of Motul and Izamal in 1918 and 1921, and like the Obregonista Socialists had done in 1926, Vidal sought to bring local anti-reelectionist affiliates together to come to collective agreements about their shared political platform. Representatives from Serranista parties across Mexico attended.[40] For umbrella organizations such as the Comité Pro-Serrano, like the Socialist parties of the Southeast, touching base with the constituent parts of the larger conglomerate was essential to at the very least give the appearance of democratic consensus regarding a unified political project. The participatory nature of conventions, which put local political leaders into direct contact with their national allies and patrons, was also symbolically important to these organizations, all of which emphasized their fundamentally democratic nature, in no small part based on their ties to their grassroots constituencies.

Vidal used Socialist organizing techniques to run Serrano's campaign, but his passionate support of Serrano's candidacy was further motivated by an abiding anxiety about the potential long-term consequences of Obregón's return to power. This was shaped by his decade of experience as a military bureaucrat who had witnessed firsthand Mexico's difficult transition from armed revolution to political consolidation, at both the local and national levels. He had returned to Chiapas after defending the government during the de la Huerta rebellion only to find himself in a protracted, violent struggle over the governorship there. He now pondered the potential consequences of what he regarded to be another presidential imposition in a series with no evident end in sight:

The only means of consolidating peace is to achieve the succession of power by institutional means, via the path of suffrage, true suffrage, freely expressed in elections, without the false installers of polls, without the false vote tallying committees, without the false bureaucratic credentials [...] those who provoke civil war are the Governments that convert themselves into political parties, and despite the protests of the public, desire that the Army stab its brothers.[41]

While Vidal may have been considering rising to that provocation by force of arms, at the heart of his apprehension about Obregón's return to power was the lack of an institutionalized means to check a caudillo's ambitions.

40 Rébora, *Memorias de un chiapaneco*, 204.
41 FAPECFT-FFT, fondo: 13, serie: 10212, expediente: 46, DISCURSOS SERRANISTAS, legajo 1/
    1, fojas 5–8, inventario: 902. Undated declaration by Vidal on behalf of the Comité Pro-Serrano.
    Whether or not he was aware of it, Vidal echoed his old mentor Salvador Alvarado, who had
    similarly argued in 1919 that politics without parties would lead to civil war. FAPECFT-FAO,
    serie: 20700, expediente A-2 30: ALVARADO, Salvador (Gral.), legajo 1, fojas 4–22, inventario:
    778. Open letter from Alvarado to Carranza, Obregón, and Pablo González, August 13, 1919.

Further, like other dissidents before him, Vidal feared that the government had become a party.[42] Vidal's opponents in Chiapas were likely to have cried foul at this, considering the undeniable overlap between his own Socialist party and state government in Chiapas. The Ministry of the Interior received extensive reports in this period that the Chiapas state government had effectively become Carlos Vidal's anti-reelectionist machine and that it was persecuting Obregonistas. A local group of Obregón supporters in Huixtla, Chiapas, complained that they were being persecuted by the Socialist government, "which has established itself as a political party."[43] The Chiapas Socialist Raymundo Enríquez, now an Obregonista, complained: "by virtue of the absolute lack of guarantees for Obregonistas, we are constantly in danger of death by assassination by the thugs who are called the Vidalista government."[44] Obregón himself wrote to the Ministry of the Interior around this time to complain of the treatment of his supporters in Chiapas, and to demand that their rights be respected.[45]

Whether it was hypocrisy or reconsideration by Vidal, it is easy to understand why the anti-reelectionists were so adamant that the federal government and political parties remain distinct entities during a presidential campaign. In Yucatán alone, Obregón's campaign was alleged to have received 135,000 pesos in contributions from the state government. This was reported to Serrano by an enraged anti-reelectionist, who added: "this is in a moment in which the campesinos of Yucatán are dying of hunger."[46] Serranista campaign workers across Mexico alleged a sharp divide between the political loyalties of government officials and those of everyday citizens. Many anti-reelectionist organizers across Mexico reported overwhelming popular support for Serrano's presidential candidacy.[47] Others reported little to no popular enthusiasm for Obregón's reelection, in spite of efforts by local

42 Jorge Prieto Laurens, the founder of the National Cooperatist Party and political leader of the de la Huerta rebellion, was particularly strident in his warnings about the dangers of parties of the state. See Jorge Prieto Laurens, *Cincuenta años de política mexicana* (México, D.F.: Editora Mexicana de Periódicos, Libros, 1968), 58, 61–62, 106.

43 AGN, Gobernación, 2/311-P(5)-1, c.96b, exp. 16. Transcribed letter from Emigdio Cosío of Huixtla, Chiapas, et al., sent to the Chiapas Senate delegation and forwarded to Gobernación, September 5, 1927.

44 AGN, Gobernación, 2/311-P(5)-1, c.96b, exp. 16. Transcribed telegram from Enríquez to the Chiapas Senate delegation, and forwarded to Gobernación, September 19, 1927.

45 AGN, Gobernación, 2/311-P(5)-1, c.96b, exp. 16. Obregón to Secretaría de Gobernación, September 7, 1927.

46 FAPECFT-FFT, fondo: 13, serie: 10212, expediente: 169, AVILEZ, Jr., Adolfo, legajo 1/1, foja 1, inventario 1025. Edmundo Rosel to Serrano, September 5, 1927.

47 See, for example, a report from an agent in Tehuacán, Puebla: FAPECFT-FFT, fondo: 13, serie: 10212, expediente: 195: TOSCANO, Vicente, legajo 1/1, foja 31, inventario: 1051. Vicente Toscano to Arturo de la Vega, September 14, 1927.

government officials to muster and/or to fabricate it.[48] In Mexico City, a confidential report to Secretary of War Joaquín Amaro by the Ministry of Agriculture cited plans by Gómez and Serrano to release documents that proved that the federal government was supporting Obregón's reelection campaign.[49]

By attempting to centralize the organization of the Comité Pro-Serrano, to unify its message, and to focus the collective efforts of its constituent parts on the singular goal of electing Serrano, Vidal created a hybrid between the personalist parties and political clubs of Mexico's past and the corporatist, quasi-official national political party that would come later. The difficulties and contradictions that arose around this effort reflect the inevitable challenges of a transition toward the institutionalization of a political system dominated by a single party before it had been fully achieved. While he condemned "a government converted into a political party," Vidal and his fellow southeastern Socialists had provided the clearest blueprint for achieving that. Two years later, Plutarco Elías Calles justified the eventual founding of the National Revolutionary Party (PNR) in strikingly similar language to Vidal's: "The same circumstance that Mexico confronts, perhaps for the first time in its history, in which the predominant feature is the lack of 'caudillos,' should permit us, will permit us, to guide national politics down the path of institutional life."[50] It remains a matter of conjecture whether or not Calles purposefully used the same name for his semi-official party of the state as Francisco Serrano had used for his anti-reelectionist party. Regardless, Calles definitively commandeered both the name and the spirit of a national "revolutionary" party, and, like Vidal, recognized that caudillo politics were unsustainable in Mexico in the long-term.

In the meantime, it was precisely the lack of national political parties with local reach that perpetuated the imposition of policies and directives from Mexico City at the local level. Lacking a party to manage the relationships and collaboration between national political leaders and grassroots constituents, Obregón and Calles sought to control local politics in Chiapas through an ad hoc network of federal agents and institutions. In May of 1927, Margarito Rios, the Agent for the Federal Public Ministry in

---

48 See, for example, a report by a Serranista party in Oaxaca: FAPECFT-FFT, fondo: 13, serie: 10212, expediente: "34"/47, DIAZ, Jesús C. PARTIDO OBRERO INDEPENDIENTE Y CAMPESINO. UNION REVOLUCIONARIO NACIONAL, legajo 1/1, foja 4, inventario 903. Jesús C. Díaz to Comité Pro-Serrano, September 25, 1927.

49 FAPECFT-FFT, fondo: 13, serie: 10207, expediente: "86"/245: SERRANO, Francisco R. (Gral.); Arnulfo R. Gómez (Gral.), legajo 1/1, foja 2, inventario 696. Undated, unsigned report, summer/fall 1927.

50 Calles, *Pensamiento político y social: antología (1913–1936)*, 240–51. Annual presidential report, September 1, 1928.

Tapachula, wrote a detailed report to Fernando Torreblanca, Calles' presidential secretary, describing his efforts in Tapachula to counter Socialist anti-reelectionist efforts there. This letter provides a rare window into efforts to organize local popular forces behind a national political campaign in this period. Rios explained that Vidal was incensed to have recently arrived in Tapachula to find his previous organizing work there on behalf of Serrano undone:

[Vidal] found that all of the agricultural colonies that he already had secured in favor of Serrano's candidacy today favor Obregón, and they [the campesinos] declined to come to town to honor him, despite the urgent summons he made to them via the legislators that he has constantly dedicated to political activities in favor of his candidate. The Governor's anger was caused by the fact that he knew that I had already foreseen that the campesinos would be summoned, and I had advised them as to what they should do (I should let you know that he has a very competent service of spies). Following my instructions to the letter, not one of them stopped for him.[51]

On presumably direct orders from the President himself, a federal agent on the ground mustered campesinos in Chiapas to turn against Vidal and to support Obregón.

Vidal and Ricardo Alfonso Paniagua were incensed. In September of 1927, Paniagua reported that while the legitimate authorities had stayed in power in Tapachula, Huixtla, and Motozintla, several municipal presidents had been arrested for sedition and sent to Tapachula, where Rios imprisoned them. "His rabid Obregonismo makes us fear for the lives of said compañeros," Paniagua wrote.[52] Vidal's friend Hipólito Rébora recalled how various forms of federal intervention complicated matters for the Chiapas anti-reelectionists: "The electoral campaign in the state in favor of General Serrano became more difficult every day, due to the decided support of the military forces, and also of the agent of the public ministry, Lic. Margarito Rios, who impudently went to visit the ejidos as a propagandist for General Obregón."[53]

This effort by Rios speaks powerfully to the value that local popular support was understood to have for national campaigns, even in far-flung Chiapas, and even for Obregón, who had never given local matters in Chiapas much attention. It also reveals the extent to which Calles and Obregón understood Carlos Vidal to be meaningfully bolstered by the

51 FAPECFT-FFT, fondo: 13, serie: 10207, expediente: "45"/221, RIOS, Margarito C., legajo 1/1, fojas 2–3, inventario 672. Margarito Rios to Fernando Torreblanca, May 31, 1927.

52 AGN-Gobernación, 2/311-P(5)-1, c. 96b, exp. 16. Vidal to Adalberto Tejeda, September 11, 1927.

53 Rébora, *Memorias de un chiapaneco*, 206.

campesinos of Chiapas, and the power that the grassroots base of the Socialist party was understood to have. It underscores that while Calles and Obregón deemed it necessary to attempt to deprive Vidal of that source of support to undermine his pursuit of his national political goals, they had no institutional mechanisms in place to do it, and so resorted to dispatching federal agents to crudely impose their political will at the local level on an ad hoc basis.

The CROM was supposed to have filled that role, but it had been handicapped in its ability to do so by the split between the Laboristas and the Socialists in Chiapas. Rios' report to Torreblanca makes clear that it was not just the Chiapas Socialists' organization of workers that was considered a threat to Obregonismo in the state, but also that the Socialists' Confederation of Workers was independent of the CROM, which meant a lesser degree of control over workers' political activities from Mexico City. Rios described the state of labor organization among the campesinos of Tapachula upon his arrival there:

I should explain to you that before my arrival here, the campesinos were at the mercy of the Governor, who had enlisted them like sheep into a Society which he formed, with the name of the Socialist Confederation of Workers of Chiapas, and separating them from the CROM, as all of them were adhered to it, they were threatened in various ways, and when I realized this, I began to encourage them with my advice that they not separate from the most respectable association that there is in the Republic. The object of separating them from the CROM was to win supporters for his [Serrano's] candidacy, and to be able to say that Serrano had the campesino element on his side. Today they only have the Guatemalan colonists that they have been able to bring from the neighboring Republic, who pass as Mexican, since they are as *prieto* as we are.[54]

The Socialist Party and PLM, once allied in Chiapas, now found themselves in direct competition for the constituents that they had collaborated in organizing for Vidal's gubernatorial campaign. This was a dramatic change from the state of affairs in Chiapas three years earlier, when a Chiapas Laborista supporter had declared, "we are all Vidalistas, first and foremost."[55] Luis Morones' eventual choice to support Obregón's reelection bid meant the final disintegration of the already fraught collaboration between the Chiapas Socialists and the CROM. The alliance between southeastern Socialists and the national labor organization was therefore yet another casualty of the fight over presidential reelection.

54 FAPECFT-FFT, fondo: 13, serie: 10207, expediente: "45"/221, RIOS, Margarito C., legajo 1/1, fojas 2–3, inventario 672. Margarito Rios to Fernando Torreblanca, May 31, 1927.
55 AGN-CAV, c. 6, f. 5. Partial letter missing attribution to Vidal, February 15, 1924.

The breakdown of the Socialist-Laborista alliance in Chiapas was emblematic of a larger trend of political realignments in the state in 1926–27. Whereas the Chiapas Socialists had once counted on the support of federal agents and soldiers stationed in the state, they now faced these as their opponents in a struggle for popular support and political control. Obregón saw to it that federal garrison commanders in Chiapas that were sympathetic to Francisco Serrano's presidential campaign were replaced with Obregonistas, to further undermine any sources of support for the Socialist anti-reelectionists. The federal military commanders also disarmed the municipal police, lest they possibly demonstrate their political dissent by force of arms.[56] "The constitutional authorities of the state of Chiapas are suffering the consequences of their virile attitude in resolutely confronting the reelectionist elements and proclaiming themselves in favor of General Serrano," Vidal protested in a press release.[57]

In Motozintla, four Vidalistas were accused of sedition and remanded to the federal authorities in September of 1927. The Comité Pro-Serrano argued in a sharply worded letter to the Ministry of the Interior that the government official handling the case was the chief of Obregonista propaganda in Chiapas, and that it was a mockery of justice to have their partisans held by their declared political enemy. A week later, on September 27, Vidal and Paniagua decried the arrest of one of Arnulfo Gómez's delegates in Chiapas. "We energetically protest this flagrant violation of constitutional guarantees," Vidal wrote. "We hope that you will order that independent elements be respected, in the exercise of their civic functions."[58]

Distant Chiapas suddenly became a highly contested piece of political territory, as the state became caught up in the ongoing struggle to define the rules of the postrevolutionary political game. Between Vidal's political rebellion against Obregón and the increasingly fraught nature of Calles' relationship to Vidal and the Chiapas Socialists, local politics in Chiapas had become a matter of considerable national political consternation. In September, the Obregonista Senator Antonio Valadez Ramírez of Jalisco denounced the abuse of Tzotzil residents of the town of Magdalena by the Vidalista government:

A great number of indigenous people, residents of the town of Magdalena, Chiapas, are taken from their homes by force, and made to work on the highways, without being paid for their work, and are the objects of many other humiliations, and these

56 Rébora, *Memorias de un chiapaneco*, 205–6.
57 FAPECFT-FFT, fondo: 3, serie: 010212, expediente: 24: BOLETINES DE PRENSA, legajo 1/2, fojas 115–16, inventario: 880. Press release, August 31, 1927.
58 AGN-Gobernación, 2/311-P(5)-1, c. 96b, exp. 16. Comité Pro-Serrano to Secretario de Gobernacíon, September 30, 1927; Vidal to Secretario de Gobernación, September 28, 1927.

attacks are caused by none other than the fact that said indigenous people are fervent Obregonistas, which is to say, they sustain a political belief that is different from that of the authorities of that unfortunate state.[59]

Valadez Ramírez went on to demand that the "Obregonista element," including the people of Magdalena, be protected from persecution and attacks for their political beliefs. In response to continued accusations of abuses of Obregonistas in Chiapas at the hands of the state government, the Ministry of the Interior sent its own secret agent to investigate the circumstances of one such claim.[60] Socialist Chiapas was now at the eye of the gathering national political storm.

The apprehension of Vidalistas in Chiapas by federal forces represented just part of a larger wave of arrests of anti-reelectionists across the whole of Mexico in August and September of 1927. Anti-reelectionists in many states complained of abuses and unfounded detentions by the federal authorities. Sometimes this was merely the destruction of campaign posters, but often it was much more serious. In Morelia, Michoacán, in August, thirty-eight anti-reelectionists were arrested after being denounced for planning a counterdemonstration at a planned campaign stop by Obregón. When Obregón was scheduled to arrive for another campaign event in nearby Uruapan, anti-reelectionists fired shots in the air to disperse the crowd gathered to greet the candidate, spreading fears among Obregón's partisans that they were planning to assassinate him. Military authorities dispatched patrols to lock down the city and prevent any further disruptions by anti-reelectionists. Serrano's partisans suspended some of their planned protests, fearing the reprisals and persecution they might provoke, but carried on with other plans to disrupt Obregon's campaign events.[61] In early September, five anti-reelectionists in Tacuba were arrested on the suspicion that they were plotting a coup on behalf of Serrano.[62] Some local anti-reelectionists continued to organize and campaign for Serrano, even anticipating that they would be the target of harassment by local officials and politicians who supported Obregón's reelection. The Serrano campaign acknowledged that likelihood, and encouraged its partisans to report any difficulties they

59   AGN-Gobernación, 2/311-P(5)-1, c. 96b, exp. 16. Senador Antonio Valadez Ramírez to Secretario de Gobernación, September 28, 1927. Camp, *Mexican Political Biographies, 1884–1935*, 275.
60   AGN-Gobernación, 2/311-P(5)-1, c. 96b, exp. 16, f. 2. Memorandum de la Oficina Confidencial, Secretaría de Gobernación, September 10, 1927.
61   FAPECFT-FFT, fondo: 13, serie: 10212, expediente: "96"/148, PIÑON B., Federico; Rafael CHAVEZ MORENO. PARTIDO NACIONAL DE TRABAJO, legajo 1/1, fojas 8–11, inventario 1004. Informe del Presidente del Partido "Nacional del Trabajo" y Presidente del Partido "Michoacano Unión," August 10, 1927.
62   FAPECFT-FFT, fondo: 13, serie: 010212, expediente: 1544: Ramírez, Eduardo, legajo 1/1, foja 1, inventario: 1010. Eduardo Ramírez to Serrano, September 6, 1927.

encountered to the Comité Pro-Serrano so that it could formulate a response.[63]

While various agents of the federal government harassed, intimidated, and in some cases murdered anti-reelectionist operatives across Mexico, Calles made no move to have Gómez, Serrano, or Vidal arrested. This seems to have reassured the leaders of the anti-reelectionist movement that they were not at risk of imprisonment, or worse. On the contrary, Gómez, Serrano, and Vidal continued to submit sharply worded letters of protest and to adamantly demand protections for their supporters from the federal government, including the release of imprisoned anti-reelectionist activists.[64] It is impossible to determine from their correspondence if the Serranistas genuinely expected their freedom of political expression to be protected by Calles' government, or whether their demands to that effect constituted a symbolic gesture as part of their larger political protest. What is clear is that the federal crackdown on anti-reelectionists only intensified. On September 7, an anti-reelectionist detainee in the state of Veracruz was accused of rebellion against federal authorities. In another case in early September, Vidal protested the arrest of General Francisco Díaz Hernández, who was working as a Serranista agent in Tampico. In yet another case, the President of the Comité Pro-Serrano for the state of Campeche was forced to flee from federal authorities, who were trying to arrest him on the pretext that he had "injured a public functionary," despite the protests of the delegate in Mérida that "his only crime is that he is Serranista." In Tepic, Nayarit, a few weeks later, a Serranista propaganda agent died in his prison cell after being arrested by federal authorities, which the Serrano campaign was quick to condemn as a political assassination. Although his death was ruled a suicide, the campaign received reports that he had sustained a bullet wound to his forehead and bruises around his neck suggesting strangulation, in addition to evidence of extensive and gruesome abuse and torture. His family was unable to find any doctors that were willing to formally testify to these facts, out of their apparent fear of retaliatory persecution by the Governor of Nayarit.[65]

63 FAPECFT-FFT, fondo: 13, serie: 10212, expediente: "7"/19, AVILEZ, Jr., Adolfo, legajo 1/1, foja 2, inventario 875. Adolfo Avilés Jr. to Serrano, August 5, 1927. (Jalisco) Arturo Lazo de la Vega to Adolfo Avilés Jr., August 15, 1927.

64 See, for example, the efforts to win the release of an anti-reelectionist in Yucatán: FAPECFT-FFT, fondo: 13, serie: 10212, expediente: "48"/170, ROSEL V., Gonzalo, legajo 1/1, foja 2, inventario 1026. Secretario General to Gonzalo Rosel V., August 20, 1927.

65 FAPECFT-FFT, fondo: 13, serie: 10212, expediente: 182, SECRETARIA DE GOBERNACION, legajo 1/1, foja 3, inventario 1038. LP Tamayo to Pedro Gómez, September 7, 1927; fojas 1–2, Vidal to Secretario de Gobernación, September 6, 1927; foja 7, Vidal to Secretario de Gobernación, September 22, 1927; foja 9, Comité Pro-Serrano to Secretario de Gobernación, September 28, 1927.

Tensions were higher than ever in Mexico City that fall, including within the Chamber of Deputies, where some anti-reelectionist legislators now found their positions imperiled. In a press release on September 27, Vidal fervently protested the expulsion legislator Domingo Acosta, "for the sole reason that this popular representative signed the patriotic manifesto of the independent anti-reelectionist bloc." He went on to accuse the Obregonistas of having sequestered Acosta in his own home and not permitting him to leave in order to defend himself or to communicate with friends and allies. In Acosta's absence, the Obregonista legislative bloc voted for his permanent expulsion from the legislature, for the alleged crime of collecting two salaries at once, as a legislator and from the Ayuntamiento of Tacuba, a charge that Vidal claimed could be easily disproved. In conclusion, Vidal wrote: "these events demonstrate that we politicians that don't participate in the reelectionist imposition are now lacking guarantees for the free exercise of our civil rights."[66]

The CROM and the PLM were also particularly susceptible to the political frictions generated by the debates over presidential reelection. The Laboristas had long supported and collaborated with parties like the Chiapas Socialist Party, some of which were now strongly anti-reelectionist. Luis Morones' decision to support Obregón's reelection additionally caused fractures within the CROM and the PLM, as some of the Laborista rank and file were thrown into a state of confusion by the seeming political realignment of their leadership. Part of the problem was that the alliances that had underwritten much of the CROM's political activity in the 1920s were driven by Morones' close relationship with Calles, and in the fall of 1927, Calles' stance on Obregón's reelection remained unclear to many of his supporters. In a press release on September 7, a Laborista delegate publicly called on Calles to definitively clarify his stance on reelection, declaring that the most recent PLM national convention had reiterated its support of Calles' policies, and that in spite of its "unanimous anti-reelectionism," the convention had voted to support Obregón's candidacy.[67]

The confusion within the PLM translated to breaks with some of its affiliates and members at the local level in the weeks that followed the Laborista convention's vote to support Obregón's reelection. The delegate from the Veracruz Labor Party wrote to Vidal that he had been sent to Mexico City to attend the Laborista convention with orders from his party to take a stand against reelection. He explained that the decision of the convention as a whole to support Obregón was the result of what he described as "a crude

66 FAPECFT-FFT, fondo: 13, serie: 10212, expediente: 24, BOLETINES DE PRENSA, legajo 2/2, fojas 228–29, inventario 880. Press release by Vidal, September 27, 1927.
67 FAPECFT-FFT, fondo: 13, serie: 10212, expediente: 24, BOLETINES DE PRENSA, legajo 2/2, foja 146, inventario: 880. Public letter to Calles by Luis Amador y Trias, September 7, 1927.

impositionist maneuver," which had contravened the true anti-reelectionist sentiment of the delegates. He went on to declare that in spite of this, the Veracruz Labor Party, and he himself, would continue to support Serrano's candidacy. "Our position has always been and always will be revolutionary, and as such, anti-reelectionist," he concluded.[68] Serrano also received messages of support from other Laborista groups that assured him that they continued to support his candidacy, no matter what the PLM convention had resolved. Rumors swirled that Morones might have to resign.[69]

The growing tension between the Laborista leadership and the rank and file was an opening that the Serrano campaign recognized and sought to exploit. In a press release, Vidal lambasted the convention's determination to support Obregón's reelection. "This is the clearest reflection of official influence in the presidential political campaign," Vidal wrote. He continued: "this resolution is in conflict with the principles of the Revolution and the unanimous sentiment of the Mexican people, as well as flagrantly contradicting the true sentiments of the workers, which were clearly and energetically expressed by their delegates at the Convention."[70] The Laborista legislator Ricardo Treviño of the Federal District gave the decidedly lukewarm defense of the PLM's support of Obregón's reelection that "we have said that it was necessary to be [reelectionist], and therefore we are."[71] If Calles, Obregón, and Morones had hoped to give the impression of a united front by pushing support for reelection through the PLM convention, the effort had the opposite effect, laying bare growing fissures in their local and regional base of popular support.

The Purge

Taken together, primary and secondary accounts of the Gómez-Serrano rebellion of October 1927 are consistent in stressing two features of the weeks that preceded it. One is the confidence and calm that all observers described Serrano and his compatriots exhibiting, including at the moment of their arrest by federal forces on October 3. The second, indubitably related, is the absolute confidence that Serrano and Vidal

68 FAPECFT-FFT, fondo: 13, serie: 10212, expediente: "89"/125, OCHOA, Antonio B., PARTIDO VERACRUZANO DEL TRABAJO, legajo 1/1, foja 2, inventario 981. Antonio B. Ochoa to Vidal, September 22, 1927.

69 FAPECFT-FFT, fondo: 13, serie: 10207, expediente: "86"/245: SERRANO, Francisco R. (Gral.); Arnulfo R. Gómez (Gral.), legajo 1/1, foja 2, inventario 696. Undated, unsigned report, summer/fall 1927.

70 FAPECFT-FFT, fondo: 13, serie: 10212, expediente: 24, BOLETINES DE PRENSA, legajo 2/2, fojas 147–48, inventario: 880. Press release by Vidal, September 8, 1927.

71 "Diario de los Debates de la Cámara de Diputados." Legislatura XXXII – Año II – Período Ordinario – October 4, 1927 – Número de Diario 15.

expressed until the last that President Calles silently supported them in opposing Obregón's return to power. Carlos Vidal's determined show of calm in the face of increasingly grim prospects for himself and the anti-reelectionist movement suggests the extent of his confidence in his long-standing alliance with Calles. It also suggests that he believed that the opposition movement was a viable one. Vidal's faith in Calles was not merely wishful thinking. The president seems to have purposefully culti-vated the appearance of total impartiality when it came to the matter of reelection, whether to draw out mutinous elements, or to ensure his own political cover, or both. It worked on all counts.

At the same time, Vidal knew well that he was on thin ice with Obregón, which only magnified the importance of his relationship to Calles. His friend Hipólito Rébora recalled that following the Obregonista presidential con-vention in mid-1927, Obregón tried to have Vidal arrested. "As Obregón knew that General Vidal was the major force behind Serrano, they accused him of I don't even know what falsehood, and the fact is that they tried to apprehend him, but he was warned in time, and hid himself, and everything was taken care of by General Serrano and President Calles."[72] If Rébora's account is accurate, Vidal's belief that Calles was on his side is greatly clarified. From Vidal's perspective, his longstanding alliance with Calles was continuing to pay dividends. This vignette also helps to make sense of Serrano's adamant belief that Calles was either his ally, or at least a neutral observer, if they were indeed cooperating to protect Vidal from Obregón.

Arnulfo Gómez also declared his faith in Calles as an ally in a toast he gave at a banquet held in Vidal's honor, in August of 1927: "General Calles has always listened to me, and I have never denied to him my aspiration to sustain the principles for which I have fought for twenty long years, and for which I have spilled my own blood on several occasions." Gómez went on to express his hope that there was no anti-reelectionist present at the banquet who intended to hide the photographs that were taken there of the event out of cowardice.[73] In a strange twist of fate, the anti-reelectionist banquet for Vidal was held at the same restaurant in Mexico City where Obregón was assassinated the following year.

Outward show of confidence aside, his own death was clearly on Vidal's mind. In press releases, Vidal described the political struggle in which he was involved as being a matter of life and death.[74] Like most Mexican politicians and soldiers of his generation, Vidal had witnessed firsthand the

72   Rébora, *Memorias de un chiapaneco*, 205.
73   FAPECFT-FFT, fondo: 13, serie: 10212, expediente: 46, DISCURSOS SERRANISTAS, legajo 1/1, fojas 13–14, inventario: 902. Transcription of speeches in Vidal's honor, August 27, 1927.
74   FAPECFT-FFT, fondo: 13, serie: 10212, expediente: 24, BOLETINES DE PRENSA, legajo 2/2, fojas 147–48, inventario: 880. Press release by Vidal, September 8, 1927.

violence that could result from political struggles – perhaps even more than most, having survived at least two assassination attempts. That spring, he changed his will, naming his wife Dévora as his sole heir and carefully documented his assets for her. "Don't get the wrong impression," he wrote to her. "It's just necessary to always be ready, even to die."[75] A few months later, he sent her a collection of his books and papers from Tuxtla to Mexico City for safekeeping.[76]

It is impossible to know precisely at what moment the anti-reelectionist movement became an armed rebellion against the Mexican government, or if it ever truly did. Certainly, anti-reelectionists across Mexico began to at least ponder the possibility that their political confrontation with Obregón would devolve into armed struggle, or even revolution. Serrano's Socialist supporters in Yucatán assured him that while all of the officials in the state were Obregonistas, the workers supported his campaign and were ready to take up arms to defend "the revolutionary principles that were won with blood," should they once again be threatened.[77] The Anti-Reelectionist Student Center of Puebla similarly promised Serrano that they would "exchange their books for carbines" should the need arise.[78]

Vito Alessio Robles, who was the President of Arnulfo Gómez's National Anti-Reelectionist Party, alleged in 1936 that it was a group of Serrano's representatives, led by Vidal, that first proposed an armed rebellion against the federal government, in September of 1927.[79] Vidal's fiery rhetoric did nothing to contradict the allegation. He wrote: "the loyalty that is demanded of the military men by the President of the Obregonista Bloc in the legislature is not to institutions, but rather, to the imposition of General Obregón, which is to say, it is a frank invitation to civil war."[80] Other sources suggest that the resort to armed rebellion that fall was agreed upon by both Gómez and Serrano together, along with their respective contingents of followers. What is clear is that in this period the two campaigns had become increasingly fused as a singular movement, and that they had meetings in late September to determine

75 AGN-CAV, c. 6, f. 11. Vidal to Dévora Rojas de Vidal, March 1, 1927.
76 AGN-CAV, c. 6, f. 11. Vidal to Dévora Rojas de Vidal, June 21, 1927. It is likely that the papers to which he referred constitute at least part of what is now the Vidal papers collection at the AGN.
77 FAPECFT-FFT, fondo: 13, serie: 10212, expediente: "46"/66, FUENTES Z., Alonso, legajo 1/1, foja 2, inventario 922. Alonso Fuentes Z. to Serrano, August 6, 1927.
78 FAPECFT-FFT, fondo: 13, serie: 10212, expediente: 43: CORTES Jr., Aureliano. CENTRO ANTIREELECCIONISTA DE ESTUDIANTES DE PUEBLA, legajo 1/1, foja 1, inventario: 899. Aureliano Cortés Jr. to Serrano, September 17, 1927.
79 Vito Alessio Robles, *Desfile sangriento* (México, D.F.: A. del Bosque, 1936), 142. Alessio Robles' assessments must be taken with a few grains of salt, considering his interest in not implicating himself in the fomenting of an armed rebellion.
80 FAPECFT-FFT, fondo: 13, serie: 10212, expediente: 46, DISCURSOS SERRANISTAS, legajo 1/1, fojas 5–8, inventario: 902. Undated manifesto: "La Provocación a la Guerra es la Imposición."

whether Gómez or Serrano should become the sole anti-reelectionist candidate.[81] Anti-reelectionist legislators subsequently argued that the opposition to Obregón's candidacy was never intended to be an armed struggle, but this interpretation was with the benefit of hindsight after the movement had failed.[82]

That fall, President Calles received numerous reports of anti-reelectionist plans to launch an armed insurgency against his government, and had agents closely scrutinize the loyalties of numerous officers and soldiers within the military. General Eulogio Ortiz worked for Calles as an investigator within the army and reported that Vidal and the Comité Pro-Serrano had been extensively attempting to recruit support for Serrano among the officer corps. He himself received a copy of a letter soliciting support for the Serrano campaign and a manifesto by Serrano that were distributed to officers.[83] These communiqués did not include anything beyond propaganda for Serrano's candidacy. Nevertheless, in early September, Ortiz recommended that an entire army corps be moved from Chiapas to another region, or at least that new officers be assigned to it.[84] Another report suggested that Serrano was in the process of arming police forces in the state of Morelos, where his ranch was located, so that they would be able to protect him. One agent reported that the anti-reelectionists were confident that they would be able to eliminate Obregón, "even if by criminal means."[85]

In September, a military officer who the anti-reelectionists had tried unsuccessfully to recruit submitted an unsolicited report to Calles that Vidal had returned to Chiapas where he was allegedly raising a force of ten thousand men to march on Tabasco and Veracruz, and that the anti-reelectionists had amassed another ten thousand troops in Nuevo León and Tamaulipas, four thousand in Cuernavaca, and another three thousand in Pachuca.[86] A later report by one of Calles' agents indicated that ammunition had been funneled to rebels who were organizing to support Serrano in

81 FAPECFT-FFT, fondo: 13, serie: 10212, expediente: 204: VIDAL, Carlos A. (Gral.), legajo 1/1, foja 4, inventario 1060. Serrano to Vidal, September 23, 1927.

82 "Diario de los Debates de la Cámara de Diputados." Legislatura XXXII – Año II – Período Ordinario – October 4, 1927 – Número de Diario 15.

83 FAPECFT-FFT, fondo: 13, serie: 10207, expediente: "101"/193: Ortiz, Eulogio (Gral.), legajo 1/1, fojas 10–12, inventario 644. Comisión de Relaciones to Eulogio Ortiz, August 1, and Manifesto by Serrano, July 23, 1927.

84 FAPECFT-FFT, fondo: 13, serie: 10207, expediente: "101"/193: Ortiz, Eulogio (Gral.), legajo 1/1, foja 5, inventario 644. Eulogio Ortiz to Fernando Torreblanca, September 2, 1927.

85 FAPECFT-FFT, fondo: 13, serie: 10207, expediente: "86"/245: SERRANO, Francisco R. (Gral.); Arnulfo R. Gómez (Gral.), legajo 1/1, foja 2, inventario 696. Undated, unsigned report, summer/fall 1927.

86 FAPECFT-FFT, fondo: 13, serie: 10207, expediente: "105"/246: SERRANO, Francisco R. (Gral.); Arnulfo R. Gómez (Gral.), legajo 1/1, foja 2, inventario 697. Unsigned report to Calles, September 21, 1927.

Jalisco, that rebel sympathizers had installed radio stations at various sites in Mexico City to use for communications during a rebellion, that several ex-Delahuertista rebels had planned an uprising in the state of Hidalgo, and that there was a plot among former rebel officers to assassinate Calles.[87]

The rebels' plan was allegedly for anti-reelectionist generals to assassinate Calles, Obregón, and Joaquín Amaro on the evening of October 2, at a military festival held in the Balbuena section of Mexico City, and then to take control of the federal government.[88] Calles and Obregón had been carefully planning for an anticipated armed uprising for some time by that point, making sure that military officers loyal to them were stationed in likely areas of anti-reelectionist rebellion, including Chiapas.[89] The Sonorans did not attend the event at Balbuena, and Calles used his knowledge of these alleged plans as a pretext to order the arrest of the anti-reelectionist leadership. Another general known to be intimately involved in the planned rebellion was immediately sent into exile, without Serrano and Vidal's knowledge. By the government's account, three military units stationed in Mexico City joined a rebellion on October 2, but most of the men involved quickly returned to their barracks. Loyal troops also swiftly defeated a battalion that rebelled in the northern city of Torreón.[90] Subsequent reports suggest that there were very limited clashes between supporters of Gómez and federal troops in Veracruz after Gómez fled there following the failure of the rebellion in Mexico City.[91] The rebellion, such as it was, was efficiently and speedily crushed before it could get off the ground.[92]

The following day, Serrano, Vidal, and a group of friends and supporters waited in Cuernavaca on Serrano's ranch to receive word of the outcome of the preliminary rebellion in Mexico City. Instead, they were apprehended by federal soldiers, and told they would be taken to Mexico City. En route, Serrano, Vidal, and twelve others were stopped on the road outside of

---

87 FAPECFT-FFT, fondo: 13, serie: 10207, expediente: "181"/292: VILLAVICENCIO, Leonel, legajo 1/1, fojas 1–3, inventario 743. Undated report from Leonel Villavicencio to Fernando Torreblanca.

88 For one account of the plan, received by Calles on September 21, 1927, see FAPECFT-FFT, fondo: 13, serie: 10207, expediente: "105"/246: SERRANO, Francisco R. (Gral.); Arnulfo R. Gómez (Gral.), legajo 1/1, foja 2, inventario 697. Unsigned report to Calles, September 21, 1927.

89 FAPECFT-FFT, fondo: 13, serie: 10207, expediente: "101"/193: Ortiz, Eulogio (Gral.), legajo 1/1, foja 4, inventario 644. Eulogio Ortiz to Fernando Torreblanca, August 26, 1927.

90 Presidential press releases reproduced in: Islas and Múzquiz Blanco, *De la pasión sectaria a la noción de las instituciones*, 47–50, 56, 62.

91 See, for example, FAPECFT-FFT, fondo: 13, serie: 10207, expediente: "231"/11: AMAYA, Juan Gualberto, legajo 1/1, foja 11, inventario 462. Report by Juan Gualberto Amaya on the last testimony of General Francisco R. Bertani before his execution, December 7, 1927. One of many such reports in this file.

92 The details of the rebellion and its aftermath have been thoroughly documented elsewhere. See in particular Castro Martínez, *A la sombra de un caudillo*.

Huitzilac, Morelos, and executed as rebels. Several gruesome firsthand accounts suggest the indignity and inhumanity of the manner in which the leaders of the anti-reelectionist movement met their ends before hastily assembled firing squads.[93] Their hands were bound with electrical wire when no rope could be found. Some of the bodies were reportedly looted by the soldiers at the scene. The corpses were stacked in the back of cars for transport to the military hospital in the capital for autopsy, and were eventually returned to their families. Serrano's autopsy revealed that he received the most physical abuse of any of the victims.[94]

The official explanation for the killings was that Serrano and his entourage had been convicted of rebellion and justly executed.[95] No records of any type of trial or a court martial for the accused rebels were ever found, although the Ministry of War searched for proof of one on more than one occasion.[96] Nor has it ever been definitely proven who gave the order to execute the anti-reelectionist leaders at Huitzilac. A multi-year investigation of the case in the mid-1930s by the Ministry of War during the government of Lázaro Cárdenas raised as many questions as it answered, with nearly all participants in the so-called Huitzilac Massacre denying any personal responsibility for the deaths of the prisoners. In lieu of evidence to the contrary, the assumption has long been, and remains, that it was President Calles who gave the order to execute the anti-reelectionist leaders, with or without the knowledge and encouragement of Obregón, who had the most invested in the outcome.[97] No one was ever tried for the killings.

The execution of Serrano, Vidal, and their companions was just the beginning of a bloody purge of their allies and associates across Mexico. One day later in Chiapas, Luis Vidal and Ricardo Alfonso Paniagua were also accused of rebellion against the government and executed.[98] Another of Vidal's brothers fled to safety in Guatemala. Several weeks later, Arnulfo Gómez was also arrested and executed. All told, in the order of 500 people lost their lives in the wake of the Gómez-Serrano rebellion. Tomás Garrido Canabal wrote to Calles two days after the massacre to request weapons to

93   This includes published accounts by witnesses, as well as sworn statements to investigators in the 1930s.
94   AHSDN-W, ACH, XI/481.5/412, tomo II, foja 500. Certified copy of Serrano's autopsy report, October 4, 1927.
95   Felipe Islas and Manuel Múzquiz Blanco, *De la pasión sectaria a la noción de las instituciones* (México, D.F.1932), 55–56.
96   AHSDN, XI/111/1–243, Serrano, Francisco R., Tomo 8, foja 1802. Othón León Lobato to Srio. de Guerra y Marina, Departamento de la Justicia, January 27, 1936. AHSDN, XI/111/1–243, Serrano, Francisco R., Tomo 8, foja 1827. Felipe Armenta Ruíz to Secretario de la Defensa Nacional, Dirección de Justicia y Pensiones, January 21, 1938.
97   Buchenau describes Obregón as "the probable instigator." Buchenau, *The Last Caudillo*, 158.
98   Islas and Múzquiz Blanco, *De la pasión sectaria a la noción de las instituciones*, 64.

fight for the government, but Calles replied tersely that the campaign against the traitors was already well in hand.[99]

In Chiapas, local politicians continued to pay the price for their association with the anti-reelectionist movement well after the leadership was dead, sometimes literally so. Beyond the bloody purges of Vidal's family and allies, the new interim state government under General Manuel Álvarez Rábago exacted a monetary price for the freedom of lower ranking Vidalistas that remained. "There were also all of the fines that they imposed on all of the people that belonged to General Vidal's government, and his friends," Hipólito Rébora recounted. "These were five thousand pesos and above, depending on rank, and to remain free, they had to pay. This was truly a plundering (it must have exceeded a million [pesos])." Rébora reported that similar extortions took place across the state, and that local authorities in Chiapas also continued to assassinate innocent people in the wake of Huitzilac.[100]

A political purge also followed. On October 4, one day after the arrest of Serrano and Vidal, a resolution was introduced in the Chamber of Deputies to strip the majority of the Chiapas legislative delegation of their seats, along with anti-reelectionist legislators from other states. They were accused of being "morally identified" with traitors, of being in open rebellion themselves, and of acting in ways that implicated them as accomplices. José Castañon, a longtime Vidalista politician, was expelled from his seat on a separate pretense. In total, twenty-eight representatives from fifteen of Mexico's thirty-one states were expelled from their elected offices as traitors. Three of these were members of the Obregonista Allied Socialist Bloc, and had attended the Alliance's convention the previous May. The Alliance, its task of reforming the constitution to make way for Obregón's reelection complete, had disbanded in February of 1927.[101]

Far from being concentrated in any region, these legislators hailed from every part of Mexico. Among these were the same seven representatives who had voted against the reform of Articles 82 and 83 in October of 1926.[102]

---

99   FAPECFT-PEC, expediente: 140, GARRIDO CANABAL, Tomás (Lic.), legajo 3/7, fojas 188–89, inventario: 2312. Garrido to Calles, October 5, 1927, Calles to Garrido, October 7, 1927.

100   Rébora, *Memorias de un chiapaneco*, 212.

101   On the dissolution of the Alliance, see Mac Gregor Campuzano, "Partidos nacionales y programas políticos en México, 1918–1928," 268–72.

102   "Diario de los Debates de la Cámara de Diputados." Legislatura XXXII – Año II – Período Ordinario – October 4, 1927 – Número de Diario 15. For a full list of all of the members of the 32nd Legislature, by state, see Camp, *Mexican Political Biographies, 1884–1935*, 393–98. The twenty-eight accused legislators were Gilberto Isaís (Baja California), Amet Ramos Cristiani (Chiapas), Jaime A. Solís (Chiapas), Carlos Flores Tovilla (Chiapas), **Ulises Vidal** (Chiapas), *Ramón Ramos* (Chihuahua), Elpidio Barrera (Coahuila), Francisco Valle (Coahuila), Luis G. Belaunzarán (Guanajuato), ***Enrique Bordes Mangel*** (Guanajuato), *Nicolás Cano* (Guanajuato), Ricardo Covarrubias (Jalisco), Joaquín Vidrio (Jalisco), Enrique A. Enríquez (México), Margarito Gómez (México), **Gilberto Fabila** (México), *Eugenio Mier y Terán*

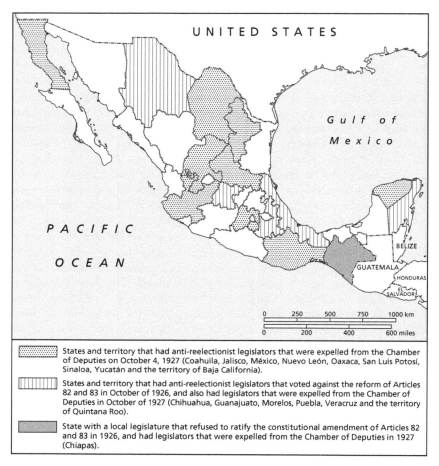

Map 2 Geographic distribution of anti-reelectionist legislators, 1926–27

The geographical distribution of the expelled anti-reelectionist legislators in 1927 is testimony to how successful the anti-reelectionist movement had been in establishing and spreading itself throughout Mexico in relatively short order (see Map 2). In removing dissident legislators from office, the

(Morelos), Francisco Garza (Nuevo León), Francisco Garza Nieto (Nuevo León), Felizardo Villarreal (Nuevo León), Carlos T. Robinson (Oaxaca), Humberto Barros (Puebla), *Antonio Islas Bravo* (Puebla), *Candelario Garza* (Quintana Roo), Antonio Trujillo Espinosa (San Luis Potosí), Fernando Cuén (Sinaloa), *José J. Araiza* (Veracruz), and Víctor Rendón (Yucatán). Names of the seven legislators that voted against the reform of Articles 82 and 83 are italicized. Names of members of the Allied Socialist Bloc are bolded.

Obregonistas followed precedent set during the de la Huerta rebellion, when over a hundred Cooperatist legislators were expelled from the Chamber of Deputies.[103]

The Obregonistas in the legislature gave numerous justifications for the purge of their colleagues in 1927. Among others was that "the accused have shown with various acts their association with elements that soak the nation with the blood of their brothers."[104] The anti-reelectionists were also charged with deviating from the path of legality in favor of violence, because they knew they could not win legally, and with opposing the reforms of Articles 82 and 83 because they didn't want to give the voters of Mexico the ability to express their desire for Obregón's return at the polls. The Obregonistas argued that it was unconscionable to have traitorous spies installed in the heart of the federal government, protected by federal *fueros*.

In the same session, the Chamber also passed a resolution to form a special commission, charged with emphasizing the legislature's absolute solidarity with the executive branch: "This commission should approach the President of the Republic and make manifest to him that all of the members of the parliamentary majority are of course ready to give all of their personal support and all of that of the members of their respective districts to the maintenance of the public peace."[105] The National Anti-reelectionist Party had insisted in its platform, published that June, that the executive branch respect the federal legislature as the true representation of the popular will, an appeal that looks especially prescient in retrospect.[106]

The Obregonista legislator Manlio Fabio Altamirano of Veracruz argued that some of the difficulties Mexico faced in 1927 were the result of Obregón and Calles having shown too much leniency with the Delahuertistas and their sympathizers three years before, and the rebellious elements in Mexico having therefore failed to learn their lesson. Altamirano evidently disregarded that Gómez, Serrano and Vidal had all actively fought against that rebellion. While many de la Huerta supporters and lower-level leaders had lost their lives, Adolfo de la Huerta and

---

103 FAPECFT-CDEEUM, expediente 090101: AGREGADO MILITAR DE ESTADOS UNIDOS, LEGAJO: 2/6. Fojas:, inventario 32. Summary of Intelligence no. 323, February 27, 1924.

104 "Diario de los Debates de la Cámara de Diputados." Legislatura XXXII – Año II – Período Ordinario – October 4, 1927 – Número de Diario 15.

105 Ibid. For biographical details on Altamirano, see Camp, *Mexican Political Biographies, 1884–1935*, 10.

106 "Plataforma de acción política del Partido Nacional Antireeleccionista." June 1927. "Partidos políticos," ed. Victoria Lerner and Berta Ulloa, *Planes en la nación mexicana, Libro 8: 1920–1940* (México, D.F.: Senado de la República, 1987), http://biblio.juridicas.unam.mx/libros/libro.htm?l=2983.

Jorge Prieto Laurens had escaped to safety in exile in the United States. (Indeed, de la Huerta outlived Calles by ten years, and Obregón by twenty-seven.) This time, Calles and Obregón were intent on ensuring that no quarter of organized political dissent remained in the army or within the branches of the federal government, particularly in the context of Obregón's ongoing presidential campaign. This was all the more pressing considering the geographic range of anti-reelectionist sentiment and influence. The understandably frightened legislators that remained were unanimous in their assent to the proposed expulsions of their anti-reelectionist colleagues, as well as in their efforts to rush to reiterate their own unconditional loyalty to the Sonorans.

Calles' ongoing public silence regarding reelection left his true disposition on the matter open to interpretation by both sides. Altamirano mused:

What the candidates Gómez and Serrano would have given for President Calles to have lost his equanimity and his rectitude that have characterized all of his acts, to have become a Carranza, the head of a political party, to lean to the side of Obregón. What these two candidates would have given to have a concrete charge of partiality to make against the President of the Republic and to be able to raise their banner of rebellion with good reason! But that could never happen, because the President of the Republic has always taken special care to maintain his impartiality.[107]

The Obregonista legislators stressed that Calles' silence when it came to the matter of reelection was not out of any sympathy for the anti-reelectionists, but rather, was motivated by his dedication to democratic principles and his unwillingness to interfere with the presidential campaign. Laborista Ricardo Treviño mocked the anti-reelectionists for claiming that Obregón's campaign represented an imposition, when the presidential race was just getting underway. "The rebellion has had no other object than to overthrow the President of the Republic," he declared. He went on to argue that it had always been obvious "to the whole world" that the anti-reelectionist movement was going to become an armed rebellion.[108]

In the Southeast, in the weeks and months following the deaths of the leaders of the Chiapas Socialist Party, Tomás Garrido Canabal began to push his version of Socialism across state lines and into Chiapas, as he actively supported the formation of ligas de resistencia there. By November of 1927, there were new ligas established just across the border, in Vidal's hometown, Pichucalco, and Salto de Agua, with Garrido's blessing and

107 "Diario de los Debates de la Cámara de Diputados." Legislatura XXXII – Año II – Período Ordinario – October 4, 1927 – Número de Diario 15.
108 Ibid.

presumably his assistance.[109] Garrido now sought to supplant one variant of southeastern Socialism with another at the regional level, permanently. For Garrido, this was an extension of the same political battles he had already been waging for years in other forums: against the upstart, opposition gubernatorial campaigns of Belisario Carrillo and Arturo Jiménez de Lara in Tabasco, in defiance of his political will at the state level, and against Vidal and the anti-reelectionists at the national level, in defiance of Obregón. But Garrido was now just one of many Mexican politicians who staked a great deal on controlling and leading "Socialism" as a political brand.

Conclusions

In July of 1928, shortly after being reelected, Álvaro Obregón was assassinated by José de León Toral, a young artist and religious fanatic, in protest at Obregón's complicity in the waging of the war against the Catholic Church during Calles' term. Conspiracy theories about Toral's possible patrons and co-conspirators abounded. Some people believed that Calles himself arranged the assassination. Others blamed Luis Morones, and still others contended that the surviving anti-reelectionists arranged it as retribution for the deaths of their leaders.[110] Whatever the truth was, if Calles had harbored any ambitions to return to power himself, these were definitively quashed.[111] The constitution was subsequently re-amended to conform to Madero's precept of no reelection. Ironically, Obregón's triumph in 1928 contributed to a strengthened commitment in Mexico to prohibit presidential reelection that remains in force today.

Obregón's reelection efforts marked the end of the era of collaboration between Calles and the Socialists of the Southeast. Although Calles sided with Obregón and brutally crushed the anti-reelectionist movement, this moment of averted crisis for the federal government left indelible marks on the course of Mexico's politics thereafter. There is no evidence to suggest that the Gómez-Serrano rebellion of 1927 ever posed a serious threat to Calles' government; an anti-reelectionist coup either never came together, or it was so poorly planned that it almost instantly came apart. Its speedy

109 See, for example, the liga de resistencia in Pichucalco, Vidal's hometown, which already existed by the end of October, just weeks after Vidal was killed: AGN-TGC, c. 115, exp. 7. Roberto Ortiz to Federico Martínez Rojas, October 31, 1927. See also Benjamin's discussion of this and of the conflict between Vidal and Garrido more broadly. Benjamin, *A Rich Land, a Poor People*, 176–77.
110 Buchenau, *Plutarco Elías Calles*, 143–45.
111 Some historians assert that Calles and Obregón had forged a secret pact in 1923 to support one another in taking turns returning to the presidency. See Meyer, "La diarquía (1924–1928)." 195–96.

defeat almost certainly did not require the murder of its leaders, but the extreme violence that Calles meted out to the anti-reelectionists was not random or capricious. It was an essential element of the confrontation over Obregón's reelection and is key to its historical significance. In leading the anti-reelectionist charge, Carlos Vidal became a liability to Calles for the same reasons he had once been an asset. His threat was precisely in his expertise at popular organizing through institutional channels – first honed in the service of his gubernatorial campaign in 1920, then as an organizer of irregular forces to defend the government during the de la Huerta rebellion, then as the leader of Chiapas Socialism, and briefly as governor. Serrano stood little if any chance of becoming president, but Vidal had the experience and proven ability to muster popular support for his candidacy, and possibly even armed popular support for a coup. No one knew this better than Calles.

Whether that threat was imminent, or even likely, mattered little. It was a time when Calles was in no mood for new popular challenges to his authority, as the Cristero War ramped up and showed no signs of abating. Southeastern Socialism had long intrigued Calles, precisely because of the power and popular legitimacy he saw that it could bequeath its leaders. Calles' choice to support Obregón's reelection doomed Chiapas Socialism and its leaders not just because they were on the wrong side of the conflict over presidential succession, but because the outcome of that conflict signaled a growing consensus among Mexico's political leaders behind the more authoritarian outlook shared by Obregón and Tomás Garrido Canabal, also labeled as "Socialist."

Although the Obregonista Socialists flirted with the southeastern model of organizing their partisans in 1926, they made no concerted effort to substantiate their stated aspirations for long-term, productive collaboration with popular constituencies. The Mexican Labor Party came a good deal closer to achieving that, but often did so by coopting preexisting local political parties organized by the likes of the southeastern Socialists. Further, the PLM leadership declared that the organization would support Obregón's return to power, irrespective of its inability to forge consensus on a presidential candidate among its own rank and file. It was Vidal who first attempted to put the southeastern Socialist model of grassroots constituency building into practice at the national level, in his failed effort to build an opposition coalition in support of Serrano and to defend the principle of "no reelection."

Although Serrano was not a Socialist, it is possible that Vidal did so precisely to obstruct the cooptation of Socialism as he understood it by those who sought to use it as political cover for a turn back toward caudillismo, or even outright authoritarianism. In an August press release, Vidal lamented not only the imposition of Obregón, but that with Obregonista control of both houses of the legislature, over a dozen governorships, various cabinet ministries, and several other important government offices, "it is impossible to triumph democratically in a presidential election, because the real pueblo is not part of any of these."[112] He anticipated that imposition of candidates for the next legislature would follow. Although Vidal failed, the applicability of the southeastern model of party building to national politics, with or without electoral democracy, was established by 1927.

The open question was whether a multi-party system would ever be able to take root in Mexico. The anti-reelectionists had made their case for one, while the Obregonistas, hewing more closely to Garrido's more authoritarian version of southeastern Socialism, moved toward a single party-dominated system. When Obregón was campaigning for reelection, he declared that once he was back in office, the ideal he envisioned for Mexico would be a two-party system, with the opposition subsidized by the government.[113] A loyal, dependent opposition party was one thing, but the prospect of facing a sincere opposition party with an organized popular base of support like the one Vidal had tried to organize was another matter entirely.

In the wake of the Gómez-Serrano rebellion, opposition politicians were hunted down and executed, and many of those who survived were forced out of their elected offices. The purges that Obregón and Calles carried out of both the Mexican legislature and the military in 1927 effectively left no opposition candidates standing, or at least either terrified any potential dissenters that remained into perpetual silence or drove them into exile.[114] Subsequently, with the discrediting of Morones and the CROM and PLM in the wake of Obregón's assassination, another potentially strong national political party was effectively disarmed. In sum, Calles' establishment of a single party-dominated political system in 1928 was made possible by Calles and Obregón's brutal, purposeful crushing of a nascent multi-party system in 1927. Obregón's assassination the following year was not the catalyst for the end of the "era of caudillos," as Calles would argue, but rather, the era's coda. Nor was Calles' foundation of the PNR a response to a vacuum of postrevolutionary political institutions in Mexico but rather, the product of a bloody fight over the character of its institutions and who would control them.

---

112 FAPECFT-FFT, fondo: 3, serie: 010212, expediente: 24: BOLETINES DE PRENSA, legajo 1/2, foja 19, inventario: 880. Press release by Vidal, August 19, 1927.

113 Dulles, *Yesterday in Mexico*, 335–36. In 1928, Calles proposed a nominally two-party system to accommodate (and politically incapacitate) conservative Catholics. See Buchenau, *Plutarco Elías Calles*, 147.

114 Camp argues that the killing of Serrano and his entourage was decisively important for Mexican politics moving forward because it served as a cautionary tale for generals with political ambitions and for civilians considering supporting them. Roderic Ai Camp, *Generals in the Palacio: The Military in Modern Mexico* (New York, NY: Oxford University Press, 1992), 80.

7

A Nation of Parties

The material and moral reorganization of the political order can only result from the action, and from the interaction of real political parties ... It is the responsibility of the Party to correct the political errors that the Revolution has committed.

Plutarco Elías Calles, May 22, 1929

During the 1920s, Plutarco Elías Calles and Álvaro Obregón stood together through many moments of peril and near-disasters for the federal government. Most critically, they survived Adolfo de la Huerta's rebellion against them. They also collaborated to face various other political and military crises throughout the decade. On several occasions, they crushed political and popular movements that might have grown powerful enough to present real challenges to their power, sometimes violently so. They used the new political order mandated by the 1917 Constitution to change how politics were done in Mexico, but they also demonstrated the flexibility of the rules of governance that the revolutionary charter outlined. They artfully manipulated gray areas of both legality and the accepted practice of politics to their own advantage as they saw fit, but conformed strictly to constitutional law and established practice when it was to their benefit. While they never publicly wavered in their alliance, by the end of the 1920s, real political differences between Obregón and Calles were becoming clear, enough so that some dissidents were willing to bet everything on their possible estrangement. Carlos Vidal and Francisco Serrano evidently both went to their graves believing that Calles was privately opposed to Obregón's reelection. They may well have been right, but they failed to appreciate that it was irrelevant. Calles' would not make such a dramatic break with Obregón while he was still alive.

Obregón's assassination in July of 1928 changed everything. In response, Calles gave his most famous speech, in which he declared that Mexico must cease to have "governments of caudillos." For all of the effusive praise that Calles and his allies lavished on the murdered president-elect, Calles' speech declaring the need for political institutions was a repudiation of not just caudillismo in general, but also of Obregón's legacy more specifically. Calles carefully cast Obregón's assassination and its destructive potential as the most powerful indictment of the political system that the deceased had endorsed. With rumors swirling about his own role in the assassination and the political class and the legislature still saturated with Obregonistas, this was a delicate political balancing act that was critical to Calles' own political survival.[1]

Obregón had consistently sought to destroy parties that opposed him and to handicap the ones that supported him in any activities beyond helping him to win election. In 1919 he had argued for the creation of a party that would unite all revolutionary factions, but by the mid-1920s he was more circumspect; the National Cooperatist Party's ability to marshal a convincing political threat to him leading up to the de la Huerta rebellion was almost certainly a particularly important object lesson. Three years later Obregón was happy to accept the support of the Alliance of Socialist Parties when he needed its members in the legislature to reform the constitution to allow him to run for reelection, but the Alliance tellingly didn't survive for long after its central purpose was achieved.[2] Following the Gómez-Serrano affair but not yet reelected to the presidency, Obregón preemptively moved to further concentrate power in his own hands once he reassumed the office, independent of any party, using his influence in the legislature to encourage the passage of a series of reforms that would give the president greater control over the judiciary, the legislature, and local government in the Federal District, ostensibly in order to reduce corruption.[3]

Obregón's death was unforeseeable, but Calles' famous speech was not an improvised response to a sudden power vacuum. Calles had spent the 1920s observing and building alliances with the southeastern Socialists and the CROM (and others), and while he did not always share their ideological commitments or long-term reformist goals, he had come to see political parties as Mexico's way forward. Although Calles evidently had no intention of fully relinquishing his own power, he was convinced that the power of individuals must be wielded through political institutions. Calles therefore recognized Obregón's assassination as a moment of political

1 On the ongoing dominance of the Obregonistas in the legislature in this period, see Dulles, *Yesterday in Mexico*, 379–81.

2 On the significance of Obregón's own party, the Liberal Constitutionalist Party (PLC) in the late 1910s, and on Obregón's relationship with the National Agrarista Party (PNA), see Garrido, *El Partido de la Revolución Institucionalizada*, 38, 40, 45-46. For a detailed discussion of the Socialist Alliance and its dissolution, see Mac Gregor Campuzano, "Partidos nacionales y programas políticos en México, 1918–1928," 247–72.

3 Medina Peña, *Hacia el nuevo estado*, 67. Medina Peña argues that this was a veiled criticism of Calles as Obregón consolidated his power.

opportunity. He argued: "The same circumstance that Mexico confronts, perhaps for the first time in its history, in which the predominant feature is the lack of 'caudillos,' should permit us, will permit us, to guide national politics down the path of institutional life."[4] He underscored that Obregón's death "intensified problems and needs of the political order that already existed."[5] After giving the most famous speech of his life, Calles exited the Chamber of Deputies surrounded by bodyguards, a none-too subtle reminder to observers of the very high human cost of caudillo politics.[6]

Obregón's suspicion and antipathy toward political parties when he was still alive turned out to be an asset for Calles in his efforts to form a unified party out of a heterogeneous and often fractious political class. In spite of Obregón's political preeminence up to the time of his assassination and Calles' reputation as the political puppet master of Mexico in the years that followed, national political power was not fully concentrated in the Sonorans' hands. The bitter struggle over Obregón's reelection makes this clear, as do the negotiations Calles had to engage in with Obregonistas following his death. Nor was there a lack of potentially viable opposition parties or candidates, as we have seen. However, the Sonorans' systematic decimation of the organized opposition to Obregón's reelection before his assassination helped to clear the way for Calles' establishment of the PNR. At their first convention, the party's founders acknowledged that their political project was possible in part thanks to the "elimination and purification" the Revolution had carried out on itself.[7]

The case that Calles made for political institutionalization and his creation of the National Revolutionary Party (PNR) was a reflection of Mexico's political reality as he understood it. In order to arrange the interim presidential succession of Emilio Portes Gil following Obregón's assassination, Calles had to negotiate with the Obregonista bloc in the legislature; in lieu of national parties, legislative blocs fulfilled their functions in many respects.[8] It must also be understood in light of Calles' particular political development over the course of the previous decade. The Socialist Southeast had provided Calles with both inspiration and valuable lessons. Above all, his collaboration with southeastern Socialist parties had helped him to solidify a crucial base of support in a region that

4 Calles, *Pensamiento político y social: antología (1913–1936)*, 240–51. "El camino hacia la más alta y respetada nación de instituciones y leyes." Annual presidential report, September 1, 1928.

5 Partido Nacional Revolucionario, *La democracia social en México: Historia de la Convención nacional revolucionaria, Constitución del P.N.R., Sucesión presidencial de 1929* (México, D.F.: Partido Nacional Revolucionario, 1929), 17.

6 Dulles, *Yesterday in Mexico*, 386.

7 Partido Nacional Revolucionario, *La democracia social en México*, 35–36.

8 For a discussion of these negotiations, see Medina Peña, *Hacia el nuevo estado*, 69–70.

had been all but impossible for both Obregón and Carranza to control. Calles' alliances with the Socialists of the Southeast remained an indispensable asset to him following Obregón's assassination, as he threaded a political needle in his efforts to control the situation and to avoid further upheaval or coups, whether by restless generals or aggrieved Obregonistas (or both).[9] This chapter examines the political aftermath of Obregón's assassination, and the long-term political trends that culminated in Calles' creation of Mexico's first "official" party of the state in 1929. It then traces the influences of southeastern Socialism on Mexican national and regional politics over the course of the 1920s, and the ways that this was reflected in both the design and political practices of the PNR and its local affiliate organizations. Lastly, it considers the many, immense challenges of putting this new political system into practice at both the local and national levels.

Mexican Socialism at the National Level, c. 1928

The creation of the PNR in 1929 was consonant with the advent of mass politics elsewhere in the world at the time, and coincided with the emergence of political parties in Latin America and elsewhere that were created to address similarly unprecedented demands of politicians by popular constituencies. Scholars have long speculated about the international influences on Calles' design of the PNR, particularly by political parties in the United States and Western Europe. While the formation of the PNR by no means occurred in political or ideological isolation, the party was carefully tailored to Mexico's postrevolutionary context and followed Mexican precedents established over the previous fifteen years. Nor was it the first time the creation of a unified national "revolutionary" party had been proposed in Mexico: Salvador Alvarado was one of the first to do so, a decade earlier.[10]

The unusually heterogeneous and regionalized character of the Mexican Revolution and its status as one of the first social revolutions of the twentieth century required new and creative solutions for forging an enduring postrevolutionary peace and a stable political system. In founding the PNR, Calles took a middle course between the personalist authoritarianism that Obregón had increasingly favored and the institutionalization of a party system that resembled the ones he had closely observed in the Southeast. He had assembled a coalition of political parties and factions to support his

9 Pedro Salmerón Sanginés, "La fundación (1928–1933)," in *El Partido de la revolución: institución y conflicto, 1928–1999*, ed. Miguel González Compeán, Leonardo Lomelí, and Pedro Salmerón Sanginés (México, D.F.: Fondo de Cultura Económica, 2000), 45–46.

10 FAPECFT-FAO, serie: 20700, expediente A-2 30: ALVARADO, Salvador (Gral.), legajo 1, fojas 4–22, inventario: 778. Open letter from Alvarado to Carranza, Obregón, and Pablo González, August 13, 1919.

presidential campaign in 1923–24, and then constructed other coalitions behind various initiatives once he was president. The PNR now assembled a diverse collection of allies in a more permanent fashion, relatively loosely bound together by mutual need more than any ideological affinity. The party of the Revolution began its long career as a hierarchical network of organizations that obviated the laborious process of convening allies for particular purposes on an ad hoc basis, which had become the standard operating procedure for national politicians during the 1920s. However, it soon became clear that Calles' adoption of the Socialist model came with further modifications. Above all, while the party was happy to accept organized popular support and praised the social justice ambitions of its affiliates, in practice, it did not prioritize the remediation of socioeconomic inequality. Nor did it insist on the enfranchisement of historically marginalized groups, particularly women, as its southeastern predecessors had done.

The PNR's stated mission belied the influence on Calles and others of observing both failures and successes in party building in preceding years. The party's organizers declared that they sought to conglomerate political parties and other groups at the state and regional levels, particularly those focused on the interests of workers and campesinos, and that the party would be dedicated to the betterment of the lives of Mexico's "popular masses."[11] This was the same solution the southeastern Socialists had crafted ten years earlier to harness the diverse revolutionary ambitions of broad and heterogeneous cross-class constituencies, but on a much larger scale.

It made strategic sense, as political parties proliferated at the local and regional levels in Mexico in the 1920s. By one estimate, they numbered at least 8,000 – most of them operating only at the local level, many highly personalist, and few having any institutional substance or staying power.[12] However, this period of intensive party creation also included a second generation of local Socialist parties as Socialism gained broad currency as a political brand across Mexico, particularly as the Socialist Alliance was near the peak of its power in the legislature in 1926.[13] Many of these new parties took direct inspiration from earlier southeastern examples, and

11 "Proyecto de programa de principios y de estatutos que el comité organizador del Partido Nacional Revolucionario somete a la consideración de las agrupaciones que concurrirán a la Gran Convención de Querétaro," January 1929. See also Córdova, *La Revolución en crisis*, 54–55.

12 Jean A. Meyer, Enrique Krauze, and Cayetano Reyes García, *Estado y sociedad con Calles*, Historia de la Revolución Mexicana, vol. 11: Período 1924–1928 (México, D.F.: El Colegio de México, 1977), 97. Meyer, Krauze, and Reyes García argue that nearly all of these parties lacked in any true institutional substance, beyond representing the ambitions of a particular politician.

13 Fowler-Salamini describes regional Socialist parties of this period as "not truly mass-based parties but rather structures which sought to bring together loose, constantly shifting, populist, middle-class and lower-class coalitions." Fowler-Salamini, "De-Centering the 1920s," 327.

some named themselves for Felipe Carrillo Puerto.[14] Despite differences in their ideologies, strategies, and the demographics of their constituencies, Socialist parties of this era commonly shared the objectives of land and labor reform; land redistribution; the expansion of public (and especially rural) education; social programs for indigenous people, campesinos, workers and children; the expansion of political rights for women; and the application of federal anticlerical laws. Like the southeastern Socialist parties, nearly all of these new organizations cited full compliance with and enactment of the 1917 Constitution, particularly of articles 27 and 123, as their central rationales.

Most prominent among them was Emilio Portes Gil's Frontier Socialist Party in Tamaulipas, which took inspiration from the Socialist Party of the Southeast of Yucatán in particular, and was founded in 1924 with Calles' support and blessing. By the time he became interim president of Mexico in 1928, Portes Gil had extensive experience forging institutionalized relationships between local parties and multi-class constituencies dating back to the late 1910s, although notably, his record of support for organized workers and campesinos was relatively weak, particularly compared to the Yucatecan example. Still, Calles' choice of Portes Gil to succeed him in the presidency in 1928 can and has been read as a ratification of Calles' ongoing favoritism toward relative radicals, even at a delicate time of marked political polarization.[15] Portes Gil would further bring this experience to bear in his capacity as a two-term PNR president in the 1930s.[16]

Examples from various regions demonstrate how many things "Socialism" meant in different contexts, in spite of a core of shared traits, as a loose interpretation of Socialist ideas and institutional forms was adapted to heterogeneous local circumstances. In 1926, the United Independent Party of Aguascalientes and Felipe Carrillo Puerto Party (of the same state) declared in their shared founding statutes their dedication to the betterment of the lives of workers and especially campesinos, and bringing an end to their economic exploitation via the creation of ligas for campesinos and consumer

14 Local organizations across Mexico honored Carrillo Puerto as their namesake following his death. See, for example, the local affiliate of the PNR in Veracruz that bore his name in 1930: FAPECFT-PEC, expediente: 218: CRUZ, Cesareo, legajo 1, fojas 4–5, inventario 1234. Cesáreo Cruz to Calles, May 5, 1930. Towns and neighborhoods across Mexico were also named for him.

15 See, for example, Frank R. Brandenburg, *The Making of Modern Mexico* (Englewood Cliffs, NJ: Prentice-Hall, 1964), 63. Tzvi Medin argues that Portes Gil encouraged Calles to marginalize Morones and the CROM. See Tzvi Medin, *El minimato presidencial: historia política del maximato (1928–1935)* (México, D.F.: Ediciones Era, 1982), 32.

16 Fowler-Salamini, "De-Centering the 1920s," 311–16. At least two local political clubs that belonged to the Partido Socialista Fronterizo took Carrillo Puerto as their namesake. See "Partido Socialista Fronterizo: programa y estatutos," May 15–17, 1924. Joel Hernández Santiago, Victoria Lerner, and Berta Ulloa, *Planes en la nación mexicana, Libro 8: 1920–1940* (México, D.F.: Senado de la República, 1987), http://biblio.juridicas.unam.mx/libros/libro.htm?l=2983.

cooperatives. They hoped to unite all of the revolutionary elements of Aguascalientes to pursue their common political goals, and to ensure that the state be led by conscientious revolutionaries.[17] On May Day two years later, the Independent Party declared its intent to organize a statewide Liga of Workers and Campesinos.[18] In 1925, the Socialist Party of Morelos, the Free Morelos Party, and the Party of Workers and Campesinos (of Morelos) likewise declared their intent to unify the workers and campesinos of their state in an organization called the Socialist Liga de Resistencia of the Campesinos of Morelos.[19] In Nayarit, the Socialist Party of the West emphasized the formation of cooperatives for producers and consumers, agricultural credit, and the restoration of ejidal collectives as central among its goals.[20] The Benito Juárez Socialist Party in Oaxaca made clear that it was above all an organization that represented its working class members against their habitual abusers, declaring that "politics will be nothing more than a defense against false leaders, mystifiers of justice and immoral people who rely on money to corrupt authorities and legislators."[21]

Like the Socialists of the Southeast, Socialist parties that emerged elsewhere in this period typically did not seek to destroy or even to undermine capitalism, but rather to harness it for the greater good of the nation and a broader swath of its population than in previous eras. In 1926, the Revolutionary Socialist Confederation of Puebla listed among its objectives "to bring about a true improvement for the working classes, the proletariat, which includes campesinos, workers and the middle class, not through hatred for capital, the existence of which takes from the wellbeing of the Nation, but through the legitimate defense of the workers against whatever entity attacks them."[22] That same year, the Socialist Party of the Federal District declared its intent to focus its energies principally on the middle class, a marked departure from the relatively more radical and adamantly popular goals of its predecessors that was tellingly not understood as a contradiction in terms.[23]

---

17   "Nuestros Estatuos. Partidos Unidos 'Independiente Aguascalentense' y 'Felipe Carrillo Puerto'. Aguascalientes," May 27, 1926. Hernández Santiago, Lerner, and Ulloa, *Planes en la nación mexicana, Libro 8: 1920–1940*.

18   "Programa Político y de Gobierno del Partido 'Independiente Aguascalientes.'" May 1, 1928. Ibid.

19   "Partidos Socialista Morelense, Libre Morelense y de Obreros y Campesinos." November 22, 1925. Ibid.

20   "Partido Socialista de Occidente" (Nayarit). June 8, 1927. Ibid.

21   In his examination of Socialism in the 1920s in Oaxaca, Smith argues that governor Genaro V. Vásquez was more radical in his rhetoric than in his political practice, particularly when it came to his policies regarding Oaxaca's large indigenous population. Smith, *Pistoleros and Popular Movements*, 38–39.

22   "Partido Socialista Benito Juárez" (Ejutla de Crespo, Oaxaca), May 28, 1926. Hernández Santiago, Lerner, and Ulloa, *Planes en la nación mexicana, Libro 8: 1920–1940*.

23   "Programa del Partido Socialista del Distrito Federal, México, D.F." February 5, 1926. Ibid.

Many of the Socialist parties of this period articulated the need to work in conjunction with other like-minded parties and organizations in pursuit of their political and social goals at the state level, prefiguring the work of the PNR to conglomerate preexisting, allied organizations within its nationwide organization.[24] By 1926, the state of Puebla was home to two different alliances of local Socialist parties.[25] Others parties were formed in this period as affiliates of the PLM, which was busy expanding its own local, state, and regional presence across Mexico in the mid-1920s, providing another important precedent for the cooptation of smaller organizations within a national party.[26] While most of these state- and regional-level confederations had little national impact or long-term significance, the experience politicians gained with local confederations of parties helped to lay the groundwork for the transition they would soon make to joining a national political confederation.[27]

Calles' formation of the PNR was a culmination of these long-term trends, as Mexico's political class embraced and selectively borrowed from the rhetoric, institutional design, and organizational strategies of regional Socialist parties. "Socialism" soon became the self-selected label of most of the competing blocs of politicians in Mexico City as a marker of revolutionary credentials, irrespective of the political programs they supported. By the time the formation of the PNR was announced, Mexican politicians already had years of experience with the kind of alliance and coalition building that it required to function. It also didn't hurt Calles' cause that for most Mexican politicians, by the end of the 1920s there were many obvious advantages of joining the PNR, rather than struggling against it. Borrowing from Tomás Garrido Canabal's playbook, Calles offered Mexican politicians a rhetorically compelling but ultimately vague set of shared goals to pursue, and sharply reminded them that their common enemies sought to exploit their disunity as their greatest weakness.

The principle enemy in question was still the Catholic Church. The PNR's anticlericalism was the closest it came to an ironclad ideological commitment, but this too was pragmatic, and employed by its leadership

---

24 See, for example, "El consejo central del 'Partido Socialista del Estado de Durango." February 4, 1926 and "Confederación Renovadora de Partidos Revolucionarios de Jalisco." February 17, 1928. Ibid.

25 "Alianza de Partidos Socialistas del Estado de Puebla," April 29, 1926 and "Confederación Revolucionaria Socialista del Estado de Puebla,* May 18, 1926. Ibid.

26 See, for example, "Partido Revolucionario Coahuilense" (Coahuila), June 12, 1926 and "Partido Independiente 'Felipe Rivera' pro Zincunegui Tercero" (Michoacán). April 22, 1926. Ibid.

27 See, for example, the Confederation of Socialist Parties of Oaxaca (CPSO), founded in 1926. Smith argues that this state level confederation was initially relatively politically weak, but laid important groundwork for the corporatist political system that did take hold in Oaxaca in subsequent years. Smith, *Pistoleros and Popular Movements*, 38–41, 46–51.

as a unifying tactic. The still-ongoing war between the Church and the Mexican state in those years was of decisive importance in shaping Calles' perspectives and long-term political goals, and the way that other politicians responded to them. Calles argued that the most urgent, but ultimately conquerable, political obstacle that Mexico faced was the enduring threat of a conservative (Catholic) reaction against the Mexican Revolution. Yet, as he advised the political class, this was a threat with no chance against them if they remained productively unified.[28] He declared at the PNR's first convention: "I could not honorably go on if I didn't insist on the dangers to all order that could result from the disunion of the revolutionary family."[29]

With the Cristero conflict ongoing, without Obregón, and still without a roadmap for how to move forward even if unified, these comments amounted to a particularly effective scare tactic that Calles leveraged to his advantage. Fears of reactionary clerics and their influence over the Mexican populace lingered within the political class long after an end to the church–state conflict was negotiated in 1929.[30] The PNR served as Calles' comfort to his allies in the face of that perceived, ongoing threat to all that they had achieved. He wrote to Manuel Pérez Treviño in September of 1929: "The clergy will undertake new activities and schemes against the Revolution, but there is no cause to be alarmed, for I have the utmost confidence that we will defeat them in whatever arena in which they appear."[31] The December 1, 1928 manifesto announcing the creation of the PNR included political polarization as one of its central justifications: us versus them, the revolution versus the reaction.[32] So did the political programs of some of its state-level affiliates.[33] Surely this would have been familiar posturing to anyone who had lived in the state of Tabasco since Garrido first took power there, particularly considering the anticlericalism,

---

28 Benjamin argues that Calles had already been working toward a symbolic unification of revolutionary leaders and factions for several years by the time he founded the PNR. Benjamin, *La Revolución*, 73–74.

29 Partido Nacional Revolucionario, *La democracia social en México*, 29.

30 Fallaw argues that in the 1930s, during the "Segunda Cristiada," "soft targets" like ejidos and federal schools were the objects of attacks by the Church's defenders, rather than the state itself, or the army. Fallaw, *Religion and State Formation*, 6.

31 FAPECFT-FPEC, serie 10803, expediente 38: PEREZ TREVINO, Manuel, legajo 1/1, foja 3, inventario 1795. Calles to Manuel Pérez Treviño, September 30, 1929.

32 "Primer Manifiesto del Comité Organizador del Partido Nacional Revolucionario," December 1, 1928. See also Dulles, *Yesterday in Mexico*, 410.

33 See, for example, the Socialist Labor Party of the State of Mexico, which in 1929 declared that it would work tirelessly to make sure the government didn't come to be controlled by reactionary elements, and prohibited anyone who had "betrayed the Revolution" from membership. "Partido Socialista del Trabajo del Estado de México." January 1, 1929. Hernández Santiago, Lerner, and Ulloa, *Planes en la nación mexicana, Libro 8: 1920–1940*.

both stated and unstated, that was deeply embedded in the new party's mission.

In most other respects, Calles' adaptation of the Southeastern Socialists' blueprint entailed tempering their radicalism, consonant with a moderation of Calles' own radicalism by the end of the decade. This was not just a matter of cynicism or political retrenchment (although it certainly contained elements of both), but another case of pragmatism by Calles and his allies.[34] Strategies for coordinating between competing factions of allies and mustering broad, cross-class support for elite-led reform projects that had been made to work on a local scale were exponentially more difficult to implement at the national level. As the experience of regional Socialist parties demonstrated, this was no mean feat at the state or regional levels either, even in places like the Southeast that were relatively untouched by the Cristero uprising. Even if there had been a critical mass of support for far-reaching social, and economic reform among Callistas in 1929, practice would have been another matter, particularly after the onset of the Great Depression.[35] This was all the more true once uniting the Mexican political class within a single partisan alliance became Calles' foremost priority.

Building the Machine

The PNR's first convention was held in the city of Querétaro in March of 1929, attended by approximately nine hundred delegates who represented existing political parties from across Mexico, including the Socialist parties of Tabasco and Yucatán.[36] Like the Socialist parties of the Southeast, the party was designed to be the institutional expression of Mexico's revolution: a taming of the conflicts that had ravaged the country for nearly two decades by that time, but also a harnessing of the political potential of the emotions the Revolution continued to evoke in both politicians and their constituents, however abstractly "revolution" was defined.

The leaders of the PNR saw the emergence of regional political parties as part of a new and necessary phase in Mexico's democratic evolution and

34 On this point, see also Arnaldo Córdova, *La Revolución en crisis: la aventura de maximato* (México, D.F.: Aguilar, León y Cal, 1995), 60. Córdova argues that the PNR charter was "a programmatic platform that was essentially conservative and stabilizing, in which the principles of social justice and popular redemption were recognized only to subordinate them to the economic development of the nation."

35 Marjorie Becker's work on Catholic resistance to revolutionary reform in Michoacán makes this particularly clear. More recently, Fallaw's examination of Catholic political responses and resistance to state-led initiatives in the 1930s demonstrates how much of a challenge the religious question posed for the postrevolutionary state, even after the single party-dominated system was relatively well consolidated. Becker, *Setting the Virgin on Fire*. Fallaw, *Religion and State Formation*.

36 Dulles, *Yesterday in Mexico*, 427. Buchenau, *Plutarco Elías Calles*, 150.

political organization. The design of their new party was meant to emulate statewide confederations of local political organizations, in order to better address the most pressing needs and issues of Mexico as a whole, in a national joint effort. They acknowledged the difficulties that previous national parties had in establishing themselves as lasting institutions, that Mexico's regionalism had always been a problem for aspiring national parties, and that imposition of political programs from the center out to the periphery had never been successful. They highlighted the case of the National Cooperatist Party, which had aspired to engender a new era of party politics through its outreach efforts to municipal governments and electoral districts. They attributed the Cooperatists' failure to their lack of effective cooperation with regional political parties. By contrast, the PNR's raison d'être was to serve as "a mechanism of vigilance, expression and support" of the Mexican Revolution that would bring about peace and equilibrium between "the living forces of the nation."[37]

Yet popular organizations were conspicuously not included in the hierarchy of the PNR, with the exception of unions and ligas de resistencia belonging to local affiliate parties.[38] Concomitantly, workers lost their representation within Calles' inner circle with the discrediting of Morones and the CROM following Obregón's assassination.[39] For its framers, and for Calles most of all, the PNR was a means of resolving ongoing political dilemmas and preventing the kind of intra-elite strife that had regularly destabilized Mexico in the 1920s, not a mechanism for redistributing land, resources, or power. The Socialist parties of the Southeast (and elsewhere too, by 1929) had demonstrated the political value of institutionalized alliances with organized popular constituencies. Calles himself had extensively praised them for that, but the PNR left the task to its local affiliates, hoping to reap the political benefits of grassroots support without providing working people with dedicated representation within the national organization. As historian Thomas Benjamin noted: "The lessons of the 'laboratories of the Revolution' were not entirely lost. Unfortunately it was not the methods or objectives of reform but the populist techniques of political control that were learned."[40] Embedded in the foundations of the PNR, Socialism became the way that politics was done, rather than a coherent core of reformist or ideological commitments.

---

37 Partido Nacional Revolucionario, *La democracia social en México*, 8–11, 35–36.
38 On the exclusion of popular organizations from the PNR, see Benjamin, "Laboratories of the New State," 83–84.
39 Portes Gil's Socialist Frontier Party of Tamaulipas set important precedents in this regard, as a "party of the state" that touted its representation of working people while giving them a relatively minimal role in the organization. See Fowler-Salamini, "De-Centering the 1920s," 308, 16.
40 Benjamin, "Laboratories of the New State."

The Early Days of the PNR

In its formative years, the new party was led by many people who already had experience with various forms of Socialist political organizing. Bartolomé García Correa, the leader of the PSS and soon to become the governor of Yucatán, was on the party's organizing committee.[41] Of the eight members of the PNR's executive committee in 1932, three had belonged to the Obregonista Alliance of Socialist Parties.[42] Although that short-lived organization had only shallowly adopted the elements of southeastern Socialism that had made it successful, its convention made clear how strong its influence was, particularly the precedents set by Carrillo Puerto. Perhaps most importantly, Emilio Portes Gil led the PNR in its early years after adapting the Yucatecan blueprint in support of his own Socialist political project in Tamaulipas.[43]

Like the southeastern Socialist parties, at least on paper, "democracy" was a central principle in the founding of the PNR. Garrido's reliance on the liga system as the symbolic bulwark of democratic practice in Tabasco, even as he and his collaborators sought to monopolize the political system, to systematically decimate political competition in the state, and to deemphasize individual political rights, was the most obvious and likely most important southeastern exemplar. Respect for its constituent organizations at the regional level was similarly fundamental to the PNR founders' assessment of its democratic character. Allowing for the independence and autonomy of political parties at the local level was one of the party's three guiding principles, much as Garrido often invoked the theoretical autonomy of the ligas de resistencia.[44]

In laying out the plans and the principles of the PNR in 1930, in his capacity as party president, Portes Gil was clear that it was a party of the state. "We will not mislead public opinion as it has been misled in the past, presuming that the National Revolutionary Party is an independent party," he declared. "The Revolution that becomes a government needs an

---

41 On the career of García Correa, see Ben Fallaw, "Bartolomé García Correa and the Politics of Maya Identity in Postrevolutionary Yucatán, 1911–1933," *Ethnohistory* 55, no. 4 (2008).

42 Members of the National Executive Committee of the PNR in 1932: Manuel Pérez Treviño, Fernando Moctezuma, Matias Rodríguez, Ernesto Soto Reyes, Rafael E. Melgar, Francisco A. Mayer, Juan de Dios Batiz, Lamberto Ortega. Moctezuma, Melgar and Batiz were all members of the Socialist Alliance. Partido Nacional Revolucionario, *Constitución del P.N.R.* (México, D.F.: PNR, 1932).

43 Fowler-Salamini writes that Portes Gil touted his party as "the corporatist forerunner of the PNR, and therefore functionally organized as the cardenista PRM." Fowler-Salamini, "De-Centering the 1920s," 318.

44 Partido Nacional Revolucionario, *La democracia social en México*, 73. Medina Peña underscores that the PNR constituted a difficult balance of centralization with decentralization. Medina Peña, *Hacia el nuevo estado*, 72.

authority for agitation and defense [...] the National Revolutionary Party will go to the communities so that they will organize and join the program of the revolution [...] It will be a collaborator with the government, a sincere administrative collaborator, that will support its revolutionary work."[45] Pascual Ortiz Rubio later claimed that when he was nominated as the PNR's first presidential candidate in 1929, he was made to understand by Calles that he would share power with the party if elected.[46]

In this, the PNR departed from the conventions of its southeastern Socialist predecessors. Although in all cases the Socialist parties of the Southeast had become effectively congruent with the governments they controlled, both in terms of activities and personnel, their formal independence from the states in question was always something that all of the Socialists of the region adamantly emphasized. Yet it was of course the closeness of the relationship between party and state in the southeastern model that proved most compelling for many Mexican politicians by the end of the 1920s. The content of Portes Gil's frank assessment of the extent of the "collaboration" that the PNR intended to have with the federal government was nothing new, but it was unprecedented in its transparency.

The creation of the PNR was an impressive political achievement by any measure, even well before its successors' many decades of unmatched dominance of Mexican politics could have been predicted. But the new party and the kind of politics it embodied were not without their doubters and critics in Mexico at the time, and the political unanimity the party's leaders aspired to was inevitably impossible to achieve. Even once Calles had largely appeased the restless and in some cases irate Obregonistas following Obregón's death, pockets of dissidence remained, particularly within the army. This was dramatically demonstrated in 1929 when General José Gonzalo Escobar led the last significant armed rebellion of the postrevolutionary era. As much as 28 percent of the army turned against the government, and the rebels enjoyed the support of Cristero forces in some places. By its end, the rebellion had caused 2,000 casualties and cost the government an estimated 25 million pesos.[47]

This was yet another rebellion that surprised no one in the know at the time, the last in a series that regularly punctuated the 1920s. Escobar had been a known political malcontent for some time, and openly worked to recruit other key players in politics and the military to join his conspiracy. By the time the rebellion happened, the only open questions were the form

45 Partido Nacional Revolucionario, *Nuevo sentido de la política: programa de acción, estatutos y presupuesto para 1930* (México, D.F.: Talleres tipográficos de El Nacional Revolucionario, 1930), 17–18. In this, Portes Gil followed the precedent of his own Partido Socialista Fronterizo of Tamaulipas. See Fowler-Salamini, "De-Centering the 1920s," 315–16. On Calles' circumspection on making the PNR a truly official party, see Garrido, *El Partido de la Revolución Institucionalizada*, 73.
46 Dulles, *Yesterday in Mexico*, 435.   47 Ibid., 442, 57.

Escobar's mutiny would take and its timing. As delegates prepared to nominate a presidential candidate at the PNR's organizing convention in Querétaro in March of 1929, the looming threat of a rebellion convinced many to throw their support to Pascual Ortiz Rubio, the least controversial option they could find. But powerful forces within the military were not so easily appeased. On March 3, the delegates received word that Escobar and his associates had rebelled. The Escobar rebels justified their uprising as being against the imposition of Calles' political will on Mexico from behind the scenes of the new party.[48]

The consolidation of the PNR may have been the final straw for the Escobar rebels, but the rebellion also reflected many of the same political uncertainties and discontents that had been simmering in Mexico for nearly a decade by that time. It included a conspicuously similar set of complaints and grievances to the rebellions of 1923 and 1927. Its leaders rightly saw their own political horizons inevitably foreshortened by the creation of the PNR. They chafed against the continued concentration of power in Calles' hands, much as the anti-reelectionists had opposed the prospect of Obregón's monopoly on power in 1927, and as the de la Huerta rebels had tried to prevent Obregón from installing Calles in the presidency in 1924, and as the Sonorans had condemned Carranza's imposition of his own successor before that, in 1920. In all cases, the rebels invoked what they understood to be the guiding principles of the Mexican Revolution and decried their wanton violation. The Escobar rebels' Plan de Hermosillo declared Calles to be the "Judas" of the Mexican Revolution, and called for the armed overthrow of President Emilio Portes Gil.[49] But much like the de la Huerta rebellion, this was a coup supported by a spectrum of rebellious elements united only in their distaste for the men in power and the political course they pursued, and it lacked the coherence necessary to mount a sustained national insurgency. Even so, it took three months for the rebellion to be defeated. The government's forces were led by Calles himself, who briefly took over as Secretary of War from Joaquín Amaro.

Just as happened following the defeat of the Gómez-Serrano rebellion in 1927, a purge of the federal legislature followed the military defeat of the Escobar rebels. This time, fifty-one representatives and four senators suspected of supporting the rebellion lost their seats.[50] In the long-term, the political triumph of Calles and the PNR over the mutinous generals and their supporters was just as important as the rebellion's military defeat.

48 Ibid., 424–32. See also Lorenzo Meyer, Rafael Segovia, and Alejandra Lajous, *Los inicios de la institucionalización: la política del Maximato*, Historia de la Revolución Mexicana vol. 12: Período 1928–1934 (México, D.F.: Colegio de México, 1978), 64–84.

49 "Plan de Hermosillo," March 3, 1929. Hernández Santiago, Lerner, and Ulloa, *Planes en la nación mexicana, Libro 8: 1920–1940*.

50 Loyo Camacho, *Joaquín Amaro*, 169–71.

If Calles' case that the military should have no role in Mexico's political future had not already been sufficiently made, the Escobar rebellion amply and definitively proved the point, as Calles reiterated in a speech that spring.[51] Still, the political class remained saturated with military men and revolutionary veterans for another political generation. Mexico did not have a civilian president serve a full term in the postrevolutionary era until Miguel Alemán, who took office in 1946.[52]

It soon became yet more starkly clear that political opposition to the PNR would be no more successful than armed resistance had been for Escobar, as former Secretary of Education José Vasconcelos launched a doomed opposition presidential campaign in 1929 as the candidate of the National Antireelectionist Party (a resurrection of Madero's party of the same name that had also supported Arnulfo Gómez's candidacy in 1926–27). Vasconcelos and his supporters ran an energetic campaign to win popular support for his candidacy, meeting with some of the same repressive responses the partisans of Gómez and Serrano had suffered two years earlier, including assassination of operatives. Undoubtedly with the crisis of 1927 in mind, Vasconcelos suggested that a secondary candidate be named should he be killed during the campaign, and worried that the government would cancel the election or use his campaign as a pretense to launch a military campaign against him. After outbursts of violence on Election Day in which nineteen people were killed in Mexico City, the legislature announced that Ortiz Rubio had defeated Vasconcelos by a highly unlikely margin of 1.8 million votes. In practice, this was little different from the "unanimous" elections of Socialist Tabasco. Vasconcelos refused to accept the results, but opted for exile when an armed rebellion in protest at the election failed to take shape.[53]

From the beginning then, selective use of violence and coercion when elections or other prescribed political procedures failed to achieve the PNR's desired result were part of the political system it now dominated. The object lessons of the de la Huerta rebellion and the Gómez-Serrano affair were decisive in the subsequent responses to organized opposition by the PNR and the government it controlled. So was the even more recent memory of the Escobar rebellion. For a nation and a political class exhausted by nearly two decades of war and regularly recurring episodes of political violence, the PNR offered a compelling alternative, one in

51 On Calles' speech, see Buchenau, *Plutarco Elías Calles*, 152.
52 On the formative revolutionary experiences of the postrevolutionary political class, see Roderic Ai Camp, *Political Recruitment Across Two Centuries: Mexico, 1884–1991* (Austin, TX: University of Texas Press, 1995), 65–76. Rath argues that considering the sheer numbers of military men in office, Calles' claims to have civilianized Mexican politics were significantly exaggerated. Rath, *Myths of Demilitarization*, 27.
53 Dulles, *Yesterday in Mexico*, 469–78.

which campaigns and elections were fundamental, but electoral results were not irrevocable if they were perceived to have the potential to cause further unrest or violence. Democratic processes remained important in this new political era, but were sometimes overruled by other considerations: above all, preventing further coups or political mutinies.

From Many, One

The notion of the PNR ushering in a "federal" system of party politics was a compromise between a single party and a multi-party system by the party's leaders that enabled the rapid construction of a diverse and lasting national political coalition for the first time in Mexico. Portes Gil declared in 1930: "[The PNR] will be the orienting organ, always respectful of the regional parties of the states [. . .] it will consider them allies in the fight for good, in the fight for what is moral, in the fight for the achievement of the advanced principles of the Mexican Revolution."[54] A measure of local autonomy of PNR affiliates was considered vital to the success and strength of the larger organization, rather than an impediment to its functioning.

In practice, unification of diverse parties and factions within a confederated system also meant bringing together parties and organizations at the local level, as in Chihuahua, where former Secretary of Agriculture Luis L. León reported to Calles in 1929 that the organizing convention of the Chihuahua Revolutionary Party had succeeded in uniting all of the revolutionary factions of the state, in spite of the fact that they had previously "found themselves divided in personalist bands."[55] But unifying diverse constituencies behind single candidates or causes, even within the same umbrella organization, was often much more difficult in practice than in theory, both at the national and local levels. Internal strife was a problem endemic to PNR affiliates at the local level from the outset. Even among factions and politicians who defined themselves and their politics as "revolutionary," there was not always consensus about what that truly meant. Much as the ligas de resistencia in Tabasco had endlessly struggled to keep members and their representatives working in productive harmony in pursuit of the same goals, local constituent organizations within the PNR discovered that the nebulous definition of "revolutionary" politics and conduct, while often convenient, could pose significant challenges when it came to political practice.

The question of the relationship between the national party and state governments also remained a fraught matter in practice, and leaders of local

---

54 Partido Nacional Revolucionario, *Nuevo sentido de la política*, 7.

55 FAPECFT-PEC, expediente 105: GONZALEZ DE AYALA GONZALEZ, Soledad (Secretaria Particular), legajo 3/9, fojas 140–41, inventario 2417. Luis L. León to Calles, June 4, 1929.

PNR affiliates frequently expressed anxiety about their relationships with state and local officials. They were protective of the degree of political autonomy they believed was due to them, and from an early point some were already concerned about its erosion in practice. In 1930, a representative of the PNR's municipal committee in the state of Querétaro complained that party president Emilio Portes Gil had unduly interfered in local politics there, and had suspiciously close ties to the governor of the state, who, he wrote, "threatens to snatch away the control that we have achieved after various political struggles." He emphasized that the group that he represented had campaigned for Calles in 1924, for Obregón in 1928, and for sitting president Pascual Ortiz Rubio, but that the local organizations that he represented were prepared to leave the PNR if their autonomy was not respected.[56]

Conversely, sometimes affiliated local parties requested the support and intervention of the PNR national organization when they felt that their members and partisans were not being sufficiently respected by local authorities. In 1934, the Socialist Labor Party of Fresnillo, Zacatecas, complained bitterly to Calles that the governor was persecuting workers and campesinos there. "Disgracefully, only the will of [the governor] rules, and he has not taken the majority into account," they wrote. Worse, they complained, in Fresnillo, politics were being dominated by Guillermo C. Aguilera, an alleged participant in the Escobar rebellion, who now had enthusiastically joined the PNR.[57]

In their effort to bring together a diverse collection of leaders and constituencies, the directors of the PNR and Calles himself were substantially aided by the identification of clear, shared antagonists, particularly those who were easily caricatured and readily vilified by their partisans. In particular, Luis Morones never recovered from the stain of his alleged participation in the assassination of Obregón, although there was never any evidence to substantiate it.[58] When he disagreed with Calles over other matters in the early 1930s, the allegation was frequently recalled. Similarly, Antonio Díaz Soto y Gama and Aurelio Manrique of the PNA were widely smeared by PNR partisans as counterrevolutionaries into the early 1930s after openly criticizing Calles following Obregón's assassination, refusing to support his nomination of Portes Gil to the presidency, and then supporting the Escobar rebellion. Manrique was

---

56 FAPECFT-PEC, expediente 85: BARRERA, Lázaro, legajo 1/1, fojas 1–2, inventario 534. Lázaro Barrera to Calles, May 6, 1930.

57 FAPECFT-PEC, expediente 1: PARTIDOS VARIOS, legajo 12/13, foja 651, inventario 4344. Antonio López et al. to Calles, March 15, 1934.

58 On Morones' alleged participation in Obregón's assassination, and the political consequences of that (false) allegation, see Clark, *Organized Labor in Mexico*, 132–33.

exiled in 1929.[59] José Vasconcelos went into his second voluntary exile in the United States the same year.[60]

The development of common enemies was a political strategy that the PNR shared with Tomás Garrido Canabal, who never forgave or forgot a political betrayal – whether real or merely alleged. In terms of its political symbolism in Socialist Tabasco, the de la Huerta rebellion was a political gift for Garrido. The perceived betrayals of the Mexican Revolution by the leaders of the CROM and the PNA were similarly politically useful to Calles and other leaders of the PNR. Along with Vasconcelos, these were the leaders of the only other political parties that might have credibly competed with the new "revolutionary" party for power, and some of the only potential opposition leaders of note that both survived the 1920s and remained in Mexico. The defaming of the leaders of these parties was not just politically convenient for the directors of the PNR; it was politically necessary. By remaining independently and steadfastly Obregonista, and by refusing to capitulate to the PNR or to allow their organizations to become its political subsidiaries, Morones, Vasconcelos, Manrique, and Díaz Soto y Gama all handed Calles political weapons that he was willing and able to wield.

One reason that this was so effective was that a relatively abstract notion of "revolution" remained the bond that most strongly held the PNR's national coalition together. As the Great University Student Party of Puebla put it in a 1933 manifesto: "Manrique, Díaz Soto y Gama and the other revolutionary rejects have gone to join the ranks of the eternal enemies, and with their false arguments attempt to denigrate the glorious achievements of that same revolution."[61] The PNR's successor parties touted their revolutionary heritage as a fundamental part of their political legitimacy in long historical retrospect, but it is worth recalling that this was the justification for the PNR's existence in the first place, as well. Local parties often cited their belief that the new national organization was Mexico's best hope to see its Revolution put into political practice. In 1929, the Agrarista Party of the State of Puebla described the PNR as "the refuge of those of us that still believe in the ideal of uplift for the

59 Dulles, *Yesterday in Mexico*, 382–83, 94–95. On Díaz Soto y Gama's break with Calles, see Jeffrey K. Lucas, "Antonio Díaz Soto y Gama and Changing Mexico: A Twentieth-Century Political Journey," *International Social Science Review* 83, no. 3/4 (2008): 139–40. On Manrique's break with Calles, see Clark, *Organized Labor in Mexico*, 124–25. On Manrique's support of the rebellion, see Loyo Camacho, *Joaquín Amaro*, 169. On the exile of Manrique: Camp, *Mexican Political Biographies, 1884–1935*, 130–31.

60 The first was during Calles' presidency (1924–28). Camp, *Mexican Political Biographies, 1884–1935*, 220.

61 FAPECFT-PEC, expediente 1: PARTIDOS VARIOS, legajo 10/13, foja 574, inventario 4344. Gran Partido Estudiantil Universitario to Calles, October 9, 1933.

oppressed classes" and "the faithful interpretation of our sacred principles achieved at the cost of so much blood."[62] This was a rhetorical strategy perfected by the southeastern Socialists at the local level in the late 1910s and early-mid 1920s, and it seems to have been equally effective for this much larger and much more diverse political organization in the years that followed.

In many cases, preexisting local parties and organizations formalized their relationships with the PNR once it was founded, sometimes coming to the national organization with their own established organizational hierarchies. In 1928, the Socialist Party of Fishermen in Veracruz, which belonged to the Socialist Party of the East, formally joined the PNR. The fishermen's stated goal was to join Mexico's "true" revolutionaries and to build a united front against the country's reactionaries, and to thereby guarantee the social interests of all workers.[63] Across Mexico, the leaders of local organizations that joined the PNR emphasized the large numbers of workers and campesinos in their respective states and communities that through them, now joined the party, and embraced the new, institutionalized era of the Mexican Revolution.[64] For the leaders of the PNR, the results spoke for themselves. As he crisscrossed the country working for the presidential campaign of Ortiz Rubio in the summer of 1929, Manuel Pérez Treviño reported to Calles that the public turnout for the campaign's rallies were without precedent. In Torreón, he found that the local PNR affiliate had organized twice as many wildly enthusiastic supporters than had greeted Obregón on his last presidential campaign event there.[65]

In the early years, many local- and state-level parties affiliated with the PNR continued to describe themselves as "Socialist." Many also adopted the basic southeastern Socialist organizational model, such as the Socialist Workers Party of the State of Mexico, which in 1929 urged its members to form cooperatives, unions, and ligas de resistencia, and declared its solidarity with all organized labor.[66] In Oaxaca, local affiliates of the PNR now belonged to a preexisting confederation of Socialist parties across

62 FAPECFT-PEC, expediente 1: PARTIDOS VARIOS, legajo 7/13, foja 391. Antonio Montes et al. to Calles, May 23, 1929.
63 FAPECFT-PEC, expediente 175: DUARTE, Rodolfo, legajo 1/1, foja 1, inventario 1641. Rodolfo Duarte to Calles, November 19, 1928.
64 See, for example, FAPECFT-PEC, expediente 1: QUEVEDO, Rafael (Dip.), legajo 1/1, foja 6, inventario 4646. Rafael Quevedo to Calles, June 29, 1930 (Aguascalientes).
65 FAPECFT-FPEC, serie 10803, expediente 38: PEREZ TREVINO, Manuel, legajo 1/1, fojas 1–2, inventario 1795. Manuel Pérez Treviño to Calles, August 30, 1929.
66 "Partido Socialista del Trabajo del Estado de México." January 1, 1929. Hernández Santiago, Lerner, and Ulloa, *Planes en la nación mexicana, Libro 8: 1920–1940.*

the state.[67] Through their membership in organizations that joined the PNR, ligas de resistencia continued operating as grassroots affiliates of the national party into the 1930s.[68]

Although many affiliate parties maintained their Socialist or sometimes "radical" self-identification, in their totality, the parties that joined the PNR were quite diverse, as is made clear by the names and namesakes of the party's local affiliates. In the port of Veracruz in 1934, twenty local PNR-affiliated parties claiming to collectively represent 10,000 workers and campesinos endorsed the same protest over the selection of candidates for the federal legislature. Some were Socialist in name, while others labeled themselves Liberals. Their namesakes included Calles, Obregón, Joaquín Amaro, Francisco I. Madero, and Venustiano Carranza, among many others.[69] In other places, parties describing themselves as "progressive" and even "feminist" also joined the PNR.[70] Old divisions and differences and even historical enmities began to fade away in this new, more unified postrevolutionary era. In Guadalajara in 1932, a group exclusively comprising revolutionary veterans formed a party that they named for Carranza. The party's first act was to write an enthusiastic message of support to Calles and to praise him for his "brilliant and eminently revolutionary conduct," an endorsement that likely would have stunned the party's namesake had he been alive to see it.[71] This counterintuitive reunification of old enemies within a new, all-embracing revolutionary "family" was a process that unfolded over time as part of a purposeful effort by the party to rewrite Mexico's recent history along more politically expedient lines.[72]

Many of the missives from local PNR affiliates in the early 1930s were addressed personally to Calles, often seeking his guidance or intervention in local matters. Leaders of parties and ligas commonly cited their allegiance to Calles himself as one of the factors that motivated them to join the PNR

67 FAPCEFT-PEC, expediente 11: GATICA NERI, Leopoldo, legajo 1/1, foja 1, inventario 2323. Presidente IV Convención Confederación Partidos Socialistas Oaxaca to Calles, March 26, 1930.
68 See, for example, the Liga Central de Comunidades Agrarias de la República: FAPECFT-PEC, expediente 7: RAMIREZ DE ARELLANO, Luis (Dip.), legajo 1/1, foja 6, inventario 4692. Luis Ramírez de Arellano to Calles, October 21, 1932. See also the third convention of the Liga Socialista de Coahuila: FAPECFT-PEC, expediente 45: VAZQUEZ, Juan F. (Dip.), legajo 1/1, foja 3, inventario 5813. Juan F. Vázquez to Calles, May 29, 1932.
69 FAPECFT-PEC, expediente 6: DARIO OJEDA, Carlos (Dip.), legajo 1, fojas 5–7, inventario 1331. Numerous political parties to Calles, February 16, 1934.
70 See, for example, the parties affiliated with the Independent Progressive Party of the Federal District: FAPECFT-PEC, expediente 1: PARTIDOS VARIOS, legajo 7/13, foja 378, inventario 4344. Manuel D. Sierra et al. to Calles, September 6, 1928.
71 FAPECFT-PEC, expediente 1: PARTIDOS VARIOS, legajo 9/13, foja 490, inventario 4344. Ignacio López and Felipe de Jesús Velasco to Calles, January 16, 1932.
72 See Benjamin's related discussion of the Monument of the Revolution (built in 1937) and its symbolism: Benjamin, *La Revolución*, 117–36.

and to participate in the institutionalization (and by implication, depersonalization) of Mexican politics. Even if Calles sincerely hoped to eradicate the figure of the *caudillo* from Mexican politics with his founding of the PNR, many of his partisans seemed determined to cast him in the role of the *Jefe Máximo* of this new postrevolutionary era.

The title of "Maximum Chief" of the Mexican Revolution was originally a pejorative epithet given to Calles by one of his harshest critics, Antonio Díaz Soto y Gama of the PNA, in protest of the concentration of power in Calles hands behind the scenes of the PNR.[73] There can be no doubt that Calles remained extremely powerful, and that he wielded that power as the president of the party's executive committee, a role roughly analogous to Garrido and Carrillo Puerto's leadership of the Ligas Centrales of Tabasco and Yucatán.[74] But historians concur that he was not as powerful as the nickname he received suggests, and that particularly by the end of the so-called *Maximato* (1928–34) other political leaders and factions had achieved significant room to maneuver politically, as well as varying degrees of independence from Calles. Nor were the dynamics of power between Calles, the party, and the presidency straightforwardly a matter of Calles imposing his will on his allies and subordinates, or three "puppet presidents" of the 1928–34 period, as myth would have it.[75]

Confusion over the true scope of Calles' power during the Maximato was (and remains) understandable, and dates from the period. The ways that the term "Jefe Máximo" was used by Calles' contemporaries suggests how complicated national politics became following Obregón's assassination. Calles' role was often oversimplified, by critics and supporters alike. His supporters' embrace of the sobriquet was characteristic of the inherent contradictions of Calles' position, and of the momentous transition in Mexico's political culture ongoing at that time. Caudillismo proved much easier to vanquish in rhetoric than in practice, even for the supposed political overlord calling for its denouement. In one such case, with no irony intended, in 1933, the Radical Party of Guanajuato explained its choice to incorporate its organization into the PNR to Calles: "today more than ever we recognize you as our Chief, as the strongman, that has known how to guide us on the institutional path."[76]

73 Buchenau, *Plutarco Elías Calles*, 155. Dulles, *Yesterday in Mexico*, 394–95.

74 On Calles' role as president of the CEN, see Medina Peña, *Hacia el nuevo estado*, 74–76.

75 See, in particular, Buchenau, *Plutarco Elías Calles*, 154–72. Buchenau describes Calles as the "arbiter of political life" rather than an all-powerful political mastermind, and Maximato as "a political stalemate that contained the elements of its own undoing" (p. 144). On the history of the *Maximato* period (1928–34), see also Córdova, *La Revolución en crisis*; Garrido, *El Partido de la Revolución Institucionalizada* (Chapter 3); Medin, *El minimato presidencial*.

76 FAPECFT-PEC, expediente 1: PARTIDOS VARIOS, legajo 12/13, foja 628, inventario 4344. Manuel L. Farias and J. Jesús Pérez Vela to Calles, December 8, 1933.

In part, the casting of Calles as Mexico's political godfather was the result of a purposeful effort by the PNR to cast the political class as a revolutionary "family."[77] This familial, patriarchal dynamic permeated political practice in the late 1920s and early 1930s. In some cases, constituents requested Calles' political blessing, much as constituents in Tabasco had sought Tomás Garrido Canabal's approval for matters both big and small. Others simply argued that the only way forward for the institutional phase of the Mexican Revolution was for Calles to return to power and to lead it himself. "Callismo over the course of time in Mexico signifies the definitive triumph of our socio-political revolution," the Pro-Durango Political Party declared in 1929. "For it to continue with all of its force and prestige, the constant and uninterrupted action of its creator, Calles, is necessary and indispensable."[78]

This seeming paradox was perhaps inevitable, considering that it was Tabasco's brand of southeastern Socialism that had emerged triumphant from the Gómez-Serrano debacle. For all its leaders' talk of popular representation and democracy, Socialism in Tabasco remained centered on the person of Tomás Garrido Canabal in practice. This same contradiction at the heart of Calles' project of institutionalization of the Mexican Revolution was the direct result of the compromise forged by the Obregonista Socialists in the mid-1920s, as they adopted "Socialism" as their own, but, led in part by Garrido, continued to embrace the political dominance of Obregón, the preeminent postrevolutionary caudillo. Not coincidentally, Garrido was also among those who urged Calles to stay on in power beyond the end of his term, after Obregón's death.[79] Presumably for the members of the Socialist Alliance in 1926–27 who went on to become founding members of the PNR, part of the allure of Garrido-style Socialism was that it provided a formula for building the alliances they desired with popular constituencies, but it did not require forswearing the concentration of power in the hands of a very few, or even one person.

The era of the PNR as a confederation of relatively autonomous organizations was short-lived. In 1933, at Calles' urging, local constituent organizations formally became subsidiaries of the national party.[80] Socialism in the

77 Buchenau, *Plutarco Elías Calles*, 155–56.
78 FAPECFT-PEC, expediente 1: PARTIDOS VARIOS, legajo 8/13, fojas 396–98, inventario 4344. Partido Político Pro-Durango to Calles, December 19, 1929.
79 FAPECFT-PEC, expediente: 140, GARRIDO CANABAL, Tomás (Lic.), legajo 3/7, fojas 199–200, inventario: 2312. Garrido to Elías, August 4, 1928.
80 Buchenau, *Plutarco Elías Calles*, 166. Buchenau argues that this move was in many ways a formality that did not transform political practice; ending the autonomy of the local parties that constituted the PNR on paper and in name did not constitute a consolidation of the national organization's power or expansion of its control at the local level. See also Medina Peña, *Hacia el nuevo estado*, 77–78.

Southeast had flourished only when its leaders had struck a functional balance between centralization and autonomy, which, as we have seen, varied a great deal from state to state. This prerequisite endured in the foundations of the PNR and shaped its compact with its local affiliates and partisans, particularly in its early days. As historical scholarship of the past several decades has emphasized, the party and its successors (the PRM and the PRI) only ever effectively exerted their political wills from Mexico City through complex and extensive processes of negotiation with local actors. Unilateral, top-down political control was unworkable at the national level just as it had been in the Southeast in previous years, even as the PNR's role as the foremost institutional mechanism for wielding political power was progressively more consolidated.

Conclusions

Socialism was widely adopted in Mexico as a political style, often unencumbered by any commitment to the ambitious reform agendas of its southeastern architects. By the end of the 1920s, it had become a catchword for countless politicians throughout Mexico, across the political spectrum. This was true to Socialism's roots in some respects. Like "revolution," "Socialism" was a term that had emotional and political resonance in postrevolutionary Mexico, even when very loosely defined; even the originators of southeastern Socialism had largely either failed or declined to define it along coherent ideological lines. This remained the case as Socialism lost its association with the idealism and reformist zeal that had inspired its creation, as its meaning was diluted through broad and often opportunistic adoption.

This lack of ideological substance and consistency did not render the designation meaningless. Nor was the adoption of Socialism as a label by so many politicians and parties purely symbolic. The formation of the PNR in 1928 was the culmination of a trend toward the institutionalization of party politics in Mexico, loosely based on southeastern Socialist precedents.[81] In a conspicuous nod to the significance of the example that the Socialist parties of the Southeast set for the nation, and in recognition of how important they were to him as allies, Plutarco Elías Calles cast his

---

81 Local political parties articulated this clearly in the mid-late 1920s, not just in the Southeast. For instance, the Revolutionary Party of Michoacán declared in 1928 that "Executive Power should only be a regulator of distinct political tendencies, represented by social groups and political parties." "Partido Revolucionario de Michoacán." April 9, 1928. "Partidos políticos estatales y locales. Relación de Partidos Políticos estatales, municipales, distritales y citadinos de la época de Calles," ed. Victoria Lerner and Berta Ulloa, *Planes en la nación mexicana, Libro 8: 1920–1940* (México, DF: Senado de la República, 1987), http://biblio.juridicas.unam.mx/libros/libro.htm? l=2983.

ballot in the election that made him president in 1924 in Mérida, Yucatán. He voted for candidates from the Socialist Party of the Southeast for both the Chamber of Deputies and the Senate, and an ally from Sonora for president. Following his mentor's lead, when Lázaro Cárdenas voted for president in 1934, it was for Tomás Garrido Canabal, rather than for himself.[82]

One of the things that made the national consolidation of the PNR possible was precisely its lack of ideological rigor. Its leaders' persistent emphasis on the unification and unity of "revolutionary" politicians and their efforts to confederate as many constituent institutions as possible within the party required maximum political flexibility. The adoption of a more rigid political philosophy would have been crippling in pursuit of those goals.[83] Here too, the southeastern Socialist example provided valuable precedents and insight. In Yucatán, Liberals faced with the political threats of Salvador Alvarado and then Felipe Carrillo Puerto had loudly proclaimed themselves reformers dedicated to the betterment of the lives of Yucatecan workers. Ten years later, the counterrevolutionary Mapaches in Chiapas enthusiastically labeled themselves as Obregonista Socialists when it was politically expedient to do so. In both cases, Socialists had changed the rules of the political game, forcing even the most conservative political factions to at least rhetorically acknowledge that workers and campesinos could no longer be excluded wholesale from participating in politics.[84]

These shallow and opportunistic nods to working people were not comparable to the reformist dedication of revolutionary leaders in these places. Rather, these precedents in the Southeast help to explain how and why the PNR was successful in uniting a very broad spectrum of Mexico's political class under one institutional roof, after a decade of bitter and often bloody infighting. Whether or not postrevolutionary politicians agreed on crucial issues such as land reform and labor rights or the extent to which

---

82 Calles voted for Ramón Ross for president. FAPECFT-APEC anexo, fondo: 3, serie: 407, expediente: 10: León, Luis (Ing. y Dip.), legajo 1/1, foja 3, inventario 1317. Luis León to Carlos Puig Casauranc, July 6, 1924. Ross was from Sonora, was a delegate to the Bucareli conference in 1923, and head of the Department of the Federal District during Calles' presidency. See Camp, *Mexican Political Biographies, 1884–1935*, 194. On Cárdenas' vote for Garrido Canabal, see Harper, "Revolutionary Tabasco," 154 (footnote 7).

83 Garrido argued that the vagueness and imprecision of the PNR's revolutionary rhetoric enabled it to win support from numerous political factions, even when the party's founding documents were "neither nationalist nor revolutionary." Garrido, *El Partido de la Revolución Institucionalizada*, 101.

84 For instance, in his study of elite landowners in Chilón, Chiapas, Aaron Bobrow-Strain cites the seeming paradox of Chiapas landowners participating guerilla warfare against the Constitutionalist Army in the 1910s in defense of state sovereignty and elite privilege, and yet quoting Marx in their formation of a workers' party less than a decade later. Aaron Bobrow-Strain, *Intimate Enemies: Landowners, Power, and Violence in Chiapas* (Durham, NC: Duke University Press, 2007), 80.

they should be implemented, the southeastern Socialist model of institu-
tionalizing bonds of mutual dependency between politicians and popular
constituencies was one that held undeniable appeal for a very large part of
the political class, irrespective of the political ends they hoped to use that
model to achieve. It was this very simple objective, unburdened by other
requirements or specifications, that was the common denominator in nearly
all political projects described as Socialist in Mexico in the 1920s and early
1930s. More than anyone, Tomás Garrido Canabal had demonstrated how
effective the system could be to achieve political control of party members
down to the grassroots, as much as to pursue economic, political, or social
reform. Applied at the national level by the PNR, the result was something
distinct from the *cacique* politics of an earlier era, in spite of superficial
similarities and shared traits.[85]

Outside influences on the design of the PNR, particularly political
parties and party systems in Europe and the United States, were real and
important, but are only part of the story. Equally incomplete is the frequent
ascription of the design of the PNR and the political system it so effectively
dominated to Calles himself. By that account, he created order out of chaos
at yet another moment of political crisis through some combination of
political scheming, backroom deals and sheer force of will. Yet Calles faced
a period of unprecedented political peril following Obregón's assassination.
There certainly were schemes and backroom deals involved, but Calles' title
of "Jefe Máximo" was originally an expression of his enemies' worst-case
scenario rather than a realistic reflection of his uncontested power. He was
able to achieve the careful compromises that kept him and his allies in
power and averted civil war because he had a blueprint to do so, and it was
a uniquely Mexican one.

Calles' ability to convince a diverse and fractious political class to join
the PNR was not a testament to his overwhelming political strength, but
the result of painful lessons that Mexican politicians had collectively taken
from a decade in which the country had been repeatedly rocked by political
crises and armed rebellions. By 1928, like Calles, many Mexican politicians
had seen what political parties like those that emerged in the Southeast
could achieve, particularly when it came to the unification of diverse

---

85 I am in agreement with Fowler-Salamini, who argues that regional Socialist parties of the 1920s
    were intended as "an alternative to traditional caciquismo." Fowler-Salamini, "De-Centering the
    1920s," 327. Recent scholarship increasingly urges re-visitation and reevaluation of *cacique*
    politics in Mexico, both before and after the Revolution, its relationship to processes of state
    building and consolidation, and the ways in which it changed over time. See the 2005 edited
    volume on the subject: Alan Knight and W. G. Pansters, *Caciquismo in Twentieth-Century Mexico*
    (London: Institute for the Study of the Americas, 2005). Knight's introductory essay to the volume
    is especially useful in considering the multiplicity of forms caciquismo took, and its many
    consequences. See also Joseph, "Caciquismo and the Revolution: Carrillo Puerto in Yucatán."

political factions and the mobilization of popular constituencies in support of elite-led political projects. Many also had firsthand experience with regional parties, as well as national partisan factions and organizations such as the Socialist Alliance and the PLM, many of which had also taken inspiration from southeastern Socialists, either directly or indirectly.

The form the PNR ultimately took and its long-term success were not foregone conclusions. However, by the time Calles and his allies founded it, the groundwork was already well established in Mexico for the formation of national political parties, and many politicians were thoroughly convinced that a functional party system was crucial for maintaining a long-term postrevolutionary peace. The precedents of party formation undertaken in the Southeast over the previous decade were essential to this transformation of Mexico's postrevolutionary political landscape.

Conclusion
Hard Lessons

When Plutarco Elías Calles declared in 1928 that Mexico must become a nation of institutions, he was not describing a nation that had made no progress in that direction up to that point. The National Revolutionary Party was not Athena to Calles' Zeus, springing forth from his mind fully formed, ready to engage in political battle from birth. To borrow Calles' own language, it was not the creation of one man, but rather, the culmination of a much longer process of experimentation with different forms of political organizing and institutionalization that ran in parallel to the process of postrevolutionary pacification, from the late 1910s onward. The formation of the modern Mexican political system was not sudden, but an integral component of the Mexican Revolution and its aftermath.

Nor did the political system the PNR and its successors so successfully controlled for so long take its final form for several more years; indeed, one of the keys to the staying power of Mexico's postrevolutionary single party-dominated system was its flexibility and adaptability over time. In their long, collective tenure in power, arguably one of the only constants of the parties of the Mexican Revolution was precisely their adamant claim to their revolutionary heritage, but this too changed in meaning over the years, until it was hardly recognizable. By the end of the twentieth century, as the PRI clung to power, some of the most credible and important opponents of the party were individuals and organizations that staked their own claims to Mexico's revolutionary heritage, condemning its betrayal of that legacy in the process.

The Socialists of the Southeast were not alone in their quests to create stable and enduring political parties that built meaningful relationships with their popular constituencies. Throughout the 1920s, there was strong consensus within the political class, including among dissidents, that Mexico needed to establish a party system as an essential part of its postrevolutionary political rebuilding. The form that system would take was the open question, and the form it did take was not inevitable; without delving too far into counterfactuals, it is fair to say that there were moments during the 1920s when it would have been reasonable to expect that

Mexico would eventually have a multi-party political system. Once credible opposition organizations were either critically debilitated or eliminated outright, as Calles and his allies convoked the PNR, instead of reinventing the wheel, they naturally looked to successful, recent precedents of party formation and constituency building. The Socialist parties of the Southeast were not the only ancestors of the party they created, but they were prominent among them, for all of the reasons outlined throughout this book.

The party that emerged at the end of the 1920s was a product of its founders' engagement with southeastern Socialist precedents in two senses. First, the institutional designs and strategies of popular mobilization and organization that they pioneered inarguably helped to give it its shape, both directly and indirectly. Calles had closely observed and collaborated with the southeastern Socialists from the outset, and repeatedly praised their political achievements. But southeastern Socialism had also contributed to a shift in Mexico's political culture, and to a broad embrace of "Socialism" as a political style by the end of the decade. This included a highly variable commitment to revolutionary reform and defense of the political and economic rights of working people, in spite of consistent, all but mandatory rhetorical insistence on those basic principles.

Second, relatedly and just as importantly, building on the work of the Socialist Alliance in the mid-1920s, the PNR's founders sought to coopt Socialism as a political brand and thereby to defuse the potential threat to their political dominance that it posed. The extreme violence that Calles and Obregón meted out to the Chiapas Socialists for their participation in the Gómez-Serrano affair underscores how much of a threat they understood it to be, as Socialists attempted to organize nationwide popular support for an opposition presidential campaign. It was not enough to exile Carlos Vidal, as they had Adolfo de la Huerta, or even to assassinate him; the other leaders of the Chiapas Socialist Party along with hundreds of their associates were also murdered, and their sympathizers were purged from the state and federal governments.

The broad and often loose adoption of the basic Socialist model by Mexican politicians over the course of the 1920s had important consequences for Mexico in the long term. First, the selective application of coercion, repression, and violence as a political tool survived the Mexican Revolution intact and was re-inscribed into the political system that emerged from it because of some of the alliances, bargains, and compromises that were made along the way. The entire political class had lived through the Revolution and its aftermath, most as active participants in one capacity or another. All of them had witnessed firsthand that state and national elections, when not thoroughly managed, had significant destructive, destabilizing potential. Many also had personal experience with political violence: Carlos Vidal was murdered at Huitzilac just over a week before the third anniversary of the attempt on his life in Tuxtla. For the first generation of the PNR, preventing further civil war, or even political unrest that might devolve into uprising, was paramount.[1] They also hoped to prevent the reinvigoration of the Catholic Church and all its power, wealth, and influence. This included generals, many of whom preferred to join the party than to meet the grim fates of their erstwhile colleagues who had rebelled over the previous decade, or to once more be put in the position of prosecuting wars against mutinous peers.

This unwritten pact was sealed for all intents and purposes when, led by the Socialist Alliance, the Mexican political class and the military over-whelmingly accepted both the return to power of Álvaro Obregón, and along with it, the ghastly retribution meted out to the anti-reelectionist leaders and the purge of their sympathizers from the legislature in 1927. As the leader of the Socialist Alliance, Manlio Fabio Altamirano, bitterly intoned in the aftermath of the Gómez-Serrano rebellion, recalling the outbreak of the de la Huerta rebellion four years earlier: "We believed that the hard lesson, the strong lesson, that the lesson of 1923 would have had its effect; we believed that our political struggles would be cured forever of the military coups that so soil the honor of the national Army, but we have been mistaken."[2] The PNR, founded a year later, was the political outcome of those hard lessons, and of the even harder lesson of Obregón's assassination that followed.

Second, the sincere dedication of many Socialist revolutionaries to make good on the Revolution's ambitious promises to Mexican citizens also survived in the DNA of the party. In the late 1920s and early 1930s it was often a latent trait, as the PNR declined to pursue any substantial, formalized alliance with organized popular groups. But no one more than Lázaro Cárdenas demonstrated that the spirit of reformism that inspired the original design of the system could still be activated, and that the party itself was the most powerful tool for putting it into practice. Cárdenas' corporatist remaking of the party as the Party of the Mexican Revolution (PRM) in 1938 much more closely resembled the Socialist parties of the Southeast than the PNR ever did, with the National Campesino Confederation (CNC) and National Worker's Confederation (CTM) harking back to the ligas de resistencia and their crucial function as the institutionalized bond between political parties and mass constituencies.

---

1   On the political consequences of the firsthand experience of violence by postrevolutionary politi-cians, see Camp, *Generals in the Palacio: The Military in Modern Mexico*, 8.
2   "Diario de los Debates de la Cámara de Diputados." Legislatura XXXII – Año II – Período Ordinario – October 4, 1927 – Número de Diario 15.

Third, the triumph of Tomás Garrido Canabal's interpretation of Carrillo Puerto's political model at the national level meant that authoritarian tendencies came along with the brand of Socialism that most directly gave rise to the PNR. Garrido had demonstrated that the liga system could be used to empower constituencies, but also to control them, sometimes in nearly equal measure. This was an innate peril of the system, as Alan Knight underscored in his seminal analysis of *Cardenismo*: its institutions could be put to different and less reformist uses than its originators intended, without substantial modification.[3] Garrido used the Socialist model to implement significant reforms and to offer his partisans substantial benefits in exchange for their participation in the liga system, which stripped them of individual political rights. The same general arrangement was sustainable for so long at the national level in part because it did promise a great deal to Mexico's working people. How much it delivered was another matter; in many places in Mexico people were still waiting for the state and the party to make good, or even to achieve pacification and political stability, decades later.[4]

Lastly, as per Garrido's example, winning a critical mass of popular support for candidates and initiatives was essential as a counterbalance to the national party's authoritarian streak in all of its iterations, even when political outcomes were foregone conclusions. Although participation in the PNR's hegemony at the local level meant the sacrifice of individual political rights, in many places the available alternatives were almost certainly much worse for working people, whether urban or rural. Again, the Southeast was a case in point. The Mapaches in Chiapas, the Liberals in Yucatán, and their counterparts in Tabasco were never able to mount a compelling case for why non-elites should voluntarily support them, and many working people had no interest in going back to the way things had been done before the Revolution when those groups and their ilk had dominated local politics without consulting popular constituencies. One of the most important projects of the Southeastern Socialists in the years immediately following the Mexican Revolution had been to disseminate information to their constituents not just about their own reform programs, but also about the promises of rights and reforms made to all Mexicans by the 1917 Constitution. Party and liga leaders may have forcibly arranged "unanimous" political outcomes, but they understood that in order to sometimes run

---

3 Knight, "Cardenismo: Juggernaut or Jalopy?," 106–7.

4 See, in particular, the cases examined by Padilla and Smith. Both authors demonstrate just how challenging and/or ineffective postrevolutionary governance and pacification were in some parts of Mexico into the mid-twentieth century, and that demands for fulfillment of revolutionary promises were sometimes met with violent responses from the state. Tanalis Padilla, *Rural Resistance in the Land of Zapata: The Jaramillista Movement and the Myth of the Pax Priísta, 1940–1962* (Durham, NC: Duke University Press, 2008); Smith, *Pistoleros and Popular Movements*.

roughshod over democratic processes and still maintain their revolutionary legitimacy, they first had to actually win a convincing measure of popular support.[5] This was true at the local level, but also at the national one; the energy and quantity of resources dedicated to presidential campaigns by the PNR and its successor parties during the rest of the twentieth century is the most conspicuous and compelling evidence of this phenomenon.

In 1935, Tomás Garrido Canabal stepped onto an airplane, and began a period of involuntary exile from Mexico – first in Costa Rica, and then later in Los Angeles. Plutarco Elías Calles was exiled the following year, as was Luis Morones. The mid-1930s was a time of tremendous political transition in Mexico, as President Lázaro Cárdenas (1934–40) consolidated his own power, maneuvered to step out of the shadow of his mentor, Calles, and began the process of empowering his own allies and disempowering the Callistas. Just a year earlier, Cárdenas had provided perhaps the greatest and best-known epigraph for any history of Mexico's Southeast in the 1920s, quipping that Tabasco under Garrido was Mexico's "laboratory of Revolution." As Cárdenas pushed hard to further institutionalize the Mexican Revolution, to pacify the country once and for all and to implement enduring social, economic, and political reforms, Tabasco's revolutionary scientist stayed true to his implacable 1920s form, and loyal to Calles. He thereby outlived his political usefulness, and instead became a liability. But southeastern Socialism had always been and then remained bigger than Garrido, or Carlos Vidal, or Salvador Alvarado, or even Felipe Carrillo Puerto. By the 1930s, the precedents established in the Southeast over the previous fifteen years continued to influence national politics, now in a way almost entirely independent of the politics of the region itself. Socialism no longer belonged to the Southeast.

5　For instance, Fallaw has shown that Catholic resistance to the state and many of its projects were decisively important to the course of Mexico's postrevolutionary state formation. Fallaw, *Religion and State Formation*, 2.

Select Bibliography

Archives Consulted

Chiapas

Biblioteca del Congreso del Estado, Tuxtla Gutiérrez
Centro Jaime Sabines, Tuxtla Gutiérrez
    Archivo General del Estado de Chiapas
    Hemeroteca del Estado de Chiapas
Universidad de Ciencias y Artes de Chiapas, Tuxtla Gutiérrez (UNICACH)
    Archivo Histórico del Estado de Chiapas (AHECH)
        Gobernación
        Hemeroteca Fernando Castañon Gamboa
            Acervos Especiales

Mexico City

Archivo General de la Nación (AGN)
    Dirección General de Investigaciones Sociales (DGIPS)
    Particulares
        Fondo Carlos A. Vidal (CAV)
        Fondo Francisco R. Serrano (FRS)
        Fondo Tomás Garrido Canabal (TGC)
    Ramo de Gobernación (GOB)
    Ramo Presidentes
            Fondo Obregón-Calles (OC)
Archivo Histórico de la Secretaría de la Defensa Nacional (AHSDN)
    Sources from the AHSDN's online archive commemorating the centennial of
           the Mexican Revolution and the bicentennial of Mexican
           Independence are cited as
    AHSDN-W (www.archivohistorico2010.sedena.gob.mx)
Biblioteca Miguel Lerdo de Tejada, Hemeroteca

Fideicomiso Archivos Plutarco Elías Calles y Fernando Torreblanca (FAPECFT)
Archivo Fernando Torreblanca
  Fondo Plutarco Elías Calles (FPEC)
  Fondo Álvaro Obregón (FAO)
  Fondo Fernando Torreblanca (FFT)
Archivo Plutarco Elías Calles (PEC)
Archivo Plutarco Elías Calles, Anexo
  Fondo Plutarco Elías Calles (APEC)
  Fondo Presidentes (FP)
  Fondo Soledad González (SGON)
Colección Adolfo de la Huerta (DLH)
Colección Documental de la Embajada de Estados Unidos en México
  (CDEEUM)
Colección Joaquín Amaro (JA)

Sonora

Archivo Histórico General del Estado de Sonora, Hermosillo (AHGES)

Yucatán

Archivo General del Estado de Yucatán, Mérida (AGEY)

Selected List of Sources Cited and Consulted

Aboites Aguilar, Luis. "En busca del centro. Una aproximación a la relación centro-provincias en México, 1921–1949." *Historia Mexicana* 59, no. 2 (2009): 711–54.
Abud, José A. *Campeche: Revolución y movimiento social (1911–1923)*. México, D.F.: Universidad Autónoma de Campeche, 1992.
  Después de la revolución: Los caciques y el nuevo estado, Campeche (1923–1943). México, D.F.: Universidad Autónoma Metropolitana, 2012.
Aguilar Camín, Héctor and Lorenzo Meyer. *In the Shadow of the Mexican Revolution: Contemporary Mexican History, 1910–1989*. Austin, TX: University of Texas Press, 2001.
Alessio Robles, Vito. *Desfile sangriento*. México, D.F.: A. del Bosque, 1936.
Alianza de Partidos Socialistas de la República. *Alianza de Partidos Socialistas de la República, primera convención, "unión, tierra y libertad."* México, D.F.: La Alianza, 1926.
Alvarado, Salvador. *Actuación revolucionaria del General Salvador Alvarado en Yucatán*. México, D.F.: B. Costa-Amic, 1918. 1965.
  El primer Congreso Feminista de Yucatán: anales de esa memorable asamblea. Mérida, Yucatán: Ateneo Peninsular, 1916.
  La reconstrucción de México: un mensaje a los pueblos de America, Volume 1. México, D.F.: Partido Revolucionario Institucional (PRI), 1919. 1982.
  La reconstrucción de México: un mensaje a los pueblos de America, Volume 2. México, D.F.: Partido Revolucionario Institucional (PRI), 1919. 1982.
Andrews, Gregg. "Robert Haberman, Socialist Ideology, and the Politics of National Reconstruction in Mexico, 1920–25." *Mexican Studies / Estudios Mexicanos* 6, no. 2 (1990): 189–211.

Shoulder to Shoulder?: The American Federation of Labor, the United States, and the Mexican Revolution, 1910–1924. Berkeley, CA: University of California Press, 1991.

Ankerson, Dudley. *Agrarian Warlord: Saturnino Cedillo and the Mexican Revolution in San Luis Potosí*. DeKalb, IL: Northern Illinois University Press, 1984.

Bantjes, Adrian A. *As if Jesus Walked on Earth: Cardenismo, Sonora, and the Mexican Revolution*. Wilmington, DE: Scholarly Resources, 1998.

Becker, Marjorie. *Setting the Virgin on Fire: Lázaro Cárdenas, Michoacán Peasants, and the Redemption of the Mexican Revolution*. Berkeley, CA: University of California Press, 1995.

Benjamin, Thomas. "El trabajo en las monterías de Chiapas y Tabasco 1870–1946." *Historia Mexicana* 30, no. 4 (1981): 506–29.

"Laboratories of the New State, 1920–1929: Regional Social Reform and Experiments in Mass Politics." In *Provinces of the Revolution: Essays on Regional Mexican History, 1910–1929*, edited by Thomas Benjamin and Mark Wasserman, 71–90. Albuquerque, NM: University of New Mexico Press, 1990.

La Revolución: Mexico's Great Revolution as Memory, Myth and History. Austin, TX: University of Texas Press, 2000.

A Rich Land, a Poor People: Politics and Society in Modern Chiapas. Revised edn. Albuquerque, NM: University of New Mexico Press, 1996.

Benjamin, Thomas and Mark Wasserman. *Provinces of the Revolution: Essays on Regional Mexican History, 1910–1929*. Albuquerque, NM: University of New Mexico Press, 1990.

Bobrow-Strain, Aaron. *Intimate Enemies: Landowners, Power, and Violence in Chiapas*. Durham, NC: Duke University Press, 2007.

Bolio Ontiveros, Edmundo. *'De la cuna al paredon.' Anecdotario de la vida, muerte y gloria de Felipe Carrillo Puerto*. Mérida, Yucatán: Compañia Periodística del Sureste, 1932.

Boyer, Christopher R. *Becoming Campesinos: Politics, Identity, and Agrarian Struggle in Postrevolutionary Michoacán, 1920–1935*. Stanford, CA: Stanford University Press, 2003.

"Old Loves, New Loyalties: Agrarismo in Michoacán, 1920–1928." *The Hispanic American Historical Review* 78, no. 3 (1998): 419–55.

Brandenburg, Frank R. *The Making of Modern Mexico*. Englewood Cliffs, NJ: Prentice-Hall, 1964.

Brush, David Allen. "The de la Huerta Rebellion in Mexico, 1923–1924." Ph.D. dissertation, Syracuse University, 1975.

Buchenau, Jürgen. *Plutarco Elías Calles and the Mexican Revolution*. Lanham, MD: Rowman & Littlefield, 2007.

The Last Caudillo: Álvaro Obregón and the Mexican Revolution. Chichester, England: Wiley-Blackwell, 2011.

Buchenau, Jürgen and William H. Beezley, eds. *State Governors in the Mexican Revolution, 1910–1952: Portraits in Conflict, Courage, and Corruption*. Lanham, MD: Rowman & Littlefield Publishers, 2009.

Buck, Sarah. "Activists and Mothers: Feminist and Maternalist Politics in Mexico, 1923–1953." Ph.D. dissertation, Rutgers, 2002.

Butler, Matthew. *Faith and Impiety in Revolutionary Mexico*. New York, NY: Palgrave Macmillan, 2007.

Popular Piety and Political Identity in Mexico's Cristero Rebellion: Michoacán, 1927–29. Oxford, England: Oxford University Press, 2004.

Calles, Plutarco Elías. *Correspondencia personal (1919–1945)*, edited by Carlos Macías. 2 vols. México, D.F.: Fideicomiso Archivos Plutarco Elías Calles y Fernando Torreblanca, 1991.

Pensamiento político y social: antología (1913–1936), edited by Carlos Macias. México, D.F.: Fideicomiso Archivos Plutarco Elías Calles y Fernando Torreblanca, 1994.

Campbell, Federico and Luis Alamillo Flores. *La Sombra de Serrano: de la matanza de Huitzilac a la explusión de Calles por Cárdenas*. México, DF: Proceso, 1980.

Camp, Roderic Ai. *Generals in the Palacio: The Military in Modern Mexico*. New York, NY: Oxford University Press, 1992.

Mexican Political Biographies, 1884–1935. Austin, TX: University of Texas Press, 1991.

Political Recruitment Across Two Centuries: Mexico, 1884–1991. Austin, TX: University of Texas Press, 1995.

Canudas, Enrique. *Tropico rojo: historia politica y social de Tabasco los años garridistas 1919/1934*. 2 vols. Villahermosa, Tabasco: Gobierno del Estado de Tabasco, Instituto de Cultura de Tabasco, 1989.

Capetillo, Alonso. *La rebelión sin cabeza: génesis y desarrollo del movimiento delahuertista*. México, D.F.: Imprenta Botas, 1925.

Carr, Barry. *Marxism and Communism in Twentieth-Century Mexico*. Lincoln, NE: University of Nebraska Press, 1992.

Carrillo Puerto, Felipe and el Partido Socialista del Sureste. *Primer Congreso Obrero Socialista celebrado en Motul, Estado de Yucatán: bases que se discutieron y aprobaron*. 2nd edn. México, D.F.: Centro de Estudios Históricos del Movimiento Obrero Mexicano, 1977.

Castro Martínez, Pedro. *Adolfo de la Huerta y la Revolución Mexicana*. México, D.F.: Instituto Nacional de Estudios Históricos de la Revolución Mexicana y la Universidad Autónoma Metropolitana Unidad Iztapalapa, 1992.

Adolfo de la Huerta: la integridad como arma de la revolución. México, D.F.: Universidad Autónoma Metropolitana Iztapalapa, Siglo Veintiuno Editores, 1998.

A la sombra de un caudillo: Vida y muerte del general Francisco R. Serrano. México, D.F.: Random House Mondadori, 2005.

Clark, Marjorie Ruth. *Organized Labor in Mexico*. New York, NY: Reissued by Russell & Russell, 1934. 1973. 1934.

Club "Chiapas Libre." *El Señor General Carlos A. Vidal, candidato al gobierno del estado de Chiapas: sus rasgos biográficos, su actuación revolucionaria*. México, D.F.: Club "Chiapas Libre," 1920.

Coatsworth, John H. *Growth Against Development: The Economic Impact of Railroads in Porfirian Mexico*. DeKalb, IL: Northern Illinois University Press, 1981.

Cockcroft, James D. *Intellectual Precursors of the Mexican Revolution, 1900–1913*. Austin, TX: University of Texas Press, 1968.

Congreso de la Unión. "Diario de los debates de la H. Cámara de Diputados, 1917–presente." http://cronica.diputados.gob.mx.

"Diario de los Debates de la H. Cámara de Senadores del Congreso de la República Méxicana, 1875–1984." www.senado.gob.mx/index.php?watch=13&mn=3.

Córdova, Arnaldo. *La ideología de la Revolución Mexicana: la formación del nuevo régimen*. México, D.F.: Ediciones Era, 1973.

La Revolución en crisis: la aventura del maximato. México, D.F.: Aguilar, León y Cal, 1995.

Díaz Soto y Gama, Antonio. *Historia del agrarismo en México*, edited by Pedro Castro Martínez México, D.F.: Ediciones Era, 2002.

Dulles, John W. F. *Yesterday in Mexico: A Chronicle of the Revolution, 1919–1936*. Austin, TX: University of Texas Press, 1961.

Eiss, Paul K. "Constructing the Maya." *Ethnohistory* 55, no. 4 (2008): 503–8.

"'El Pueblo Mestizo': Modernity, Tradition, and Statecraft in Yucatán, 1870–1907." *Ethnohistory* 55, no. 4 (2008): 525–52.

In the Name of el Pueblo: Place, Community, and the Politics of History in Yucatán. Durham, NC: Duke University Press, 2010.

"A Measure of Liberty: The Politics of Labor in Revolutionary Yucatán, 1915–1918." In *Peripheral Visions: Politics, Society, and the Challenges of Modernity in Yucatan*, edited by

Edward Davis Terry, Ben Fallaw, Gilbert M. Joseph and Edward H. Moseley, 54–78. Tuscaloosa, AL: University of Alabama Press, 2010.

Enríquez, Ignacio C. *The de la Huerta Disloyalty: Events in the Pre-Election Presidential Campaign of 1924 Which Led to the Betrayal of Mexico by Some of Its Politians and Army Leaders*. Mexico, D.F., 1924.

Falcón, Romana. *Revolución y caciquismo: San Luis Potosí, 1910–1938*. México, D.F.: El Colegio de México, 1984.

"Veracruz: los límites del radicalismo en el campo (1920–1934)." *Revista Mexicana de Sociología* 41, no. 3 (1979): 671–98.

Fallaw, Ben. "Bartolomé García Correa and the Politics of Maya Identity in Postrevolutionary Yucatán, 1911–1933." *Ethnohistory* 55, no. 4 (2008): 553–78.

"Cárdenas and the Caste War That Wasn't: State Power and Indigenismo in Post-Revolutionary Yucatán." *The Americas* 53, no. 4 (1997): 551–77.

Cárdenas Compromised: The Failure of Reform in Postrevolutionary Yucatán. Durham, NC: Duke University Press, 2001.

"Dry Law, Wet Politics: Drinking and Prohibition in Post-Revolutionary Yucatan, 1915–1935." *Latin American Research Review* 37, no. 2 (2002): 37–64.

"Felipe Carrillo Puerto of Revolutionary-Era Yucatán: Popular Leader, Caesar, or Martyr?" In *Heroes and Hero Cults in Latin America*, edited by Samuel Brunk and Ben Fallaw, 128–48. Austin, TX: University of Texas Press, 2006.

"Los Límites de la Revolución: Plutarco Elías Calles, Felipe Carrillo Puerto y el Socialismo Yucateco, 1921–1924." *Boletín* 52 (2006): 1–31.

Religion and State Formation in Postrevolutionary Mexico. Durham, NC: Duke University Press, 2013.

"The Southeast Was Red: Left-State Alliances and Popular Mobilizations in Yucatan, 1930–1940." *Social Science History* 23, no. 2 (1999): 241–68.

Fallaw, Ben and Terry Rugeley, eds. *Forced Marches: Soldiers and Military Caciques in Modern Mexico*. Tucson, AZ: University of Arizona Press, 2012.

Fenner, Justus. *La llegada al Sur: la controvertida historia del deslinde de los terrenos baldíos en Chiapas, en su contexto internacional y nacional, 1881–1917*. San Cristóbal de las Casas, Chiapas: CIMSUR, 2015.

Fenner, Justus and Miguel Lisbona, eds. *La Revolución mexicana en Chiapas un siglo después: nuevos aportes, 1910–1940*. San Cristobal de las Casas, Chiapas: Programa de Investigaciones Multidisciplinarias sobre Mesoamérica y el Sureste, 2010.

Fowler-Salamini, Heather. *Agrarian Radicalism in Veracruz, 1920–38*. Lincoln, NE: University of Nebraska Press, 1978.

"De-Centering the 1920s: Socialismo a la Tamaulipeca." *Mexican Studies / Estudios Mexicanos* 14, no. 2 (1998): 287–327.

García de León, Antonio. *Resistencia y utopía: memorial de agravios y crónicas de revueltas y profecías acaecidas en la Provincia de Chiapas durante los últimos quinientos años de su historia*. 2nd edn. México, D.F.: Ediciones Era, 2002.

Garrido, Luis Javier. *El Partido de la Revolución Institucionalizada: la formación del nuevo estado en México, 1928–1945*. México, D.F.: Siglo Veintiuno Editores, 1982.

Gillingham, Paul. *Cuauhtémoc's Bones: Forging National Identity in Modern Mexico*. Albuquerque, NM: University of New Mexico Press, 2011.

"Who Killed Crispín Aguilar? Violence and Order in the Postrevolutionary Countryside." In *Violence, Coercion, and State-Making in Twentieth-Century Mexico: The Other Half of the Centaur*, edited by Wil G. Pansters, 91–114. Stanford, CA: Stanford University Press, 2012

Gillingham, Paul and Benjamin T. Smith, eds. *Dictablanda: Politics, Work, and Culture in Mexico, 1938–1968*. Durham, NC: Duke University Press, 2014.

Ginzberg, Eitan. "State Agrarianism Versus Democratic Agrarianism: Adalberto Tejeda's Experiment in Veracruz, 1928–32." *Journal of Latin American Studies* 30, no. 2 (1998): 341–72.

Gómez Estrada, Jose Alfredo. *Lealtades divididas: camarillas y poder en México, 1913–1932.* México, D.F.: Instituto Mora; Universidad Autónoma de Baja California, 2012.

González Compeán, Miguel, Leonardo Lomelí, and Pedro Salmerón Sanginés. *El Partido de la revolución : institución y conflicto, 1928–1999.* Sección de obras de política y derecho. México, D.F.: Fondo de Cultura Económica, 2000.

González Oropeza, Manuel. *La intervención federal en la desaparición de poderes.* México, D.F.: Universidad Nacional Autónoma de México, Instituto de Investigaciones Jurídicas, 1983.

Gordillo y Ortiz, Octavio. *Diccionario de la revolución en el estado de Chiapas.* San Cristóbal de Las Casas: Programa de Investigaciones Multidisciplinarias sobre Mesoamérica y el Sureste, UNAM, 1999.

Greene, Graham. *The Power and the Glory.* Norwalk, CT: Easton Press, 2000.

Greene, Kenneth F. *Why Dominant Parties Lose: Mexico's Democratization in Comparative Perspective.* Cambridge, England: Cambridge University Press, 2007.

Gruening, Ernest. *Mexico and Its Heritage.* London: Stanley Paul & Co. Ltd., 1928.

Guardino, Peter F. *Peasants, Politics, and the Formation of Mexico's National State: Guerrero, 1800–1857.* Stanford, CA: Stanford University Press, 1996.

Guzmán, Martín Luis and Antonio Lorente Medina. *La sombra del caudillo.* Madrid: Editorial Castalia, 2002.

Hale, Charles A. *Emilio Rabasa and the Survival of Porfirian Liberalism: The Man, his Career, and his Ideas, 1856–1930.* Stanford, CA: Stanford University Press, 2008.

Mexican Liberalism in the Age of Mora, 1821–1853. New Haven, CT: Yale University Press, 1968.

"Political Ideas and Ideologies in Latin America, 1870–1930." In *Ideas and Ideologies in Twentieth Century Latin America,* edited by Leslie Bethell, 133–205. Cambridge, England: Cambridge University Press, 1996.

Hall, Linda B. *Álvaro Obregón: Power and Revolution in Mexico, 1911–1920.* College Station, TX: Texas A&M University Press, 1981.

Hamilton, Nora. *The Limits of State Autonomy: Post-Revolutionary Mexico.* Princeton, NJ: Princeton University Press, 1982.

Harper, Kristin A. "Revolutionary Tabasco in the Time of Tomas Garrido Canabal, 1922–1935: A Mexican House Divided." Ph.D. diss., University of Massachusetts Amherst, 2004.

"Tomás Garrido Canabal of Tabasco: Road Building and Revolutionary Reform." In *State Governors in the Mexican Revolution, 1910–1952: Portraits in Conflict, Courage, and Corruption,* edited by Jürgen Buchenau and William H. Beezley, 109–11. Lanham, MD: Rowman & Littlefield Publishers, 2009.

Hart, John M. *Anarchism & the Mexican Working Class, 1860–1931.* Austin, TX: University of Texas Press, 1978.

Hernández Santiago, Joel, Victoria Lerner, and Berta Ulloa. *Planes en la nación mexicana, Libro 8: 1920–1940.* México, D.F.: Senado de la República, 1987. http://biblio .juridicas.unam.mx/libros/libro.htm?l=2983.

Hofstadter, Richard. *The Age of Reform: From Bryan to F.D.R.* New York, NY: Knopf, 1955.

Islas, Felipe and Manuel Múzquiz Blanco. *De la pasión sectaria a la noción de las instituciones.* México, D.F. 1932.

James, T. M. *Mexico's Supreme Court: Between Liberal Individual and Revolutionary Social Rights, 1867–1934.* Albuquerque, NM: University of New Mexico Press.

José Valenzuela, Georgette Emilia. *El relevo del caudillo: de cómo y porqué Calles fue candidato presidencial.* México, D.F.: Ediciones El Caballito, 1982.

La campaña presidencial de 1923–1924 en México. México, D.F.: Instituto Nacional de Estudios Históricos de la Revolución Mexicana (INEHRM), 1998.

"1920–1924: ¡ ... Y Venían de una Revolución!" In *Gobernar sin mayoría, México 1867–1997*, edited by María Amparo Casar and Ignacio Marván, 157–93. México: Taurus, CIDE, 2002.

Joseph, Gilbert M. "Caciquismo and the Revolution: Carrillo Puerto in Yucatán." In *Caudillo and Peasant in the Mexican Revolution*, edited by D. A. Brading, xi, 193–221, 311. New York, NY: Cambridge University Press, 1980.

"The Fragile Revolution: Cacique Politics and Revolutionary Process in Yucatan." *Latin American Research Review* 15, no. 1 (1980): 39–64.

Rediscovering the Past at Mexico's Periphery: Essays on the History of Modern Yucatán. Tuscaloosa, AL: University of Alabama Press, 1986.

Revolution from Without: Yucatán, Mexico, and the United States, 1880–1924. Durham, NC: Duke University Press, 1988.

Joseph, Gilbert M. and Jürgen Buchenau. *Mexico's Once and Future Revolution: Social Upheaval and the Challenge of Rule since the Late Nineteenth Century.* Durham, NC: Duke University Press, 2013.

Joseph, Gilbert M. and Daniel Nugent, eds. *Everyday Forms of State Formation: Revolution and the Negotiation of Rule in Modern Mexico.* Durham, NC: Duke University Press, 1994.

Justo Sierra, Carlos, Fausta Gantús Inurreta, and Laura Villanueva. *Breve historia de Campeche.* 2nd edn. México, D.F.: Fondo de Cultura Económica, 2011.

Katz, Friedrich. *The Secret War in Mexico: Europe, the United States, and the Mexican Revolution.* Chicago, IL: University of Chicago Press, 1981.

"Violence and Terror in the Mexican and Russian Revolutions." In *A Century of Revolution: Insurgent and Counterinsurgent Violence during Latin America's Long Cold War*, edited by Greg Grandin and Gilbert M. Joseph, 45–61. Durham, NC: Duke University Press, 2010.

Kiddle, Amelia M. *Mexico's Relations with Latin America during the Cárdenas Era.* Albuquerque, NM: University of New Mexico Press, 2016.

Knight, Alan. Cardenismo: Juggernaut or Jalopy?" *Journal of Latin American Studies* 26, no. 1 (1994): 73–107.

The Mexican Revolution. 2 vols. Cambridge, England: Cambridge University Press, 1986.

"The Mexican Revolution: Bourgeois? Nationalist? Or Just a 'Great Rebellion'?" *Bulletin of Latin American Research* 4, no. 2 (1985): 1–37.

"The Myth of the Mexican Revolution." *Past & Present* 209, no. 1 (2010): 223–73.

"Peasants into Patriots: Thoughts on the Making of the Mexican Nation." *Mexican Studies / Estudios Mexicanos* 10, no. 1 (1994): 135–61.

"Popular Culture and the Revolutionary State in Mexico, 1910–1940." *The Hispanic American Historical Review* 74, no. 3 (1994): 393–444.

"Populism and Neo-Populism in Latin America, Especially Mexico." *Journal of Latin American Studies* 30, no. 2 (1998): 223–48.

Knight, Alan and Wil Pansters, eds. *Caciquismo in Twentieth-Century Mexico.* London, England: Institute for the Study of the Americas, 2005.

Kourí, Emilio. *A Pueblo Divided: Business, Property, and Community in Papantla, Mexico.* Stanford, CA: Stanford University Press, 2004.

Lear, John. *Workers, Neighbors, and Citizens: The Revolution in Mexico City.* Lincoln, NE: University of Nebraska Press, 2001.

León, Luis L. *Crónica del poder: en los recuerdos de un político en el México revolucionario.* México, D.F.: Fondo de Cultura Económica, 1987.

Lewis, Stephen. *The Ambivalent Revolution: Forging State and Nation in Chiapas, 1910–1945.* Albuquerque, NM: University of New Mexico Press, 2005.

"Dead-end *Caudillismo* and Entrepeneurial *Caciquismo* in Chiapas, 1910–1950." In *Caciquismo in twentieth-century Mexico*, edited by Alan Knight and Wil Pansters, 151–68. London: Institute for the Study of the Americas, 2005.

"Efraín Gutiérrez of Chiapas: The Revolutionary Bureaucrat." In *State Governors in the Mexican Revolution, 1910–1925*, edited by Jürgen Buchenau and William H. Beezley, 139–55. Lanham, MD: Rowman & Littlefield, 2009.

Leyes y decretos del gobierno socialista de Yucatán. Mérida, Yucatán: Talls. Pluma y Lápiz, 1924.

Lomnitz-Adler, Claudio. *Death and the Idea of Mexico*. Brooklyn, NY: Zone Books, 2005.

Deep Mexico, Silent Mexico: An Anthropology of Nationalism. Minneapolis: University of Minnesota Press, 2001.

The Return of Comrade Ricardo Flores Magón. Brooklyn, NY: Zone Books, 2014.

Lorenzana Cruz, Benjamín. *Del maderismo al mapachismo en Chiapas: La Revolución Mexicana en la región de Tonalá*. Biblioteca Chiapas: Investigación del patrimonio cultural. Tuxtla Gutiérrez, Chiapas CONACULTA / CONECULTA, 2013.

Loyo Camacho, Martha Beatriz. *Joaquín Amaro y el proceso de institucionalización del Ejército Mexicano, 1917–1931*. 2nd edn. México, D.F.: Miguel Ángel Porrúa, 2003.

Lucas, Jeffrey K. "Antonio Díaz Soto y Gama and Changing Mexico: A Twentieth-Century Political Journey." *International Social Science Review* 83, no. 3/4 (2008): 132–57.

Lurtz, Casey Marina. "Exporting from Eden: Coffee, Migration, and the Development of the Soconusco, Mexico, 1867–1920." Ph.D. dissertation, The University of Chicago, 2014.

MacGregor Campuzano, Javier. "Partidos nacionales y programas políticos en México, 1918–1928." PhD dissertation, El Colegio de México, 2005.

Magaloni, Beatriz. *Voting for Autocracy: Hegemonic Party Survival and Its Demise in Mexico*. New York, NY: Cambridge University Press, 2006.

Marcial Gutiérrez, Silvia Teresa. *Los tranvías: Un medio de transporte y su importancia social, económica, cultural, política y en la traza urbana de la ciudad de Campeche (1883–1938)*. Campeche: Universidad Autónoma de Campeche, 2002.

Martínez Assad, Carlos R. *Breve historia de Tabasco*. 2nd edn. México, D.F.: Colegio de Mexico Fondo de Cultura Económica, 2006.

El laboratorio de la revolución: el Tabasco garridista. 5th edn. México, D.F.: Siglo Veintiuno Editores, 2004.

Martínez, Óscar Janiere. *General Fausto Ruiz Córdoba: apuntes biograficos*. Tuxtla Gutiérrez, Chiapas: Consejo Estatal para las Culturas y las Artes de Chiapas, 2011.

Medin, Tzvi. *El minimato presidencial: historia política del maximato (1928–1935)*. México, D.F.: Ediciones Era, 1982.

Medina Peña, Luis. *Hacia el nuevo estado: México, 1920–1994*. 2nd edn. México, D.F.: Fondo de Cultura Económica, 1995.

Invención del sistema político mexicano: forma de gobierno y gobernabilidad en México en el siglo XIX. México, D.F.: Fondo de Cultura Económica, 2004.

Meyer, Jean. *The Cristero Rebellion: The Mexican People between Church and State, 1926–1929*. New York, NY: Cambridge University Press, 1976.

La Cristiada. 24th edn. 3 vols. México: Siglo Veintiuno Editores, 2007.

"La diarquía (1924–1928)." In *Gobernar sin mayoría, México 1867–1997*, edited by María Amparo Casar and Ignacio Marván, 195–234. México: Taurus CIDE, 2002.

Meyer, Jean A., Enrique Krauze, and Cayetano Reyes García. *Estado y sociedad con Calles*. Historia de la Revolución Mexicana, vol. 11: Período 1924–1928. México, D.F.: El Colegio de México, 1977.

Meyer, Lorenzo. *El conflicto social y los gobiernos del Maximato*. Historia de la Revolución Mexicana, vol. 13: Período 1928–1934. México, D.F.: Colegio de México, 1978.

"La Revolución Mexicana y sus elecciones presidenciales: una interpretación (1911–1940)." *Historia Mexicana* 32, no. 2 (1982): 143–97.

Meyer, Lorenzo, Rafael Segovia, and Alejandra Lajous. *Los inicios de la institucionalización: la política del Maximato*. Historia de la Revolución Mexicana vol. 12: Período 1928–1934. México, D.F.: Colegio de México, 1978.

Middlebrook, Kevin J. *The Paradox of Revolution: Labor, the State, and Authoritarianism in Mexico*. Baltimore, MD: Johns Hopkins University Press, 1995.

Monroy Durán, Luis. *El último caudillo: apuntes para la historia de México, acerca del movimiento armado de 1923, en contra del gobierno constituido*. México, D.F.: J.S. Rodríguez, 1924.

Moreno, Daniel A. *Los partidos políticos del México contemporáneo*. 8th edn. México: B. Costa-Amic, 1982.

Morton, Ward M. *Woman Suffrage in Mexico*. Gainesville, FL: University of Florida Press, 1962.

Navarro, Aaron W. *Political Intelligence and the Creation of Modern Mexico, 1938–1954*. University Park, PA: Pennsylvania State University Press, 2010.

Nolan-Ferrell, Catherine A. *Constructing Citizenship: Transnational Workers and Revolution on the Mexico-Guatemala Border, 1880–1950*. Tucson, AZ: University of Arizona Press, 2012.

O'Malley, Ilene V. *The Myth of the Revolution: Hero Cults and the Institutionalization of the Mexican State, 1920–1940*. New York, NY: Greenwood Press, 1986.

Obregón, Álvaro. *Discursos del General Álvaro Obregón*. 2 vols. México, D.F.: Talleres Gráficos de la Nación, 1932.

Olcott, Jocelyn. *Revolutionary Women in Postrevolutionary Mexico*. Durham, NC: Duke University Press, 2005.

Olcott, Jocelyn, Mary K. Vaughan, and Gabriela Cano, eds. *Sex in Revolution: Gender, Politics, and Power in Modern Mexico*. Durham, NC: Duke University Press, 2006.

Olea, Héctor R. *La tragedia de Huitzilac*. México, D.F.: B. Costa-Amic, 1971.

Osten, Sarah. "Trials by Fire: National Political Lessons from Failed State Elections in Post-Revolutionary Mexico, 1920–1925." *Mexican Studies/Estudios Mexicanos* 29, no. 1 (2013): 238–79.

Pacheco, José Emilio. *Crónica de Huitzilac*. Cuadernos mexicanos. México, D.F.: SEP-Conasupo, 1980.

Padilla, Tanalís. *Rural Resistance in the Land of Zapata: The Jaramillista Movement and the Myth of the Pax Priísta, 1940–1962*. Durham, NC: Duke University Press, 2008.

Pansters, Wil G., ed. *Violence, Coercion, and State-Making in Twentieth-Century Mexico: The Other Half of the Centaur*. Stanford, CA: Stanford University Press, 2012.

"Zones of State-Making: Violence, Coercion and Hegemony in Twentieth-Century Mexico." In *Violence, Coercion, and State-Making in Twentieth-Century Mexico: The Other Half of the Centaur*, edited by Wil G. Pansters, 3–39. Stanford, CA: Stanford University Press, 2012.

Paoli Bolio, Francisco Jose, and Enrique Montalvo Ortega. *El socialismo olvidado de Yucatán: elementes para una reinterpretación de la revolución mexicana*. México, D.F.: Siglo Veintiuno Editores, 1977.

Partido Nacional Revolucionario. *Constitución del P.N.R.* México, D.F.: PNR, 1932.

La democracia social en México: Historia de la Convención nacional revolucionaria, Constitución del P.N.R., Sucesión presidencial de 1929 México, D.F.: Partido Nacional Revolucionario, 1929.

Nuevo sentido de la política: programa de acción, estatutos y presupuesto para 1930. México, D.F.: Talleres tipográficos de El Nacional Revolucionario, 1930.

Partido Socialista Radical de Tabasco. *Código obrero*. Villahermosa: Talleres de Redención, 1925.

Pérez Bertruy, Ramona Isabel. *Tomás Garrido Canabal y la conformación del poder revolucionario tabasqueño, 1914–1921*. Villahermosa: Gobierno del Estado de Tabasco, Secretaría de Educación, Cultura y Recreación, Dirección de Educación Superior e Investigación Científica, 1993.

Plasencia de la Parra, Enrique. *Personajes y escenarios de la rebelión delahuertista*. México, D.F.: Instituto de Investigaciones Históricas, UNAM, 1998.

Portes Gil, Emilio. *Historia vivida de la Revolución Mexicana*. México, D.F.: Cultura y Ciencia Política, 1976.

"The Presidential Dilemma in Mexico." *Foreign Affairs* 3, no. 1 (1924): 78–89.

Prieto Laurens, Jorge. *Cincuenta años de política mexicana*. México, D.F.: Editora Mexicana de Periódicos, Libros, 1968.

Purnell, Jennie. *Popular Movements and State Formation in Revolutionary Mexico: The Agraristas and Cristeros of Michoacán*. Durham, NC: Duke University Press, 1999.

Rabasa, Emilio. *La evolución histórica de México*. Paris: La Vda. de C. Bouret, 1920.

Rath, Thomas G. *Myths of Demilitarization in Postrevolutionary Mexico, 1920–1960*. Chapel Hill, NC: University of North Carolina Press, 2013.

Rébora, Hipólito. *Memorias de un chiapaneco*. México, D.F.: Editorial Katún, 1982.

Reed, Alma M. and Michael Karl Schuessler. *Peregrina: Love and Death in Mexico*. Austin, TX: University of Texas Press, 2007.

Reyes Ramos, María Eugenia. *El reparto de tierras y la política agraria en Chiapas, 1914–1988*. México, D.F: Universidad Nacional Autónoma de México, Centro de Investigaciones Humanísticas de Mesoamérica y del Estado de Chiapas, 1992.

Rico, Juan. *Yucatán: la huelga de junio*. 2 vols. Mérida, 1922.

Ridgeway, Stan. "Monoculture, Monopoly, and the Mexican Revolution: Tomás Garrido Canabal and the Standard Fruit Company in Tabasco (1920–1935)." *Mexican Studies / Estudios Mexicanos* 17, no. 1 (2001): 143–69.

Robledo Santiago, Edgar. *Valores Humanos de Chiapas*. Tuxtla Gutiérrez: Universidad Autonoma de Chiapas, 1992.

Rugeley, Terry. *Yucatán's Maya Peasantry and the Origins of the Caste War*. Austin, TX: University of Texas Press, 1996.

Rebellion Now and Forever: Mayas, Hispanics, and Caste War Violence in Yucatán, 1800–1880. Stanford, CA: Stanford University Press, 2009.

Rus, Jan. "The 'Comunidad Revolucionaria Institucional': The Subversion of Native Government in Highland Chiapas, 1936–1968." In *Everyday Forms of State Formation: Revolution and the Negotiation of Rule in Modern Mexico*, edited by Gilbert M. Joseph and Daniel Nugent, 265–300. Durham, NC: Duke University Press, 1994.

"The End of the Plantations and the Transformation of Indigenous Society in Highland Chiapas, Mexico, 1974–2009." Ph.D., University of California, Riverside, 2010.

El ocaso de las fincas y la transformación de la sociedad indígena de los altos de Chiapas, 1974–2009. Tuxtla Gutiérrez, Chiapas: Universidad de Ciencias y Artes de Chiapas, 2012.

"Revoluciones contenidas: los indígenas y la lucha por Los Altos de Chiapas, 1910–1925." *Mesoamérica*, no. 46 (2004): 57–85.

Salmerón Sanginés, Pedro. "La fundación (1928–1933)." In *El Partido de la revolución: institución y conflicto, 1928–1999*, edited by Miguel González Compeán, Leonardo Lomelí and Pedro Salmerón Sanginés, 33–105. México, D.F.: Fondo de Cultura Económica, 2000.

Santamaría, Francisco Javier. *La tragedia de Cuernavaca en 1927 y mi escapatoria célebre*. México, D.F.: F.J. Santamaría, 1939.

Santos, Gonzalo N. *Memorias*. 5th edn. México, D.F.: Grijalbo, 1986.

Servín, Elisa, Leticia Reina, and John Tutino, eds. *Cycles of Conflict, Centuries of Change: Crisis, Reform, and Revolution in Mexico*. Durham, NC: Duke University Press, 2007.

Smith, Benjamin T. *Pistoleros and Popular Movements: The Politics of State Formation in Postrevolutionary Oaxaca*. Lincoln, NE: University of Nebraska Press, 2009.

Smith, Stephanie. "'If Love Enslaves ... Love be Damned!': Divorce and Revolutionary State Formation in Yucatán." In *Sex in Revolution: Gender, Politics, and Power in Modern Mexico*, edited by Jocelyn Olcott, Vaughan, Mary K., and Cano, Gabriela, 99–111. Durham, NC: Duke University Press, 2006.

"Salvador Alvarado of Yucatán: Revolutionary Reforms, Revolutionary Women." In *State Governors in the Mexican Revolution, 1910–1952: Portraits in Conflict, Courage, and Corruption*, edited by Jürgen Buchenau and William H. Beezley, 43–58. Lanham: Rowman & Littlefield Publishers, 2009.

Spenser, Daniela. *El partido socialista chiapaneco: rescate y reconstrucción de su historia*. México, D.F.: Centro de Investigaciones y Estudios Superiores en Antropología Social, 1988.

Stumbling Its Way Through Mexico: The Early Years of the Communist International. Tuscaloosa, AL: University of Alabama Press, 2011.

Sullivan, Paul. *Xuxub Must Die: The Lost Histories of a Murder on the Yucatán*. Pittsburgh, PA: University of Pittsburgh Press, 2004.

Taracena, Alfonso. *Historia de la Revolución en Tabasco*. 3rd edn. Vol. 1, Villahermosa: Consejo Editorial del Estado de Tabasco, México, 1981.

Terry, Edward Davis, Ben Fallaw, Gilbert M. Joseph, and Edward H. Moseley, eds. *Peripheral Visions: Politics, Society, and the Challenges of Modernity in Yucatan*. Tuscaloosa, AL: University of Alabama Press, 2010.

Tostado Gutiérrez, Marcela. *El intento de liberar a un pueblo: educación y magisterio tabasqueño con Garrido Canabal, 1924–1935*. México, D.F.: Instituto Nacional de Antropología e Historia, 1991.

Trens, Manuel B. *Vidal y Chiapas: su campaña política y su administración*. México, D.F., 1927.

Turner, John Kenneth. *Barbarous Mexico*. Austin, TX: University of Texas Press, 1969.

Vaughan, Mary Kay. *Cultural Politics in Revolution: Teachers, Peasants, and Schools in Mexico, 1930–1940*. Tucson, AZ: University of Arizona Press, 1997.

Vaughan, Mary Kay and Stephen E. Lewis, eds. *The Eagle and the Virgin: Nation and Cultural Revolution in Mexico, 1920–1940*. Durham, NC: Duke University Press, 2006.

Vidal, Carlos A. *Dos meses de gobernador en Tabasco: del gobierno pre-constitucional al constitucional*. Mérida: La Voz de la Revolución, 1919.

Viqueira Albán, Juan Pedro. *Encrucijadas chiapanecas: economía, religión e identidades*. México, D.F.: Tusquets Editores, 2002.

Wasserstrom, Robert. *Class and Society in Central Chiapas*. Berkeley, CA: University of California Press, 1983.

Wells, Allen. "All in the Family: Railroads and Henequen Monoculture in Porfirian Yucatan." *The Hispanic American Historical Review* 72, no. 2 (1992): 159–209.

"Family Elites in a Boom-and-Bust Economy: The Molinas and Peóns of Porfirian Yucatán." *The Hispanic American Historical Review* 62, no. 2 (1982): 224–53.

"Forgotten Chapters of Yucatán's Past: Nineteenth-Century Politics in Historiographical Perspective." *Mexican Studies/Estudios Mexicanos* 12, no. 2 (1996): 195–229.

Yucatán's Gilded Age: Haciendas, Henequen, and International Harvester, 1860–1915. Albuquerque, NM: University of New Mexico Press, 1985.

Wells, Allen and Gilbert M. Joseph. "Clientelism and the Political Baptism of Yucatán's Urban Working Classes, 1876–1929." In *Citizens of the Pyramid: Essays on Mexican Political Culture*, edited by W. G. Pansters, 66–106. Amsterdam: Thela Publishers, 1997.

Summer of Discontent, Seasons of Upheaval: Elite Politics and Rural Insurgency in Yucatán, 1876–1915. Stanford, CA: Stanford University Press, 1996.

Womack, John. *Zapata and the Mexican Revolution*. New York: Vintage Books, 1968.

Young, Julia G. *Mexican Exodus: Emigrants, Exiles, and Refugees of the Cristero War*. New York, NY: Oxford University Press, 2015.

Zebadúa, Emilio. *Breve historia de Chiapas*. México, D.F.: Fondo de Cultura Económica, 1999.

Index

Institutional Revolutionary Party. *See* Partido
  Revolucionario Institucional
International Harvester, 20, 23, 27
Iturralde, José, 121

Jalisco, 108, 111, 217, 225
Jiménez de Lara, Arturo, 151, 152, 154, 155,
  156, 158, 231
Joseph, Gilbert M., 21

Katz, Friedrich, 5
Kaxatah, 130
Kini, 46
Knight, Alan, 263

Labor Day, 47
Laboristas. *See* Confederación Regional de
  Obreros Mexicanos
Las Margaritas, 193
Lazos León, Florinda, 177–8
legislative blocs, 104, 198, 201, 202, 204, 205,
  220, 223, 227, 236
legislative purges, 130, 220, 227–30, 247, 261, 262
Lenin, Vladimir, 48, 201
León, Luis L., 204, 205, 249
Lerma, 84
Los Angeles, 264
Lugo, Juan, 151, 154

Madero, Francisco I., 18, 21, 22, 24, 64, 68, 100,
  168, 180, 195, 203, 205, 231, 248, 253
Magdalena, 217
Mam people, 176
Manrique, Aurelio, 104, 250, 251
Mapaches, 68–9, 70, 71, 72, 78, 88–90, 91, 95,
  122, 161, 162, 164, 165, 166–7, 168–9,
  170, 171, 172, 174, 175–6, 178, 179, 181,
  183, 184, 190, 191, 204, 207, 208, 209,
  257, 263
  and Álvaro Obregón. *See* Obregón, Álvaro
Margalli, Homero, 140, 141, 148–9, 150,
  151, 152
Mariscal, 72, 176
Mariscal (Chiapas), 190
Marx, Karl, 32, 47, 48
Marxism, 9, 50
Maximato, 254–6
Maycotte, Fortunato, 108, 113
Mena Brito, Bernardino, 34, 55
Mendoza, Ismael, 78
Mérida, 38, 51, 55, 113, 114, 117, 118, 219, 257

Mestre Ghigliazza, Manuel, 64
Mexican Labor Party. *See* Partido Laborista
  Mexicano
Mexican Liberal Party. *See* Partido Liberal
  Mexicano
Mexican Revolution, 3, 6, 8, 12, 18, 21, 22, 34,
  43, 54, 58, 59, 68, 70, 73, 77, 78, 82, 96,
  106, 116, 129, 154, 193, 196, 199, 202,
  203, 205, 207, 236, 237, 242, 243, 244,
  245, 247, 249, 251, 252, 255, 260, 261,
  262, 263, 264
México (state), 85, 102, 252
Mexico City, 18, 31, 108, 113, 225
Miami, 18
Michoacán, 10, 85
Michoacán Socialist Party. *See* Partido Socialista
  de Michoacán
Mier y Terán, Eugenio, 203
military of Mexico, 15, 90, 99, 106–7, 109, 110,
  111, 121, 122, 126, 134, 152, 167, 170,
  174, 196, 197, 205, 214, 215, 217, 218,
  223, 224, 225, 226, 233, 247, 248, 262
  reform of, 107, 131
Ministry of War. *See* military of Mexico
Mireles, Luis T., 133
Moctezuma, Fernando, 201
Morelia, 218
Morelos, 18, 32, 203, 224, 240
Moreno Cantón, Delio, 32
Morones, Luis, 52, 136, 155, 172, 173, 183, 196,
  216, 220–1, 231, 233, 244, 250, 251, 264
  and Chiapas Socialists, 165
Motozintla, 73, 163, 168, 173, 176, 215, 217
Motul, 47, 130
Mucel Acereto, Joaquín, 63, 73–4, 75
Múgica, Francisco, 10, 56, 65, 69, 73, 80

National Revolutionary Party. *See* Partido
  Nacional Revolucionario
Nayarit, 85, 240
New Orleans, 126, 156, 158
New York City, 100–2, 107, 128
Nuevo León, 224
Nunkiní, 73

Oaxaca, 108, 113, 197, 210, 240, 252
Obregón, Álvaro, 15, 31, 49, 53, 54, 55, 59, 60, 74,
  76, 82, 90, 92, 99, 100, 104, 106, 108, 109,
  111, 113, 119, 122, 128, 131, 164, 165, 168,
  194, 196, 203, 206, 207, 214, 221, 225, 226,
  232, 233, 237, 242, 247, 253, 255

PNR. *See* Partido Nacional Revolucionario

political violence, 2, 3, 4, 5, 11, 14–15, 34, 37, 57, 71, 72, 75, 93, 96, 104, 152, 153, 154, 165, 169–70, 181, 223, 225–7, 229, 232, 233, 248–9, 261–2

Pomuch, 77

Porfiriato, 18, 19–21, 31, 179

Portes Gil, Emilio, 10, 113, 236, 239, 245, 246, 247, 249, 250

PPPC. *See* Partido Político Pro-Campeche

PRI. *See* Partido Revolucionario Institucional

Prieto Laurens, Jorge, 103, 104–5, 108, 111, 127, 230

PRM. *See* Partido de la Revolución Mexicana

Pro-Campeche Political Party. *See* Partido Político Pro-Campeche

Pro-Campeche Socialist Agrarian Party. *See* Partido Socialista Agrario Pro-Campeche

Proudhon, Pierre-Joseph, 201

PRT. *See* Partido Radical Tabasqueño

PSS. *See* Partido Socialista del Sureste

Puebla, 108, 203, 223, 240, 241, 251

Querétaro, 85, 243, 247, 250

Quintana Roo, 61, 85, 87, 118, 203

Rabasa, Emilio, 29

Radical Socialist Party of Tabasco. *See* Partido Radical Socialista Tabasqueño

Ramírez Corzo, Luis, 166, 168, 171

Ramírez Garrido, José Domingo, 94

Rébora, Hipólito, 215, 222, 227

Reed, Alma, 112, 116, 117

reelectionism, 195, 196, 198, 202–3, 262

Rico, Juan, 39, 46, 54, 56, 111–12, 172

Rios, Margarito, 214–16

Rojas de Vidal, Dévora, 78, 223

Ruiz, Fausto, 183

Rus, Jan, 179, 191

Russia, 5

Sales Guerrero, Gonzalo, 75, 76, 77, 83

Salto de Agua, 230

San Cristóbal de Las Casas, 67, 123

San Juan Chamula, 68, 70, 179, 180, 181

San Luis Potosí, 104, 123, 131, 199, 201

San Pedro Remate, 176

Sánchez, Guadalupe, 108, 115, 116, 125

Santa Anna, Justo A., 119

Santos, Gonzalo N., 199, 202, 203

Secretaría de Educación Pública (SEP), 145, 248

Senate (Mexico), 104, 109, 168, 171–2, 198

Serrano, Francisco R., 15, 109, 110, 196, 198, 204, 205, 206, 214, 219, 221, 222, 225, 232, 234, 248

in the Southeast, 121–2, 127

presidential campaign, 196, 204, 206, 209, 211, 213, 214, 215, 216, 217, 219, 221, 223, 224, 232

Sinaloa, 23, 196

Socialism (nationwide), 195, 199, 200–1, 205, 207, 231, 232, 238–41, 244, 252–3, 255, 256–8, 261

Socialist Agrarian Party (PSA). *See* Partido Agrario Socialista (PSA)

Socialist Agrarian Party of Campeche. *See* Partido Socialista Agrario de Campeche

Socialist Party of the Southeast (PSS). *See* Partido Socialista del Sureste

Socialist Party of Yucatán. *See* Partido Socialista de Yucatán

Socialist Workers' Party of Yucatán. *See* Partido Socialista de Yucatán

Soconusco, 165, 176, 190

Soconusco Union of Workers and Peasants. *See* Unión de Obreros y Campesinos de Soconusco

Solís, Jaime, 163

Sonora, 23, 31, 196, 257

southeastern Mexico

demography, 95

physical characteristics of, 7–8, 61

political significance, 100, 112, 131

southeastern Socialism, 95, 160, 161, 187, 189, 194, 195, 201, 205, 212, 232

and Plutarco Elías Calles. *See* Calles, Plutarco Elías

as compared to parties elsewhere, 10, 104, 260

characteristics, 8–9, 96, 160, 192–3

conception of democracy, 9, 46, 160, 245

ideology, 9–10, 256

internal divisions, 96–8, 115, 129, 156–8, 177, 189, 207–9, 230–1

national influence of, 1–2, 6, 10–11, 13–14, 17, 35–6, 95, 115, 132, 195, 199, 201, 237–8, 240, 243, 244, 245, 256, 257, 258, 259, 261, 262, 264

organizational model, 9, 81, 195, 198, 199, 201–2, 232, 233, 238, 246, 256, 258, 261, 263

origins, 58–9

prohibition of alcohol, 39, 49, 65